Armaments and Politics in France
on the Eve of the First World War

GERD KRUMEICH

Armaments and Politics in France on the Eve of the First World War

The Introduction of Three-Year
Conscription 1913–1914

Translated by STEPHEN CONN

With a Foreword by JAMES JOLL

BERG PUBLISHERS

Berg Publishers Ltd,
24 Binswood Avenue, Leamington Spa,
Warwickshire CV32 5SQ, UK
51 Washington Street, Dover,
New Hampshire 03820, USA

British Library Cataloguing in Publication Data

Krumeich, Gerd
    Armaments and politics in France on the eve of
    the First World War: the introduction of three-
    year conscription 1913–1914.
    1. France—Politics and government—1870–1940
    I. Title II. Aufrüstung und Innenpolitik in
    Frankreich vor dem Ersten Weltkrieg. *English*
    944.081'3   DC340

ISBN 0–907582–34–6–PBK

Library of Congress Catalog Card Number 84-73480

Printed in Great Britain by Billings & Sons, Worcester

For Sebastian

Contents

Foreword

Recent discussion of the causes of the First World War has often suggested that we must look for an explanation of the decisions which led to war in the pressures of domestic politics on the governments concerned. Much has been written over the past twenty years about the *Primat der Innenpolitik* in the case of Germany, but a similar analysis of the relation between domestic and foreign policy in the other belligerent countries is only just beginning.

The case of France is a particularly interesting one, and less attention has been paid to France's role in the crucial years between 1911 and 1914 than to that of Germany, Britain or Russia. Between the crisis over Morocco in 1911, when there was talk of war between France and Germany, and the outbreak of hostilities in 1914, the French were re-shaping their military policy, tightening up their alliance with Russia and experiencing a serious domestic political crisis both over financial policy, with the proposal to introduce an income tax, and over defence, with the proposal to extend the period of compulsory military service from two to three years. Gerd Krumeich, using an impressive range of French archives both in Paris and the provinces, including the unpublished diary of President Poincaré, has traced in detail the interaction between diplomatic, military and financial factors in influencing French policy. He analyses clearly the complicated personal intrigues and party divisions and compromises in French political life. He shows the apparently growing polarisation in France between a reviving nationalism on the Right and an increasing anti-militarist activity on the Left which led some observers, including the German ambassador, to believe that France was on the verge of a crisis comparable to that of the Dreyfus Affair; and he explains why the characteristic divisions and compromises within the French Socialist Party helped to prevent this.

The apparent deep division of opinion over the question of national defence in fact, as Dr Krumeich shows, masked a fundamental agreement on the need to defend *la patrie*, however great the disagreement about the ways and means, so that in the crisis of 1914 a remarkable unity of sentiment was established and enabled the *Union Sacrée* to be declared. At the same time, this book demonstrates the gap between the popular conceptions of strategy and the actual plans of the general staff and suggests that much of the anti-militarist agitation was probably misdirected. Finally, the book illustrates the extent to which French policy, both domestic and foreign, was dominated by the alliance with Russia. The importance of the law extending military service from two to three years was that it was as much a gesture to the Russians demonstrating that the French took the alliance seriously, as it was a practical contribution to France's military strength. Domestic and foreign policy were inextricably bound together so that each determined the other and it is hard to decide where the primacy lies.

Gerd Krumeich preserves an admirable impartiality in a field in which prejudice and acrimony often bedevil scholarly discussion, and he has written a book which is a major contribution both to the political history of France, to which he brings a sensitive and perceptive understanding, and to the continuing discussion about the origins of the First World War.

London, October 1984   *James Joll*

Preface to the English Edition

The origin of this study was a PhD thesis, completed under the supervision of Professor Wolfgang Mommsen and submitted at the University of Düsseldorf. It was published in Germany in 1980 and has since been thoroughly revised for this English edition. I have now omitted both material which appears dated and that which, from a few years' distance, no longer seems so important. In its place, I have incorporated much recent literature and the quotations which appear in French in the original have been translated into English.

It is, of course, a great pleasure for an author to see his work published in translation and the fruits of his research which, because of language barriers are not easily accessible to all those interested in his field, presented for evaluation and discussion by scholars in other countries. That this opportunity exists now (and to a greater extent than ever before) is due mainly to the initiative taken by Berg Publishers to make work by German historians available to English-speaking scholars. I would like to thank the Franz Steiner Verlag, Wiesbaden, who have given permission for this English edition. Stephen Conn has not only undertaken the labour of translating the text but has succeeded in rendering my complicated thoughts into simpler (and more comprehensible) language. Many friends have helped me with their criticism; the responsibility for all mistakes must rest with me.

Gerd Krumeich

3

Introduction

This study on armaments and politics in France on the eve of the First World War originated in a vague feeling of uneasiness on the part of the author with Fritz Fischer's account of the relationship between German and French military preparations in *Krieg der Illusionen*.[1] Fischer's theory that Germany's aggressive aspirations towards world power status—and this factor alone—had left France with no alternative but to take defensive measures, appeared to be too simplistic a challenge-and-response model, particularly in view of the fact that the arms race among the rival imperialist powers was flanked by nationalist mass movements in countries other than Germany. To a large extent following in Fischer's footsteps, German research in the 1960s came to the conclusion that German imperialism and aggressive nationalism were the result of the socio-structural upheavals and subsequent malfunctioning of the political system in Wilhelmine Germany.[2] All this research focused exclusively on Germany. The question now was, were similar or even identical structural problems to be found in other countries? If so, might the general crisis in European politics not be interpreted as the outcome of an accumulated series of internal and social antagonisms, bridged only temporarily by the mechanisms of secondary integration (e.g. nationalism) which, in turn, led to the crisis and the débâcle in European politics?

A comparative study of this period had so far been conducted only in broad outline. In this respect Arno Mayer's 'Causes and Purposes of War in Europe, 1870–1956' and his case-study 'Domestic Causes of the First World War'[3] can be regarded as both unique and pioneering. Observing the exacerbation of internal and social tensions all over Europe in the immediate pre-1914 period, which Mayer describes as a 'symbiotic growth of domestic and international tensions', he concludes that as social conflict grew, the early years of the century witnessed an 'erosion' of the Centre, traditionally orientated towards

5

domestic and social compromise, in all the European countries which were soon to go to war. This erosion, he continues, finally led to a polarisation between the 'forces of order' and the 'forces of change', if not to a head-on clash between revolutionary and counter-revolutionary tendencies. Further, this social disintegration in the states of pre-war Europe had a destabilising effect on foreign policy, since the conservative élites were now increasingly tempted to strengthen their internal position by recourse to a 'diversionary war'.[4] In Mayer's opinion these counter-revolutionary trends gained increasing momentum from the time of the modernisation crisis in the 1870s when the conservative élites succeeded in rallying mass support among both the *petite bourgeoisie* and the small farmholding classes who felt threatened by socio-economic change and were therefore susceptible to jingoism, chauvinism and theories of conspiracy.[5] The conservative élites exploited and encouraged these tendencies in order to prevent this crisis strata from falling into the revolutionary camp. Mayer, therefore, regards the pre-war armament campaign as a fundamentally domestic tactic, an integral part of the struggle between the forces of order and the forces of change.[6]

Mayer concedes in principle that a comparative study of the domestic developments in the nations of Europe before the First World War must allow for the fact that the prevailing political system—which he classifies as either autocratic or democratic—may have restricted the 'necessity, possibility and extent' of the techniques of manipulation.[7] However, he does not expound on this aspect, which may indeed be of considerable heuristic value when one is assessing the degree of external aggressiveness of the various national systems. With his penchant for model Platonism and the predominance of his theorem of erosion, he tends to focus his research upon the analogies in the internal developments of the various European nations.

So far as France is concerned, Mayer regards the 1913/14 armament debate and the controversy over tax reform as the culmination of political and social polarisation. In his opinion it was in particular the strident anti-militarism of the socialist and syndicalist Left—which the Right also regarded as a social threat—that provoked the formation of the conservative and nationalist bloc, as a result of which even a number of left-wing Republicans (the so-called Radicals) went over to the counter-revolutionaries. The armament question, he claims, made the traditional cooperation between moderate Socialists and the bourgeois Centre taboo. The Centre—hitherto moderately reformist—turned towards the militarist, nationalist and socially conservative Right, endeavouring to lure mass support away from the socially progressive and anti-militarist alliance of left-wing bourgeois and socialist groups by means of nationalist rallying slogans.[8]

Although the revolutionary counterpole is not entirely tangible in his case-study, Mayer nevertheless seems to attribute to it considerable charisma, presumably owing to the landslide victory of the 'bloc of the Left' (Socialists and bourgeois Radical-Socialists) over the 'bloc of the Right' in the 1914 parliamentary elections. Mayer is convinced that it was this phenomenon which led Poincaré, as an exponent of the anti-revolutionary camp, to opt for war in the July crisis of 1914 which, true to conservative doctrine, he regarded as an antidote to revolution. Fear of German aggression was stirred up with the aim of splitting the bloc of the Left—a diversionary tactic which proved successful.[9]

Mayer's approach—a combination of the phenomenon of pre-war domestic bloc formation, long observed by French research, and an analysis of the long-term malfunctioning of French society, which resulted in political antagonism—initially appears quite convincing. A phenomenon portrayed as a secular conflict between two political temperaments with changing actors and political groups in Goguel's famous *ordre-mouvement* dichotomy—reproduced by Mayer word for word—is derived by Mayer in a much more tangible way from the socio-structural framework conditions of the time. However, and we shall return to this later, such direct appraisals of political behavioural patterns are highly questionable from a methodological point of view. How, for example, did a society polarised to such an extent succeed in demonstrating such a degree of unanimity at the decisive moment— that is, in August 1914? Why did no group of any social relevance offer any resistance to the *Union Sacrée* in August 1914? If the social divide between the forces of order and the forces of change was so deeply entrenched in the clash between nationalist/conservative and anti-militarist/progressive elements that a diversionary war seemed to be the only solution to the intransigent élites, recourse to the theory of German aggressiveness in July 1914 is actually quite absurd, for, according to the same theory, this issue had been an integral part of the counter-revolutionary strategy for years, or even decades, and had as such been resisted by the counter-bloc.

The dilemma inherent in this polarisation theory confronts all the historians who since Seignobos's *Évolution de la IIIe République*[10] have stressed the erosion of the left-wing bourgeois parties owing to growing social tensions since roughly 1905, but who have nevertheless observed that a new socially and politically progressive bloc emerged in the course of the defence and tax debates in the years 1913/14. This bloc of the Left triumphed over the socially conservative and national-ist counter-bloc in the 1914 parliamentary elections.[11] Even Seignobos could not bridge the gap between the theory of the formation of domestic blocs, on the one hand, and the phenomenon of national unity, on the other; and the same applies to a whole series of studies on domestic developments in the Third Republic before the First World War. In the *Manuel des partis politiques en France*—unsurpassed even today—Georges Bourgin offers a solution which has been applied time and again: 'The effect the war had on France was to create the *Union Sacrée*, in which the parties, in the face of external danger, renounced their own views and united to accomplish the common and imperative task: to halt the invasion and pave the way for victory.'[12]

Although the catalysing effect of external events cannot be denied, such eclectic explanations are not satisfactory. Moreover, the theory that the domestic conflict subsided as war loomed ahead, is particularly doubtful in this case, its being almost universally accepted that the peak of the domestic crisis was the antagonism between pacifist and militarist tendencies.[13] One therefore has the impression that these explanations are based on the assumption that, despite domestic controversies and bloc formation, a fundamental national consensus still remained. However, the theory of a national consensus in France in this period has seldom been advanced and only partially elaborated upon. One example is perhaps Chastenet's 'Jours inquiets et jours sanglants'. Chastenet maintains that, against the background of socio-economic and institutional stability, the effervescence in France before the First World War was relatively secondary and surmountable.[14] Stanley Hoffmann also observes a relative consensus, despite the dissidence and wrangling within the *société bloquée*, and maintains that the traditional class divides had been at least bridged by the predominance of republican tradition. The republican constitution and its institutions, he claims, had even secured the national integration of the Socialists. Thus, since all the political tensions were expressed within this framework of national integration, the wave of nationalism in the pre-1914 years, and above all the armament debate, could not possibly have had a polarising effect on French society: 'The French were tearing themselves apart, but to a great extent on behalf of the one and the same divinity—the nation . . . if there was disagreement it was nevertheless on the base of unity.'[15]

A third approach differing from both the polarisation and consensus theories could be classified in very general terms as the 'theories of decadence'. These theories merit particular attention, since they have provided the basis for the key studies on armaments and politics in pre-war France by Michon and Weber.[16] Madeleine Rebérioux's *La République radicale?* can be regarded as the most impressive and coherent example of this approach.[17] Rebérioux questions the topos according to which, in the years between the turn of the century and the outbreak of war, the Third Republic's institutional and political life was determined by the left-wing bourgeois Radicals as the protagonists of a democratic Republic and the representatives of the *petite bourgeoisie* and the peasant farmers. According to Rebérioux, the post-1907 period was characterised by a degradation of political life resulting from the new alliance between the business world (banking and industrial capital) and part of the socially heterogeneous middle classes. As links between banking and industrial capital tightened, the savings capital of the *petite bourgeoisie* also began to play a more important role. As a result of this *complicité* of economic interests, the *petit bourgeois* groups' political label 'Left' gradually became devoid of meaning.[18] On the other hand, the lack of social homogeneity within the middle classes prevented outright political polarisation. This tension produced a fundamental political malaise which affected above all the Radical Party as the representative of the middle classes. The Radical Party was therefore faced with a gradual process of disintegration.

As a result of the sclerosis of left-wing republicanism, Rebérioux continues, many Radicals now became susceptible to anti-socialist and nationalistic rallying-cries. Pre-war neo-nationalism, which actually originated in the common interests of socially conservative bourgeois groups (as personified by Poincaré) on the one hand, and the traditionalist Nationalists (Barrès) on the other, therefore became a mass movement solely because of the susceptibility of the middle classes.[19]

Rebérioux also regards the 1913/14 armament campaign—the debate on three-year military service—as the peak of this new wave of nationalism. In her opinion it was not the expansion of the German army in 1913 which was behind French rearmament, but the desire of the nationalist and socially conservative groups to exploit this *thème mobilisateur*[20] in order to accelerate the final disintegration of left-wing republicanism. Although the nationalist alliance fell to pieces after the adoption of the defence bill in the autumn of 1913, this goal had nevertheless been attained. Rebérioux admits that a change took place several months before the outbreak of war when a radical/socialist counter-bloc emerged against the nationalist and socially conservative elements and won a landslide victory in the 1914 elections, but nevertheless insists that this change was of no political consequence. The bloc of the Left, she argues, had come about only because the Socialists' popular appeal—as a result of their decided stand against nationalism and militarism—had sparked off a process of reflection in the minds of many Radicals. A number of left-wing republican deputies had come out in favour of an amendment to the defence bill for purely tactical reasons in view of the coming elections. The Radical Party was divided on the key issue of the time—the defence question—so a real *rassemblement* of the Left against nationalism and war had not been established. This internal dissent was in the final analysis the political consequence of the complex liaisons of part of the middle classes—represented by the Radicals—with the interests of the national *grande bourgeoisie*.[21] In Rebérioux's opinion the *Union Sacrée* of August 1914 was the result of this complexity: the cooperation between the left-wing republican Premier, Viviani, and the champion of socially conservative nationalism, Poincaré, was possible only because of the affinity of interests which bound together the social groups the two politicians represented. Thus, all in all, Rebérioux paints the picture of a society in which fundamental social upheavals led to a domestic and socio-psychological change. However, this process of change was not yet sufficiently mature to produce clear-cut political polarisations in 1914. Her picture is dominated by an amorphous Centre, an element which had catastrophical effects, in that as a result democratic, pacifist and socially progressive forces failed to resist nationalistic rallying-cries.

Therefore, similarly to Michon,[22] Rebérioux explains the domestic developments in the pre-war period in terms of shifts in socio-economic structures and political erosions. Eugen Weber, in contrast, has attempted to illustrate the interaction between foreign policy and domestic affairs in pre-war France.[23] In his study, *The Nationalist Revival in France*, Weber also starts from the assumption that social unrest from roughly 1905 had resulted in a moderate reaction—that is, a *rapprochement* between moderate bourgeois and traditionalist/nationalist forces. Even the left-wing Republicans had increasingly evolved into a conservative force on account of social developments.[24] However, in Weber's opinion social developments do not provide an adequate explanation for the fact that 'by 1914 practically all French political parties had come round to support drastic measures of military preparedness against Germany and to supporting Poincaré'.[25] Weber regards the Agadir crisis of 1911 as a catalyst for domestic development, in that from this time onwards the precarious situation abroad laid the foundations for open cooperation between all the significant élites, regardless of their political colours. With the exception of the Socialists and a minority group of the bourgeois far Left, from 1911 onwards all the parties were reorientated according to principles such as 'social order, discipline, firm government, and strong policies at home and abroad'.[26] Weber concedes that this 'new nationalism' served the interests of socially conservative groups and had partly originated in the swing to the Right of the republican Left (partly on the grounds of the social defence). However, he insists that the new nationalism was able to gain the momentum it did only because Poincaré, Millerand, Delcassé and other politicians from the 'national' Centre had the same fears, so far as foreign policy was concerned, as the main groups of the bourgeois Left. They were all 'frightened and resentful men, seeking national union and preparedness, not for attack but for defence'.[27]

Given this consensus on defence between the Right, the Centre and the bourgeois Left, what explanation can be found for the heated debate on the conscription bill in 1913 and the subsequent swing to the Left, culminating in the victory of the Left in the elections of 1914—which in Weber's opinion clearly demonstrated the population's rejection of the policy of national unity and rearmament? Weber offers an explanation for this 'intriguing aspect of the phenomenon', as he himself admits, which largely corresponds with Mayer's dichotomy of the 'intransigent élites' and Rebérioux's 'tactical considerations' of the Radicals. Weber maintains that the nationalist revival was essentially confined to Paris, traditionally open to such movements, and that it did not spread into the provinces. The leading figures of the new nationalism—namely, authoritarian Conservatives like Poincaré, Barthou and Millerand—had been able to exert considerable influence on Parliament and the press, but not, however, on the *petite bourgeoisie* and the small farming classes in the provinces. For this reason the nationalism of Paris was a major factor of influence, but failed to leave its impact on the election results and the 'machinery of the democratic system of government'.[28] The discrepancy in the *rapprochement*, on the basis of defence policy, between the left-wing, moderate and conservative élites, on the one hand, and the resistance of above all the socialist and left-wing republican electorate, on the other, had led to the fateful disintegration of the Radical Party: 'If the radical leaders tended to side with the moderate wing, their troops moved in large numbers nearer to the socialist position.'[29] In Weber's view it was this phenomenon which prompted a substantial number of radical deputies and the upper echelons of the party to adopt a policy of extreme caution and opportunism following Parliament's adoption of three-year military service. On the one hand, they had been loath to abandon the defence bill, considered as imperative for the defence of the nation, whereas on the other hand they were equally loath openly to adopt this stance in public for fear of arousing the displeasure of the electorate. With the exception of a minority of deputies who clearly came out on one side or the other of the *Trois Ans* fence, for the majority of left-wing republican deputies the defence issue was a 'burning poker, so hot that many did not know by which end to pick it up'.[30] Thus many deputies

promised the electorate that the three-year law would soon be repealed, although in actual fact they were convinced that the law was
necessary and were determined to uphold the *Trois Ans*.

In Weber's eyes it was this confusion, the disparity between defence
requirements and the inability to explain these requirements to the
people, which made the victory of the Left in the 1914 elections such
an ephemeral phenomenon. The bloc of the Left—Socialists and
Radicals—was smashed 'on the morrow of victory' because the majority of the Radicals refused to support the Socialists' demands for the
immediate repeal of the defence bill.

Weber therefore neither observes a clearly defined bloc of the Right
in this period, nor gives the bloc of the Left much hope of survival
following the 1914 elections. For him the key to the dynamics of the
nationalist revival is the inconsistent behaviour of both the Radical
Party deputies and its leaders. This element, and this element alone,
enabled the leading figures of new nationalism—to implement their
policy—a defensive line in foreign affairs, and a mildly conservative
domestic policy. On account of the ineffective mechanisms of parliamentary transmission, the electorate's rejection of this policy in
1914 had no effect on foreign policy decision-making. The political
leaders were therefore in a position to act on their views in the July
crisis.[31]

In view of these different interpretations of domestic developments
in France on the eve of the First World War, the author was originally
concerned with the following questions:

1. How deep was the schism between nationalist and anti-militarist
   forces?
2. What was the extent of the polarisation between socially conservative and progressive movements?
3. How far had left-wing republicanism been eroded by the increase
   of social antagonisms?
4. To what extent could the 'intransigent élites' exert their influence?

At this point it should be stressed—and we shall return to this
later—that this original interest in French *domestic* affairs sparked off
in the present writer a deeper and more complex interest in examining
the relationship between domestic and foreign policy in French affairs
on the eve of the First World War.

In the above-mentioned studies the controversy over the introduction of three-year military service in 1913/14 is regarded both as a
paradigm of the polarisation theory, a peak of the nationalist revival
and, last but not least, as a significant indication of the inner decay of

radicalism. The objective of the following analysis of the political debate is to overcome the rather peculiar discrepancy between the great importance historical research has attributed to the debate and the fact that historians have so far devoted very little attention to the conflict.[32] This study cannot be confined to an analysis of the debate in Parliament and agitation in the press. Precisely because of Weber's theory concerning the fundamental difference between Parisian nationalism and politics in the provinces, the author has endeavoured, in so far as sources were available, to examine how the 'man in the street', not affiliated to any political party or organisation, viewed the rearmament issue. Attention is focused on the left-wing Republicans—the *radicaux* and the *radicaux-socialistes*—since, although their attitude towards the nationalist revival and the extension of conscription is the very core of all the theories of decadence and polarisation, the politics of this group has been subject to much less scrutiny than for example that of the *Section Française de l'Internationale Ouvrière* (SFIO) or the nationalist Right. Was it really the case—as for instance Rebérioux maintains—that the *radicaux-non-radicaux*, who had just adopted a socially conservative stance, really helped the nationalist bloc of the Right and the moderate Republicans to victory? And, if so, how could this bloc, based on economic *complicité*, fall to pieces so soon after the adoption of the three-year law, opening the door for the victory of the Left in the 1914 elections? Can this really have been due to the opportunistic electioneering tactics of pseudo left-wing deputies and party bodies? This may indeed be true of individual cases, but to apply this theory to entire groups of society is a highly questionable approach. If social structures and problems at grass-roots level were so evident in political behavioural patterns, as the theories of polarisation and decadence assume, what is the heuristic value of the interference of intransigent leaders and decision-makers observed by critical historians such as Mayer, Weber or Rebérioux? The dilemma apparent in rashly judging the political behaviour of groups of society in terms of structural patterns seems to be that gaps resulting from the attempt to interpret political history on the basis of relatively short-term sociostructural parameters have to be bridged by constructing personalisation theories.

Our first aim therefore had to be to conduct a comprehensive analysis of the political debate on the defence question and the related issue of the introduction of progressive income tax. The object of this exercise was to pinpoint whether and to what extent social malfunctioning determined political developments. This question has been examined on the basis of both contemporary publications (sources such as the minutes of parliamentary proceedings, the press, pamphlets, etc.) and a series of previously unknown or neglected sources. New light has been shed on the background to the three-year law and the problems surrounding its implementation at domestic level by the minutes of the *Conseil Supérieur de la Guerre* (CSG), the Chamber Army and Finance Committees, and above all by Poincaré's diary and correspondence. (These sources were also of significance to the foreign policy and strategic motives to army reform—see below.)

The archives of the French Ministry of the Interior were also a particularly fruitful source. Although the prefects' reports, ministerial instructions and similar documents from this period have as a rule not been preserved, all the files on the introduction of the three-year law are still available for the whole of the country. This extensive material has been assessed with particular reference to the behavioural patterns of both the left-wing bourgeois, Socialist and Syndicalist groups, and the non-organised population in the various departments. It also gives a relatively exact picture of the policies used by the government to implement the conscription law. Alongside this material from the archives of the Ministry of the Interior, files from the Ministry of Justice and the Préfecture the Police in Paris, as well as from various departmental archives, have also been studied and evaluated. These sources also highlight the intensity and the problems of the Socialists' and Syndicalists' campaign against rearmament. However, this is not so much thanks to the regular reports of political police informants as to the fact that, when the local Socialist and Syndicalist offices were searched in May 1913, files were seized which in some cases provide a valuable substitute for party archives, unfortunately not available. Further information on the problems faced by the Socialists' campaign can be found in Jules Guesde's estate, which is kept at the International Institute for Social History in Amsterdam. Evaluation of the newspapers and periodicals of a variety of political colours provides a broad spectrum of public opinion, which can naturally not be identified *a priori* with it. The contemporary press was above all a source of information for all the resolutions, demonstrations, and so forth, of the various parties and other relevant groups connected with the armament debate. Since no party archives or detailed studies of the domestic developments in this period are available, this was the only way of compiling a relatively precise and complete outline of the facts.

At first glance the debate in the press and in Parliament seemed to confirm the theory of polarisation. There is perhaps no better illustration of the bitterness which characterised the defence debate—for some time at least—than the statement made by Raoul Villain, the murderer of Jean Jaurès, following his arrest on 31 July 1914: 'I committed this crime because M. Jaurès has betrayed his country by conducting the campaign against the three-year law. I believe that traitors must be punished and that one can give one's life for such a cause. I have a profound feeling of having accomplished my duty.'[33] Villain had doubtless acted on his own initiative. No evidence was ever found that he had links with extreme nationalist groups—for example, the *Action Française*. Nevertheless, it cannot be denied that the chauvinistic and anti-socialist campaigns in the press of the bourgeois right of Centre, the Conservatives and the anti-republican Right against the 'anti-patriots' and the *Prussiens de l'Intérieur* were a fertile breeding ground for individual idiosyncrasies.[34]

However, one major observation went against the grain of the polarisation theory: this campaign seems to have had virtually no effect on the Radical Party, which was after all the numerically strongest and politically most significant party of the time. Although the leading figures of the party expressed great concern at the upsurge of chauvinism in the wake of the introduction of the conscription bill in 1913, they were nevertheless not prepared to join forces with the Socialists and the Syndicalists to form an *antitroisanniste* bloc. The reason for this reticence seems to lie in the curiously ambiguous line of argument of the left-wing Republicans. Most Radicals in Parliament, in the press and among the public considered the defence bill as a further expression of socially conservative, anti-radical tendencies which had already manifested themselves under Poincaré's ministry (1912) and Poincarés' election to the presidency in January 1913. What the Radicals, however, never called into question—with few exceptions—was the readiness to endorse any steps which would serve to safeguard national defence in the wake of the recent German armament bill which seemed to pose an immediate and ominous threat to France. It was not only the *radicaux-non-radicaux* (to use Rebérioux's term), 'infected' by the Centre and the Nationalists, who wondered whether the three-year law might be the only adequate means of warding off an attack from Germany, despite its reactionary side-effects at domestic level.

This fundamental difference between the domestic and defence aspects of the extension of military service ran like a leitmotiv through the statements of left-wing Republicans, both in Paris and in the provinces. And in view of the key role of radicalism in French society, it also dominated the entire arms debate up until the outbreak of the First World War. The opposing poles—the *Troisannistes* and the *Antitroisannistes*—were increasingly forced to enter into this dual argument in an attempt to win the left-wing Republicans wavering between domestic scruples and defence considerations over to their respective sides. This constraint, furthermore, led to a curious change in the Socialists' arguments and political tactics: although initially resolute opponents of the three-year law on grounds of international-ism and pacifism, as the debate continued the SFIO gradually changed its line to denounce the domestic reactionary and anti-republican motives behind rearmament. The opposition of the SFIO and the danger that the three-year bill might not gain a majority in Parliament (apparent in the series of amendments proposed by the left-wing Republicans) made the other pole—the *Troisannistes*—change its argu-ment. This was an aspect which initially the present writer could not quite fathom. In the opening phase of the campaign (February–May 1913) the government, backed by the unconditional support of the far Right and the moderate bourgeoisie, tried to stir up feelings of hysteri-cal fear as a means of pushing through the three-year bill as quickly as possible. However, as the debate continued—prolonged in fact by the SFIO counter-agitation—the *Troisannistes*, with the exception of the extreme Nationalists, attempted to dispel the left-wing Republicans' doubts. Thus it was stressed that three-year conscription was not to remain in force indefinitely. The bill was no more than a provisional measure, imperative because of the acute danger France was facing, and in no way represented a break with the traditional republican and democratic army constitution. It was this argument alone which convinced the Radicals—and by no means only the centrist *radicaux-non-radicaux*—that the defence bill was after all a technical issue and domestically neutral.

These empirical findings with respect to the character of the first phase of the defence debate—the domestic tensions after the·adoption of the bill will not be examined at this point—raised a fundamental heuristic problem. Like almost every 'critical' historian, the present writer originally assumed that the expansion of the French army could not be interpreted simply as a response to the 1913 German arms bill. Historians such as Michon and Weber, and more recently Rebérioux, have pointed out that, since 1911, both nationalist and French army circles had been openly demanding the amendment of the republican and egalitarian conscription law of 1905. This fact, along with the curiously swift presentation of the three-year bill in 1913, when the actual content of the German arms bill was still unknown, implies that the French government had had a ready-made defence bill 'up its sleeve' (Herzfeld) for some time, which it now produced at the appropriate moment, the intention being to strengthen the nationalist/ militarist and socially conservative trends which had been gaining momentum over the years and to exploit the armament campaign as a means of winning over faltering left-wing Republicans into the nat-ionalist and conservative camp once and for all. However, if we assume that the three-year law was a symbol and vehicle of this swing in domestic politics, why did the government and the conservative groups (with the exception of the Nationalists) try to present technical and objective arguments in the course of the debate? And why, in particular, did they stress again and again that the three-year law was in no way a break with the left-wing republican and egalitarian principles of the 1905 conscription law?

These unanswered questions made it necessary to conduct more detailed research into the motives behind rearmament. Was it perhaps really true that the German arms bill at the beginning of 1913 threatened France with an 'attack', which she could ward off only by reinforcing her regular army?

There are virtually no sources available on the origins of the three-year law. No minutes of the proceedings at cabinet meetings had been preserved; there was no record of official reports of the meetings of the *Conseil Supérieur de la Guerre*, the body responsible for the bill; and the minutes of the Chamber Army Committee meetings had not been published. Fortunately, however, many of these sources could be exploited. Poincaré's diary in the National Library in Paris which, as we shall see, greatly differs from his memoirs on many essential points, provides a welter of highly interesting references to developments at home and abroad in these years, and, above all, a valuable insight into the cabinet meetings where the three-year law and related issues were discussed.[35] The minutes of the meetings of the *Conseil Supérieur de la Guerre* in the army archives in Paris-Vincennes reveal the military and political motives and problems involved with the armament issue. And, finally, the minutes of the Chamber Army Committee (*Archives Nationales*) bear witness to the—successful—attempts of the military and political leaders to hide these motives from Parliament and the public. It should be pointed out, without going into detail, that it was the discovery of these three sources which led the author to expand his field of investigation and, along with other sources, to make the constant interaction of foreign and domestic policy the core of this study.

The above-mentioned sources led to the following conclusions:

1. The three-year law was definitely not prepared before January 1913.
2. The German arms bill in early 1913 was the reason for the introduction of the French defence bill.
3. The motive behind the French armament measures was *not* the fear of an imminent German assault. The *only* reason for these measures was the fact that the expansion of the German army was a threat to French strategic plans, above all the new operational plan, in draft since 1911, which was based on an unconditional

offensive.

4. The offensive strategy of the French general staff, laid down in Plan XVII in 1913, was one of the essential components of the military agreements with Russia. To call this strategy into question would be to jeopardise the entire network of French foreign and security policy.

5. French military and political leaders were aware of the fact that these considerations of foreign policy and strategics would not be accepted by the left-wing Republicans in Parliament, not to mention the Socialists, or the population as a whole. For this reason army reorganisation, which had been planned on the basis of long-term considerations of foreign and military policy and which was now indispensable in the light of the new German armament plans, was presented to the public as an urgent emergency measure necessary to protect the country from a German attack.

If, in view of these facts, one does not opt for theories of conspiracy but attributes contemporary decision-makers with at least a hypothetical sense of responsibility, it is necessary to clarify the origins of the offensive strategy, its relevance to defence policy and its relation to the problems of the Russian alliance and the *Entente* with Britain. It transpired that the Agadir crisis was of particular relevance in this context, which is why this study begins 'after Agadir'.

In view of the fact that developments in foreign policy were constitutive for French military planning, the theory, based on the pre-eminence of domestic policy, that the three-year law was a vehicle of socially conservative policy, cannot be substantiated. On the other hand, there is no reason to conclude a primacy of foreign policy. Although it must be conceded that French military and political leaders followed the imperatives of foreign and defence policy, their action was nevertheless subject to insurmountable domestic and social constraints.

The observation that a concept of foreign and defence policy, dovetailed with the framework conditions of foreign policy, could be implemented only at domestic level with the aid of extreme manipulation and, as a result, remained constantly unstable, leads to four fundamental theories on the relationship between domestic and foreign affairs in pre-war France:

1. At this stage the internal system of the 'Radical Republic' had not been eroded to such an extent that the necessary support for an open swing in foreign and military policy could be found in

Parliament and in public. Given the predominance of traditional left-wing republican topoi (in particular, the concept of the purely defensive nation in arms and the reductionist identification of national defence with territorial defence), military measures resulting from changes in the system of foreign policy could be given only secondary legitimation.

2. The mechanisms of secondary legitimation were inducive of domestic crisis (not, however, of polarisation!), because although the objective difference between the left-wing republican concept of national defence and the three-year law could not have been completely obscured, this question was never openly discussed in public. For this reason the suspicions of the Left that the defence bill was first and foremost a vehicle of domestic reactionary aspirations could never be completely dispelled. Under the pre-eminence of domestic policy, the three-year law—and with it the entire calculations of foreign policy and strategics—remained in danger.

3. This *de facto* primacy of domestic policy and the reductionist identification of foreign policy with national defence were inducive of crisis in foreign policy in two ways:

   (*a*) The joint foundations of French foreign and strategic policy from the time of the Agadir crisis—the Russian alliance and the three-year law—were never explicitly called into question by the relevant political groups; nor were they confronted with alternative concepts of foreign policy. This fact stands unaltered, despite certain attempts by the SFIO and minority groups of the bourgeois Left, which could never fully rid themselves of their idiosyncratic, narrow perception of foreign policy.

   (*b*) The continuity of the non-radical élites' decision-making in foreign policy was severely threatened by the slide to the Left in the 1914 elections. An amendment of the conscription law now seemed imminent—for purely domestic reasons. It was the resultant impending (but unintentioned!) challenge to the whole of French foreign policy and strategical calculations—military agreements and strategic planning which permitted no short-term modification—which determined the behaviour of the French government in the July crisis of 1914. It was this awareness that internal constraints would soon jeopardise French foreign policy calculations that led French decision-makers to give their unconditional support to Russia and accept the German challenge on the motto 'now rather than later'.

4. Meanwhile, the result of the national defence stereotype was that, over and above social antagonisms of every kind, the whole of French society, including the Socialists, was convinced that France must be armed against the impending German onslaught. It was this basic consensus, which had been confirmed time and again in the course of the parliamentary and public debate on the defence question, which paved the way for the *Union Sacrée* and secured it at the decisive moment.

In conclusion, therefore, the actual turn of events in pre-war French domestic politics does *not* confirm the theory that a socio-political polarisation had emerged in this period or that the intransigent élites were resorting to a 'diversionary war' to preserve their social status. However, the theories of decadence are not so simple to assess. On the one hand, political history from 1911 shows that the alleged social erosion of left-wing republicanism had no direct influence on political developments; the predominance of the 'national defence' stereotype can also be regarded as a clear indication of the unchallenged prevalence of radical ideology in contemporary French society. On the other hand, perhaps this stereotype in itself indicates a lack of political innovation which, in turn, was due to a particular socio-historical development. Jean Touchard, for example, has pointed out that in the wake of the social upheavals from the 1890s the left-wing Republicans had increasingly sought cover behind defence stereotypes on all political and social issues—for example defence of *la patrie*, 'order', 'local interests', 'peace', 'republican defence'.[36] However, the story of this long-term social immobility and its political effects, which must take account of the actual interaction between social processes and phenomena at 'superstructural' level, has yet to be written.

The following account of the arms debate in France on the eve of the First World War shows that to interpret directly political developments as a basis of short-term social malfunctioning may lead to an underestimation of the influence which long-term developments—institutional framework conditions, established political ideologies and behavioural stereotypes—may have on fundamentally heterogeneous decision-making.

CHAPTER 1

After Agadir

Strategic Planning and Foreign Policy

The Franco–German confrontation over Morocco in 1911 was of decisive importance for the overall development of French foreign and military policy in the final years before the outbreak of the First World War. The occupation of Fez by French troops in May 1911, necessary to reinforce informal French rule in Morocco but at the same time a violation of the Algeciras agreement of 1906, provided German diplomacy with a welcome opportunity to reopen the debate on the Moroccan question and to secure something in the nature of 'compensations'.[1] Although after painstaking negotiations the crisis was ironed out, for the time being, the *Panthersprung* on 1 July 1911 had nevertheless left a distinct impression upon a large section of French public opinion, as well as governmental and military circles, that Germany was willing to resort to military means in order to achieve her imperialistic aims.[2]

However, during this crisis it became apparent that in military terms France was not sufficiently prepared for a war with Germany. The Chief of Staff, Joffre, bluntly remarked to the Premier, Caillaux, that the French 'did not have even a 70 per cent chance of victory'.[3] Joffre's scepticism as largely due to the confused command structure of the French army. As a result of the Dreyfus affair in the 1890s the organisational relationship between military command and military planning had become somewhat distorted—a state of affairs which could have devastating effects in the event of a war. The civil authorities tended to be distrustful of the officer corps, still basically anti-republican and traditionally monarchist,[4] which had led to a strictly defined delimitation of responsibility between the military command on the one hand and military planning and organisation on the other. Responsibility for strategic planning and army organisation lay in the

21

hands of the various departments of the general staff, subordinated to the Ministry of War. In peacetime the *généralissimé désigné*, supreme commander in the event of war, had no influence whatsoever on the staffing of the *État-Major* or on its strategic planning, the authority to issue commands and instructions being the sole responsibility of the Minister of War.[5] Thus the only link between the general staff and the Commander-in-chief was the Minister of War; but in 1911 alone three different men were to be entrusted with this portfolio.

In practical terms this constant reshuffling at the head of the army meant that the subordinate army authorities gained a considerable degree of independence. The consequences of this situation were particularly evident at the time of the Agadir crisis when the most important of these bodies, the *Troisième Bureau*, responsible for military planning and organisation, was dominated by the so-called 'Young Turks', a group of high-ranking officers rallied around Lt-Colonel Grandmaison and openly opposed to the strategically defensive approach of the operational plan of the time, Plan XVI (1908).[6] The Young Turks, inspired by A. du Picq's and Foch's theories on warfare, advocated an out-and-out offensive approach to the conduct of war.[7] Grandmaison's famous *deux conférences* in the spring of 1911 are paradigmatic of this theory. Starting out from the immense destructive power of modern artillery and its demoralising effect on the attacking troops, Grandmaison advocated a change in the soldiers' morale rather than steps to modernise the army, such as the procurement of modern heavy artillery. This new morale was to be achieved in an 'immediate and total attack' in which the soldiers, in a state of 'over-excitement' would overrun the enemy fortifications: 'Our conclusion shall be that we must be prepared and prepare the others for this by cultivating with passion, excess and in the finest details of training, everything that bears . . . the mark of the offensive spirit. Let us take this to the extreme. . . !'[8] The fact therefore that a group of officers who had for some time been advocating an offensive approach were entrusted with the implementation of a basically defensive operational plan, and not thereby subject to permanent control, is sufficient illustration of the confusion within the army and makes it seem rational that—*rebus sic stantibus*—a war with Germany had to be avoided at all costs.

The Agadir crisis had thus shown that the French army was not really prepared for action. The government immediately set about dismantling the dualistic army command structure. In a decree from the Minister of War, Messimy, on 28 July 1911, the *généralissimé désigné* was replaced by the Chief of General Staff who, as his title suggests, was to be at the head of the general staff, responsible for military planning and in command of the main army in wartime.[9]

On Messimy's recommendation General Joffre was entrusted with this newly created post on the very same day. The appointment seemed to the government to be politically unproblematic, since Joffre was not really considered as a representative of the caste still predominant within the officer corps despite a decade of republicanisation. Joffre was rated as a technician, a specialist in questions of logistics.[10] Although he rejected some of the theories of the offensive theorists as exaggerations,[11] Joffre nevertheless endorsed the principle of an out-and-out offensive approach to warfare on both technical and moral grounds.[12] His new position of strength as Chief of General Staff provided him with the opportunity of gradually dovetailing the French operational plan into the offensive doctrine. The result of this planning, which lasted from August 1911 until the spring of 1914, was the famous—or infamous—Plan XVII. This plan embodied the dogma of an *offensive à outrance* which, following the experiences of the First World War, was later to become a target of criticism from both the military and political points of view.[13] The frontier battles in the autumn of 1914 were to illustrate the absurdity of the basic premises of Joffre's strategy 'that a victory will be won only by him who looks for a battle and fights it offensively with all his might'.[14]

Nevertheless, it is unwarranted to describe the drafting and implementation of Plan XVII as no more than the product of the unrealistic and idiosyncratic thought patterns and the 'continuing ineptness'[15] of Joffre and his collaborators at general staff. This interpretation disregards the fundamental issue, namely: why did the political leaders—who had undoubtedly gained the upper hand since the end of the Dreyfus affair—tolerate (as did Caillaux) or even actively encourage (Poincaré) the 'Plan games' of the general staff? Indeed, the lie of the land in alliance and military policy in 1911–14 gave Joffre's offensive strategy a degree of rationality which no politician in office—no matter what his colours—could deny. It was in fact also a fundamental reason for the introduction of three-year conscription in 1913.

The reorganisation of the army high command by Caillaux's left-wing republican government provided a catalyst for the release of the offensive doctrine. However, this was not a reflection of militaristic intentions or evidence that the civil authorities were acquiescing to their military counterparts. Caillaux and his Minister of War, Messimy, were convinced that, despite the concentration of power in the hands of Joffre, rational from a military point of view, constant surveillance could ensure that political decision-making would retain its hold over military planning. When in December 1911 Joffre outlined to the head of government his new strategic plan, in which war operations were concentrated on an offensive on the Franco-German border, Caillaux pointed out to the Chief of Staff that decision-making was ultimately the responsibility of the civil authorities.[16] And although Joffre repeatedly pressed the political leaders for a precise account of how France actually stood in external affairs, and in particular for an indication of the stance Britain and Russia were likely to adopt in the event of a war, his pleas fell on deaf ears. For, unlike Joffre, Caillaux was of the opinion that it was first of all up to the general staff to draw up plans expedient from the military point of view. These would then be submitted to the government for critical examination, with particular reference to the overall situation in foreign policy, and if necessary amended.[17] In his memoirs Caillaux emphasises that, unlike his successor, Poincaré, he had not accepted Joffre's plans without question. Owing to a lack of awareness of political responsibility, writes Caillaux, Poincaré had neglected the civil authorities' responsibility of control and was therefore at least partly responsible for the 'inept operational plan'.[18]

Caillaux's self-justification must be viewed with a certain degree of scepticism. Although the relationship between the civil and military authorities had been clearly defined under his government, this did not eliminate the concrete problems of French diplomacy in the wake of Agadir, which were in fact at the root of the offensive approach to strategic planning.

The fact that strategic planning depended on circumstances within the alliance was confirmed at the beginning of 1912 when Joffre was forced to abandon his original plans on account of the attitude of Britain. Plan XVI, as amended by Joffre from September 1911, had in fact not yet been aimed at an *offensive toutes forces réunies*. It did admittedly reflect a new priority—strictly offensive warfare—but was nevertheless not yet entirely focused on an offensive in Lorraine. Joffre clearly recognised the dilemma that a plan of this kind presented, since it forced the French army to concentrate its efforts on the Metz-Strasbourg line. This line was on the one hand not only highly fortified but unfavourable terrain for mass manoeuvres. On the other hand, however, it was virtually official doctrine at that time that the opening battles along this line would determine the final outcome of the war.[19] For this reason Joffre's strategic considerations initially included the possibility of an offensive via southern Belgium. This manoeuvre would have a twofold advantage: first, the French army, on favourable terrain, could cut off the Germans wheeling through Belgium (it was taken for granted that the Germans would attack through this route); second, the British Expeditionary Force (BEF) could join in the offensive.[20]

It was clearly due to the fundamental political problems involved in this operational plan that in the course of 1912 the French general staff began to concentrate the French offensive entirely in Lorraine, despite serious misgivings. The reason for this change in policy was that Joffre's repeated demand for the political leaders' go-ahead to a violation of Belgian neutrality by allowing French troops to enter Belgium (this being the only means of applying the more favourable strategic alternative) was turned down by both Caillaux and his successor Poincaré. Whether or not the two politicians were motivated by the same reasons, or whether Caillaux was more influenced by the fundamentals of international law than Poincaré, is of no significance in this context. Objectively decisive for both presidents was the certainty that Britain, as the guarantor power of Belgian neutrality, would not fight on the side of a power which had violated it. At the end of 1912, when Anglo-French relations had become consolidated after the failure of the Haldane mission, the British government once again insisted on the fact that if French troops were to march into Belgium prior to a German invasion, Britain would be forced into a position of neutrality.

As from 1912, on account of the British veto, the French general staff orientated all its strategic plans towards the *offensive à outrance* in Lorraine.[21] To renounce completely the large-scale offensive at the beginning of the war was inconceivable for the dogmatic Young Turkish strategists for whom purely offensive warfare was a 'superior' form of warfare.[22]

In these circumstances the military agreements with Russia began to assume a major role in the French war plans. The coordinated offensive of Russian and French troops was particularly decisive in this context. The starting-point of the French offensive on the highly fortified Lorraine border was basically unfavourable, and French prospects of success in a war could be enhanced only if a substantial number of German contingents were held back by a Russian offensive on the German–Russian border.

However, for both political and military reasons it was highly questionable at this point whether Russia would be prepared to launch an offensive attack, either in time or with the full strength of her army. Although the 1892 Franco-Russian military convention was still in force, the strategical planning of the two countries was no longer sufficiently coordinated. Since around 1906—that is, after Russia had been weakened by the Russo-Japanese War—French operational plans had no longer been based on the principle of a simultaneous Russian offensive. On the contrary, on the assumption that the Russians would delay in launching their offensive, strategically defensive manoeuvres had been planned at the initial stage.[23] The Agadir crisis had confirmed these reservations. At the peak of the crisis the Russian government had informed France that it did not regard the Franco-German dispute over Morocco as a *casus foederis*. The Russian ambassador in Paris, Izvolsky, explained to Caillaux that the reticence of his government was largely due to the fact that the Russian army was unprepared for a war in Europe and that it would take at least two years to reorganise the army in order to meet the provision of the 1892 convention, according to which a rapid and simultaneous advance of Russian and French troops was to be launched on Germany.[24] At a conference of the representatives of the Russian and French general staffs in August 1911 these doubts were again confirmed. Although the Russian general staff agreed to do all it could to launch an offensive against Germany with the main body of its army on the sixteenth day following mobilisation, it nevertheless argued that the reorganisation of its army, necessary to achieve this goal, would take at least two years. The French could therefore not expect a Russian offensive on the eastern border of Germany until the twentieth day following mobilisation. Moreover, Russia might be forced to retain part of her army to ward off an Austrian offensive.[25] The very fact that only a few days before the outbreak of the First World War French army officers and politicians were by no means convinced that Russia was actually prepared to launch the main offensive against Germany—and not Austria![26]—proves just how fragile the 1911 agreements were considered to be.[27]

In view of the latest problem that the *offensive à outrance* in Lorraine could be launched only in conjunction with simultaneous Russian relief attacks, the French officers and the Poincaré cabinet, reshuffled at the beginning of 1912, now made a determined effort to improve military and political relations with Russia. In the following phase, which lasted until the so-called 'Liman von Sanders affair' at the end of 1913,[28] the pressure on the French to bear upon Russia to carry out her military planning in accordance with the 1892 convention was so intense that the policy of France towards her ally was basically characterised by preliminary concessions in the political, military and financial fields:

> Apart the reasons which logically prompted us to concentrate operations on our front by as swift an offensive as possible, the will to respect the letter of the convention also compelled us to assume this attitude. And we can affirm that in each contact with our general staff the Russian general staff has been shown with certainty that we are adopting an offensive approach and respecting the provisions of the convention. This has made a great contri-

bution to the increase in the Russian general staff's efforts. If they had felt that we were not so resolute, there can be no doubt that our allies would have been more reserved at the outbreak of the war.[29]

This quotation clearly reflects the great concern and doubts of the French officers with regard to Russia's reserved attitude to French strategic demands. This uneasiness was again confirmed during the Franco-Russian general staffs' conference in July 1912, at a time when the French offensive plan had already been drafted. In these discussions Joffre once again insisted on the essential point of strategic calculation and impressed upon his Russian colleagues that 'it is in the interest of the Germans to advance successively and separately, first against France and then against Russia. The plan of the allies, in contrast, must be to launch a simultaneous attack on both fronts with the maximum combined effort'.[30]

The crucial importance this principle had already assumed for French strategy at this early stage was underlined when Joffre presented the French concentration plans showing that almost the entire French army would be concentrated on the Franco-German border at the beginning of the war. However, the Russian general staff could not be convinced of the wisdom of such a one-sided approach to strategic planning. The Russian Chief of Staff, Zilinsky, stated quite unequivocally: 'Austria has greatly expanded her military power and improved her railway lines. She is obviously aiming at an offensive. Russia cannot expose herself to a failure on the Austrian front. The moral effect would be disastrous. She must therefore divide her forces to face this power as well as Germany.'

Joffre was admittedly given the assurance that the Russian army would henceforth be in a position to launch its offensive operations against Germany a day earlier. Nevertheless, the French officers seem to have been extremely worried by the negative turn of these discussions, fearing that Russia was not prepared to coordinate fully her military preparations with French strategic calculations for political reasons. Furthermore, in view of the inadequate strategic railway links, it still remained doubtful whether Russian troops could be concentrated on the eastern border of Germany with the speed required.[31]

As this uneasiness about how Russia would react in the event of war grew in the minds of the French officers, the government, which also had doubts about the stability of the alliance,[32] intensified its endeavours to reinforce the alliance at all costs. Poincaré, in office since the beginning of 1912,[33] was absolutely convinced that Germany's intentions were basically hostile and accordingly geared his entire policy towards preparing France 'materially and spiritually, at home and abroad, for the threatening crisis'.[34] This policy was to be carried out by cultivating the alliances and ententes in foreign policy and reinforcing France's military striking power.[35] This policy, later to be described as 'Poincaristic', was mainly focused on the alliance with Russia. Poincaré's policy towards Russia seems to have been characterised essentially by major concessions to the Russians in the interpretation of the *casus foederis* stipulated in the treaty of the alliance—a policy aimed at persuading Russia to respect the letter of the political and military agreements between the two countries. Poincaré's objective was to safeguard France from Germany's hegemonic ambitions. Since he considered no alternative but the Russian alliance, he endeavoured to strengthen this alliance at all costs so that military agreements would be respected and the effectiveness of the French operational plan guaranteed. This aim was also the fundamental reason for his state visit to St Petersburg in August 1912, a few weeks after the aforementioned general staffs' conference. With hindsight it can be assumed that the commitments made by Poincaré in St Petersburg with respect to the *casus foederis* went far beyond the original purely defensive aims of the alliance, in that he promised Russia that France would come to her aid in a war with Austria-Hungary over the Balkans. Although this pledge was qualified, to be applicable only in the case of German intervention in such a war, its significance was none the less far-reaching, since Germany was bound under the Dual Alliance to come to the assistance of Austria if she were attacked by Russia.[36] Although Poincaré's concession on this point by no means implies that he was a warmonger, as was often insinuated following the First World War, it is nevertheless characteristic of a policy 'at the edge of a plunging precipice'. For, since Russia considered herself the protecting power of the Slavic peoples, Poincaré had little hope of warding off the potential consequences of these concessions. He could in fact only cherish the hope that Russia basically wanted peace and trust in the skill of his own diplomacy. Poincaré believed that the Russians could be persuaded into coordinating permanently with their French allies so that the potential risks of a Russian policy geared towards Russia's Balkan interests could be kept in check.[37]

However, even before Poincaré had made these concessions in St Petersburg, it was evident that the aspirations and problems of Russian policy in the Balkans could hardly be squeezed into the corset of advance consultations with France. French enquiries about the aims of the military alliances of the Balkan states set up under Russian patronage in the spring of 1912 were not even answered by the Russian government.[38] And, at the latest, it was during the course of the St Petersburg discussions that Poincaré became convinced that the

Balkan military alliances were tantamount to a pact of war led by Russia.[39] Yet he was not prepared to steer clear of this danger but continued to level his gaze on Germany, 'dominated by so many bad instincts', whose desire to hegemony was inducing France to reinforce the Russian alliance at all costs.[40]

Poincaré later justified his policy of granting far-reaching political concessions to Russia with the argument that France would otherwise have had no hope of Russian assistance if she were attacked by Germany.[41] Poincaré's self-justification in answer to accusations in the innocentistic literature of the post-war period was at least partly true; for, despite the assurances given by Russia with regard to the stability of the political alliance, French political leaders at the beginning of 1912 were most dubious about the military effectiveness of this alliance. And indeed in the course of the St Petersburg talks Poincaré did insist of Sazonov, Kokovcov and the Tsar that Russia must complete the network of strategic railway lines on the eastern border of Germany. He directly referred to Joffre's concern: '. . . it was our general staff which brought up the question of these shortcomings, even more serious in view of the fact that our mobilisation is to take place more quickly so that they may pose a threat to the first military efforts of the two countries'.[42]

Sazonov, although aware of the importance of this matter, intimated that Russia was more concerned with expanding the strategic railway network on her border with Austria. The French were informed that the Russians would 'probably' look into their requests 'within the bounds of possibility'.[43] The Tsar referred Poincaré to his Finance Minister, Kokovcov, on this matter. Without mincing his words Kokovcov expressed his distrust of the already very reticent promises made by the army officers: 'These gentlemen . . . would be capable of committing us without due reflection. They talk and talk with virtually no concern of financial possibilities or even diplomatic considerations.'[44]

Despite the Russians' cool reaction to French military demands the Poincaré government did not amend its foreign policy. On the contrary, the Poincaristic line of French policy was enforced even further as a result of the First Balkan War.

The outbreak and repercussions of the First Balkan War were a clear illustration of the limits to the traditional statemanship of the Great Powers in Europe. Despite latent conflicts of interest between the Great Powers, alliance systems and conference diplomacy had hitherto been regarded as a possible means of securing peace. The new self-assurance of the victorious Balkan states had suddenly cast a shadow on this principle. French policy—and the policy of other nations—was

now dominated by the fear that this change in the *status quo* could lead
to a general European conflict. In August 1912 Poincaré had informed
the Russian government that 'matters of concern purely to the
Balkans'—without German intervention—would not be considered a
casus foederis.[45] Meanwhile the French government had apparently
become convinced that matters that concerned 'only' the Balkans
simply did not exist and that, on the contrary, the entire strength of the
alliance and its preparedness would have to be put to the test.[46] On
repeated occasions towards the end of 1912 the French stressed their
own preparedness and urged the Russians to follow their example and
show a greater degree of firmness *vis-à-vis* the political and military
alliance.[47]

The French reaction to the new German arms bill at the beginning of
1913 must be seen against this background. On the one hand the
French offensive strategy required coordinated Russian measures; on
the other, Russia seemed to be wavering, both politically and militarily. The fact that the French government did all it could to come up
with an immediate response to the 'German challenge', even before the
precise details of the German armament bill were known, can be
explained by the fact that the French general staff believed that its own
offensive plan would be jeopardised by the German armament plans if
retaliatory measures were not taken at once.[48] A further ominous
possibility for France was that the German army bill, regardless of the
precise form it would finally take, might make Russia even more
reluctant to coordinate her military policy along French lines. The
French government therefore now began to put across its strategic
demands to the Russians more firmly. In the first place the French
ambassador in St Petersburg, Georges Louis, known as a 'dove', was
recalled and replaced by Delcassé. The new ambassador was ordered to
do all he could to ensure that the Russians adjusted their military
policy once and for all to meet the requirements of the alliance.
Furthermore, the French government hastened to assure its reluctant
ally that France herself was prepared to keep her military power 'at a
level prepared for all contingencies', which was why it had already
been decided to extend military service to a period of three years.[49]

Poincaré's Policy of 'National Unity'

The crisis of 1911 not only sparked off a reorientation of
French foreign and military policy but led to a change in power
structures in the French domestic scene. Now that attention was

focused on foreign policy—or, to be more precise, national defence—the influence of the left-wing Republicans, who had dominated the domestic scene since the Dreyfus affair, began to subside:

> Internal affairs gave way to foreign. Political promises and programs had come to nothing so often that they met with increasing scepticism. Now it seemed that internal affairs would look after themselves, if only the new ministry [the Poincaré government] could settle the imbroglio of foreign policy. The new interest in foreign affairs permeated a world heretofore preoccupied almost solely by local and national questions.[50]

This new mood[51] among wide sections of the public has been referred to as a 'nationalist revival'. In actual fact it was a spontaneous reaction, an expression of national pride in the wake of what was regarded as the blackmailing policy of Germany, and had little in common with the old doctrinaire form of nationalism, of for example the *Action Française*.

It was this general mood which gave Poincaré's government, formed at the beginning of 1912, its stability. It is impossible to give a precise definition of Poincaristic policy in terms of party politics. Poincaré's policy of national unity found support not only among the ranks of the national Centre and the nationalistic Right. Even the radical Left endorsed at least the foreign policy of Poincaré's government. Throughout 1912 hardly a word of opposition was voiced by left-wing Republicans against Poincaré's doctrine of strength and energy in foreign policy and—its counterpart in internal affairs—the policy of national unity. Even the Socialists offered little resistance to Poincaré's policy; their campaign against chauvinism and reaction was not launched until 1913, parallel to their campaign against the introduction of three-year military service. Indeed, Poincaré's election to the presidency in January 1913 was essentially due to the Socialists' refusal to support the left-wing candidate who had been fielded against Poincaré, not on grounds of foreign policy but on purely domestic issues.[52]

The key to Poincaré's governmental declaration on 16 January 1912 was his call for the national unity of all the groups of the Radical Party. In those 'difficult hours' of international politics, said Poincaré, it was Parliament's duty to 'follow the example of the country' and set aside its traditional domestic squabbles such as anti-clericalism, always at the heart of radical republican domestic policy. Parliament's conduct should be geared towards the public interest. This 'superior' interest had to be pursued, and domestic issues suspended to a certain extent, because it was a priority to cultivate the French system of alliances and to ensure the continuity of French interests. These words reflect a specific interest which had already become apparent in the electoral reform of July 1912: to provide the executive with a considerably greater degree of independence from the fluctuating parliamentary majorities which generally led to frequent changes of government throughout the Third Republic. In his governmental declaration Poincaré also called for the strengthening of national defence in view of the alarming events of the previous months: 'Although our country is profoundly pacifist, she is not the master of all eventualities and intends to respect all her obligations. We shall devote careful attention to our army and navy which, like you, gentlemen, we regard as the sacred pillars of the Republic and *la patrie*.'[53]

The link between strength in foreign policy, military strength and domestic—moral—unity alluded to in Poincaré's governmental declaration was to be the leitmotiv of all the new President's public statements throughout his term of office. A speech he gave in Dunkirk on his return from St Petersburg in the autumn of 1912 is a typical example:

> The Republic has upheld France's position in the world by a policy of wisdom, sang-froid and dignity. Only our material and moral strength can give value to our friendship and maintain our position above persistent circumstances. Let us therefore endeavour to preserve and enhance the vital energy of our country, and I am referring not only to her military and naval strength but above all to this political confidence and this unity of national feeling which endows a people with grandeur, glory and immortality.[54]

The policy of moral unification was applied above all in the military field, with the government's measures aimed at both increasing the prestige of the army among the public and strengthening the moral force and inner cohesion of the regular army.[55] Poincaré's War Minister, Millerand, wrote in a report on his activities: 'The general idea which guided me . . . was to provide the command with all the necessary material and moral requirements to fulfil its duties.'[56]

Accordingly, particular efforts were made to tighten up military discipline, although this went against the traditional doctrine of the 'citizen soldier' which older generations of republican politicians had used as a weapon against the anti-republican spirit of 'military society'. A decree dating from 1910 had defined military discipline as follows: 'You shall obey all the orders of your commander for the good of the service, the execution of military regulations and the upholding of the law.'[57]

Under Poincaré's government these 'rational' regulations on military discipline were replaced by a decree stipulating that the soldier must give 'total obedience' and yield 'constant submission' to the orders of his superiors. A further attempt to increase army homogeneity and the officers' authority was the *Loi Millerand* of 31 March 1912. The real purpose of this act was to curtail syndicalist agitation in the ranks. Defamation of the army, incitement to disobey orders and desertion were henceforth subject to extremely severe punishment—namely, transfer to a delinquent battalion of the colonial army.[58]

Alongside these repressive measures, efforts were made to improve the image of the army among the public, in order to demonstrate the 'harmony of the patriotic feelings' of all Frenchmen at home and abroad.[59] Thus public military retreats, prohibited following the Dreyfus affair in the 1890s to prevent any manifestation of the anti-republican 'military society' were now reintroduced. The enthusiasm of the Paris mob for these weekly military parades attracted a great deal of attention both at home and abroad, since they often ended up in rallies with a clearly chauvinistic overtone.

Republicans, fearing that this mass enthusiasm could lead to a new wave of Boulangerism, followed these events with the utmost concern.[60] All the more so, since the nationalist Right interpreted the enthusiasm for the army which was being orchestrated by the government as a sign that the national Republic—identified with Poincaré—was *nolens volens* becoming reconciled to the militarist and anti-republican doctrine of the 'integral Nationalists'.[61] Recent historical research has gone a step further, suggesting that this militarism was a general indication that the Poincaré government had deliberately initiated a conservative swing in domestic politics, and that in the final years before the Great War this new form of mass nationalism had become the basis for a conservative 'catch-all' policy.[62] However, these theories are exaggerated interpretations which can be refuted. Precisely, the events of 1913 prove beyond doubt that there could be no question at that time of chauvinistic and militaristic feelings among wide sections of the public. The enthusiasm for the army seems rather to have been a spontaneous reaction to the 'shame' of Agadir. Moreover, the curious observation that in the years 1911–13 there was a continual fall in the number of *sociétés de préparation militaire* applying for official registration, illustrates the transcience of this state of nationalistic agitation.[63] We must bear in mind that, despite their scepticism about a 'flood of Boulangerism', the vast majority of the left-wing republican deputies in Parliament endorsed the repressive measures embodied in the *Loi Millerand*. This law was in fact no more than the continuation of the attempts of previous governments, including left-wing republican ministries, to curb the anti-militarist agitation of the revolutionary Syndicalists.[64] Even the Socialists, whose newspapers continually protested against the systematic stimulation of 'military reaction',[65] clearly repudiated anti-militarist and anti-patriotic agitation in the parliamentary debate. Although the socialist parliamentary group tabled an amendment to the *Loi Millerand* providing for milder punishments in certain cases other than those originally stipulated, only about half of the socialist deputies in Parliament voted in favour of a motion to repeal the law.[66]

Moreover, at this time a crisis in anti-patriotic doctrine had emerged within the syndicalist movement itself. More than all the appeals for national unity or other verbal expressions of patriotism, the crisis is a clear illustration of the deep impression Agadir had left on French society, even among the diehard opponents of the bourgeois class state.

To resume briefly upon this crisis, one of the fundamental elements of revolutionary syndicalism embodied in the *Confédération Générale du Travail* (CGT), founded in 1895, was strict anti-militarism. This line had originally been regarded as purely corporate and as a reaction to the fact that strike movements were often put down by the army. However, in the years of social unrest following 1905, this anti-militarism within the CGT had become a hardened doctrine, an expression of the anarcho-syndicalist struggle against the bourgeois state.[67] A resolution adopted at the CGT congress in Amiens in 1906 expressed this doctrine in its classical form: 'Congress affirms that anti-militarist and anti-patriotic propaganda must become increasingly intense and audacious. In every strike the army is on the side of the employers. In every European conflict, in every international or colonial war the working class is the victim of the parasitic, bourgeois employers' class. . . .'[68]

Despite the opposition of the reformist syndicates to the intemperately anti-militarist and anti-patriotic CGT slogans—which quite openly spoke of sabotaging mobilisation and declared that the outbreak of a war would be an appropriate opportunity to push through the 'social revolution'—this policy was reaffirmed in the congress resolution of 1908 in Marseilles and 1910 in Toulouse.[69]

However, in the wake of the Agadir crisis the anti-patriotic doctrine lost a considerable degree of its momentum, both within the CGT leadership and at grass-roots level—that is, among the revolutionary syndicates. At the CGT *Conférence des Fédérations et des Bourses* in 1911 almost all the delegates declared that 'they could not count upon their syndicates to join in a general strike if war broke out'.[70] And in a statement from CGT headquarters on 20 August 1912, later known as the 'Encyclical of Syndicalism', 'politicising anti-patriotism' was condemned as a form of 'mindless excitation' which was eroding syndicalism.[71] Although the CGT congress in Le Havre reaffirmed the

principle of anti-patriotism in September 1912,[72] it has appropriately
been pointed out that this confirmation of the new obsolete principles
was lacking in substance and was not accompanied by any precise
plans for action in a war which at that time certainly seemed imminent.
On the contrary, the CGT leaders informed their members that, in the
event of war, they could not count on orders from the CGT and that
the workers' reaction would be left to their own spontaneity.[73] The
basic assumption of anti-patriotism—that war was in effect only an
instrument used by the ruling classes to intensify the class struggle—
apparently lost its relevance at a time when revolutionary syndicalism
was actually faced with the real threat of a war for the first time in its
history. In a report on the Le Havre congress the famous Socialist
Charles Rappoport concluded that the CGT had in practice abandoned a number of its earlier chief dogmas: 'In the past, anti-
militarism and anti-patriotism were considered by many as the essential tasks of the CGT. Now these principles are being restrained. In
theory anti-militarism is maintained, but it produces no enthusiasm
among the majority.'[74]

The statement made at the Le Havre congress by Péricat, secretary
of the—extremely revolutionary—federation of construction workers,
is characteristic of this attitude. According to Péricat, anti-militarism
and the principles of syndicalism were inseparable. However, agitation
had to serve purely corporate aims—that is, the soldiers were to be
persuaded to refuse to be exploited as the defenders of capitalism in
labour disputes. And Merrheim, leader of the revisionist lobby within
the CGT, stressed that the *Sou du Soldat*[75] should not be misused for
the propagation of anti-patriotic doctrine.[76]

This line of restraint gradually becoming apparent among the upper
echelons of the CGT reflected a new orientation among the rank and
file. At a special CGT congress on 24/25 November 1912 it was
decided that, in view of the danger of the Balkan war escalating into a
general European conflict, a general strike would be held on
16 December 1912. The strike was to serve as a warning to the
bourgeois state that it could not expect the support of the workers in a
'wager of war'.[77] However, no more than 50,000 workers joined in this
general strike. Its failure can doubtless be at least partly explained by
the energetic intervention of the government.[78] It is nevertheless
interesting to note that even leading revolutionary Syndicalists considered the failure as a sign that anti-militarism and anti-patriotism had
diminished among the organised workers. At the same time they
hoped that the organisation of resistance to the government's plans,
announced early in 1913 to extend military service, would provide a
new impetus for anti-patriotism.[79] It was in fact only in the course of

the dispute over the three-year law in 1913–14 that the extent of the severe erosion of anti-patriotic ideology within revolutionary syndicalism, manifest since 1911, really became clear.

Without exception, the measures and developments in the wake of the Agadir crisis so far referred to were of more or less direct concern to the military sector. However, *the* event in domestic politics in 1912 was without any doubt the adoption of the great electoral reform which had already been on the parliamentary agenda for some years. This issue merits our attention on two grounds. In the first place the 1912 electoral reform is the most important testimony to the decline in influence of the left-wing Republicans who had hitherto dominated domestic politics—a decline due to the above-mentioned nationalist revival. Second, and more important, on account of their experience on the issue of electoral reform, many radical politicians in 1913–14 saw the three-year bill as a direct continuation of the anti-radical, Poincaristic line of domestic policy and were therefore bitterly opposed to the bill only on these grounds.

The introduction of proportional representation had been one of the main demands of both the socialist Left, the moderate bourgeois groups and the 'rallied' Catholic and monarchist Right for years. The majority system of uni-nominal voting in small constituencies—generally identical with the administrative districts of the various departments—stipulated the election of a candidate who won a majority of the total votes in the first ballot. If no candidate gained an overall majority, a second ballot was held, in which a relative majority guaranteed a seat.[80] This system of proportional representation meant that the outcome of an election was frequently determined by only a nominal majority, and the losing party was not represented in Parliament at all. It was generally considered as unjust, and this unjustice was only partially offset by the fact that in the second ballot a candidate defeated in the first ballot often withdrew in favour of another more promising candidate of similar political colours. Since constituencies particularly in rural areas, often had no more than 10,000 voters, parish-pump politics were often more decisive for the electorate's choice and pacts made for the second ballot than party political manifestos, even more so because, in the pre-war period, the organisation of the French political parties was extremely rudimentary. Since the rise of the Radical Republic in the 1890s this electoral system had given the radical Republicans—representing in particular the interests of the rural lower middle classes and the farmers—distinct over-representation in Parliament.

Reform of this electoral system had been before the Chamber since 1909. Two amendments to the system were under discussion: first, the determination of an electoral ratio to ensure parliamentary representation of the minorities in each constituency; and second, the list system to replace the present uninomial principle. It was generally considered that these reforms would involve major changes in the system of representation, because the list system would force the loosely organised political groupings— especially the bourgeois 'parties of notables' —to draw up a firm political programme and to form more distinctly organised parties. This reorganisation was seen as a prerequisite without which deputies would not be in the position to devote their attention to the interests of the nation as a whole, as opposed to merely parish-pump politics.

These arguments were energetically disputed by the Radicals of the day and still give rise to controversy in modern political science.[81] In his study on the influence of electoral systems on political developments, Goguel has come to the conclusion that proportional representation generally tends to promote the formation of rigid and influential political parties whose existence leads to major difficulties when it comes to forming coalitions and governments, since the political intransigence of the centrally organised parties generally tends to be more marked than that of their representatives in Parliament, who are responsible only to their own electorate. In Goguel's opinion this explains the great difficulties with regard to the continuity and stability of French governmental policy.[82] When extrapolating these conclusions to the 'French experience', we must bear in mind that the left-wing parliamentary bloc formed after the Dreyfus affair in the 1890s virtually disintegrated in 1905, since from then on this bloc, originally formed as a united front against anti-republican reaction and covering a spectrum ranging from the far Left to the moderate bourgeois *gauche démocratique*, had become more and more divided over its conflicting views on social policy. Against this background of dissent, continuity in governmental policy could be guaranteed only by the 'skill' (Briand) or 'strength' (Clemenceau, Poincaré) of individuals who could steer governmental policy, not as representatives of a particular party but as personalities in their own right.[83] Parliamentary control of this means of government consisted of no more than the obligation of these politicians to ensure again and again—and *ad hoc* —that they had the confidence of the *majorité républicaine* in Parliament behind them. The tone for this politically left-wing but socially heterogeneous majority was set by the two groups of the Radical Party —the more centrist *gauche radicale* and the *gauche radicale-socialiste*, the left wing of the bourgeois parties. Since the 1910 elections these parties between them had 252 of the 597 seats in Parliament[84] and could therefore form a parliamentary majority, either with the Social-

ists or the centrist *républicains de gauche*, depending on the question
at issue.

In his governmental declaration in January 1912 Poincaré had
shown express consideration for this republican majority by stating
that the necessary reform of the electoral system could be carried
through only with its help. However, in actual fact proportional
representation was adopted by the Chamber in July 1912 against the
wishes of the vast majority of left-wing republican deputies. The most
important result of this reform—which still had to get through the
Senate, where the Radicals were in the majority, before being definitively adopted—was the concrete evidence that in republican France a
parliamentary majority could be formed against the traditional radical
majorité républicaine. However, this majority was a coalition between
the far Left and the anti-radical groups of the bourgeois Centre and far
from a new or stable governmental majority.[85] It is therefore wrong to
describe the majority formed on the issue of electoral reform as a
'majority of the right of Centre'.[86] The Poincaré government's main
preoccupation with regard to the electoral reform issue seems to have
been to underline the unreality of the old *majorité républicaine* and
reinforce the independence of the executive from Parliament. Briand
had had a similar aim in mind in 1909/10 when, as head of government,
he had tried to make electoral reform the basis for his policy of
appeasement—that is, a general reorientation of policy in line with the
supposed interests of the whole of society. However, it would have
been impossible for Briand to have offered serious resistance to the
radical majority's influence in the Chamber without provoking his
own downfall, which was why he had been forced to drop electoral
reform in the midst of the debate.[87] The policy of *divide et impera* in
domestic politics and the consolidation of the executive's power over
the *majorité républicaine* bore fruit only when foreign policy arrived
on the centre of the stage after the Agadir crisis. In a period of tensions
in foreign policy and with the threat of war looming on the horizon, it
seemed absolutely essential to both Parliament and public opinion to
have a strong government. The Radical Party was traditionally devoid
of doctrines on foreign policy and, given that Poincaré's government
was conducting foreign policy with apparent success, and thus enjoy-
ing a high degree of public prestige, no Radical could now dare to try
to overthrow the government over a matter of internal dissent. When
the Chamber voted in favour of the electoral reform by 339 votes to
217 (the votes against coming from the Radicals alone), on 10 July
1912, the Radicals demanded the government's resignation on the
grounds that the majority in favour of proportional representation had
not been a purely republican one. However, there was no attempt to

overthrow Poincaré in a vote of no confidence.

Therefore the stability of Poincaré's government seems to have been a result of the critical situation in foreign affairs. It is doubtful whether this government could have survived in different circumstances; for, in view of the parliamentary majority and the mistrust of the radical groups in Parliament on account of the electoral reform, it was very likely that Poincaré would be forced to resign if there were a relaxation of tensions in foreign policy.

Poincaré's decision to stand in the presidential elections of January 1913 was consistent with his aim of guaranteeing continuity in French foreign policy, the major element of which was the—ever problematic —alliance with Russia. Even though a number of the constitutional prerogatives of the presidential office had become virtually meaningless since the rise of the parliamentary regime in the 1880s, the President still played a major role within the executive under the Third Republic.[88] One of his undisputed prerogatives was the nomination of the Premier, whereby he would generally have to follow certain indications ensuing from the parliamentary majority but on principle had a free hand, all the more so since throughout the history of the Third Republic clear-cut, unanimous parliamentary majorities were few and far between. Moreover, there was also the *secteur réservé*— not actually guaranteed to the President under the constitution but which had traditionally become part and parcel of his office over the years: the right to exert direct influence upon decision-making in the fields of military and foreign policy. For this reason it was customary for a premier designate, who could otherwise form his cabinet at his own discretion, to submit the names of his war and foreign ministers to the President for his approval. Again, according to tradition and not the constitution, the President also chaired the cabinet and, since 1912, the Supreme Council of War.[89]

Poincaré justified his decision to run for the presidency as follows: the presidential office with its traditional prerogatives had given him the opportunity, with all due consideration to ministerial responsibility, to watch over the 'lasting and indestructible interests of French foreign policy'.[90] In his address of thanks following his election he declared to the National Assembly: 'I shall remain the faithful guardian of the constitution and the law. I shall keep the interests of our national defence far from any attack and in agreement with the responsible ministers I shall look after the unity of our foreign policy.'[91] In his memoirs Poincaré attributes the possibility of a president being active in politics to the moral authority inherent in his office, which offsets his constitutional duty to remain above party politics and to refrain from exerting direct influence on political decision-making. Poincaré fails to mention that in actual fact it was only in the course of the debate on the three-year law in 1913/14 that this restraint was in part forced upon him.

However, at the beginning of 1913 there was as yet no indication of the problems looming ahead in the months to come as a result of Poincaristic foreign policy. In a report dated 29 January 1913 the Russian ambassador, Izvolsky, commented as follows: 'I have just spoken at some length to Poincaré. He told me that in his capacity as President of the Republic it would still be possible for him to exert direct influence on French foreign policy. He said that throughout his term of office he would not fail to use this opportunity to ensure the continuity of a policy based on a close alliance with Russia.'[92]

Poincaré later confirmed that these words were a faithful reflection of his opinion, but he categorically denied what Izvolsky said in the following—famous—passage of his report—namely, that the President had asked the Russian government not to go to war in the Balkans without previously consulting France, to enable the French government to prepare public opinion for participation in such a war.[93] It is certainly true, as was generally known at the time, that Poincaré's political thinking was based on the possibility of war. Nevertheless, to assume, as did the innocentists following the First World War, that this was directly linked with a secret diplomacy of war mongering is going too far. The essence of Poincaré's power politics was that peace could be preserved only if France were permanently prepared for a war, both materially and morally, and in the contemporary perspective at least this may imply a concern to safeguard peace just as much as belligerent aspirations.

Poincaré's charisma was based precisely on the fact that, whereas he continued to stress that French policy was aimed at preserving peace, he nevertheless left no doubts about his determination to use power politics to maintain the position of France in European politics. As has often been stated, the nationalist Right endorsed Poincaré's policy of strength as a preparation for the inevitable, and indeed desirable, war.[94] The Right saw Poincaré as a leader whose domestic policy was likely to triumph over the 'abject' regime of the radical Republic.[95] Nationalistic feeling had always been especially strong on the streets of Paris, and the enthusiasm of the Paris mob for Poincaré's national policy indeed reminded many contemporaries of the plebiscitary Boulangerism of the 1880's.[96] On the other hand—and this is an aspect which has so far not been given due consideration—even the Socialists, critical of Poincaré, did not have the impression that he was conducting a war mongering policy. Despite his criticism of the fact that France was allied to the tsarist regime, Jaurès seems to have assumed at the time that the existing system of diplomatic blocs in Europe was the very essence of a policy of peace for the whole of Europe.[97] And, following Poincaré's election to the presidency, the famous Socialist, Compère-Morel, one of the leading *Guesdistes*, declared:

> One must admit that the population was pleased with the result of this election. The entire press was favourable to Poincaré and public opinion was on his side. He reaped the seeds of the popularity he sowed during the last stormy months of his premiership. The *petite bourgeoisie* in particular was grateful to him for having declared that war would be disastrous and that he would do all he could to prevent it.[98]

The ambiguity of Poincaré's policy is further illustrated by the fact that the staunchly left-wing republican newspaper *La Lanterne* was a decisive supporter of Poincaré in the presidential election campaign on the grounds that he was a determined opponent of war mongering nationalism.[99] The leaders of the *républicain-socialistes*, generally to the left of the *radicaux-socialistes*, called on all their followers to vote for Poincaré, since his policy was a guarantee not only for peace but for the preservation of national dignity.[100]

Regardless of the broad spectrum of Poincaré's popularity, the Radicals stirred up a 'wild campaign'[101] against Poincaré's candidacy, both in the Chamber and the Senate. The reason for this campaign, in which the Senate and parliamentary radical leaders, Clemenceau and Caillaux, were especially predominant figures, was the mistrust of the anti-radical course in domestic policy in 1912—that is, introduction of the electoral reform against the *majorité républicaine*.[102] It was later maintained that Poincaré's candidacy had been opposed because his policy of national unity had been regarded as a threat to peace in Europe[103]. But this is not true. On the contrary, it should be stressed that in the years 1912–14 Poincaré was never accused by the left-wing Radicals, either in Parliament or in public, of being a warmonger. The agitation against his candidacy was based on no more than domestic and parliamentary issues.[104] Poincaré asked Clemenceau to explain why he was opposed to his candidacy, which Clemenceau did in a letter dated 31 December 1912. The contents of this letter are indicative of the arguments of the parliamentarians opposed to Poincaré's candidature. Clemenceau accused Poincaré of having exploited the leeway the parliamentary Radicals had granted him throughout 1912, because of the difficult situation in foreign affairs (a waiver on interpellations), in order to establish a heterogeneous coalition of the far Left, right-wing republican and anti-republican groups against the *parti républicain* majority with the aid of the electoral reform. Poincaré, Clemenceau maintained, had aimed at exploiting the moderation of the Radicals as a result of the situation abroad in order to strengthen his own personal hold on Parliament. Therefore his candidature for the presidency was no more than the continuation of this policy, which represented an act of violence against the sovereignty of Parliament. This fact alone explained why the anti-republican groups so heartily welcomed Poincaré's decision to stand for the highest office in the land: 'You have widened the split within the Republican Party by constituting a governmental majority which owes its short-lived power to the enemies of the Republic. This fact alone suffices to deprive you of the uniting authority which must be the first attribute of the supreme magistrature.'[105]

Poincaré's election was made possible by three factors. The first was socialist refusal to support the radical candidate against Poincaré, Pams, and their insistence on fielding their own candidate. Poincaré himself regarded this as decisive for his success.[106] The Socialists saw no reason on the grounds of either foreign or domestic policy to prevent Poincaré's election and to form a left-wing bloc along with the Radicals gathered around Caillaux to this end. Although they were to change their minds several months later when the arms race had gathered momentum and the three-year bill was introduced, at this point they were not ill-disposed towards a defeat of the Radicals. 'For us as Socialists Poincaré will always be the President of a class government. The only lesson we can learn from the election is that the Radical Party, the party and the hope of the middle class, is gradually disintegrating.'[107]

From the political point of view, the most significant factor in the election was the equal share of votes won by both Poincaré and Pams within the traditional *majorité républicaine* groups in the Chamber and the Senate.[108] This dissent among the bourgeois Left and the Centre meant that the anti-republican and nationalist Right played the decisive role in Poincaré's election. Nevertheless, to describe Poincaré on these grounds as the 'chosen one of the Right'[109] is going too far. There is no evidence that Poincaré was deliberately seeking their favour. Throughout 1912 he had made very few substantial concessions to the Right in internal affairs[110] and, similarly, he granted them very few concessions in return for their support of his candidature.[111] The bond was an objective one: Poincaré's national policy bound the Right to his cause without these ties being consolidated in domestic affairs in the years 1913–14.

The 'du Paty de Clam affair' was indicative of this situation. On 10 January 1913—a week before the election—a decree on behalf of the War Minister, Millerand, was published in the *Journal Officiel* ordering Lt-Colonel du Paty de Clams' readmission into the army. News of this triggered off a wave of indignation within the parliamentary Left—du Paty had been one of the officers most severely compromised in the Dreyfus affair and had therefore been dismissed from the army. The only plausible reason why Millerand should have opted for this sudden action so soon before the presidential elections is that he wanted to extend a token of good will to the Right. Albert de Mun, leader of the 'rallied' Catholics, interpreted Millerand's act as demonstration of a new patriotic pact and as a deliberate eradication of the old demarcation line between 'Republic' and 'Reaction'.[112] Poincaré, however, disowned Millerand and accepted the War Minister's resignation. He considered Millerand's conduct unacceptable,[113] although de Mun warned him not to show such weakness: 'You shall not disarm your enemies by breaking the solidarity which bound us.'[114]

Finally, the dispute over the three-year law showed that until the outbreak of the First World War the national consensus between the Right and the bourgeois national Centre could be achieved only when the overriding concern was to protect and guarantee national defence —and even then, only in the short term. It is nevertheless true that at this time of crisis in foreign policy Poincaré—and with him the national Centre—steered away from the formula of the 'unity of all Republicans' against the anti-republican Right, which had characterised the Republic's years of struggle, and instead began to accept the cooperation of the Catholic, 'rallied' and anti-republican Right on national issues: *Pour la France avec les Français, pour la République avec les Républicains*, as the *Alliance Républicaine Démocratique* (ARD), the reservoir of the moderate bourgeois groups, formulated the slogan of their policy in the light of the latent crises in foreign policy.[115] However, Eugen Weber's overriding theory, that patriotic unity had initiated a process in which a long-term stable coalition of the republican Centre with the anti-republican Right had been formed against 'foreign and social danger', can hardly be substantiated on the basis of the real developments in internal affairs in the years 1913/14.[116] The essence of these internal developments, which began with Poincaré's election as President of the Republic, was the attempt to set up a coherent governmental party by combining the Left and Right of Centre[117] with a national and liberal form of political ideology.[118]

The efforts of the Socialists, and to a certain extent of the Radicals, to revive the now defunct bloc of the Left against this burgeoning centralism, was a major aspect of the debate on the defence bill in the years 1913/14.

CHAPTER 2

The Origins of the
Three-Year Law

Early in 1913 news filtered through of the new German
rearmament plans. The main argument of the champions of three-year
military service in 1913 was that it was imperative for France to take
immediate retaliatory steps to protect her territory from a sudden
German attack. This theory is still advanced by modern historical
research.[1] On the other hand, during the war-guilt debate following
the First World War, it was suggested by various sources that the 1913
German arms bill had not in fact been at the root of the three-year law
and that the German plans had simply provided the French officers
and politicians with a welcome opportunity to pull their own long-
planned and ready-made arms bill 'out of their hats'.[2] Let us now
attempt to trace how the expansion of the German army in 1913
became the 'detonating agent'[3] of French rearmament. The indisput-
able link between German and French rearmament cannot be explained adequately in simple terms of a challenge-and-response model.
The three-year law was not triggered off by the danger that the newly
expanded German army would be capable of overrunning France in a
very short time, as many of its protagonists—and many historians
since—believed. The decisive factor was that German rearmament had
made the French operational plan null and void. This was in fact the
only reason why the French army officers and the government considered retaliatory measures absolutely indispensable.[4]

The first reports of the German general staff's new military demands
in *Die Post* on 8 January 1913, followed by the denial of this report in
the semi-official *Norddeutsche Allgemeine Zeitung* on 18 January,
received little if any attention from the French press.[5] Likewise French
diplomatic staff in Germany had little to report about the aims and
extent of German rearmament.[6] On 31 January, several days after

agreement had been reached between the German general staff and the War Ministry on the scope of the new German defence bill,[7] Serret, military attaché in the French embassy in Berlin, made his first report of any length on the German rearmament plans. The military principle behind these plans was that, following the French cadre bills of 1912,[8] which provided for a greater integration of reserve units into the regular army, Germany intended to secure the superiority of her regular front-line forces. Since France had a lower population than her neighbour, she could not hope to keep up with Germany in a 'race of numbers' but would now have to try to re-establish her 'military superiority' (*sic*) by a considerable 'improvement in the quality' of her army.[9] However, this objective could be reached only if the French cover troops (*couverture*) were comprised mainly of regular service-men and were not principally dependent on reserve units, at least in the opening battles of a war which were considered as decisive.[10]

Serret's analysis does indeed reflect the actual military context in which the German arms bill of 1913 posed a challenge to the overall network of Poincaré's foreign and security policy, not yet completed. The German armament plans posed a great threat to the unconditional offensive strategy, which, as we have seen, had been the linchpin of the plans of the French general staff since 1911. The French army leaders believed that these plans would make it possible to launch an *attaque brusquée* before troop concentration had been fully accomplished.[11] Joffre's interpretation was that an *attaque brusquée* was identical with an *attaque partielle*—that is, an attack on the French cover troops launched by the German units on the spot at the beginning of mobilisation.[12] However, one of the basic postulates of the French general staff's Plan XVII, ready to be submitted for approval at the beginning of 1913, was that a strong *couverture* was necessary against such offensive strikes as a guarantee that troops could be concentrated closer to the German border than under the then current operational plan and to ensure that troops could assemble and launch their united offensive without being hindered by an *attaque brusquée*.[13]

Since Plan XVII and the offensive strategy were regarded as the *sine qua non* of French power in foreign policy, the German challenge made it essential to reinforce the French cover troops—that is, to respond to the German armament plans by increasing the numbers of regular soldiers without delay. However, unlike matters of foreign policy and strategic planning, this step required the approval of Parliament. The painstaking and at times extremely controversial discussions between the government and the general staff on the contents of French armament measures demonstrate what a mammoth task it obviously was to reconcile the imperatives of the offensive strategy (an effective reinforcement of the *couverture*) with the republican theory of national defence. In the subsequent public and parliamentary debate on the three-year law it was confirmed time and again that both Parliament and the public were prepared to sanction French rearmament only if it could be justified as the only means of safeguarding national territory against an apocalyptic German 'onslaught'. To understand the following it is therefore indispensable to distinguish between the strict military and strategic sense of the term *attaque brusquée* and the use of the term in the wider sense—namely, the justification of rearmament by invoking the prospect of French territory being swiftly and decisively invaded by the entire German army. Until July 1914 the debate in France on the three-year law concerned just the latter concept of the term *attaque brusquée*. A detailed account will follow of the actual consequences of this discrepancy between military strategy and intentions, on the one hand, and the public justification of rearmament in terms of domestic and military policy, on the other.

In the first half of February 1913 the Premier, Briand, chaired six conferences attended by the War Minister, Étienne, the Finance Minister, Klotz, the Chief of Staff, Joffre, and the chairmen of the Chamber and Senate Army Committees.[14] Poincaré, the newly elected President, was not present at these discussions and ostensibly was not informed of their content either.[15] It was not until 15 February that the War Minister, Étienne, informed the President that, in view of the German armament plans, he was convinced that military service must be increased to three years.[16] On 17 February *Le Temps* unofficially announced that the conference had come to the following decisions:

1. Parliament was to be asked to approve an additional emergency credit of 70–80 million francs, so that already scheduled improvements to the army's technical equipment could be carried out immediately.
2. A bill earmarking a further credit of 500 million francs was to be introduced for the implementation of longer-term reforms, above all the improvement of fortifications and a reinforcement of the army's heavy artillery strength.
3. The War Minister had been charged with submitting proposals to the cabinet in the coming week on how the increase in the army's effective strength, now seen as indispensable, could be achieved. Three alternatives had been taken into account: an extension of military service to three years for specific branches of service (cavalry), an extension of service in all branches of the regular army to thirty months or, finally, a combination of both. The

War Ministry had already come to the conclusion that a general extension of service in all branches was the appropriate solution. The government had decided to adopt the War Minister's proposals as soon as they had been submitted to the cabinet, to present the whole package to Parliament immediately and to call for a vote of confidence on the issue.[17]

These reports in *Le Temps* were not a faithful reflection of opinion within the government. The Premier, Briand, was most indignant about this leak, which he described to Poincaré as a 'magnification of his intentions'.[18] On the following day, 18 February, Briand had *Le Temps*'s reports denied. There was no question of the introduction of three-year conscription. All that had been planned was to take better advantage of the scope of the 1905 recruitment law: the 'shirkers'— conscripts employed in the military administration—should, so far as possible, be called to arms. In addition, the government intended to ask Parliament for an additional credit of 500 million francs for the improvement of military equipment.[19] According to Poincaré's notes, the Finance Minister, Klotz, was even more categorical than Briand in his opposition to the army's plans to raise the effective strength of the regular army, and other ministers similarly expressed serious doubts to Poincaré about the War Minister's intentions.[20] In Klotz's opinion the extra-budgetary credit of 500 million francs he had suggested would suffice to strengthen fortifications to withstand an *attaque brusquée*. He asked for permission to put his arguments across to the *Conseil Supérieur de la Guerre*, but this was refused on the grounds that the Finance Minister was not a member of the CSG. On 27 February Klotz therefore presented the cabinet with a counter-proposal(!) to the War Minister's plan to raise conscription—a supplementary credit of 500 millions.[21]

On 25 February, amidst this split within the ranks of the government, *Le Temps* confirmed its semi-official report of 17 February, adding that the government had meanwhile decided to propose a general extension of military service to three years.[22] This affirmation of the republican principle that military service should be of equal length for all citizens is to be assessed as a fundamental concession to public opinion. In the public debate on the government's intentions it had at this early stage already become quite clear that Parliament and public opinion would sanction an increase in the military burden only if the principle of equality were upheld.[23] It should, however, be noted that this report in *Le Temps* was again not a true reflection of opinion within the government and the general staff. Not only Joffre but other members of the general staff, and even Poincaré and his confidant,

Millerand, actually considered a general extension of service for all conscripts as superfluous,[24] in that the concession to the principle of equality went far beyond the general staff's demands[25]—obviously the War Minister, Étienne, had gone 'too far too soon'.[26] Thus at the cabinet meeting on 1 March agreement could not be reached on the content of the army bill: according to Poincaré, Étienne's proposals still seemed 'a little too imprecise'.[27]

The government therefore decided to convene a meeting of the *Conseil Supérieur de la Guerre* to iron out all the contentious points.[28] Poincaré remarks that the list of questions to be submitted to the CSG was drawn up at a special cabinet meeting on 3 March.[29] However, since the contentious issues were not even discussed at this meeting, the War Ministry's assessment of the situation and its conclusion that three-year service was necessary had evidently become generally accepted.[30] This implies that Étienne had meanwhile succeeded in convincing his colleagues in the cabinet of his position. In view of the doubts of Briand, Klotz and Poincaré, it is difficult to explain how this could have happened so quickly—and there are no minutes available of cabinet meetings. However, there is an interesting reference in a letter from Paul Cambon, the French ambassador in London, to his brother Jules, ambassador in Berlin: 'We have talked at length to General de Castelnau. He told me that you have played an important role in the government's resolve to propose three-year service. He said the cabinet was very reluctant. Your despatches and those of your military attaché were read to the cabinet and submitted to the Ministry of War to provide them with arguments. . . .'[31]

In this letter Cambon can have been referring only to his and Serret's telegrams of 27 February and 1 March which, in contrast to the initial cautious reports on the objectives and extent of the German arms bill, now insisted on the moral aspect of French armament measures with regard to foreign policy. Cambon wrote that the entire German public had been impressed by the rigorous reaction of French opinion to the potential threat to their country. The government must therefore be aware of the moral importance of its own decision, precisely because of the impression it would leave on German opinion. 'Thus the question of three-year service has been presented in such a way that if we do not substantially increase military service, it will be seen by the German press as a sign of weakness. It is absolutely indispensable that the German people should not be given this impression, in the very interest of peace.'[32]

These arguments apparently succeeded in convincing a number of sceptical members of the government that an extension of military service was the order of the day. Moreover, the list of questions submitted to the cabinet on 3 March showed a means of reconciling the wishes of the general staff and the doubts of some of the ministers. At the meeting of the *Conseil Supérieur de la Guerre* on 4 March an agreement was subsequently reached, on the basis of which the government could justify the three-year bill to the public.

The War Minister's memorandum provided the CSG with the following main points of discussion on 4 March:

1. Is it necessary, in view of the German effort, to expand our armed forces, in particular our frontier cover troops?
2. Can an expansion of our armed forces be achieved other than by an increase in the length of regular service of conscripts?
3. [Technical data.]
4. Considering that *in the present circumstances the principle of an equal military burden for all citizens is regarded as unalterable*, should 27-month service, 30-month service, three-year service be adopted?
5. *In view of the abundance of resources* as a result of three-year service, would it be appropriate in the application of this system to provide for a reduction of the length of active service for service-men from large families?[33]

The Chief of Staff, Joffre, was categorical: there was no alternative, he said, but to expand the army. In his opinion the scheduled increase in the German army of up to approximately 850,000 men implied that in the event of war Germany could decisively accelerate mobilisation so that her army, then comprised exclusively of regular units, 'could knock down our cover troops and *create havoc among our debarkation*'.

If three-year conscription were introduced and the French regular army also reinforced, the total number of troops that could be mobilised in the event of war would admittedly not be increased, he continued, but mobilisation would at least be facilitated by the higher ratio of regular units, as a result of which '*our units would obviously have considerable offensive power*'.

Poincaré, who as President of the Republic chaired this meeting, does not seem to have been satisfied with these purely technical arguments, which in fact outlined the essence of Joffre's strategical line of thought. He raised the following objection: '. . . to enable the government to justify these proposals to Parliament, one must first of all provide a precise definition of exactly what effort Germany has made to increase her military strength'.

General Pau then took the floor to give this 'precise definition'. Following a brief outline of the history of German military expansion since 1815 (!), the General came to the following conclusion: 'They [the Germans] are aiming at an army whose fighting units can be mobilised without calling in the reservists. This reveals our neighbours' aggressive intentions. An army formed in this way is indeed a first-rate offensive instrument, always ready for action.'

Briand agreed with Pau's demagogic 'precise definition' of Joffre's technical arguments:

> The government is willing to do all it can to prepare the army for any eventuality it may have to face. But the burden will be a heavy one. To make the reform lasting, so that in the future when the fervour of patriotism has calmed down the issue will not be called into question again, the measures taken must be backed up by serious, convincing arguments, not only by technicalities which will not be understood.[34]

The alternatives to the three-year law—that is, items 3 and 4 of the list of questions submitted to the CSG—were rejected unanimously without serious discussion. This is an important point, in that these alternative solutions were later to play an important role in the public and parliamentary debate on the three-year issue. Throughout the parliamentary debate the government maintained again and again that all these counter-proposals had been carefully examined by the military experts in the CSG, discussed in detail and finally rejected as unsuitable. In actual fact, discussion was limited to a statement from Joffre that none of these alternatives to the three-year law could be applied in practice, since they would all involve several call-up dates per year.[35]

The discussion on the fifth question is of great importance, since it clearly reveals the discrepancy between the public justification of the three-year law and the demands of the general staff. At the beginning of the CSG meeting General Legrand, on behalf of the general staff, had estimated that a total of some 130,000 additional regular servicemen were required. If it were decided to introduce three years of service for all able-bodied citizens, the army would be left with a surplus of approximately 50,000 soldiers. According to the general staff's calculations, the total annual recruitment quota was 210,000; after deduction of the usual losses, approximately 180,000 would carry out service in the regular army.[36] However, Poincaré ruled out a reduced period of military service for the sons of large families as politically inexpedient. He was convinced that the surplus in resources resulting from three-year military service for all conscripts could be utilised somewhere in the army. The generals agreed, at least for the time being, and Pau stated laconically: 'We'll always manage to utilise the left-overs'. Concluding the meeting, Briand again pointed out in no uncertain terms that public opinion (but not the press!) could be kept on their side only if it were stipulated and clearly demonstrated that the present legislation was no longer adequate and that the three-year law would uphold the principle of the absolute equality of the military burden for all able-bodied citizens.[37]

A comparison of the results of the CSG's discussions with the official communiqué on this meeting, received by the public with considerable attention,[38] shows that the government was using demagogic arguments to 'sell' an arms bill to Parliament and the public which quite obviously had its origins in considerations of power politics and offensive strategy. The official communiqué stated that on the basis of the general staff's report, the CSG had come to the unanimous decision that 'in the interests of national defence it was absolutely indispensable to increase the strength of the army'. Given that the individual companies of the French army had an effective strength of no more than some seventy men,[39] the French cover troops, continued the communiqué, were too weak to withstand an *attaque brusquée*. The CSG had ascertained that Germany would soon have at least 300,000 regular servicemen more than France, the majority of whom would be deployed in the front line.[40]

On 5 March the cabinet adopted the CSG's decision and resolved to submit the three-year bill to Parliament without delay and with no provisions on exemptions from service.[41] The next day the War Minister, Étienne, briefed the Chamber on the reasons for the government's bill.[42] Étienne was constantly interrupted by the heckling of the Socialists whose campaign against the 'criminal' law was at that time just as strong as agitation for national defence.[43] In his statement the Minister emphasised that with its bill the government had fully committed itself to the spirit of the 1905 conscription law, which stipulated 'absolute equality of the military burden' for all conscripts. The security of France, he affirmed, would continue to be guaranteed by the enlistment of all the nation's able-bodied citizens who, expressing the will of the entire nation, were to stand up for the defence of France. However, in the present circumstances only the three-year law could guarantee the nation's security. The government, he concluded, therefore called upon Parliament to adopt the bill in its present form and without delay, since its only intention was the continued application of the emergency paragraph 33 of the 1905 conscription act.

Article 33 of the 1905 act stipulated that, in times of diplomatic tension with the imminent threat of war, the government could 'provisionally' retain conscripts who had just concluded regular service in the forces.[44] Étienne's affirmation that the government was actually planning no more than the general application of the provisions of Article 33/1905 was put across to the public as the most important argument in favour of the three-year law. This clearly established the purpose of the bill as a means of defending French territory from an onslaught. Even before Étienne's statement to Parliament, *Le Matin, the* Paris daily, had declared that it had been authorised to state that the new defence bill was in effect no more than an extension of the emergency provision of the 1905 act.[45] Thus, the offensive strategical problem of an *attaque brusquée* was projected as the imminent threat of a calamitous German invasion. This *attaque brusquée* ideology alone determined the subsequent public and parliamentary debate on the three-year law. The gulf between the real interest in the *Trois Ans*, on the one hand, and the gripping arguments put before the CSG by Briand and reiterated again and again, on the other, produced an incoherence and discrepancy between the arguments used by the government and general staff before the public and the course of action they actually followed. The opponents of the three-year law could not be kept blind to this disparity indefinitely.

This discrepancy between the reality and the ideological justification of French armament policy was to have serious consequences. The confusion in French internal affairs up to July 1914—the swing from the nationalist revival to the sweeping victory of the Left in the 1914 elections—can indeed be explained only by this disparity. It could even be said that the three-year law was not the 'apex of the nationalist revival'[46] but the beginning of its end.

CHAPTER 3

The Early Stages of the Public Debate on the Defence Bill

The Campaign for 'National Defence'

Agitation for an amendment of the defence bill began in the press of the non-radical Centre, the Conservatives and the nationalist Right immediately after *Le Temps*'s first reports on the government's plans. The moderate, conservative and right-wing press were united in their demands that the necessary rearmament measures should be implemented *d'accord entre Français*, above party lines and without a parliamentary debate.[1]

Until the end of February 1913 reports in the semi-official *Le Temps* reflected a degree of uncertainty as to whether the new defence proposals should be justified to the public as part and parcel of European alliance policy, necessary to maintain the balance of power, or as the only possible means of defending France from the Germans' plans to launch an *attaque brusquée*.[2] However, coinciding with the formal presentation of the three-year bill, the arguments on grounds of foreign and strategic policy gave way to the demagogic campaign on the *attaque brusquée*. The main reason for this was probably the realisation that, if the patriotic consensus were not to be destroyed *a priori*, consideration would have to be given to bourgeois Left and radical opinion. In this context we should recall Premier Briand's statement to the Supreme War Council (see p. 50 above), in which he pointed out that, if long-term public support for the new defence measures were to be maintained, it would be necessary to bring emotional rather than technical arguments into the public debate.[3]

The conditions in which the public was prepared to accept an extension of military service were spelt out in the first reports of the Radical press[4] and in *Le Temps*'s own poll, *Le Pays et les Trois Ans*. This poll was begun at the end of February and was carried out on a daily basis until mid-April. The interviewed representatives of the so-called *République des Comités* (mayors, chairmen of local associations and party committees) all stressed the need to extend military service—since 850,000 German troops could sweep down on the weak French cover troops in next to no time, measures would have to be taken to defend the French frontier.[5] No reference is to be found in the poll to rearmament as an aspect of overall foreign policy. It was stated again and again that everything must be done for the defence of the country; an invasion by 'Teutonic hordes' must be prevented; aggressive Germany should not be given the opportunity of doing to the French what the Americans had done to their 'redskins'. However, it is interesting to note that the defence proposals did not as a rule muster up any enthusiasm. There were frequent references to the 'patriotic resignation' with which the great sacrifices would have to be made to defend *la patrie*. At the same time it was generally maintained that if military service were extended, the military burden should be shared equally by all citizens.[6]

It is doubtful whether all the points of this 'consultation of the people' by an interested party truly reflected a broad spectrum of public opinion. The chauvinistic undertone of the readiness for national defence, which *Le Temps* brought to the fore, hardly corresponded with the real attitude of a broad spectrum of the population. Nevertheless, *Le Temps*'s survey was highly significant. This first attempt to mobilise a broader spectrum of public opinion beyond the boundaries of Paris made it quite evident that the only means of justifying an extension of military service was to put forward the argument that additional measures were necessary to defend the country against an *attaque brusquée*. This probably explains why the semi-official press now attempted to steer the course of the public and parliamentary debate on the *Trois Ans* in one direction only: for or against the safeguarding of national defence? From the very outset this polarisation implied the attempt to exclude the Socialists from this so abstractly construed national solidarity, for the SFIO had never left any doubts that it would oppose the three-year law with all its might.[7]

In view of the fact that the left-wing Republicans were bound to regain a position of decisive influence in Parliament—precisely on account of this new exclusion of the SFIO from the heterogeneous anti-radical coalition of 1912—it was now necessary to show consideration for this group, otherwise it would not be possible to demonstrate France's patriotic *élan* by quickly pushing the three-year bill through

Parliament. For this reason *Le Temps* endeavoured to make it clear that approval of a new defence bill did not imply that the Radicals who had pushed through the 1905 bill would now have to 'eat humble pie', since the egalitarian principles of the previous bill would be maintained in its successor. The nationalist Right, it wrote, therefore had no grounds to maintain that the three-year bill represented acquiescence to their ideas on military policy and thereby a general concession on the part of the Republic's leading politicians that a democratic form of government in France was incompatible with strength and security in French foreign policy. This argument, continued *Le Temps*, was unfounded, since the only reason for the introduction of the bill was the imperative of safeguarding the survival of France in response to the threat posed by the German rearmament plans. It was for this reason and this reason only (!), it concluded, that the population had already fully accepted an increase of the military burden.[8]

A task of even greater urgency was to appease the Radicals. When the government's proposals were published, the campaign of the Republicans on the far Right, as well as of the monarchist Conservatives and the nationalist Right, concentrated on the one theme: the necessity to prolong military service in view of the German threat was irrefutable proof that the entire policy of the left-wing republican regime since the Dreyfus affair had been a failure. The 1905 conscription law with its egalitarian principles, symbol of the triumphant Republic and the principle of the citizen soldier, the 'law of the Dreyfus men', the 'detestable measure of the bloc', simply did not suffice to safeguard national defence. Thus the need for the three-year law was proof that the Republic's entire military policy had been a disaster and that democracy was anti-French.[9] This controversial criticism of one of the main achievements of the 'radical Republic' was also expressed in the massive campaign of the Right in favour of the planned increase in the army on militaristic and anti-democratic grounds. Many high-ranking officers voiced their opinions in the right-wing press at this time, justifying the three-year law from the purely military point of view. Particular emphasis was placed on the moral dimension of the offensive strategy—quite in accordance with the doctrine of Grandmaison and his disciples on the general staff. In view of the alleged plans of the Germans to launch an *attaque brusquée* on France, it was maintained that a spirit of sacrifice and soldierly discipline—the ability to withstand the enemy 'head-on'—were of decisive importance for the defence of *la patrie*. This spirit of sacrifice and the passive obedience required would have to be imparted to the soldiers by a lengthy spell within the confines of barracks, since 'today's recruit' was subject to a welter of democratic and anti-patriotic influences before he began his military service, such that he was not prepared to obey his military commanders unquestioningly. Thus the main aim of military service should be to discipline a conscript in such a way that his French soul would no longer be disconcerted by his republican spirit.[10]

The Right also tried to capitalise on the national *élan* by calling on all patriots to unite in a new political party which was to be a 'patriotic' bloc comprising all the groups from the far Right to the right of Centre as a front levelled against the radical Republicans.[11] The chairman of the *Alliance Libérale Populaire* (ALP), Piou, declared at a party congress in mid-February that his 'rallied' Catholic party would be prepared to withdraw from the opposition, and he offered the government his full support on the *Trois Ans*.[12] In fact the Right continued to support the government's bill, and parliamentary cooperation between the non-radical Centre and the Right on the defence issue lasted until the passing of the bill. The Briand and Barthou governments willingly accepted 'patriotic petitions' from Paris students, the most outstanding of which had been drafted by Barrès himself, and also supported the campaign of the Right in other ways.[13] As a result many Radicals came to the conclusion that the government was a prisoner of 'reaction' and that the campaign in favour of the *Trois Ans* therefore had an anti-republican overtone.

However, cooperation between the government and the nationalist Right, along with the bourgeois Centre, advocated by the ALP (Piou, de Mun) in particular,[14] was to pose problems from the very outset. It soon became evident that interests were so heterogeneous that it would hardly be possible to set up a patriotic bloc with objectives going beyond the enactment of the three-year law. The 'rallied' Catholics' demand that, in view of the patriotic pact, Parliament and the government must now abandon anti-clerical traditions in educational and Church policy met with frosty silence on the part of the government and demonstrative rejection in the press of the Centre.[15] None the less, de Mun's demand was not totally unfounded: the Centre had for some time been scorning the Radicals' sectarian fanaticism on anti-clericalism as reactionary, now that the Republic was geared towards the interests of the nation as a whole.[16] The only plausible reason why the Centre was loath to enter into a coalition with the Right over and above the *Trois Ans* was that it hoped to win over at least some of the Radicals in support of the three-year law and was thus interested in preventing an extreme polarisation between Right and Left.[17]

Questions of parliamentary tactics were not the only obstacle to the consolidation of a patriotic bloc between moderate and conservative bourgeois groups, on the one hand, and the nationalist Right, on the other. A further stumbling-block was conflicting ideas on the question of how rearmament was to be financed. The Right adopted an unequivocal and radical position on this issue from the very outset: here, too, the national emergency required a demonstration of French unity and radical measures. At an early stage Albert de Mun spoke out against all forms of privileges; the nationalist *Oeuvre* warned French industrialists not to try to feather their nests at the expense of the national emergency, since this could trigger off an anti-capitalist revolt.[18] At least the positions of de Mun and the ALP were not at all verbally demagogic. Soon afterwards the ALP members of the budgetary committee helped carry through the socialist/radical motion that the new defence measures must be covered by additional levies on property and capital.[19]

Unlike the nationalist Right, the moderate and conservative bourgeois groups in Parliament and public were categorically opposed to emergency measures of a financial nature. Immediately after new military measures had been announced, it was rumoured on the stock exchange that the government was intending to finance the *Trois Ans* and the material improvement of army equipment not by additional taxation but by contracting a loan,[20] an approach which was unanimously welcomed by Centre and conservative opinion, which categorically rejected the financing of the new defence measures by further taxation.[21] The opposition to this idea was based on the justified fear that, in view of the dictates of safeguarding national defence, the Radicals and Socialists would now reintroduce their old demand for the introduction of a personal and progressive income tax—and would this time have more success in doing so. As a deterrent the Conservatives tried to prove that the new military burden would not be so heavy that new fiscal resources would have to be tapped to cover its costs, and they concluded that the Radicals' demands were 'demagogic'.[22] Even though this reasoning could perhaps be substantiated from an objective point of view, it was nevertheless incompatible with the call to all Frenchmen to be willing to make sacrifices. Hence the criticism that this 'egoism of the bourgeoisie' had proved the call for national unity to be purely ideological, an attempt to justify socially reactionary aims.[23] Aims of this kind were indeed mentioned both in the Centre and conservative press with a great lack of consideration for public opinion. The costs of the loan, it was stated, were to be offset solely by cuts in the social budget (workers' pensions, sickness insurance, etc.) and by further cuts in the regular budget—for example, denationalisation of the state railways.[24] These demands were justified by the argument that sound finances were at least as important for national defence as a strong army.[25]

This argument was also advanced by the main trade associations. At an early stage the *Union des Intérêts Économiques*, which was closely linked, both in its leadership and its political stance, to the ARD, stated that the industrialists would be prepared to make sacrifices on behalf of national defence only if the state took steps to maintain the competitiveness of French industry (e.g. by denationalisation of the railways, reforms in infrastructures).[26] However, the most significant statement came from the *Comité Central d'Études et de Défense Fiscale* (CCEDF), to which twenty-nine heavy-industry trade associations were affiliated (e.g. the *Comité des Forges, Comité Central des Chambres Syndicales, Comité Central des Armateurs de France, Fédération des Industriels et Commerçants Français, Comité Central des Houillères de France*).[27] In its first statement on the issue the CCEDF warned of the 'political reformers' who were aiming to exploit the threat to France from the German defence measures by reforming the French tax system: 'To overthrow the tax system of France at this hour would be a grievous weakening of national defence.' This was the objective of the 'enemies of the social order', which, given 'the present state of Europe', was no less than 'criminal': 'More than ever before, national defence requires guaranteed resources, the assurance of internal peace, the guarantee of prosperity and the maintenance of a tax system which has proved its worth.'[28]

Thus in this initial phase of agitation 'for national defence' there was already a considerable degree of dissent within the camp of the staunch *Troisannistes*, as supporters of the three-year bill were often referred to at the time. Admittedly the conflicting views on the social and party political aspects of the defence issue did not lead to a split between the nationalist Right and the national Centre in the following phase. Nevertheless, the fact that the Centre, unlike the Nationalists, was in favour of including the Radicals in the joint patriotic front, was to prove crucial. The campaign of the Centre and the Conservatives against the anti-patriotic SFIO and emergency financial measures convinced many left-wing Republicans that the three-year law was basically the offshoot of domestically reactionary motives. In view of this suspicion, whether or not it would be possible for Republicans and Socialists to join forces against the government's bill depended not least of all on the line adopted by the SFIO on the defence issue.

The Campaign of the Socialists and Syndicalists: Theory and Practice

When *Le Temps* published its reports on the forthcoming French army bill, the SFIO *Commission Administrative Per-*

manente (CAP) immediately called for a meeting of the International Socialist Bureau (ISB) to draft a joint resolution on an international response to the arms race. Should a resolution similar to that approved at the Basle congress[29] be adopted, or would it be advisable to 'decide on measures against the offensive of military imperialism and rearmament, especially in Germany and France?'[30] The German and Austrian Social Democrats (SPD) rejected the principle of direct ISB involvement, since, like the French Socialists, they were of the opinion that the Balkan war would not spark off any further international conflict. So the SFIO and SPD bureaux simply agreed on a joint public statement, published simultaneously in French and German on 1 March 1913 in both *L'Humanité* and *Vorwärts*.

The fact that the International went no further than this joint Franco-German statement against militarism and chauvinism has been described by Haupt as a turning-point in the policy of the International.[31] The validity or otherwise of this viewpoint will not be examined here. What is of importance in this context is the fact that the International's step back confirmed the policy of the French Socialists. The SFIO leadership did not regard the activities of the International—which as an institution could exert pressure on national governments—as an essential factor for the preservation of peace, but was more concerned with achieving 'a pacifist orientation of public opinion' at national level, 'which, thanks to the International's efforts, has even reached the unorganised masses of the proletariat'. This movement would have to be reinforced if peace were to be maintained.[32] The CAP's position was clearly outlined by Jaurès in his first public statement on the three-year law when, in one of his famous *synthèses*,[33] he established the link between foreign and domestic policy. The Socialist Party, said Jaurès, would secure peace by means of a constant appeal to the workers and peasants of France and thus halt the wave of rearmament which was making war inevitable. This action on behalf of international peace would, moreover, provide a new impetus for democratic aspirations, since the 'effrontery' of reactionary domestic politics would not last long faced by an enlightened public.[34]

The *Consultation du Pays*, carried out with great vigour since the beginning of March 1913, originally provided the core of socialist agitation against the 'three years'. In two articles in *L'Humanité* on 6 March, the day the government presented its bill, Jaurès declared that the reason for the 'appeal to the workers and peasants of France' was the fact that reactionary politicians were trying to push the defence bill through Parliament as quickly as possible without any debate on the issue, so that the people would be taken unawares and have no chance of finding out the real motives behind the new defence measures. It would be no problem, he went on, to provide evidence that the bill was not in response to the 'threat from Germany' but an expression of a policy of domestic reaction, for which there was every reason for uneasiness abroad, and which was therefore a threat to peace.[35] Confronted with chauvinistic surprise tactics, Jaurès went on, the SFIO would prove to Parliament and the public that German rearmament was solely due to the events such as the Balkan wars and the weakening of Turkey: 'The debate shall be neither stifled nor restricted. The Chamber shall be faced with the responsibilities reaction has entailed and the country . . . will have the time to organise resistance.'[36] However, this threat to stir up the opposition of the country against Parliament, if necessary,[37] did not mean that Jaurès and his supporters advocated an anti-parliamentary mass movement. For Jaurès the attempt to win over the 'Radical masses' for socialist aims[38] did not exclude the hope of setting up a parliamentary coalition of all 'true democrats' against the forces of 'reaction'.[39]

Nevertheless, the question of whether or not it would be advisable to join forces with the public and the left-wing bourgeois groups in Parliament against the 'three years' seems once again to have brought to the surface the differences there had always been between the *Jaurèsistes* and the Marxist-inspired *Guesdistes* within the SFIO. The latter group believed that the interests of the party were the only yardstick for socialist policy, the concrete issue at stake being of secondary importance, and that socialist policy should basically serve to strengthen party organisation and socialist propaganda. For this reason prominent *Guesdistes* were totally opposed to Jaurès's policy of both mobilising the 'Radical masses' and cooperating with the left-wing Republicans in Parliament.[40]

This dissension within the ranks of the party raised its head at the SFIO annual party congress in Brest (23–25 January 1913). The CAP, chiefly pro-Jaurès, moved that discussion on all structural and organisational questions should be postponed to a special session in November so that the delegates assembled in Brest could concentrate on the three-year issue. This proposal met with sharp criticism, especially from the pro-Guesde faction, and even more so because Jaurès and other leading SFIO politicians were not present at the congress, since 'in view of the defence debate their continued presence in Parliament and/or the Army Committee was indispensable'.[41]

As had been the case so often at party conferences since the 1905 merger, the impression of party unity on the question of the three-year law and the form of struggle to be adopted was only superficial and created on the basis of a *motion nègre-blanc*.[42] The *Guesdiste*

Compère-Morel tabled a motion declaring that the conference should entrust the SFIO deputies in Parliament and the CAP with the mandate to 'launch both in Parliament and in the country the most energetic and resolute action on behalf of Franco-German *entente*, international arbitration, a national militia and against the three-year law'. What this motion in effect amounted to was that the SFIO's campaign was to be directed not only against the 'three years'. This issue was to be used as a general platform for socialist propaganda.[43] The conference spokesman on behalf of the *Jaurèsistes*, Vaillant, conceded that agitation against the defence bill should also be beneficial to party recruitment. However, this aspect was watered down by a 'point of detail' in the *Guesdiste* motion: 'It is in fact a question . . . of eliminating the immediate obstacle to all proletarian and socialist progress and to fight against the three-year law.' This, it was maintained, must be the goal of the *oeuvre socialiste et républicaine* (*sic*). The masses had to be spurred on with boundless hatred, 'mercilessly and relentlessly', and mobilised to defend the Republic from the reactionary onslaught. This mobilisation also meant exerting pressure on the electorate to confront the pro-*Trois Ans* Radicals with the will of their voters.[44]

So although a head-on collision between *Jaurèsistes* and *Guesdistes* was again warded off at the congress of Brest, the activities of the party executive in the following phase made it quite clear that it was not willing to bow down to the *Guesdistes'* demands. Following the congress a circular was sent to all the party federations, in which the conference resolution was interpreted strictly in terms of Vaillant's 'point of detail'—the motion of the *Guesdistes* that the three-year law should be exploited for 'socialist propaganda' was not even mentioned.[45] The following circulars from the party executive[46] also clearly implied that the *Guesdiste* approach had been rejected. In all these circulars—instructions on the practice of socialist agitation—the instrumental function of the campaign against the *Trois Ans* as a means of recruiting new members was mentioned only once, and even then it was couched in rather cautious terms as a postscript:

> From the point of view of their recruitment, the federations must endeavour to take advantage of the agitation. . . . Evidently, among the signatories of the protest who are not yet affiliated, many could be recruited to the Party. The federations should therefore keep a record of the names and addresses of the signatories so that they can be found at the appropriate moment. We shall draw up the same list which, in conditions to be determined, can be submitted to each group concerned.[47]

Thus from the beginning of the campaign the SFIO party leadership conducted a pragmatic policy in order to maintain links with the left-wing Republicans. Meanwhile, the fear of the *Guesdistes* that the campaign against the *Trois Ans* would lead to the 'disappearance of socialism'[48] was in fact not unfounded. The attempt to create a common front with the bourgeois Left could succeed only if the campaign were dominated by domestic issues. As we shall see later, the radical Republicans who were opposed to the *Trois Ans* saw the bill as a fresh manoeuvre of 'a reactionary domestic policy', a continuation of the Poincaristic policy of 1912. The Socialists tried to adjust their campaign accordingly, and as a result issues such as disarmament, international understanding and arbitration tended to be played down in their campaign. In so doing the Socialists also helped to hide the foreign policy and the strategical background to rearmament from the French public up to the outbreak of war.

At the same time as the SFIO, the CGT launched its campaign against the extension of military service.[49] The assertion of the Prefecture of Police that the SFIO and the CGT were conducting a joint campaign[50] was pure speculation—at least at this initial stage. In actual fact leading Syndicalists at first tried to take advantage of the agitation against the *Trois Ans* to improve the image of syndicalism as a movement independent of socialism. It was only in the course of the campaign that various endogenous and exogenous factors led to cooperation with the Socialists—and this cooperation in fact amounted to a new form of syndicalist subordination to the Socialists in political matters.

On 25 February the CGT *Comité Confédéral* (CC) called on all its affiliated syndicates and syndicate unions to organise meetings in protest against the new military proposals which were 'directed particularly against the proletariat'.[51] Identical resolutions were to be passed at all these meetings and then sent to the prefecture of the respective departments, the deputies and senators of each constituency, the Army Committee of the Chamber and to the regional and local press. These *ordres du jour* gave a résumé of the subjects mentioned in the CGT manifesto, *Contre la loi de trois ans et la réaction militariste*.[52] This manifesto proclaimed that the object of the ruling classes in both Germany and France was to compete in an arms race and make war inevitable. This 'murderous activity' could be halted only by a *rapprochement* between the two peoples. The syndicalist International having already launched a campaign to this end, it was now the task of the French Syndicalists to block the three-year bill in order to achieve the final goal. However, the internationalist part of the CGT manifesto made no concrete reference to possible forms of international cooperation against rearmament. This shortcoming can be explained by the fact that French syndicalism had for years been isolated within the international union movement. Unlike other Western trade-union federations, French syndicalism had remained faithful to its theory that links between union and political action could not take the form of open cooperation between the Socialist Party and the unions.[53] Griffuelhes had recently reaffirmed this stance in rather arrogant terms at the 1912 Le Havre congress: 'I maintain that we are somewhat isolated in the International because we are ahead. . . . It is not up to us to fall back in step. *We are ahead*. . . . Our isolation is due to the fact that *we are ahead* of our comrades abroad.'[54]

The CC manifesto focused not so much on international cooperation as on the conclusion that the warmongering of the 'reactionaries' was levelled 'most particularly' against the proletariat, whose emancipation under the leadership of syndicalism was possible only in times of peace. For this reason the manifesto urged all syndicalist organisations and the entire proletariat not to remain passive but to demonstrate the hostility of the working classes to the *Trois Ans*. The government's plans to prolong 'military servitude', claimed the manifesto, was a threat to the proletariat, not only on account of the imminence of war, but also because of the rise in the cost of living (additional indirect taxation to finance armaments, shortfalls in production owing to reduced labour supply). Furthermore, the small farmer who would have to do without his son's labour for a further year, would suffer 'even greater misery'.

However, as a result of the 'return to corporatism' and the diminishing authority of the CGT central office over the locally organised syndicates—a phenomenon which had its origins in the long-term development of French syndicalism and had just become apparent in the general strike of 1912[55]—even the CGT leaders were dubious about how effective this call for action would be. A police informer reported from the CC meeting on 25 February that the CGT leaders were extremely doubtful about the possibility of organising a real mass movement against the *Trois Ans*. Since, he continued, a great number of provincial labour exchanges and syndicates had been only 'lukewarm' of late, resolute agitation at grass-roots level could not be expected. The CGT leaders now intended to try *au prix de tous les sacrifices* in the campaign against the defence bill in order to regain lost ground. 'Before gaining satisfaction, we must', said Jouhaux—and this was repeated by Yvetot—'revive syndicalism, which is falling asleep.'[56]

Nevertheless, if the campaign against rearmament were really to succeed in regaining the ground lost at grass-roots level, the CGT leaders must not only clarify the theoretical stance of syndicalism on the *Trois Ans* but also demonstrate the practical presence of syndicalism to the proletariat by effectively organising agitation. However, in this case theory and practice could not be divided: the theory of revolutionary syndicalism was based on the assumption that every form of agitation in terms of direct action had a consciousness-raising effect and thus served to strengthen the organisation. Yet if syndicalism could not come up with a stance which could be clearly differentiated from the political line of the Socialist Party, CGT agitation against the *Trois Ans* might not strengthen its own organisation but serve only the interests of the SFIO's mass agitation. This was even more true, since many labour exchanges and syndicates tended to see their role under reformist corporatism as purely economic and corporatist and therefore accepted the presence of a political party in the form of the Socialist Party.[57]

This theory that it was the syndicates' responsibility to fight against the *Trois Ans* on their own account was to remain inconsistent and somewhat confused. Jouhaux justified the Syndicalists' opposition to the new military bill with the argument that the three-year law was unacceptable to the workers, since militarism would check the process of industrial development indispensable for the realisation of the 'historic task' of the working classes. From this task arose the need for international workers' solidarity against militarism as an expression and means of socio-economic reaction. Jouhaux believed that these facts made further political arguments by the Syndicalists against the *Trois Ans* superfluous: 'We are sheltered behind a plain and blunt refusal. We refuse to examine or discuss the arguments advanced by the other parties.'[58]

The dialectic of this refusal was that to dispense with their own specifically syndicalist argumentation, on the one hand, while stressing the independence of syndicalism on the other, brought syndicalism to a certain degree closer to Jaurès's position. This probably explains why precisely Jouhaux was prepared to cooperate with the SFIO on specific political issues,[59] whereas Yvetot, the main champion of the old anarcho-syndicalist anti-militarism, tried clearly to differentiate between *action ouvrière* and the political campaign of the SFIO, and to use the campaign against the *Trois Ans* to promote the interests of syndicalism. According to Yvetot, the argument that France had to be protected from the threat from abroad was only a pretext for the build-up in troops, the real aim of which—as always—was internal suppression. Thus the introduction of three-year military service was no more than 'a peak of the cynicism' *vis-à-vis* the workers, following in the tradition of the 1912 *Loi Millerand*.[60] And if there really were any justification for the *Trois Ans* on grounds of foreign policy, one would simply have to appeal to the people's instinct for self-preservation and their reluctance to be led like lambs to the slaughter on account of a would-be *patrie*: 'Let us remain simple and straightforward. Our protests will then be better understood. . . . Our opposition is based on uncomplicated interests.' So, continued Yvetot, nothing could better set the 'decelerated' (*sic*) process of anti-militarism and anti-patriotism back into motion than the arms bill, against which the revolutionary Syndicalists would, if necessary, use force. The struggle against the *Trois Ans* would, he prophesied, lead to a 'revival of our intense syndicalism of 1906'.[61]

On 6 March the CGT published a circular from the *Fédération Nationale du Bâtiment*[62] in an attempt to reconcile the various positions mentioned above. The circular began with the statement that the only reason for the defence bill was the government's plan to 'tame the working class'. This target was to be achieved in two ways: first, by stepping up the use of military force against striking workers; and second, by extending military service to break the bonds of worker solidarity. Thus the organised proletariat was to be crushed and class-conscious workers transformed into potential 'yellow dogs' by the soul-destroying barracks life. This first part of the circular concerning the 'actual' position of the workers on the three-year law was followed by the second section, which provided the arguments to be used by Syndicalists when speaking out against the bill in order to win public opinion: syndicalism advocated *la paix à outrance*. Thus Syndicalists should have the courage to stand up at meetings and declare that 'we do not want to march against the German workers who share our opinion that the emancipation of the working class can take place only in times of peace'. The *ordres du jour* were also to be used to influence public opinion. The circular concluded with a reference designed to appease the reformist syndicates—that the necessary and categorical protest against the *Trois Ans* would by no means dissuade syndicalism from pursuing other specific syndicalist objectives (reduction of the working day, etc.).[63]

This circular is sufficient proof of the doctrinarian dissent typical of the ambiguity of syndicalism of the day. Whereas the first part of the circular was virtually a paraphrase of Yvetot's theories, the second part—designed for the attention of the public—was a condensed version of the Jouhaux approach which, by stressing the syndicates' unconditional will for peace (*paix à outrance*), opened the door to the possibility of their joining forces with the SFIO. The final part of the declaration, in view of its dichotomy and distinction between political and economic action, represented a concession to the Reformists.

The CGT's theoretical dilemma hardly seems to have detracted from the belligerency of many militants at the initial stage of the debate on the three-year law when attention was centered on the fight against the military bill itself. The failure of the CGT leadership to formulate a uniform policy on the defence issue increased the concrete opportunities for practical cooperation between revolutionaries, reformist Syndicalists and Socialists on the three-year issue. A police informer reported from a meeting of the leaders of the CGT syndicates and federations that the majority of the delegates were very pleased about the determined fight of the SFIO (and many Radicals!), and that the reformist syndicates 'saw eye to eye with the anti-militarist revolutionaries' on the defence issue.[64] A little later the leaders of the *Union des Syndicats de la Seine*, the largest of the syndicate unions within the CGT, even moved an—unpublished—resolution on cooperation with the SFIO on action against the three-year law: 'If the Socialists ask to speak at meetings . . . we shall let them, because even if their approach is not quite the same as the Syndicalists', we must not disregard the support of all the parties opposed to the three-year law.'[65]

It was typical that the Seine union should be the first to launch real mass agitation. Its call for the first large demonstration against the three-year law on the Pré St Gervais on 16 March was addressed to 'everyone': 'Wake up, everyone! Workers and employees . . . fathers and mothers, boys and girls, all of you, stand up against the CRIME which is being perpetrated!'[66] To make its intentions absolutely clear, the Seine union specified its manifesto immediately before the demonstration: 'It [the Seine union] hopes that all groups outside syndicalism struggling against military reaction will join its forces to give a more spectacular and universal tone to the demonstration.'[67]

This first mass demonstration in Paris was to act as a signal: 'To get the peasants and workers of France on their feet the revolutionary proletariat of Paris must raise its voice against the three-year law'.[68] Apparently the CGT leaders were actually planning to concentrate their agitation in the provinces rather than Paris. At a meeting of the general committee of the Seine union its secretary, Bled, stated that the CGT would be unable to organise any large-scale May Day rallies in Paris that year, since it had been decided to send the top speakers into the provinces, above all to fight against the *Loi de Trois Ans*.[69]

In view of the fact that both the SFIO and the CGT intended to concentrate their extra-parliamentary action against the three-year bill in the provinces, it will be necessary to give a more detailed analysis of agitation at grass-roots level, not only to gain an insight into the political and organisational potential of the SFIO and the CGT, but to determine the attitude of the French population towards the proposal to extend military service in the opening phase of the debate. On 7 March—only the day after the presentation of the government's bill—the directors of the political police instructed all the departmental superintendents to monitor and keep them informed of the agitation of Socialists, Syndicalists and anarchists 'against the army and the government'.[70] Apparently these instructions were generally followed and the reports, along with those of the Prefecture of Police on agitation in Paris itself,[71] give at least an outline of the dimensions of the early stages of the socialist and syndicalist campaign.

The first striking fact is that relatively few CGT demonstrations were held in the capital, and the attendance at those that did take place was generally low. It was not until 14 March that the first meeting was held by the *Jeunesses Syndicalistes*. Throughout the rest of the month a total of six demonstrations were held, with an average of some 100 participants. Moreover, the organisation of these demonstrations was always the joint effort of several syndicates.

In the SFIO camp the picture at this initial stage was a quite different one: twenty-five meetings with an average attendance of approximately 500 were reported between 6 March and the end of the month. If we deduct the four mass rallies organised by SFIO headquarters, with an average of some 1,200 participants, from this total and consider only the meetings held by the SFIO Paris *arrondissement* sections, we are still left with a total of twenty-one meetings with on average 320 participants, fairly evenly distributed throughout the city, though with a slight predominance in the traditionally 'red' *arrondissements*. Thus, in the case of the SFIO, there was a considerable degree of activity among the rank and file.[72]

It is difficult to find a precise explanation for this disparity between concrete CGT and SFIO action in the capital. The lack of CGT activity—only one mass rally on 16 March—may have been due to the fact that agitation was to be concentrated in the provinces. However, this still does not explain the extraordinary inactivity of both the individual Paris syndicates and the *Comités Intersyndicaux*. It therefore seems plausible that, despite the fact that the CGT leaders had stressed the difference between their own *action ouvrière* and the political activity of the SFIO, many syndicalist workers were nevertheless attracted by the political action and approach rather than the syndicalist action against the three-year law, particularly since the ideological barriers had already been partly broken down by the *Union des Syndicats'* pragmatic approach to joint action.

Considering CGT intentions of stirring up the whole of the country against the *Trois Ans*, the concrete results of its action in the provinces were also rather meagre. The poster *La Loi de Trois Ans et la réaction militariste*, intended as the main instrument of the CGT's appeal, was to be seen in only half of the fifty-two departments investigated.[73] The poster campaign had admittedly been impeded from the very outset by the CGT's lack of funds[74] and the illegal intervention of the police authorities who had torn down or covered over the CGT poster in many areas.[75]

It is surprising to note that few delegates from CGT headquarters attended the meetings of the local labour exchanges and syndicates. Yvetot seems to have been the only prominent CGT member who was active at departmental level, and in fact he attracted large crowds.[76] However, even the few larger demonstrations held in the departments cannot hide the fact that syndicalist propaganda against the *Loi de Trois Ans* aroused relatively little interest, even among the CGT groups at grass-roots level. In his final report on his campaign in the department of the Loire, Yvetot lamented the 'sad state' of syndicalism in this old industrial centre which seemed to have become a perpetual 'fief of that swine Aristide [Briand]'.[77] In fact, in the department of the Loire there was a relatively high level of protest action among syndicalist workers; Yvetot's main concern was that this action did not respect the confines of his own strategy. The St Étienne bookbinders' syndicate, associated with the reformist *Fédération du Livre*, was the first syndicate to send a letter of protest to the Prefect.[78] In this letter the syndicate stressed that it disdained 'uncontrolled demonstrations' and was concerned only with defending its own economic interests. At the same time it quoted the political grounds for protest as being the fact that the three-year law had established a coalition of united 'reactionaries', which threatened to wash away the Republicans in a 'wave of chauvinism'.[79]

On the whole there was little activity among the organised workers in the provinces. In twenty-eight of the fifty-two departments investigated, no independent local syndicate or labour exchange action was carried out. In most cases action amounted to no more than the passing of the *Comité Confédéral* resolution. Campaigns of any magnitude at all got off the ground only in the departments of Cher, Ille-et-Villaine, Nord, Saône-et-Loire (Montceau), Somme and Pas-de-Calais. In these regions the organised workers printed a number of posters and held meetings and protest marches. Given the general disinterest, even among the rank and file, in *action ouvrière* against the *Trois Ans*, with only scattered platonic activities being carried out,[80] the forecasts of the prefects in a number of departments, that the Syndicalists had little hope of mobilising large sections of the population against the bill, seemed to have been true.[81]

In this opening stage of the public debate the SFIO leaders followed a strategy similar to that of the CGT. The CAP's first circular on the issue to the departmental federations called on them to display the

Franco-German socialist manifesto of 1 March in huge format in their departments and to organise local rallies coinciding with the mass demonstration in Paris on 16 March. At these rallies, as at those organised by the CGT, identical resolutions were to be passed and submitted to the authorities and the prefects. However, in contrast with the CGT *ordre du jour*, the Socialists' was extremely moderate. It condemned the 'intimidation of public opinion' by the 'reactionary and capitalist press', described the *Loi de Trois Ans* as a waste of public funds, and demanded that it should be repealed and replaced by a 'methodical' reorganisation of the army (militia), regardless of the 'whims of neighbouring nations'.[82]

Judging from the available sources, the readiness—or ability—of the SFIO departmental organisations to carry out these meetings of protest against the three-year bill was not very substantial. Rallies were held in only eleven of the fifty-two departments investigated, and although they were organised either along with the local syndicates or in some cases even along with the radical *comités*, only three of these rallies were really successful.[83] Despite the announcement that Jaurès would attend an SFIO mass rally in the department of Tarn, only 600 people turned up, while other mass rallies in the traditional SFIO strongholds in this department (Décazeville!) even had to be cancelled owing to a lack of interest among the workers.[84] Not even the poster campaign was completely successful. The Franco-German socialist poster condemning the arms race was distributed in only twenty-six of the fifty-two departments investigated, and in many areas suffered the same fate as the CGT poster, being torn down or covered over. SFIO headquarters seem to have had little interest in effectively distributing this poster in any case. The individual federations each received only one copy, with a revenue stamp already attached, and additional copies had to be ordered along with the obligatory revenue stamp.[85] Moreover, the poster campaign was not even mentioned in the second CAP circular.[86] This seems to have been due not only to financial and administrative difficulties but also to the poster's lack of appeal to the public. 'It's too long', remarked a prefect laconically, and other prefects confirmed that the population was neither reading nor discussing the Franco-German manifesto.[87]

In view of the disappointing results of the opening phase of its campaign, the SFIO now began to concentrate its protest action in the departments on collecting signatures for a mass petition to be presented to Parliament. This activity began in mid-March, roughly coinciding with the Brest conference. It was hoped that these petitions, which were to 'voice the opposition of the masses', would reach every corner of France and would be a means of inexpensive propaganda requiring little organisational effort. Particular efforts were to be devoted to the constituencies of deputies who supported the bill or had not quite made up their minds, and above all to the constituencies of radical deputies who were traditionally dependent on the local *comités* and could therefore best be impressed by the 'will of the people'.[88] Since the petition was addressed not only to Socialists but to all citizens who for one reason or another were opposed to the defence bill, no particular motives for the protest were given on the petition forms, which were apodictically entitled *Contre la Loi de Trois Ans*.

This new form of *Appel au Pays* had a surprising degree of success. According to *L'Humanité*'s statistics, almost 20,000 signatures were collected daily in the first two months.[89] It was this surprisingly high response which led to the remarks in a number of prefecture reports from the end of March that the majority of the population was mistrustful of the government's bill, even in some of the departments whose prefects had been convinced at the beginning of the month that the vast majority of the population was prepared to accept the defence bill.[90] This development in public opinion certainly did not make it easier for the Radical Party to define its position on the three-year law.

The Position of the Radical Party

Parliamentary radicalism had lost its unchallenged position as a governmental party in Poincaré's cabinet and was now being more and more suppressed in the grip of national unity. Poincaré's election to the presidency against the wishes of the Radicals had been sufficient evidence of this.[91]

Since public interest was immersed in the *Trois Ans* issue, it was absolutely imperative for the Radical Party to define its stance on rearmament. All the statements in the pro-radical press conceded that German rearmament, aggressive or not, naturally made it necessary for France to make a considerable effort. For example, *L'Aurore*, opposed to the *Trois Ans*, commended the French and German Socialists' poster as an expression of pacifism, but added that in view of German rearmament the Socialists were flogging a dead horse. Germany was forcing France into making new efforts to redress the 'proportion of strength'. *Le Siècle*, which commented on the government's proposals almost daily, declared that the three-year law was the expression of a 'magnificent wave of patriotism all over the country in the wake of the threat from Germany'.[92] Despite these comments, the radical press was generally of the opinion that, regardless of the objective 'threat from

Germany', the German army would not be in a position to launch an *attaque brusquée* as long as France fully utilised the potential of the 1905 conscription law. General Percin, a former member of the *Conseil Supérieur de la Guerre*, tried to demonstrate this in the columns of *L'Aurore*.[93] On 19 February, directly following the first reports on German rearmament plans in *Le Temps*, *Le Radical* proposed that the cover troops on the French eastern border should be reinforced by enlisting the 'shirkers',[94] calling in the colonial troops to defend *la patrie* and by 'organising reserves more rationally'.

These proposals were reiterated on a number of occasions and were also taken up by the other radical newspapers.[95] Agreement in principle to all the necessary material improvements to the army— additional heavy artillery equipment and reinforcement of fortifications—was stressed time and again. The radical press was thus striving not only to emphasise the left-wing Republicans' patriotism but to prove that its own concept of national defence was still viable, and therefore it viewed the three-year bill with scepticism. The government's intransigence and the nationalist campaign were both seen as a sign that the 'three years' were to be used to drive home the anti-radical line of Poincaristic domestic policy.[96] *Le Radical* nevertheless stated on 26 February that the Radical Party would go along with the *Trois Ans* if evidence were provided that the government's bill was the only means of meeting the requirements of national defence.

The weakness of the Radicals' line of argument lies in its rather peculiar and unbalanced combination of political and non-political elements. Whereas military measures in retaliation for the 'German threat' were advocated, no analysis of the political context of the arms race or an application of this analysis to political theory took place. The radical press tried to reinforce the old line that radicalism was a bulwark of the Republic against domestic reaction—that is, against *Poincarisme*—but this defensive approach was not a solid basis for a real alternative to the government's proposals. The three-year law had been justified to the public as the only means of safeguarding national defence. Thus it was argued that the government bill contained no more and no less than the necessary sacrifice advocated by the Radicals.

Particular public attention was aroused by the statement of the 'patriarch of radicalism', Clemenceau, immediately after announcement of the CSG vote. Clemenceau, who had been one of the champions of the republican conscription bill of 1905, was asked whether he regarded the amendment of this bill as a sign that Parliament was 'confessing its sins'. He answered as follows: 'One can after all confess one's sins on behalf of *la patrie*. I don't mind at all. I would be prepared to go to confession all day long if it meant saving *la patrie*.'[97]

Another prominent radical politician, C. Dumont, assured the 600 people assembled at the inaugural meeting of the Quimper party section that the Radical Party would lend its support to any measures necessary to defend the country from the threat of German rearmament, so that any 'conscious Frenchman' would back the government's plans as long as the principle of equality of the military burden was upheld.[98] Garreau, who had been the Senate spokesman on the 1905 conscription law, also stated that he would give his full support to the government's plans if equality were maintained, 'because in peacetime, with no provocation whatsoever, Germany sees fit to draw up her formidable armaments against us'.[99]

Initially, most radical deputies seem to have been concerned at the vehemence of the campaign of both the Right and the SFIO. The fiery heckling from the socialist benches as the bill was read to Parliament was condemned by the Radicals, who considered this 'blind obstructionism' as detrimental to an objective debate on the government bill which might indeed be misconceived but which could not be dismissed from the outset as 'reactionary'. As a traditional parliamentary party, the Radical Party stated that it would be unable to define its position on the issue until the bill had been seriously examined and debated in Parliament; it would agree to 'only what was necessary, but nevertheless to everything that was necessary'.[100] Thus, in their initial statements, both groups of the Radical Party in Parliament, the *gauche radicale* and the *gauche radicale-socialiste*, were unanimous in their call for a 'serious and calm examination' of the issue.[101]

Both parliamentary groups also demanded—with remarkable unanimity—that the costs of rearmament would have to be paid for 'by the rich'.[102] Along with forty other members of his group, the *gauche radicale* deputy Jacquier tabled an amendment to the government bill on 10 March proposing that the costs of the material improvement of army equipment should be covered by a 'war tax' to be levied on incomes above a ceiling of 10,000 francs.[103] On the same day the *gauche radicale-socialiste*, led by Durafour, further stipulated that the costs of the three-year law itself should be covered by this tax, adding that this did not, however, imply their approval of the government's bill.[104] The fact that the Jacquier group did not subscribe to this more explicit motion implies an underlying dissent between the two radical parliamentary groups. Moreover, the *gauche radicale* did not even refer to the *Trois Ans* in its statement, which can be interpreted only as an indication that it was impossible for the whole of the parliamentary party to agree on a joint stance.

It was probably because of this confusion and disagreement of the radical position on the three-year law that the Radical Party executive committee (CE) did not issue its statement until 24 March.[105] The party leaders declared that their party was prepared to meet the requirements of national defence but added, in accordance with the Jacquier and Durafour amendments, that the rich would have to bear the brunt of the costs in order to safeguard the defence of the country, and that before a decision was taken on the bill, Parliament should carefully examine the possible alternatives.[106] So although inclined to accept the bill, the CE put forward this stereotype demand for careful examination despite the fact that the public debate on the *Trois Ans* had been launched over a month previously, and despite that all the political groups concerned had emerged with a clear-cut position. It was only the Radical Party which failed to come down on either side of the fence. This ambiguity in the radical camp was sharply criticised by Jaurès. The Radicals were so 'slow-witted', he said ironically, that they lamented the awakening of 'reaction' but would actually prefer to have the *Loi de Trois Ans* 'today', since the Socialists had so far not managed to 'awaken the country'.[107]

Perhaps the main reason for the Radicals' reticence was the fact that the Briand ministry (formed following Poincaré's election to the presidency on 18 March 1913) was overthrown by the Senate, where the Radicals were in a majority, on 18 March 1913. Although to all extents and purposes the fall of the government was due to a disagreement between the government and the Senate on the question of the electoral reform,[108] Poincaré hit the nail on the head when he exclaimed: 'It's the revenge of the Radicals against my election!'[109] Clemenceau, the undisputed leader of the Radicals in the Senate, declared that his party's opposition to proportional representation was because a vote in favour of electoral reform would represent an endorsement of the 'Caesarean spirit' at the root of the bill. The Caesarean danger was that, as heads of government, Poincaré and his successor Briand had backed a bill which had not gained a real *majorité républicaine* in the Chamber but had been passed by a heterogeneous majority of the far Left, Conservatives and the nationalist Right. So it was now up to the Senate as the 'bulwark of the Republic' to prevent the traditional *majorité républicaine* from being deprived of its political powers.[110]

Now that the government had been brought down by the Senate, leading radical politicians and publicists hoped to regain their traditional position as a governing party which they had lost under Poincaré in 1912. It was expected that Briand's successor would form a cabinet not of national but of Republican unity, which could be possible if the government did not make a dogma of the three-year law. The Radicals were prepared to meet the government half-way to form a new partnership against anti-radical and nationalist policy.[111]

The fact that the defence question was considered purely in terms of domestic issues does not imply just that the Radicals were thinking along unrealistic or idiosyncratic lines. This disregard of the international dimension was fostered by the Right's obvious attempts to exploit the national consensus in order to achieve their domestic aims. Moreover, the ambiguity and intentional vagueness of the government's arguments to the public and Parliament also served to kindle the suspicion of many Radicals that the defence bill was first and foremost a manoeuvre of domestic policy. The government's cover-up tactics were clearly exposed at the first meeting of the Chamber Army Committee when, in strict confidence, the War Minister, Étienne, put forward an extremely candid explanation for the governmental bill.[112]

When a radical deputy enquired why the government had decided on the three-year law 'all of a sudden', given that on 2 December 1912 Millerand, the War Minister, had emphasised that the French troops were in 'fine fettle', Étienne replied that 'the situation in Europe has changed since December 1912'. Germany would soon boast 850,000 men-at-arms compared with a regular French army of 478,000. Étienne commented as follows on the German troop reinforcement:

> Why does Germany want to increase her armed strength to such a high level? Quite frankly, and I mean this most sincerely, I do not think that at this moment, as I utter these words, or even yesterday, Germany has or had the intention to pounce upon France. I do not think this is what the Kaiser has in mind. But it is impossible for him not to take account of the general situation in Europe and he has examined the consequences of the troubles and the upheaval in Eastern Europe, in the Balkan Peninsula [involving Austria, which was why Germany would have to do without Austria's help and face France alone] . . . who would be in a very favourable situation. [He has also considered] Russia, which, by the virtue of the very fact that she has a population of 116 million, could draft enormous numbers of men, and that his situation could then be precarious. To ward off this danger he therefore had the idea of increasing his military strength—I won't say to a maximum but to a level at which he could resolutely face both France and Russia as they stand at the moment.

Thus—again according to Étienne—France must augment her striking power so that Germany would never be tempted to attack, for external factors could lead to Germany having to 'march' without her actually wanting to. Then, owing to the sluggishness of Russian mobilisation, Germany, with her army mobilised inside three days, could launch an assault on France and, having subdued her, turn all her troops against Russia. Only if France increased her troop-level on the frontier, concluded Étienne, could this plan be thwarted and Germany forced into moderation.

A radical member of the Committee, General Pédoya, retaliated that, if there were a threat of an attack from Germany, the emergency paragraph of the 1905[113] conscription law would suffice for the reinforcement the troops on the border. Étienne replied,

> Article 33 gives us the possibility to keep a class in the ranks for an additional year. But do you think this is an appropriate system for a nation which has a sense of duty both now and in the future? . . . Must we not provide for what may happen in the future? . . . France must be put in a position where her military force is such that she can guard permanently against the future, and speak with authority to the outside world in order to gain respect for and uphold her rights and her dignity. . . .[114]

Étienne added a further military argument to these strategic considerations, which led to a storm of protest from Jaurès: whereas Germany would not integrate the reservists into her regular army, the effective peacetime strength of France was so low at present that she would be compelled to integrate too many reservists into the individual companies in order to put them on a war footing. However, if these reserve units were to be in a state of readiness, they would have to be trained together over a long period of time—and this was not guaranteed by the present system.

Étienne's reasoning was a true reflection of much of the real background to the three-year law, so far as both foreign policy and the military sector were concerned. What was missing was the crucial link between these points and the offensive strategy. Moreover, the vital problem of the Russian alliance was touched upon only briefly.[115] Étienne had insisted that the three-year law aimed only at reinforcing troops on the front to ward off a sudden German attack. As a result of this discrepancy between the military concept of the *attaque brusquée* and the danger of a German assault haunting the public, Étienne's arguments seemed most incongruous. The government was not in a position to provide the evidence, demanded above all by the Radicals, that the three-year law was the only adequate means of safeguarding national defence. From the Radicals' point of view, 'national defence' was synonymous with the securing of the borders by all the forces of the 'nation in arms' and the strengthening of fortifications. And if these premises were accepted, it could hardly be disputed that, faced with the imminence of war, a German invasion could also be prevented on the basis of the Radicals' defensive concept.

All that filtered through to the public about the Army Committee's meeting was Étienne's statement that the three-year law was not aimed at preventing a 'direct danger' but at providing for a general 'future situation'. The radical *Lanterne* concluded from this that Parliament did not need to take any rash decisions but had time for an in-depth examination of the bill.[116] Therefore Étienne's demand at the second meeting of the Army Committee on 18 March that the discussions should be wound up as quickly as possible, and the bill voted on before the parliamentary recess,[117] certainly did not help to remove the suspicion from many radical minds that the three-year law was no more than a manoeuvre of domestic reaction.

CHAPTER 4

The Hardening of the Fronts Under the Barthou Government

The Barthou Government and the Amendment of the Defence Bill

As we have already seen, Briand's cabinet was overthrown by the Senate on the issue of electoral reform. This was undoubtedly a challenge to the anti-radical policy of national unity and its suspected Caesarean overtone. However, Poincaré refused to pick up the gauntlet, despite right-wing demands that he must now justify the confidence France had entrusted in him. On the day the government was overthrown A. de Mun, leader of the Catholic 'rallied' *Alliance Libérale Populaire*, commented in a letter to Poincaré: 'This war of malice and hate on the body of France is abominable! I implore you, remain firm! Abandon nothing, neither foreign affairs nor the war. Make the three-year law an absolute condition. The country is behind you just as the day [you were elected to the presidency] in Versailles!'[1]

Poincaré now entrusted Louis Barthou[2] with the task of forming a new government. Barthou had been proposed by Briand basically because he was a 'most determined supporter of the three-year law' who could be counted on to defend the government bill 'with vigour and talent'.[3] However, although this choice illustrated Poincaré's determination to carry through the *Trois Ans*, it nevertheless represented a concession to the Radicals, since Barthou had never been committed to electoral reform.[4] Moreover, two leading radical politicians were given portfolios in the new cabinet,[5] although for the first time since the Dreyfus affair a *Progressiste* was also given a seat in cabinet—a decision which Barthou justified with the argument that he wanted all the republican groups in Parliament to participate in the 'law of national salvation'.[6]

This motley political composition of Barthou's cabinet demonstrates that its only *raison d'être* was to push the three-year bill through Parliament. Before forming his cabinet, Barthou had made it quite clear that he would accept this task only if all his ministers were unequivocal supporters of the *Trois Ans*. He was 'quite obstinate' on this point.[7] So, from the very outset, Barthou totally excluded any compromise on the defence issue, thus dashing the hopes of leading Radicals.

Barthou's governmental declaration on 25 March[8] concentrated accordingly on matters of national defence and the three-year law. The new Premier also spelled out the principles of anti-clericalism with a greater degree of clarity than Poincaré and Briand had done in their governmental declarations (1912 and January 1913, respectively). For instance, Barthou declared that the new government would 'protect state schools against the slander and manoeuvring [of the Right] which was becoming more and more intolerable'. Moreover, Barthou also referred to the need for tax reform to 'compensate' for the great sacrifices to be made on behalf of national defence, above all by the rural population. These statements may be written off as trivial and 'ritualistic',[9] but they were nevertheless most ingenious.

Many left-wing republican deputies now apparently saw fit to abstain in the vote on the governmental declaration, since, despite their scepticism, the argument that the *Trois Ans* was part and parcel of an overall reactionary domestic strategy no longer appeared absolutely tenable. Characteristically enough, of the 162 votes against the government, only fifty-five came from the ranks of the *gauche radicale-socialiste*, whereas fifty-six members of this group abstained along with thirty-nine *gauche radicale* members. The remaining abstentions were mainly on the Right, an expression of discontent with Barthou's anti-clerical declarations. The SFIO and the vast majority of the *républicain-socialistes* voted against the government.[10]

Therefore, although Barthou had no coherent parliamentary majority on his side, his government was not directly threatened, since the left-wing groups were split over the three-year issue. This became clear shortly after the division on the governmental declaration at the meeting of the chairmen of the left-wing republican groups to decide whether or not to present a joint interpellation.[11] Significantly enough, the agenda of this meeting ignored the *Trois Ans* issue, referring only to the 'scandal' that a *Progressiste* had been appointed as a member of the government and that there had been no left-wing majority in favour of the governmental declaration. Only the *républicain-socialistes* were unequivocal in their rejection of any form of support for the government. The radical-socialist group was not prepared to follow their example. Caillaux, who had been elected chairman of the *gauche radicale* group the previous day, declared that his group could not support an interpellation either.[12] This reluctance was even more remarkable, since only the day before, on 24 March, the executive committee of the Radical Party had urged the deputies of both groups to vote against the government on account of Barthou's dogmatic stance on the military question. Many radical politicians obviously believed that defence policy was a technical issue which had to be detached from issues of domestic policy.

This basic differentiation, which was to become more and more apparent as time went on, was fostered by Poincaré's attempts to dispel the feelings of mistrust the Radicals had towards him and his policy, which they suspected as being latently Caesarean. Several days after the formation of the Barthou government Poincaré gave a speech in Montpellier, the chief town of the department of Hérault and one of the strongest bastions of radicalism.[13] The *discours de Montpellier*, which attracted considerable attention, was Poincaré's first public appearance since his election as President. Without even mentioning the three-year bill, Poincaré commended the population's 'peaceful patriotism', and stressed that the role of the President of the Republic was 'impersonal and anonymous'. The President, he said, could hope for no more than to be the 'first servant of the Constitution and the laws of the land'.[14]

The Montpellier speech has often been regarded as evidence that Poincaré was a 'party president', a 'chief executive with a programme', who identified with the political programme of particular parties, thus breaking out of the bounds of non-partisanship inherent in the presidential office.[15] However, this historical assessment does not reflect contemporary public opinion. Jaurès, for example, interpreted Poincaré's speech as a sign of the President's will to disassociate himself from the Boulangist campaign which had been sparked off by the chauvinists and reactionaries around him, fearing that it might sweep away not only himself but France and the Republic with him. *Le Radical* declared that Poincaré's speech was proof that his patriotism was not to be confused with 'provocative chauvinism' and that he did not intend to project himself as an anti-radical political leader, despite the hopes of the Right.[16] The press of the Centre and the Right were extremely cautious in their comments and did not try to interpret Poincaré's speech in terms of party politics as an attempt to 'play off' his charisma against Parliament. On the contrary, in a letter to the War

Minister, Étienne, A. de Mun complained that Poincaré had not wanted to broach the 'vital subject'—the *Loi de Trois Ans*—in Montpellier because of 'excessive scruples'. The President's reticence, wrote de Mun, was inappropriate, since Parliament could be persuaded to pass the bill immediately only if subjected to the pressure of public opinion. 'What is at stake is sacred! We [the Right] will do . . . all we can. But we need help!'[17]

The attempt to coordinate the mobilisation of public opinion with right-wing agitation to put pressure on Parliament was in fact to constitute part of the Barthou government's domestic strategy.[18] This, however, was Barthou's personal policy, which is not to be confused with Poincaré's efforts to dispel the Radicals' doubts about his Caesarean domestic policy, that of gaining a stable parliamentary majority in favour of the three-year bill.

At first sight it seems that one reason for the Barthou government's extreme intransigence towards Parliament might have been the deterioration of Franco-German relations at this point (late March 1913), which could have led the government to increase pressure on Parliament so that additional defensive measures could be introduced as soon as possible. Poincaré in particular later insisted that German chauvinism had assumed alarming proportions throughout the spring of 1913. The first sign of this had been the 'Störenfried' article in *Die Post*. The next was the German government's reaction to the Lunéville incident. This was followed by Bethmann Hollweg's speech in the Reichstag on the reasons for the expansion of the German army. And the final straw was the 'Ludendorff memorandum'.[19] Joffre for his part declared that the Ludendorff memorandum had strengthened the determination of the French government to carry through its defence bill at all costs.[20] If it were true, as the editors of the *Documents Diplomatiques Français* maintained, that French army officers and politicians in 1913 believed that this document was authentic,[21] the French government's concern about the now official chauvinistic aggression of Germany could, objectively, seem justified. However, the version of the Ludendorff memorandum circulating among French governmental circles was in all probability a red herring contrived by the French general staff—and the government must also have been in the know.[22] If not, why was this memorandum neither directly nor indirectly mentioned at the meetings of the Supreme Army Council on 18 and 24 April?[23] The fact that the Foreign Minister, Pichon, sent his ambassadors in London and St Petersburg the faked version of the Ludendorff memorandum, adding that there could no longer be any doubt about Germany's aggressive intentions towards France,[24] is to be considered as no more than a manoeuvre of traditional 'statesmanship'.

Nevertheless, it cannot be disputed that there was a link between German rearmament and the hardening of the position of the Barthou government *vis-à-vis* Parliament. This link, albeit rather indirect, is revealed by the fact that, when informed of the content of the official German defence bill on 28 March, the French government felt compelled to drop its own plans and adopt the position of the general staff, sceptical of the three-year bill owing to the concessions—within the domestic context—to the principle of equality.[25] This amounted to an about-turn in the Barthou government's military policy, since the cabinet now adopted the Reinach-Montebello counter-proposal regarded by the generals as a means of maintaining Plan XVII despite the expansion of the German army.[26] Barthou's determined words were probably designed to detract from this about-turn in policy and to keep the little confidence left-wing republican public opinion had in the government on his side.

The essence of the Reinach-Montebello counter-proposal was that it stipulated precisely the effective strength of individual companies: 140 men for companies stationed within the *Métropole*, and 200 men for the cover-troop companies. Officially the aim of stipulating the numbers in this way was to safeguard the expansion of the army against any subsequent attempt (e.g. by means of budgetary legislation) to cut back its numbers. In practice it meant that the number of those soldiers who had already been in service for two years would be added to the number of those who had been serving for one year. Then, on the basis of this addition, the number of soldiers above the legally stipulated effective strength would be discharged in advance from the group which had already served two years. This 'second portion' would include the sons of large families and especially distinguished soldiers.[27] General Legrand of the Army Committee estimated the necessary overall effective strength at 600,232 men-at-arms, which in real terms would mean an increase in the regular army of approximately 130,000 men (compared with its strength as of 1 February 1913). Therefore, since the overall strength of one conscript class was approximately 195,000 men, roughly 60,000 could be discharged in advance.[28]

In contrast with the original version of the government's bill, this counter-proposal corresponded exactly with the general staff's ideas, its offensive strategy and Plan XVII.[29] The original draft had aimed above all at expanding the regular army but had lacked provisions stipulating the composition of the army in wartime—that is, the ratio between the number of regular soldiers and reservists in a mobilised unit, essential to the offensive Plan XVII which army officers considered could be applied only if the respective units consisted mainly of

regular troops. At the CSG meeting on 18 April, at which the definitive decision on this operational plan was taken, General Pau, in reply
to a question from Étienne, replied that the plan would be feasible only
if each unit under mobilisation had a maximum of one-third reservists.
General Galliéni added that any measure reducing recourse to reserve
battalions to a minimum in wartime was welcome. Germany, according to Pau, was in the process of setting up an army consisting of only
professional soldiers (*sic*). Thus it was up to France to ensure that no
reserve battalions were deployed in the decisive opening battles of a
war. Reserve units could be used only to guard fortifications, trains,
and so forth. Pau's plea against the deployment of reserve units
culminated in a cynical remark suggesting that the reservists could at
least have some value as 'cannon-fodder': 'They [the reservists] could
also perhaps be used as a type of mobile depot to fill in the gaps in the
front-line units until the men from the depots arrive.'[30] The *Bases du
Plan* (XVII), published after the war, provide sufficient evidence of the
general staff's resistance to the integration of the reserves into the
regular units, despite attempts to cover this up by appropriate omissions. For example, one of these omissions, which gives a description
of the function of reserve units, is an·exact reflection of Pau's remarks
at the CSG meeting on 18 April 1913.[31]

A further link between the Reinach-Montebello counter-proposal
and Plan XVII can be found in the minutes of the CSG meeting on
24 April, when the proposal was discussed and adopted without any
wide-ranging amendments. According to the *note de présentation*, the
stipulation of minimum effective strength in the Reinach-Montebello
proposal had two aims. In the first place it was to enable the cover
troops to play their 'special role'—that is, the offensive!—without
having to call in any reserve units. Second, the effective peacetime
strength of troops stationed within the country could be organised in
such a way that reservists would account for much less than 50 per cent
of each mobilised unit. Only then could these units maintain their
'offensive value and cohesion'.[32]

The next day, on 25 April, the principle of the stipulation of effective
strength was put before the Chamber Army Committee and adopted,
despite vehement protest from the Socialists and a number of Radicals.
General Legrand, spokesman for the government, informed the Committee that minimum effective strength had to be stipulated in order to
guarantee sufficient periods of training for the recruits. The strategical
intention to dispense with the reservists so far as possible was thus
concealed from the deputies.[33]

Given the dictates of Plan XVII, the government's adoption of the
Reinach-Montebello counter-proposal was technically rational. On

the other hand, this step could give rise to considerable complications, since it practically wiped out the whole of the government's original arguments in favour of the three-year bill. The discrepancy between the intentions of the government and the general staff, on the one hand, and the egalitarian principle which was the main prerequisite for the approval of the left-wing Republicans in Parliament and public, on the other, represented a real threat to the whole bill, since even before this about-turn, which was incompatible with the government's dogmatic language, Barthou had the support of only a very fragile parliamentary majority.

Repression at Home and the Danger of Political Polarisation

In these circumstances the campaign against the military bill gained new momentum, especially since the Socialists had decided to use the parliamentary Easter recess to intensify their public agitation.[34] Barthou retaliated with a massive pre-emptive strike: on 29 March a circular ordered the prefects to ban all street demonstrations for or against the three-year law. On 26 April these instructions were reissued, this time including a ban on the workers' traditional May Day celebrations.[35]

Although these rigorous steps had been taken against the advice of a number of prefects who considered that the ban on demonstrations was bound to lead to public disorder and provoke heavy clashes, especially since it included the May Day demonstrations,[36] they were nevertheless carried out in most departments.[37] In some cases prefects and police went even further and put a ban on protest meetings in labour exchanges and in municipal premises. These measures were also given the government's seal of approval.[38] Another indication of repression was that, under instructions from the Minister of the Interior, the police authorities drew up a black list of professors and teachers who had participated in action against the *Trois Ans* which was then passed on to the Minister of Education for further action.[39] Barthou obviously intended to curtail public protest against the *Loi de Trois Ans* as far as he could without actually breaking the law, and he paid no attention to the danger of a hardening of the fronts this policy implied.

The government did not stop at this administrative suppression of protest. At the beginning of the parliamentary Easter recess the members of the government appeared in public for the first time to speak on behalf of the 'three years'. This campaign was launched with a speech by the War Minister to the Paris *Société Hippique*. Étienne declared that, in view of the German army of 850,000, any protest against the government's bill must be regarded as an attempt to 'disarm France'. The government, he continued, would do all it could to persuade Parliament to carry out its 'patriotic duty' and accept the government's bill in its present form. Étienne made statements of a similar vein at a meeting of high-ranking officers in Paris and again at a large public meeting in Rouen.[40] On another occasion the War Minister declared that the task of a responsible government must be to express in 'word and deed' the 'deep-rooted and subconscious national hopes'· of a people who were aware of their historic task and accordingly did not want to 'die'. Regardless of 'customs and prejudices', the government would continue to defend its army bill in 'clear and decisive' terms. This bill had been presented on account of 'sudden necessity' and it was the only means of safeguarding the defence of France 'in her hour of need'.[41]

The Premier, Barthou, also entered the public debate. At a meeting in Caen he described the *Trois Ans* as a necessity which the country 'in its instinctive clear-sightedness' had already generally accepted as its national duty. The government was highly gratified to see that the people were not letting themselves be influenced by the 'fallacies and illusions of pacifist internationalism'. Alluding to the government's policy of taking disciplinary action against teachers and professors who had publicly protested against the government's bill, Barthou said that the government considered any criticism of its plans by civil servants as incompatible with their special status.[42] A few days later, at a meeting of the *Association Générale des Étudiants de Paris*, the Vice-Chancellor of the University of Paris, Liard, made a number of proposals to the Premier, present in person, on how in the opinion of professors and students military service could be prolonged without the rather disagreeable interruption of university studies. Assuring the Premier that everyone accepted his military duty, Liard suggested that it might be more appropriate to calmly examine the possible options rather than indulging in 'outbreaks of verbal patriotism'.[43] This was bluntly rejected by Barthou. It was indeed an important task to continue to develop French culture, he replied, but at the present time considerations of this kind had to give way to the necessity of effectively protecting French territory. Barthou advised the professors and their students 'not to create too wide a gap between the intelligentsia and the rest of the nation'.[44]

The energetic tone of members of the government coincided with a new spurt in the campaign of the Right. Agitation was no longer limited to the usual daily attacks against socialist and radical 'anti-patriots' in the press. A. de Mun now encouraged 'all patriots' to join forces in support of the *Loi de Trois Ans* throughout the country. The aim of this agitation must be to launch a 'massive protest among the people' to force the 'lazy' deputies—who for fear of upsetting their *comités* had still not passed the law—to fulfil their duty to *la patrie*. Early in April 1913 the *Echo* published a poster entitled *Appel à la France*. Printed in blue, white and red, it referred to the vote of the Supreme Army Council and contained only the following reminder: 'Germany will soon have a regular army of 900,000. At present the French army stands at 480,000.'[45]

The *Action Française* also stepped up its agitation against the 'Prussians inside our country'. The Royalists had always regarded the 'Dreyfusard intellectuals', the *sorbonicoles*, as German agents in league with Jaurès and out to destroy the 'true France'.[46] In the lycées and universities the *Action Française* youth organisation, the *Camelots du Roy*, began to run riot in the classes and lectures of any teachers and professors who had uttered even the slightest criticism of the three-year law.[47] Some of these incidents created so much havoc that, a few days before his above-mentioned argument with Barthou, the Vice-Chancellor of the University of Paris had declared a number of *camelots* out of university bounds.[48]

In response to the hardening of the government line and the new wave of agitation from the nationalist Right, the left-wing republican press and organisations also became more vociferous. Sharp criticism was fired at the government whose apodictic language was regarded as a strange contrast to its actual indecision. The *Ligue des Droits de l'Homme* warned of the 'revival of nationalism', declaring that the very fact that the government had adopted the Reinach-Montebello counter-proposal justified the left-wing Republicans' aims to prevent the government's proposals from being 'approved too rashly'. The amendment to the governmental bill, it claimed, was an indication that Barthou was prepared to abandon the sacrosanct principle of equality with regard to the sharing of the military burden.[49] Furthermore, the left-wing Republicans now blamed the government for supporting the attempts of the Right to exploit the 'admirable movement of patriotism', which had its origins in the threat from Germany, for politically reactionary purposes. The government, it was maintained, saw eye-to-eye with the Right on two scores. On the one hand, the government supported the Nationalists' campaign. On the other, it wanted to muzzle parliamentary and public debate and was not prepared to wait for Parliament to vote on the issue and accept its decision. This showed that 'a bit of bluff on the part of the government and mass hysteria' were behind the campaign for the *Loi de Trois Ans*.[50] Further evidence that the left-wing Republicans were becoming increasingly sceptical about the line of the Barthou government is that, from the beginning of the parliamentary Easter recess, spontaneous cooperation began between radical *comités* and local socialist branches. In particular, Radical Party groups signed the SFIO petition or even helped in its distribution.[51]

On the basis of these developments *L'Aurore*, one of the leading left-wing republican newspapers, made an urgent appeal to the Radical Party executive committee. After two months of debate on the three-year issue, it was high time, it wrote, for the CE to adopt a clear-cut stance and launch a campaign against the government bill. The responsible bodies in the party, wrote *L'Aurore*, were simply 'dozing away'. This was a 'danger to the nation': if the Radical Party continued to abstain on such a fundamental issue, it would be renouncing its key role in internal affairs, leading to a polarisation between socialist and nationalist agitation which would ultimately tear the country apart.[52]

Despite this criticism the party leaders remained adamant that there was a fundamental difference between the defence issue, on the one hand, and the nationalist campaign, on the other. In response to *L'Aurore*'s demand, the CE therefore refused to 'simplify in such a brutal manner'. In contrast with the Socialists and Nationalists, it intended to weigh up the pros and cons of an extension of military service and live up to the 'permanent responsibility' of radicalism by defending the interests of France. The party, however, intended to adopt a hard line against the chauvinists who were intent on turning the defence issue into the core of a reactionary internal policy.[53]

The opinion of the party leaders was largely confirmed by the votes of the *Conseils Généraux* (CG), regional parliaments of the individual departments which provided a forum of discussion for matters of local interest, in their annual session beginning on 15 April.[54] A clear majority for or against the *Loi de Trois Ans* was obtained in only very few departments; generally Parliament was urged not to give in to nationalistic and chauvinistic demands. The *Conseils Généraux* declared that Parliament should adopt an extension of military service only if, after careful examination, this was considered necessary to protect France from attack and provided that the principle of equality was strictly observed. In addition, it was frequently affirmed that any increase in the military burden should be financed by new forms of taxation.[55]

Although the regional parliaments were sceptical about the government's proposals, their resolutions were in no way directed against the three-year bill. In many departments a sceptical resolution was adopted against the socialist vote, which rejected the bill in its entirety. However, these resolutions generally gave the *Troisannistes* no grounds for satisfaction, as illustrated by *Le Temps's* final commentary on the opinions of the *Conseils Généraux*. The newspaper deplored this new 'indecision' of the population, which originally had willingly accepted the 'three-year' sacrifice, and blamed the sudden change in public opinion on politicians and publicists who, with their 'vague objections', had put it into people's minds that this sacrifice was basically unnecessary.[56]

Caillaux was the first leading Radical Party politician to draw up alternatives, on the basis of the resolutions of the *Conseils Généraux*, which could be endorsed by all Republicans concerned about national defence. At a series of Radical Party meetings in his department, Sarthe, he criticised the reactionary and anti-democratic form of the campaign on behalf of the *Loi de Trois Ans*, but nevertheless took care not to qualify the bill itself as reactionary. Unlike the Nationalists, he said, the Radical Party wanted to maintain the democratic principle of equality in the army. However, the Radicals' commitment to the democratic principle of equality, he continued, was inseparable from its readiness to use all the might of the nation to secure national defence. The party was therefore prepared to accept a certain extension of military service and to support all the financial demands of the government if the necessary costs were covered not by indirect taxation but by newly created income and property taxes. In Caillaux's opinion, the government was too 'shy' when it came to financial matters. On the basis of its proposals the necessary strengthening of fortifications could not be carried out with sufficient speed. Thus the national effort meant above all 'dipping one's hand into a pocket. But let's not get it wrong. We must dip into the pocket where there's money'.[57]

As Caillaux outlined in his memoirs, and as his action in 1913 confirmed, the aim of his policy at this time was to force the government to break with the Nationalists to prevent a polarisation of internal fronts. On concrete terms this meant pursuing a policy in which the *Loi de Trois Ans* lost its dogmatic character and was no longer the vehicle of chauvinism and domestic reaction. At the same time he wanted to make it easier for the government to break away from its nationalist 'cronies'. The Radical Party was to adopt a line of extreme caution to prevent a further hardening of the fronts. This desire for 'domestic *détente*' was also the main reason why he was prepared to come to terms with the government and accept an extension of service in the regular army of about six months. This olive branch was offered to the government not only on the grounds of domestic calculation. Like many Radicals, Caillaux was not convinced that an extension of military service was fully superfluous and intrinsically reactionary; it was only the three years' dogma which he viewed as a 'concession to aggressive nationalism'.[58]

The actual limits—and the dilemma—of Caillaux's strategy were that he too concentrated on the domestic context of the three-year bill, and was blind to the wider framework of foreign and military policy. Under the dictates of the offensive strategy and 'diplomacy of strength', the government could not accept Caillaux's compromise. None the less, there was still a danger of Caillaux's succeeding in winning over a great number of republican deputies for his compromise proposal, which took shape in the form of the Paul-Boncour/ Messimy counter-proposal before the end of the parliamentary recess.[59] Barthou's prompt response—the application of the emergency paragraph of the 1905 conscription law—can be explained by this objective disparity between the government's intentions, on the one hand, and the internal motives behind Caillaux's compromise, on the other. This step was to lead to a further hardening of the domestic fronts.

The Application of the Emergency Paragraph of 1905 and the Counter-Proposal of the Left

On 4 May, a few days before Parliament reconvened for its orderly 1913 session, Barthou declared in a speech in Caen that the government had decided to apply Article 33/1905 as from the autumn. This meant that conscripts due to complete their service at this point would be retained in the army. The emergency paragraph of the 1905 conscription law—Article 33, section 6—ran as follows: 'If deemed necessary by circumstances, the Minister of War and the Minister of the Navy are authorised provisionally to retain in the ranks the class which has completed its second year of service. The Chambers shall be informed of this decision as soon as possible.'[60]

This step made it quite clear that the government was intending to anticipate Parliament's decision on its bill. Even before Barthou's statement in Caen, the great Paris dailies had reported and played up the news that this measure had been adopted by the cabinet. Since the debate was progressing so slowly, and in view of the obstruction in the Army Committee, they wrote, the government considered recourse to the emergency paragraph of the 1905 law as indispensable, for it would enable the army to begin increasing the number of men in uniform immediately without having to wait for Parliament's decision, which would not be taken until July at the earliest.[61] To anticipate Parliament's decision in this way was very dubious not only from the constitutional point of view. Barthou's interpretation of the circumstances justifying the government's application of the emergency paragraph did not correspond with the spirit of the 1905 law, the original intention of which had been to prescribe a very narrow interpretation of the circumstances in which a conscript class could be 'provisionally' retained in the ranks.[62]

When the government decided on this measure it was presumably unaware that it would spark off unrest in the barracks, which in turn would lead to a further hardening on the domestic fronts.[63] Barthou was in hot water. Without a clear-cut parliamentary majority, confronted with the votes of the *Conseils Généraux* and up against Caillaux's compromise proposals, there was a real danger that the three-year bill would not gain a parliamentary majority on the basis of the Reinach-Montebello amendment. Thus Parliament might unconsciously prevent the implementation of Plan XVII, thereby destroying the centre-piece of the government's overall strategy for foreign and military policy. On 2 May, the day before the cabinet's decision to apply Article 33, the War Minister, Étienne, had approved the general staff's guide-lines for Plan XVII, whereupon it had set to work on the technical details of the new operational plan.[64] It should be emphasised once again that the general staff was of the opinion that only the amended version of the *Loi de Trois Ans* (with the Reinach-Montebello amendment) would adequately permit army reorganisation in accordance with the guide-lines of the new plan.[65] A number of CSG generals—that is, army corps commanders—threatened to resign if the government complied with Caillaux's proposals.[66]

The reaction sparked off by Barthou's measure was fervent, both in public and in Parliament. The Socialists and Syndicalists immediately began to intensify their campaigns against the *Loi de Trois Ans*—although naturally in different directions. *L'Humanité* declared that the 'revolting flippancy' with which Barthou was trying to force his will on Parliament by means of this 'authoritarian gesture' could serve the interests only of the SFIO's campaign against the defence bill. This step, it stated, was bound to show the Radicals that their intention of coming to a reconciliation with the government was unrealistic.[67] The SFIO cherished the hope that a parliamentary majority against the government might yet be achieved, as can be seen in a circular from the CAP to the federations on 6 May appealing for a new effort, since it must by now have become clear to everyone that the government was opposed to any form of reconciliation. The circular added that the petition campaign must be reinforced to give more weight to the parliamentary (!) struggle of the Socialists.[68] A few days later the local branches were sent a poster: '*Contre le maintien de la classe libérable sous les drapeaux.*' This poster, of which 50,000 copies were printed, denounced Barthou's measure as a 'misuse of power' which gave the soldiers the right to appeal to the Council of State as the 'watch-dog' of the government. 'All Socialists, proletarians and real Republicans' now had to unite in the struggle. Another CAP circular on 9 May encouraged members to step up the petition campaign. The socialist organisations, it stated, still had a month to stir up the very soul of the country before the opening of the parliamentary debate.[69] These circulars show that the party leaders basically saw the *Appel au Pays* as a means of achieving a parliamentary majority against the bill. The *Guesdiste* aim of using public agitation to promote 'socialist propaganda' and to recruit new members had been pushed into the background and was in fact mentioned only in a postscript to the circular of 9 May.[70]

The reaction of the CGT was even more fervent—verbally at least. On 11 May the *Comité Confédéral* decided to publish and circulate a poster in various departments (which, however, was not mentioned in the press until 17 May). The poster campaign, which caused quite a stir, coincided with the soldiers' unrest, for which the CGT was largely held responsible, and the police therefore destroyed every single copy of the poster they could lay their hands on. In this poster the CGT called on the proletariat to rise *en masse* against the government's *coup de force*. The proletariat, under the yoke of the arms manufacturers, Morocco politicians and chauvinistic reactionaries, would be able to save their brothers locked up in their barracks from a further extension of military servitude. Mass demonstrations in seven cities on 1 June were to mark the beginning of the mass uprising.[71]

The bourgeois Centre and right-wing press unanimously welcomed Barthou's announcement as an opportune anticipation of the *Loi de Trois Ans*. No constitutional scruples were voiced. On the contrary, the government was particularly complimented for having adopted a strong line and shown the right path to the timid and hesitant deputies. According to *Le Temps*, only 'unpatriotic fellows' could criticise the government's approach.[72]

The Radicals were extremely cautious in their assessment of Barthou's proposals. Their comments were generally limited to the optimistic statement that Barthou's intentions could in no way prejudice Parliament's decision.[73] The reason for this confidence was that Caillaux's alternative proposals were beginning to take the shape of a concrete counter-proposal to the three-year law. On 8 May the *Délégation des Gauches* decided to examine all the counter-proposals and amendments to the three-year bill already tabled and to draft its own counter-proposal as a common republican platform. At this meeting of all the chairmen of left-wing parliamentary groups it was agreed that a common proposal would have to guarantee the reinforcement of the cover troops and a better 'amalgamation of the classes'.[74] On 15 May Caillaux was elected chairman of this *Délégation*, which naturally strengthened his position *vis-à-vis* the government.

Several days later the *Délégation des Gauches*, backed by the Radical Party CE, actually put forward a joint counter-proposal on behalf of the Left. There was now an irrefutable danger of the government's either being forced to give in or being overthrown by a compact left-wing majority.[75] This proposal, based on two earlier counter-proposals tabled by the deputies Paul-Boncour (Republican-Socialist) and Messimy (Radical), became known as the 'Paul-Boncour/Messimy counter-proposal'. It proposed a six-month extension of service in the regular army, and twenty-three additional days of reserve exercise for each of the eleven classes of the regular army reserves.[76] Boncour and Messimy thus aimed at amalgamating the regular army and the reserves on the assumption that a mobilised unit's striking power would be maintained if it were comprised half of regular soldiers and half of reservists. This proposal corresponded with the government's wishes, in that the annual call-up of the eleven reserve classes meant that three classes would be permanently retained in the forces. Whether or not this concept was realistic depended on the function the reservists were to play in the event of war.

The opinion of the general staff on this problem has already been mentioned. Messimy hit the nail on the head when he criticised the general staff and the CSG for having taken only the effective peacetime strength of the regular army into consideration, regardless of the reserves. The strength of the Boncour/Messimy amendment, or rather its power of persuasion, was that it not only took account of the alleged concern of the government and the general staff but laid particular emphasis on the republican principle of a nation in arms. The sharp contrast between this principle and the concept of a military society is clearly illustrated in Messimy's memoirs:

> 'Should I appear a Utopian, I do not believe that keeping . . . the majority of soldiers in barracks for a very long time will improve their military training or bring much comfort to the morale of the nation. And for men who are asked to sacrifice their lives, morale is a factor of inestimable value which nothing will make me underestimate!'[77]

Poincaré's correspondence shows how this development seemed to jeopardise the government's bill and illustrates the concern of the

Troisannistes in view of the counter-proposal of the Left. On 16 May both Albert de Mun and Joseph Reinach addressed a virtual cry for help to the President. De Mun described the 'great and real danger' resulting from the concerted action of the Left in Parliament: 'They will try to get the government to accept this deal [the Paul-Boncour/ Messimy counter-proposal], putting it across as a token of the Radicals' goodwill, and, if it does not accept, they will overthrow the government in this duel, less odious than for example the rejection of the three-year law.' To ward off this danger, wrote de Mun, the government would have to use 'precise military arguments, presented with authority', and win Parliament over to its side. Since General Pau was the only person in France with the necessary degree of authority, he would have to be appointed as the governmental spokesman in the parliamentary debate. De Mun had already convinced Barthou of this, he continued in his letter, but the War Minister, Étienne, was still wavering, not wanting to offend the present spokesman, Joffre. However, these scruples would have to give way to the 'higher authority of General Pau'.[78]

Reinach, who addressed a letter to Poincaré at the same time, stressed that if Parliament were to pass the Paul-Boncour/Messimy or a similar amendment the consequences would be 'first a parliamentary, followed by a political and military', disaster. If the government dropped the three-year bill, he wrote, France would have made not an *acte* but only a gesture which would lead to a direct loss of French authority and influence in world politics. Furthermore, it was known from reliable sources that a number of generals on the CSG would tender their resignation in such a case. Reinach believed that the Paul-Boncour/Messimy or similar amendments would be rejected only if General Pau addressed Parliament: 'Montebello will speak, Bénazet will speak, Étienne will speak, Barthou will speak. But our speeches will be like Jomini translated by Demosthenes . . . and a hundred, a thousand times less [meaningful] than a half-hour speech by General Pau.' Barthou and Briand had already given the go-ahead for this strategy, continued Reinach. Étienne still had misgivings, not wanting to offend Joffre who had been the government's spokesman so far. But Joffre would also have to agree with Pau's being appointed to 'command the first army in the Chamber'.[79]

Bearing in mind Pau's statements at the CSG meeting on 4 March, it is clear why de Mun and Reinach wanted General Pau to address Parliament. Unlike Joffre, who had justified the *Loi de Trois Ans* on purely military grounds and within the context of strategic planning, Pau had formulated the gripping argument called for by Briand: the planned expansion of the German army illustrated the 'aggressive intentions of our neighbours'.[80] A few days after receiving the letters from de Mun and Reinach, Poincaré had a lengthy discussion with Pau on 'questions in connection with the three-year bill',[81] and when the debate in the Chamber on the *Trois Ans* was opened Pau did indeed replace Joffre as the government's spokesman.[82]

To prevent the Left from joining forces against the three-year bill, Poincaré intervened in the public debate on the issue for the first time. The President felt he had no alternative, since in his letter on 16 May Reinach had drawn his attention to 'Caillaux's intrigues'. According to Reinach, Caillaux and his followers in Parliament were spreading the rumour that Poincaré had promised Caillaux that he would succeed Barthou,[83] a rumour which would, in view of the rather peculiar structure of the *République des camarades*,[84] influence the vote of many deputies and could be seen as token of Poincaré's goodwill towards Caillaux's conciliation proposals. Poincaré lost no time in reacting to Caillaux's would-be attack. On 23 May he let it be officially announced in the press that he had invited his most bitter enemy since the January 1913 presidential elections, Clemenceau, for talks. Poincaré told his closest confidant, Paléologue, that this was his way of showing Parliament that if the cabinet were overthrown on account of the defence issue, Clemenceau, and not Caillaux, would be entrusted with the reins of government. If the Chamber voted against Clemenceau as Premier, he (Poincaré) would assert his constitutional rights and ask the Senate to dissolve the Chamber. If the Senate refused to do so, he himself would resign.[85]

The next day *Gil Blas* published what it claimed to be an authorised summary of Poincaré's talks with Clemenceau. Poincaré's aim had been to convince Clemenceau of the necessity of the *Loi de Trois Ans*, since the government was concerned that Clemenceau supported the Paul-Boncour/Messimy counter-proposal. The President had therefore informed Clemenceau that the key to the bill lay in the Russian alliance, since in the St Petersburg talks in 1912 the Russian government had been very sceptical about France's ability to implement the military arrangements.[86]

Since there are no further sources available on this subject, it is difficult to assess whether this report in *Gil Blas* was authentic or not. In the course of the war-guilt debate the report was regarded by various sources as irrefutable proof that the three-year bill was not linked with German rearmament, but had been promised by Poincaré to the Russian government in St Petersburg.[87] Apart from the fact that the report did not go that far but, reversing the facts (!), alluded only to the general problem of the military and international context of the bill, it should not be forgotten that *Gil Blas* could not at this time be regarded as part of the semi-official press but was, on the contrary, generally considered as the organ of Caillaux—it was in fact Caillaux who financed the newspaper. Therefore it cannot be denied that the report may have been a move on the part of Caillaux to counter Poincaré's offensive and to bolster the suspicions of the Left that the *Trois Ans* had been proposed not only to defend the country against an *attaque brusquée*.[88] The fact that the government did not issue an official denial of the *Gil Blas* report suggests that it may indeed have been semi-official. On the other hand, how could the government deny the report without arousing the suspicions of their ally, Russia?

Thus between the end of March and mid-May 1913 a considerable swing took place, both in public opinion and in the position of the left-wing groups in Parliament. The Reinach-Montebello counter-proposal amending the *Loi de Trois Ans*, the government's repressive measures and the new wave of nationalist agitation had all served to heighten the left-wing republican public opinion's mistrust of the bill. Finally, the joint counter-proposal of the left-wing groups in Parliament, presented only two weeks before the opening of the parliamentary debate, made it seem extremely doubtful that there would be a parliamentary majority in favour of the *Trois Ans*. Against this background, soldiers' riots broke out in the middle of May 1913. These riots were to transform the internal landscape once again and were a considerable set-back to the concerted action of the Left against the three-year law.

The Soldiers' Revolts and Their Political Consequences

Between 17 and 22 May 1913—that is, immediately after Parliament had approved Barthou's decision to apply the emergency paragraph of the 1905 law—there was an outbreak of protest in a number of garrisons against this decision in particular and against the *Loi de Trois Ans* in general. This movement, generally known both at the time and in historical research as the *mutineries* (mutinies), was launched on 17 May in the Toul garrison when soldiers on leave banded together, formed a column of some 300 men and marched through the town shouting 'Down with the three years!', at times even singing the 'Internationale'. Officers who attempted to oppose the march were insulted and even threatened. A little later the commander of the Toul garrison gave the signal for mobilisation, whereupon the 'mutineer' soldiers immediately returned to their barracks.

The garrison commanders were apparently not very concerned about this incident, since leave was not cancelled the next day. However, on the following day another demonstration broke out and this time more than 2,500 soldiers joined in. The striking soldiers explained to threatening civilians that 'We are not refusing to fight. But we don't want to stay here for three years'. The cavalry was brought in to disperse this second and final demonstration. Similar demonstrations took place on the following days in the barracks of Paris (Neuilly, Clignancourt), Belfort, Toul, Nancy and Rodez. The 'instigators' of these protests were immediately given severe sentences by the military courts. By 25 May more than twenty soldiers had been banished to disciplinary battalions in Africa, some thirty had been court-martialled, and roughly fifty had been imprisoned for a period of between thirty and sixty days.[89]

These incidents produced a storm of public protest. The press of the Right and Centre used the revolts to revive their campaign in support of the three-year bill and from the very outset tried to create the impression that the *mutineries* had been staged by the anti-militarist and anti-patriotic CGT. *Le Temps* and other newspapers, including those on the Left, reported that these protests were not a spontaneous expression of discontent but had been 'staged from the outside' and 'in preparation for some time'. For example, on 20 May *Le Temps* reported that in the first searches General Pau had ordered carried out in Toul 'instructions from Paris' had been found in some of the soldiers' lockers; civilians who had played a leading part in the demonstrations had also been arrested. On 22 May the Paris daily *Le Matin*, soon followed by other newspapers,[90] published a 'CGT circular', bundles of which had allegedly been found in the Toul barracks in the course of General Pau's searches. It ran as follows:

> The time has come to revolt against the veritable *coup d'état* decided by the government and sanctioned by the Chamber. . . . You will have to bear the consequences of this military folly. Will you hesitate to resort to force or illegal action? Demonstrations will be taking place simultaneously in all the regiments. Your conscience demands that you join in. . . .

This circular was obviously a forgery: the Toul authorities had to admit that no incriminating evidence had been found against the CGT.[91] However, to back up the claim that the CGT had been behind the unrest, further 'facts' were published in the following days 'proving' that the CGT had for some time been planning to prevent mobilisation by organising mutinies. In making these allegations the press was supported by the police; for example, a police report on the activities of the *Sou du Soldat* was passed on to *Le Matin*, which gave it extensive coverage.[92] And the editor-in-chief of *Le Temps*, André Tardieu, published a widely acclaimed essay in the conservative *Revue des Deux Mondes* giving an account of the 'campaign against *la patrie*' on the basis of other information provided by the political police.[93]

Even the government—in a way which, in view of the actual state of the inquiries, can be qualified only as demagogic—tried to give the public the impression that the CGT was behind the 'mutinies'. On 21 May General Pau informed the press that the inquiries of the military authorities had shown that the riots had not been 'mutinies' at all, but a 'political movement' organised by the Syndicalists who had been 'rabble-rousing' in the barracks for some time. Unfortunately the military authorities could intervene only when riots actually broke out. The task of taking pre-emptive steps against such riots breaking out was the work of other authorities.[94] In a similar vein the War Minister, Étienne, declared to the Senate that the government was convinced that the unrest had been planned well in advance. The government, furthermore, was determined to 'stamp out' this movement 'at its roots' and eliminate the syndicalist organisation, the *Sou du Soldat*. This statement was greeted with applause by the Senate.[95]

The government was thus intent on finding evidence to back up its allegations against the CGT. Repeated instructions were issued to the prefects to find out whether 'civilian agitators' had recently appeared on the scene in their respective departments. It was 'beyond all doubt that these demonstrations were connected with an overall movement'.[96] However, the answers provided no grounds for this assumption. After thorough investigations all the prefects had to concede that there was no evidence that the riots had been the work of civilian agitators.[97]

Although the government had no legal grounds for prosecuting the CGT, it was not dissuaded from its intentions. During the night of 25/26 May more than 600 syndicalist and socialist offices were searched throughout the country.[98] It would be impossible to go into all the details of this operation at this point, but it can be concluded that no evidence was forthcoming that the soldiers' riots had been instigated by a third party or that the CGT could be held responsible.[99]

The government, unabashed nevertheless, immediately took further steps against the CGT. On 29 May the Premier, Barthou, declared to the Senate that the acts of the CGT were 'illegal, wicked and criminal'; the searches had left no doubt about the link between the riots and CGT propaganda. Legislation would have to be brought in to avoid this happening in the future. Following Barthou's speech the Senate voted that a bill should be presented to this effect.[100]

The CGT vehemently rejected the accusation that it had inspired the soldiers' revolts. Following the searches, the *Bureau Confédéral* stated that the *Sou du Soldat* had always operated strictly within the law, which explained why no incriminating evidence had been unearthed.[101] Nevertheless, the CGT continued to stress the solidarity of the proletariat with the 'mutineer' soldiers, whose anger at the government's *coup d'état* was more than justified. Moreover, Jouhaux and other leaders even declared that they were proud that their own protest against the *Loi de Trois Ans* had been heard in the barracks.[102] These incidents had convinced the CGT that their organisation was recognised by the people as the leader in the struggle against militarism. Now it would find the strength to step up its campaign against the extension of military service.[103]

Moreover, at this stage there was also a revival of the revolutionary verbalism of previous years among the CGT rank and file. Yvetot, for example, whose discontent with the form of the CGT agitation against the defence bill has been outlined above,[104] regarded the riots as a confirmation of the old anarcho-syndicalist doctrine of anti-militarism and direct action. His first commentary on the unrest was entitled 'Bravo Barthou'. In this article Yvetot ironically congratulated Barthou for having acted as an *'agent provocateur* of revolt and insubordination'. In view of the Premier's action, he wrote, there was 'quite a lot in store for us between now and October'.[105] In a somewhat involved turn of phrase, yet in terms which would be clearly understood by a contemporary reader, Yvetot expressed the hope that the soldiers' riots would gain momentum and culminate in a general soldiers' strike in October 1913 when the class to be kept in uniform would otherwise have been due for discharge.[106] A little later, but *after* the searches, a number of militant syndicates demanded that the CGT should be prepared to take the forthcoming soldiers' riots under its wing and organise a general strike. Some syndicates even voiced the hope that this general strike could be the spark to ignite the 'social revolution', since the government would never dare send in the troops against striking workers representing the direct interests of the soldiers.[107]

Records of these and similar statements were carefully compiled by the political police and used as evidence for the arrests of prominent Syndicalists.[108] However, it was unlikely that CGT leaders really believed that the soldiers' strike would lead to a general strike. There was no reference to such a possibility in the official CGT newspaper, the *Voix du Peuple*, and even the generally 'revolutionary' *Bataille Syndicaliste* was very cautious on this point. The great concern of CGT leaders about the storm of public opinion and the 'crack-down' of the authorities is illustrated by the fact that, following the soldiers' riots, the CGT openly declared its subordination to the SFIO for the first time: the Socialist Party succeeded in dissuading the CGT from its plan to organise demonstrations all over the country at the beginning of July against the retention of the conscript class due for discharge. On 24 May—that is, *before* the searches—the CGT *Comité Confédéral* revised its resolution of 11 May on this point and instead called upon all its syndicates to join in an *ad hoc* demonstration organised by the Seine federation of the SFIO. The Syndicalists were given strict orders to follow the instructions of the organisers: there were to be no shouts or cries likely to disturb the peace, and strict discipline was to be maintained throughout the demonstration.[109] Under these auspices the demonstration went off very peacefully, despite the underlying tension on the internal scene at the time. Jaurès's opinion that the cooperation with the Syndicalists had decisively strengthened the SFIO and the *démocratie républicaine*[110] sheds further light on the government's campaign against the CGT: the repressive measures had accelerated the revisionistic swing latent within the CGT for some time, thereby strengthening political socialism as opposed to revolutionary forces. However, this growth in the influence of the Socialists could prove to be another spanner in the works, so far as the *Loi de Trois Ans* was concerned.

For this reason the Socialists' reaction to the government's *coup* was rather ambiguous. On the one hand, sharp protest was raised against Barthou's attempt to 'assassinate the working class', while, on the other hand, leading socialist politicians expressed the hope that the government's measures would once and for all stamp out the anarchist and revolutionary groups within the CGT so that the subordination of the CGT to the SFIO in political affairs would be permanent.[111] A development of this kind would have served the *Jaurèsistes'* aims of joining forces with the left-wing Republicans in Parliament and in public. Nothing better illustrates the extent of SFIO support for the idea of a left-wing bloc than the following statement by Gustave Hervé, long-standing leader of the far Left of the SFIO, most sympathetic towards the CGT:

I had a dream. The CGT and the Socialist Party, the only two organised and disciplined popular forces, had formed a bloc.... Alas! it was only a dream.... We are not yet united enough, or organised enough, or disciplined enough, or brave enough, to fight such a battle. Because we do not yet have the strength or the virtues we would need to fight this battle so that the united proletarian bloc could hold back this wave of nationalism which is surging down upon us, I am for the other bloc, the moderate republican bloc, which has already proved three times that it is more than a dream.[112]

However, at this stage few Radicals or members of other left-wing republican groups were prepared to enter into a political alliance with the SFIO. At a banquet on 18 May leading Radicals had called for the 're-establishment of the bloc' to counter political reaction,[113] but these voices seem to have been almost completely stifled by the soldiers' revolts.[114] The radical vote in the ballot, on an interpellation presented by the Socialist deputy Vaillant, is perhaps the best illustration of the aversion of both groups of the *Parti Républicain Radical et Radical-Socialiste* towards uniting with the SFIO against the forces of reaction. Vaillant had presented his interpellation against the government on 23 May because of the ban on the traditional socialist ceremony in commemoration of the anniversary of the end of the Paris Commune in the Père Lachaise cemetery. In reply to the interpellation, the Minister of the Interior, Klotz, read out the circular of 29 March[115] containing the ban on all demonstrations for or against the three-year law. This ban, he argued, had had to be extended to the Père Lachaise ceremony, since the Socialists and Syndicalists had publicly announced their intentions of using this year's event to protest against the *Loi de Trois Ans* and the 'retention of the class'.[116] There was a great furore in the Chamber when Klotz added that the government's decision was aimed at preventing public clashes between patriots and anti-patriotic demonstrators. Even Deschanel, the President of the Chamber, protested against the opponents of the defence bill being classified as 'anti-patriots'. Nevertheless, despite the storm of protest from all the Republicans opposed to the *Trois Ans*, a large majority in the Chamber adopted a motion presented by the deputy Delaroche-Vernet (*radical-socialiste*), in which the government's ban was expressly approved.

Compared with the last vote by call of political significance, the result of the ballot—330 to 168 in favour of the Delaroche-Vernet motion—reflected a considerable stabilisation of the governmental majority. This was basically a result of the soldiers' revolts, which had made many deputies have second thoughts about their links with the SFIO. Only ninety-nine deputies voted along with the SFIO against the government. These included sixty-one *radicaux-socialistes* and a mere six *gauche-radicale* deputies.[117] Caillaux was one of the radical deputies who voted along with the government, a fact which *Le Temps* welcomed as a sign of the 'return of the prodigal sons'.[118]

Although the soldiers' unrest had prevented the establishment of a clear left-wing coalition in the Chamber with the inclusion of the Socialists, the governmental majority was still anything but stable. This majority was based neither on a uniform line on the *Trois Ans* issue nor on a homogeneous form of social ideology; in fact its only common denominator was its rejection of 'anti-patriotic intrigues'. The first parliamentary debate on the financing of rearmament revealed the incoherence of this majority. A combination of various factors[119] forced the government to bring this question before Parliament precisely at the time of the 'mutinies'—an opportunity which Caillaux used as a platform for a renewed attack on the government.

On 19 May the government asked the Chamber to approve an additional credit of 440 million francs to cover the costs accruing from the application of the emergency paragraph of the 1905 law. This sum, along with the additional credit of 550 million francs requested in February for the improvement of fortifications,[120] was to be covered by the raising of a loan of around 1 billion francs. Since the interest rates and redemption costs of the loan (about 70 million francs per annum) were to be covered by the regular budget, the rates of a number of excise taxes were to be raised.[121]

The government's plan did not correspond with the Radical Party's line on this question. A few days earlier the Radical Party executive committee had called on all its member deputies to ensure that the costs of rearmament were covered by a tax on property.[122] The budgetary committee, in which the Radicals had a majority, thus rejected the government's proposals and instead pressed the government to submit new legislation to cover the costs in question.[123] The government did in fact soon come up with a new proposal. A national tax on income to cover the interest rates and redemption costs of the proposed loan was to be levied on income above 10,000 francs, with a maximum progression of 3 per cent.[124] Owing to this sudden shift in policy and the application for the first time of the principle of progressivism to the French taxation system, which had long been one of the left-wing Republicans' main demands, the 'national tax' was interpreted by the entire press, regardless of political affiliation, as a victory by the Radicals over the government.[125] The fact that the government had climbed down on this issue proved that the support it had gained among left-wing Republicans as a result of the soldiers' unrest in no way implied a substantive stabilisation of the governmental majority. It became apparent that Barthou's majority was extremely fragile, held together only by the dangers inherent in the international situation and the fear of internal unrest, revolution and anti-patriotism. Nevertheless, these political issues did not affect most left-wing Republicans' preference for a progressive financial policy.

The compromise between the government and the Left on the tax question was viewed by conservative opinion and interest groups with suspicion and downright disapproval. The famous liberal economist Yves Guyot candidly expressed the concern of these groups: the government's plan to cover the costs of the proposed loan by only 240,000 taxpayers was the 'first step towards capital being taken over by common ownership'.[126] The plan was criticised by newspapers such as *Le Temps* as a 'social war machine'.[127] The *Union Générale des Syndicats* addressed a public letter to Barthou warning him not to break the bonds of patriotic unity of all 'good Frenchmen'.[128] The objective consequences of the government's compromise tactics were analysed and criticised with no regard to the political situation and the predicament faced by the Barthou government on the eve of the parliamentary debate on the *Loi de Trois Ans*. With almost disarming cynicism and a form of class-consciousness totally unruffled by the ideology of national unity, conservative public opinion reiterated its views on how rearmament could be financed.[129] Any form of property tax was rejected unanimously, and instead an increase in various excise taxes was proposed. All Frenchmen, according to the League against Income Tax, would have to 'do their bit' to save *la patrie*.[130] The heated reaction of *La Petite République* to these declarations of 'cynical egoism' illustrates the concern of moderate Republicans that the unheralded question of the financing of rearmament might prematurely break the 'patriotic consensus': 'In fact all the propagandists of revolutionary action are not in the CGT. The *grands bourgeois* skinflints are the greatest enemies of social order and patriotism.'[131]

Caillaux immediately tried to use the financial question to widen the gulf between the government and its conservative associates, on the one hand, and between the progressive and conservative elements, on the other. Since his original compromise formula had been rendered null and void by the soldiers' riots, Caillaux now intended to set up a left-wing majority, including a substantial number of deputies from the Centre, on the basis of the financial question.[132]

Shortly after the government had presented its bill on the proposals for the loan and taxation measures, Gheusi, supported by Caillaux and other members of the *Délégation des Gauches*, presented an interpellation on the guide-lines of the government's financial policy.[133] In his first speech to Parliament in almost two years, Caillaux, at great length, presented the programme of the opposition as an alternative to the reticent proposals of the government, in which military expenditure, being 'unproductive', was to be covered exclusively by taxes on acquired wealth. Barthou turned down a motion to this effect on the grounds that it was 'purely political' and instead called for a vote of confidence.

This fresh attack from Caillaux obviously intimidated the government, since, following this interpellation, Barthou accepted a motion that there should be no debate on the issue, although he had just called for a vote of confidence. Even on this basis he gained a majority of only 312 votes to 240. Caillaux had admittedly not been successful. Yet the difficulties inherent in a majority of the amorphous Centre, bound together by the fear of danger both at home and abroad, had become apparent. It was not the right of Centre which declared a vote of confidence in the government against the Gheusi/Caillaux motion but the 'rallied' and nationalist Right.[134] This demonstrates beyond all doubt that the socially conservative supporters of the government were disgruntled with the Barthou cabinet. At this point it also became obvious that the government might well be forced to make further concessions to the Left. On 2 June—the first day of the debate in the Chamber on the *Loi de Trois Ans*—the committee on financial legislation, to which the national tax proposal had to be submitted, ruled that the costs of rearmament should be covered by a single levy on capital, distributed over a number of years.[135]

In view of all these events and developments, when the parliamentary debate on the three-year law finally began on 2 June it was still open as to whether there would be a majority for or against the bill. On the one hand, the government had not succeeded in gaining a political coherent majority; on the other, the 'mutinies' had ruled out the possibility of the establishment of a left-wing bloc against the *Trois Ans*.

CHAPTER 5

The Parliamentary Debate

The Obstacles to Political Polarisation

The Socialists' parliamentary campaign against the military bill was concentrated in the slogan 'Resistance to anti-republican reaction'.[1] A. Thomas, the only SFIO deputy to take the floor in the general debate,[2] was adamant that the SFIO would do all it could to ensure that the old political groups of the pre-Agadir era would once again be 'face to face'.[3] He therefore advocated a return to the bloc of the Combes era, which had symbolised the victory of the republican state over monarchist, clerical and militarist reaction following the Dreyfus affair in the 1890s. Moreover, throughout the general debate the Socialists confined their action to heckling and interpellations intended to 'prove' that the *Loi de Trois Ans* was part and parcel of a reactionary and anti-republican strategy. At the very first sitting they found an opportunity to demonstrate to the Chamber that 'reactionary, military intrigues' were going on. During the speech of a left-wing republican deputy who accused the military of not having correctly implemented the 1905 conscription law owing to class prejudice, General Pau, present in his capacity as the government's spokesman, rose to leave the Chamber in protest. It was only thanks to the War Minister Étienne's assiduous efforts that Pau was finally calmed down, although shortly afterwards Pau's anger was aroused anew by an attack on the military authorities.[4]

There was a storm of protest in Parliament against this incident. The monarchist Right chanted its traditional *Vive l'armée! Vive la France!*, while the socialist Left retorted with *Vive la République!*[5] All at once the shadow of the Dreyfus affair had been cast on Parliament, for at the time of the affair the upper echelons of military power had often challenged Parliament in such a way, albeit with greater persistence. Jaurès immediately tried to deepen this traditional wedge between the 'two Frances'[6] by declaring that Pau's protest was a threat to the sovereignty of the civil authorities which had been intact since the end of the Dreyfus affair and which all Republicans had to defend.[7]

The next day the debate on the conscription law was once again interrupted by an interpellation. The grounds for this were that a demonstration of a number of left-wing republican and socialist youth organisations in honour of Joan of Arc had been disbanded, because the police officer responsible was of the opinion that slanderous banners had been on display which were liable to disturb public peace and order.[8] This again raised a storm of protest in Parliament, since the demonstration had been organised in response to a mass demonstration of the *Action Française* and other radical right-wing groups in honour of Joan of Arc, yet in which the police had not interfered.[9] To prevent left-wing Republicans from showing solidarity towards the Socialists on this issue, the government immediately dissociated itself from the incident and declared that the police officer involved would be suspended at once. The Socialists then had no option but to withdraw their motion of censure. However, a few days later Barthou, greeted with applause from the benches of the Right and the Centre, declared that, since the police officer concerned had acted in good faith, the government had decided not to impose a penalty.[10]

Nevertheless, the Socialists continued in their efforts to win over the bourgeois Left by producing evidence of the 'anti-republican aggression' of the military and civil authorities. On 6 June *L'Humanité* published a circular from the War Minister, Étienne, instructing the garrison commanders to ensure that no officer voiced any criticism of the government's defence bill. Disciplinary action would be taken against any officer who did not follow these instructions. Jaurès entered another interpellation on the basis of this circular, which he tried to project as further evidence of Barthou's deliberately reactionary domestic policy. The government, he said, was aiming not only to crush the organised working class but to stamp out any form of republican thought.[11] However, the government triumphed again. Étienne dismissed any knowledge of the document and read out a circular, dated 4 June, instructing officers not only to use repressive measures against the unrest in the ranks but to try to improve their day-to-day contacts with the soldiers, setting up a fatherly relationship, in order to isolate all the revolutionary agitators.[12] Extended applause from the Right, the Centre and the vast majority of the benches of the Left once again illustrated that many deputies regarded the Socialists' action as an inadmissible attempt to divert attention from the real problem of national defence.

The Radical Party, following the general trends in Parliament, greeted the Socialists' attempts to establish a joint republican front with the utmost reserve. When, in the course of a further interpellation, the SFIO called upon the Radicals to defend the achievements of the Republic along with the proletariat,[13] the Radical Party CE published a declaration of principle rejecting the establishment of a bloc of the Left at the price of reducing all French domestic problems to two issues—reaction and the *Loi de Trois Ans*—as 'too simple'. Cooperation between Radicals and Socialists, even in the form of a parliamentary bloc of the Left, could be meaningful, continued the declaration, only on the basis of a precise and foreseeing programme of social reform.[14]

The executive committee's decision was certainly influenced by the fact that, a few days earlier, the strong Rhône federation of the Radical Party had rejected the local SFIO federation's proposal of cooperation 'against the three-year law and military reaction'.[15] The Rhône federation had resolved that, despite the Radical Party's scruples about the military bill and given the present domestic circumstances, it saw no analogies with the time of the Dreyfus affair, republican institutions being in no way endangered. Cooperation with the SFIO was indeed desirable but could be established only when and if the Socialists abandoned their policy of 'demagogic instigation'.[16]

The SFIO's endeavours in Parliament were backed by a number of radical-socialist deputies who tried to prove that the three-year bill had not been introduced as a result of the imperatives of national defence, and was no more than a manoeuvre of domestic politics carried out by a government tending towards the Right and a traditionally anti-republican general staff. It was the express intention of the representatives of 'military society', they argued, to use extended military service to train the recruits for passive obedience, to deprive them of their status as 'citizen soldiers' and gradually to phase in the professional army once again, thus abandoning one of the main achievements of the Radical Republic—the 'republicanisation' of the army.[17] A further argument was that the present 'crisis' in national defence had come about as a result of the officer corps' deliberate 'sabotaging' of the provisions of the 1905 law. From the quantitative point of view the army could still guarantee the defence of French territory against an *attaque brusquée*, if two-year military service were retained. One of the grounds for this argument was the large number of conscripts assigned to non-combat duties. General Pédoya (*radical-socialiste*) estimated the number of these 'shirkers'—orderlies, kitchen staff, batmen, secretaries, bandsmen, and so on—as 80,000 conscripts.[18] Moreover, a number of left-wing republican deputies maintained that the size of the army in the event of a war was irrespective of whether service in the regular army lasted two or three years.[19] The 1905 law had laid the emphasis of the French army on the reserves—the actual 'nation in arms'. It had rejected all militarist[20] tendencies in defining the aim of two-year military service as being confined to purely technical training in soldiering. In its hour of need, they argued, the trained 'nation in arms' could protect *la patrie* from any invasion. If acts of aggression were to be warded off, the citizen soldier's belief in the justice of his task was more important than an additional year of drilling in barracks. These deputies rejected the government's bill, since in practice it ignored the overriding principle of the citizen soldier. The theory supported by nearly all the *Troisannistes* inside and outside Parliament, that the reservists should be integrated into the regular army, was emphatically rejected as 'reactionary'.[21]

This line of argument was unrealistic and unconvincing to contemporaries, in that it idealised a military constitution which has never been achieved in this pure form. The then advocates of the citizen soldier—and a number of historians since[22]—overlooked the fact that the idea of the 1905 conscription law was never actually put into effect. As Jaurès had analysed in his *Armée Nouvelle* in 1911, the 1905 law had itself been a compromise between the traditional priority of a standing army and the idea of a militia system—which had originally been part of radical republican ideology and was now advocated by the Socialists.[23] In the post-1905 years, the heyday of the left-wing Republicans, the 1905 law had not in fact been regarded as a source of republican ideas or a model republican policy to be preserved and developed, and many provisions of the law had been amended to guarantee its military effectiveness. Even out-and-out opponents of the *Loi de Trois Ans* frankly admitted that it was not only the officer corps which had 'sabotaged' the 1905 law on account of anti-republican convictions or class prejudice.[24] The conservative press and deputies now often commented ironically that the Republicans, for whom the 1905 law had become a dogma, had never paid any attention to its military effectiveness in the past. In the pre-Agadir period, they maintained, Parliament, with its mainly left-wing majority, had tended to consider 'national' defence as an idiosyncratic appendage to the 'defence of anti-clericalism'.[25]

The actual course of the 'three-year' debate in the Chamber is the best evidence that for the majority of left-wing republican deputies the problems of national defence were in no way significantly linked with republican doctrine *per se*, or with the idea of defending republican institutions against militaristic tendencies. On the contrary, attitudes tended to be pragmatic, even among the determined opponents of the government bill. This prevented a polarisation within Parliament along ideological lines, so that the debate was dominated by the real question at hand—how to respond to what was considered the real danger of a German assault. For this reason even the Left warmly applauded the speech made by the moderate deputy Lefèvre. On the basis of an analysis of German arms expenditure since 1905, the build-up of strategic railway lines in the west of Germany and the theories of the German general staff on the *kurzer Krieg* (von Bernhardi), Lefèvre tried to prove that Germany intended to take France unawares with its regular army at as great an effective strength as possible. This danger could be warded off only by reinforcing the French cover troops. Lefèvre therefore warned the Chamber not to let the debate be overshadowed by political issues or party squabbles. In the present situation there was no point playing off republican measures against reactionaries. 'What would be reactionary . . . would be a reduction of France in Europe.'[26] Even *L'Humanité* agreed with *Le Temps* that the applause for Lefèvre's speech was an indication that the SFIO was totally isolated in Parliament.[27] Furthermore, the extremely radical *Lanterne*, from the outset a determined opponent of the 'three-year dogma', conceded that this speech had won many sceptical deputies over to the government's side.[28]

At the root of this wish for a pragmatic debate on the military question above party political lines was the overriding belief, both in Parliament and among the public, that there was a danger of a German 'assault'. The need to have an 'army always ready'[29] to face the threat of an *attaque brusquée* was the main argument of all those in favour of the *Trois Ans*, even in Parliament. However, since neither the *Troisan-nistes* nor their opponents were prepared or even in a position to bring the problems of the offensive strategy and strength in foreign policy into the parliamentary debate on national defence, the crucial reasons why the government and the general staff intended to expand the standing army remained taboo. On the other hand, only a profoundly political debate along these lines could have clarified the role of both the nation in arms and the standing army in the French military system. The slogans of 'national defence' and *attaque brusquée*, and the refusal to bring questions of ideology and politics into the debate, persuaded the majority of the Republicans in the Centre and on the Left to accept this concept in good faith as technically rational. Thus distracted, they remained unaware of its real political and military significance.

The tenacious debate on whether the integration of the reserves into the regular army would be better assured by the three-year bill than present legislation was typical of this situation. This question was of fundamental importance, as Joffre explained, because the quality of troops depended on two factors: the training of the recruits and the inner cohesion of the various army units. Recruits' training should be not only in soldiering, but should essentially prepare soldiers for action at the height of battle. This could only be possible on the basis of a lengthy period of military service, during which the recruit could develop automatic reflexes. The inner cohesion of the various troop formations as a whole could, in turn, be guaranteed only if each formation were trained together in barracks, so that over a period of years the soldiers would grow accustomed to each other and their officers and thus develop into a real 'unit'. Only a unit 'welded together' in this way could really form the solid core upon mobilisation 'around which heterogeneous elements from the reserve would gather'. Only an *ensemble* of this kind could function as the instrument of the commander, swiftly obeying 'his orders alone on the basis of his years of drilling'.[30] Given the *sine qua non* of the offensive strategy in Joffre's Plan XVII, these comments on the necessity of troop cohesion were even rational, since the basic assumption of Plan XVII was in fact an 'offensive of all forces united', the precise tactics of which had been left to the discretion of the individual *chef*. The automatic reflexes of the drilled troops were the correlative of the sole responsibility of the commander for decision-making.[31]

However, it was not the offensive strategy which was before the Chamber, but the problem of how to ward off an *attaque brusquée* from Germany. This discrepancy, deliberately fostered by the government and the general staff, led Parliament up the wrong path, as the Army Committee's report on the government's proposal illustrates. This report, which partly quoted Joffre word for word, nevertheless stated that the basic premise of a purely defensive 'nation in arms' was not called into question by the *Loi de Trois Ans*, which was no more than a 'transitional measure' (*sic*) 'dictated by the direct interests of *la patrie*'.[32] The Radical, Paté, who had drafted this report, explained to the press that the Army Committee considered the three-year law as a 'solid dyke' necessary only at that time of tension and that it did not imply a general reorganisation of the French army.[33]

The criticism from the Socialists and some of the Radical-Socialists that these theories were anti-republican and tantamount to militarism was indignantly rejected even by some of those on the benches of the Left, with reference to the supposed objective and technical bases of a measure which served only the interests of national defence.[34] Objectively these military and technical arguments were certainly linked with a number of premises of conservative ideology.[35] For this reason the alleged technical argument seemed natural to conservative Republicans and anti-republican traditionalists on two counts. Nevertheless, the statements on the 'three-year' issue cannot be clearly attributed to overall social ideology. Regardless of their other political views, the left-wing Republicans were not specifically concerned with defending the Republic against the forces of reaction on this issue, but against an *attaque brusquée*.[36]

The best illustration of the pragmatic approach of the majority of republican deputies was the resounding success of the Paul-Boncour/Messimy counter-proposal,[37] supported by more than 260 left-wing deputies, despite the final success of the government's diversionary tactics.[38] The strength of this proposal was that it adopted the *attaque brusquée* theory in its widest sense. In justifying the bill to the Chamber, Paul-Boncour emphasised that he was as convinced as the government that German rearmament was forcing France into making 'great efforts of military reorganisation'.[39] Messimy and Paul-Boncour also saw virtually eye-to-eye with Joffre on the question of the integration of the reservists into the regular army. Paul-Boncour stated that on the basis of his proposal—which not only extended regular service to thirty months but provided for annual one-month reserve exercises for all the eleven reserve classes—this integration could be carried out smoothly. Reserve exercises, he added, were moreover aimed not only at keeping the reservists prepared both physically and militarily for war, but served to maintain permanent contact between reservists, officers and fellow-soldiers in peacetime, a factor which was essential for 'unity in the battlefield'.[40] Messimy was even more categorical. It would be mad, he said, to maintain that all-reservist units could be thrown into battle before mobilisation had been concluded—that is, when the danger of an *attaque brusquée* was greatest. The core of a powerful army must remain the regular regiment which, like a living organism, could absorb a varying number of reservists, depending on the circumstances.[41] Paul-Boncour objected to the government's proposal on the grounds that it was solely concerned with the stipulation of the effective strength of the standing army, whereas he and Messimy wanted to concentrate army reorganisation on permanent resources of trained reserves. In this way it would be technically possible to enlist the whole of the nation in arms for the defence of *la patrie* so that, regardless of the new demands, 'the logic of the army system which a forty-year development has produced [could be] maintained'.[42]

By introducing this criticism Paul-Boncour had unconsciously put his finger on the sore point of the government's bill. In his memoirs Joffre was later to maintain that the Paul-Boncour/Messimy counter-proposal 'could not have solved the problem'[43] but that at the time the government and the general staff were not prepared to enlighten

Parliament as to the real reasons behind the three-year bill. The government could therefore go no further than dogmatically to assert that both qualitatively and quantitatively the *Trois Ans* were the only means of bringing the army up to the requirements of national defence. However, many deputies believed that the same pragmatic principle was behind both the 'thirty months' and the 'three years'. The counter-proposal therefore appealed to a great number of deputies, since it not only underlined the will to make an effort on behalf of *la patrie* but gave the deputies the opportunity of appeasing voters who were liable to be satisfied with the Paul-Boncour/Messimy counter-proposal on the grounds that it greatly reduced the sacrifice the government expected from the people.[44]

In his memoirs Joffre confirmed that Paul-Boncour's statements had posed a real threat to the *Trois Ans*: '. . . at the end of the meeting[45] I had the very clear impression that our proposal would have been jeopardised if we had voted directly after this speech. Fortunately the vote did not take place until a few days later. The effect of Paul-Boncour's speech had meanwhile had time to evaporate'.[46]

The Passage of the Three-Year Law through Parliament

Faced with this danger to the three-year law, the government now tried to break the front of the deputies likely to vote in favour of the counter-proposal.

Since the Socialists had come out in support of the Paul-Boncour/Messimy counter-proposal, the government was intent on preventing a bloc socialist and left-wing republican vote. Barthou therefore stepped up his campaign against the CGT, denouncing the Socialists' connivance with the 'revolutionary anti-patriots'. These tactics proved very effective and in fact played a decisive role in the defeat of the amendment in Parliament, as a closer examination of the course of the events will illustrate.

On 1 and 2 July—that is, just after Paul-Boncour's speech and immediately prior to the vote on the counter-proposal—thirteen leading CGT members were arrested in a sudden police swoop and charged with having organised the soldiers' revolts.[47] The SFIO protested vehemently against this 'useless and grotesque comedy', declaring that its sole purpose was to stabilise the governmental majority.[48] The CGT issued an official statement to the effect that the arrests were in no way connected with the soldiers' revolts and that the government, afraid of losing its majority to the Paul-Boncour/Messimy counter-proposal, had totally fabricated this 'red herring'.[49]

This reproach doubtless hit the nail on the head, although the government had ordered the arrests not only for reasons of parliamentary interest. Reference has already been made to a memorandum of the political police, dated 26 June, advising the arrests of militant CGT leaders as a precaution against further soldiers' revolts in the autumn of 1913,[50] and there are other indications that the government really was expecting another outbreak of unrest.[51] Nevertheless, it can still be concluded that the government hardened its line against the CGT precisely at this point in order to influence Parliament's choice between its own bill and the Paul-Boncour/Messimy counter-proposal to its own advantage. The fact that the CGT leaders were arrested immediately prior to the vote on the proposal suggests that this was indeed a red herring. Joffre's statement, already quoted, that the vote 'fortunately' took place a few days after Paul-Boncour's speech, would also seem to back up this theory.[52]

On 3 July Parliament rejected the counter-proposal by 312 votes to 266.[53] It is of course impossible to pinpoint exactly how many left-wing Republicans voted along with the government out of conviction and how many rejected the counter-proposal in order to disassociate themselves from the SFIO.[54] However, the following sitting of the Chamber showed that the latter motives were decisive for many left-wing Republicans. On 4 July the Chamber debated an interpellation presented by the socialist deputy Claussat condemning police abuses during the searches in May. In his reply Barthou pointed out that Jaurès, allegedly concerned with the defence of the Republic, doggedly refused to disassociate himself from the 'criminal' Syndicalists.[55] A motion for the *affichage*[56] of Barthou's speech, tabled by a Centre deputy, was adopted with only 141 votes against. All the members of the *gauche radicale* and almost 100 Radical-Socialists supported Barthou's line against the Syndicalists and Socialists.[57] In the press of all political creeds this almost unanimous protest of left-wing Republicans against the alleged SFIO solidarity with the CGT was seen as a sign that Parliament would vote in favour of the three-year law. Moreover, a number of newspapers commented that the Left's obvious rejection of the SFIO's aspirations towards a 'bloc against reaction' had opened up a wide gulf between all the defenders of *la patrie* and internal law and order, on the one hand, and the 'accomplices of the saboteurs', on the other.[58] It is true that, following the rejection of the Paul-Boncour/Messimy counter-proposal and the subsequent aloofness of the bourgeois Left with regard to 'anti-patriotism' and the 'sabotage' of the social order, the *Loi de Trois Ans* had no further obstacles to surmount. Whether the wider-ranging social perspectives would be fulfilled nevertheless remained doubtful. The financing of the three-year law had still to be settled and this matter alone could easily lead to a new transformation of the political fronts. The reorganisation of the French taxation system would have to be discussed again in the Chamber—a demand which both Socialists and left-wing Republicans had been making for some time and which could now bring them together again.

A first opportunity to consolidate relations between the Socialists and left-wing Republicans arose in the final days of the parliamentary debate on the defence bill. Directly before its adoption, a governmental initiative added a new and far-reaching amendment to the bill, which confirmed the suspicions the SFIO had had all along that the three-year law had been introduced not only as a measure to guarantee national defence.

On 5 July, two days after the rejection of the Paul-Boncour/ Messimy counter-proposal, the government adopted an amendment proposed by the right-wing republican deputy Paul Escudier, which provided for enlistment at the age of twenty. From now on recruits were to be enlisted at the end of their twentieth year and not, as previously, at the age of twenty-one. Escudier's motion reflected the wish, frequently expressed by the public, that the country's socio-economic burdens resulting from the *Trois Ans* should be reduced as much as possible. A regulation to this effect had been requested at the meeting of the presidents of the French chambers of commerce at the beginning of June, so that young people would not have to wait until they were twenty-four before they could enter the economic process, establish a family, and so forth.[59] The government, with the approval of the Army committee of the Chamber and the Advisory Committee on Hygiene and Epidemiology, had originally rejected this proposal on the grounds that such young recruits would not have adequate physical resistance.[60] It was following an initiative from Poincaré that the government had dispelled these doubts and included 'incorporation at the age of twenty' in the military bill. Poincaré later explained that he had taken this initiative in order to remove one of the most serious objections to the *Loi de Trois Ans* so that the bill would finally be passed.[61] However, the following entry in Poincaré's diary shows what the President really had in mind: 'The immediate result of incorporation at twenty—which I had great difficulty in persuading Barthou to accept—shall be the immediate call-up of the class of 1913. Consequently the class of 1910, retained in the ranks, will shortly be discharged.'[62]

Interest was therefore focused on the matter of discharging the oldest class in the regular army, which was in the offing, while retaining three conscript classes in the barracks. This measure would considerably mitigate the government's earlier decision to apply Article 33 of the 1905 law—that is, to retain the 1910 class in the autumn of 1913, which had in fact directly sparked off the soldiers' revolts in May. The government seems to have been very apprehensive about the prospect of further unrest in the autumn of 1913, which radical CGT members had predicted and intended to exploit.

Jaurès pointed out to Parliament that the ostensible reason for the three-year law had in effect now been eliminated, exposing the 'reactionary farce' behind the military bill. It was domestic concern, he claimed, which had led the government to repudiate the apparent necessity of a 'solid backbone' against the *attaque brusquée*; for, if the classes of 1912 and 1913 were to be enlisted simultaneously, there would be no alternative but to discharge immediately the class of 1910, since there was simply not enough room in the barracks for four classes of recruits. On the other hand, to discharge the class of 1910 would mean that in the autumn of 1913 the regular army would be left with only one conscript class with a fairly adequate level of training, the class of 1911. By contradicting itself in this way, the government, he concluded, was simply asking for an *attaque brusquée*. Barthou tried to refute these weighty objections by arguing that the government had never intended to retain the class of 1910 for a whole year; and that this class would be discharged to ease the strain on the barracks as soon as the two new classes had reached a level of training to match the 'international situation.'[63]

However, this plan of the government totally contradicted the principle of equal military service for all citizens, since retention of the 1910 class could no longer be justified on the basis of the emergency article of the 1905 law. Now two conscript classes were to be called in at the same time, not on account of danger lurking abroad, but because of considerations of internal expediency.

The government's dilemma became irrefutable when on 7 July the Radical-Socialist deputy Daniel Vincent tabled an amendment to Article 18 of the governmental bill, proposing that the following be added: 'All men deemed fit for service shall effectively complete an equal period of service.'[64] This sentence, which categorically excluded the possibility of any professional or social groups being exempted from military service, embodied the much-alluded-to 'republican spirit' of the French army constitution. The strength of this republican principle was so overwhelming that even its most determined adversaries did not dare to oppose it in public. The Vincent amendment was adopted by 564 votes in favour and one against (!), virtually without debate, whereupon the entire Article 18 of the government bill—that is, the principle of three-year service—was approved with a relatively clear majority (i.e. compared with the vote on the Paul-Boncour/Messimy counter-proposal) of 330 votes to 223.[65]

The Chamber's decision that all able-bodied citizens were to complete an 'effectively' equal period of service made it impossible for the government to retain the class of 1910 at short notice. The government was therefore faced with two alternatives. Either it could persist in its intention to call up conscripts at the age of twenty and discharge the class of 1910 immediately, or it could drop incorporation at the age of twenty and retroactively apply the three-year principle to the class of 1910 in accordance with the original government bill. If the government opted for the former alternative, the argument that the *Loi de Trois Ans* had been introduced only as an emergency measure against the threat of an *attaque brusquée* would be exposed as purely ideological, whereas the latter might trigger off another wave of unrest in the barracks. There were already signs of discontent among the class due for discharge, which the prospect of hopes being dashed was bound to exacerbate.[66]

At first the government tried to avoid taking a decision in either direction. Barthou declared that he would go along with the vote of the Chamber on this issue, since the Escudier amendment had not been the result of a governmental initiative and did not concern the substance of the government's bill. Although even *Le Temps* denounced this attempt to pass the buck to the Chamber as 'unserious',[67] Barthou was successful and, following a brief debate, the Chamber adopted Article 6 of the three-year bill in the form of the Escudier amendment by 376 votes to 199. Many deputies were obviously not aware of the military implications of this additional clause; others may have been convinced by the social advantages of the provision. Not only all the Socialists and a group of Radical-Socialists, but many right-wing deputies and other supporters of the *Loi de Trois Ans* (e.g. Lamy, Montebello and A. Lefèvre) voted against the amended version of Article 6. However, both Joseph Reinach and, on the other side of the fence, Caillaux, voted in favour of it. A number of politicians otherwise prominent in parliamentary debates (Delahaye, Driant, de Mun), the chairman of the Army Committee, Le Hérissé, and its spokesman, Paté, did not vote in the ballot.[68] A few hours before the final division on the three-year law (on 19 July), the Escudier amendment was taken a step further. The Chamber, again with a completely incoherent political majority, ruled that three-year military service would first apply to the class of 1913, which meant that the aim of retaining two adequately trained conscript class plus a recruit classes in the ranks could not be achieved until 1916. The contradictions of this decision were clearly spelled out by Jaurès—'Never shall the country have paid more dearly for such a mystification'—and he subsequently continued to refer to the 'madness' that, instead of guaranteeing a 'solid backbone', the extension of military service had finally come to no more than over-crowding the barracks with two classes of untrained recruits.[69]

Since virtually the only justification the public had been given for the *Trois Ans* was that it was the only adequate emergency measure which could be taken against the threat from Germany, Jaurès's argument was a forceful one. It was virtually impossible to cover up the contradiction between the original line of argument based on fear, which had also been advanced in the Army Committee's report,[70] and the final *status quo* following the Escudier amendment. Various factors helped to gain a parliamentary majority for the *Loi de Trois Ans*. A psychological reason was that after so many months of public and parliamentary debate, many deputies were loath to go back to their electorate empty-handed and face the criticism that they had prevented the strengthening of national defence simply because there was no alternative.

Another reason, perhaps decisive for many left-wing Republicans, became apparent when the Senate with its radical majority gave the go-ahead to the *Trois Ans* on 7 August 1913, the final stage in the enactment of the bill.[71] The Senate spokesman, Paul Doumer,[72] did not even mention the *attaque brusquée* in his report. He admitted that the new conscription law would be fully effective only from 1916, but added that this was the responsibility of Parliament and not of the government, since incorporation at the age of twenty had been decided by Parliament, independently of the government, against its will (*sic*) and purely on the basis of economic and social considerations.[73] However, this delay would not compromise the heart of the govern-ment's bill—the stipulation of effective strength in order to improve the training and cohesion of the regular units and the integration of the reservists. Doumer's report concentrated almost wholly on this 'tech-nical' argument, which had already left a deep impression on the Chamber. Clemenceau, the *spiritus rector* of the radical majority in the Senate, admittedly criticised the government's 'improvisation' and 'incoherence'—despite the threat from Germany, a fully trained con-script class was to be discharged and replaced by two recruit classes for purely domestic reasons—but was nevertheless convinced by the military and technical arguments.[74] Étienne justified the government's acceptance of conscription at the age of twenty as follows: 'We must undoubtedly take the strength of the German army into consideration, but in reality (*sic*), gentlemen, is not the essential factor on this point to achieve a parallelism . . . a simultaneous process and the equilibrium of mobilisable forces that must guarantee our security!'[75]

Following this statement no one asked why the government had originally justified the *Trois Ans* on the basis of an *attaque brusquée* of the 900,000-strong German army. If we can assume that the 'military and technical' argument was decisive for many left-wing Republicans in the Chamber, it must nevertheless be noted that this swing in opinion—from the fear of an *attaque brusquée* to the belief that it was necessary to improve the integration of the reservists—never explicitly took place. Parliament's final vote on the *Loi de Trois Ans* on 19 July clearly illustrates that the republican Left in particular was still not aware of the importance of three-year service for national defence and had still not adopted a common stance on the issue.

Before the final vote was held, the spokesmen of the various parliamentary groups issued statements to the Chamber explaining why their group was voting for or against the bill. It was symptomatic of the previous days' events, which had polarised opinion even further, that on the republican Left and in the Centre the party whip was enforced only by the Socialists, the anti-republican Right, the 'rallied' Catholics and the right-wing republican *Progressistes*. All these groups fully supported their spokesmen's speeches. The Centre and the Left, however, could not muster such a degree of unanimity. The *Entente démocratique et sociale*, founded in June as a new reservoir for the parliamentary Centre, gave Joseph Reinach, one of the leading *Troisannistes*, the task of reading out a declaration on behalf of the roughly 100 members of this group.[76] However, only fifty-five deputies actually signed Reinach's statement, which more than any other spelled out the actual goal of the three-year law. The *Loi de Trois Ans* did not have just a quantitative aspect—that is, the balance between German and French regular forces—said Reinach. Of equal importance was to expand each regular unit in such a way that the reservists could be absorbed upon mobilisation without upsetting the balance in the respective units. Thus, he concluded, the French army would be capable of 'facing up to all eventualities'.[77] A small group of twenty-two deputies from a motley of left-wing republican groups voted in favour of the government's bill although, as its spokesman E. Chanal stressed, the Paul-Boncour/Messimy counter-proposal should really have been the 'maximum'. On the other hand, it was preferable to go 'too far' in improving the country's preparedness rather than 'not far enough'.[78] Caillaux, speaking on behalf of 140 deputies 'from the four groups of the Left', rejected the government bill on the grounds that the *Trois Ans* would serve only to strengthen the regular forces. Since the Escudier amendment had removed the argument that the law was necessary to guard France against an *attaque brusquée*, only reactionary domestic motives, he declared, could lie behind the bill.[79]

On 19 July the Chamber adopted the *Loi de Trois Ans* by 358 votes to 204.[80] A rough analysis shows that the number of out-and-out supporters or opponents of the bill—that is, those who signed the declarations of the various groups—was approximately equal on both sides. Reinach's fifty-five supporters, and the twenty-two deputies who had signed Chanal's declaration, joined ranks with the 130 *progressiste*, ALP and monarchist Right deputies.[81] The entire SFIO group (seventy deputies) and some 130 deputies of Caillaux's group voted against the bill. However, since there were about 600 seats in Parliament, more than 150 Left and Centre deputies must have voted in favour of the bill without justifying their decision! What tipped the scales in the government's favour was the vote of a large number of Left and Centre deputies who refused to recognise the link between general options of domestic and foreign policy and national defence. This is confirmed by the fact that only fifty-five deputies from the various left-wing groups came out in favour of Reinach, although he could not be suspected of anti-republican intentions and although it was common knowledge that he had played a key role in the drafting of the government bill. This is perhaps the most convincing evidence of the much-alluded to ideological distortion of the three-year issue: the vast majority of the republican deputies who finally voted in favour of the government's bill did so either because they did not grasp or because they rejected Reinach's justification of the bill on grounds of foreign policy and power politics.

Jaurès's prediction that the new conscription law would prove to be the 'Pyrrhic victory of chauvinism and reaction'[82] was not altogether unrealistic. Although the Socialists had not succeeded in convincing the majority of left-wing Republicans that the bill was the result of domestic reactionary manoeuvres, the government had no reason to be satisfied either, as little remained of the original patriotic *élan*. The Paul-Boncour/Messimy counter-proposal had shown that there was still a majority in Parliament in favour of the purely defensive approach to army organisation, which was unrealistic in terms of strategic calculations. Since the majority in favour of the *Trois Ans* was not formed on the basis of a common and explicit concept of national defence in its true context of French military and foreign policy, this majority was a very fragile one. This meant that there were further dangers on the internal front looming ahead for the *Loi de Trois Ans*.

The Completion of Plan XVII *and the* Question of the Russian Railway Loan, 1913

Although the amendments to the *Loi de Trois Ans* in the course of the parliamentary debate made the ideology of an *attaque brusquée* seem rather fragile, this had little effect on the long-term strategic planning of the French general staff. After the bill had been adopted by Parliament and the Senate, Joffre set to work on the drafts for the mobilisation and concentration plans to complete Plan XVII, the basic ideas of which had been passed by the Supreme Army Council (CSG) on 18 April and adopted by the government early in May.[1] The core of the implementing regulations of the strictly offensive war plan was the 'regulation on the conduct of large army corps', which in the future was to provide the basis for instruction in the military academies. This regulation was given the legal status of a decree on 28 October 1913 and was thus legally binding. 'Like a type of dogma', as Joffre put it, the decree advanced the theory that one could succeed in war only 'by looking for a battle and being able to tackle it offensively'. Like the German general staff, the French high command was convinced that for socio-economic reasons a war between the Great Powers could be only a short one. In the regulation of 28 October 1913 this was stipulated as the main reason why it was necessary for a battle to take place as soon as possible to decide the outcome of the war.[2] These guide-lines were extremely disdainful of the defensive strategy: defensive facilities, fortifications, and so forth, were important only because in certain circumstances they could facilitate the commander's offensive manoeuvres. A second decree on 2 December 1913 laid down that a defensive approach was permissible only if and when it had been decided to withdraw contingents of troops from given areas to reinforce troops involved in offensive action elsewhere.[3] Joffre's instructions on 21 November 1913 on the implementation of the 1912 cadre laws were also part and parcel of this series of instructions and decrees.[4] By February 1914 the strategic and logistical details of Plan XVII had been drafted. At the end of the month, after almost two years of preparation, the new operational plan could finally be implemented.[5]

It is important to note that fresh information received by the French general staff at the end of 1913 was not included in the drafting of the offensive doctrine. The prospect that the German army might not only wheel through Belgium but was prepared to deploy reservists in the front lines, was not followed up by the drafting of any alternatives to Plan XVII.[6] In his memoirs Joffre tried to justify the pointless and catastrophic sacrifice of blood during the frontier battles in August 1914 with the argument that, unlike the general staff, who had moved away from the 'excesses' of the offensive theory, the subordinate cadre officers had not fully grasped the tactical conditions of an offensive strategy, which to them was a sacrosanct dogma—as a result of which the troops, 'prepared to make any sacrifice', had exposed themselves to enemy fire with no regard to local topography and with inadequate artillery preparation.[7] This rather disloyal attempt of Joffre to shift the blame for the failure of French strategic calculation from the high command to the misguided and one-sided subordinate officers and their over-enthusiastic, self-sacrificing soldiers (*sic*) is not very convincing. The discrepancy between the technical concept of the overall offensive and the enthusiasm for national defence at the outbreak of war is quite evident in this apology. The reason for the absurd 'misunderstandings' at the beginning of the war seems to lie in the *attaque brusquée* ideology and the gap, never bridged during the debate on the *Loi de Trois Ans*, between offensive and strategical considerations, on the one hand, and the citizen soldier's willingness to fight to the bitter end on behalf of his country, on the other. As a result, tens of thousands of soldiers followed an unrealistic offensive theory to their deaths.

The offensive strategy and the basic ideas of Plan XVII included swift mobilisation and the simultaneous concentration of French and Russian troops at the outbreak of war. The bases of Plan XVII adopted by the CSG on 18 April 1913 assumed that the Russian army had made 'considerable progress' and could now begin warfare on the fifteenth day following mobilisation in order to launch an offensive attack on Germany 'with the bulk of [its] regular troops' from the twentieth day. Further progress in speeding up mobilisation and concentration were considered imminent.[8]

This confidence was based on the supposed success of the Delcassé mission, the chief objective of which had been to persuade the Russians to implement and speed up the military arrangements of 1912.[9] The central issue in both these arrangements and Delcassé's talks with the Russian government was the improvement of Russia's strategic railway lines, upon which the speed of the Russian army's operations was basically dependent. In his first reports in March 1913, Delcassé was very optimistic that the Russian government was prepared to implement the programme drafted by the general staffs in 1912 as soon as possible.[10]

However, in actual fact Russia was not willing to comply fully with the French demands.[11] In mid-June 1913 the Russian government let it be known that the Duma would certainly not give the go-ahead to a railway project designed 'along exclusively military lines', being more concerned with the development of an economically relevant railway project to increase the 'wealth and power' of Russia.[12]

The French government therefore sought to comply with the Russians while at the same time looking for an opportunity to take advantage of the fact that the Tsar's government was in need of capital to implement its strategic interests. Such an opportunity arose in June 1913 when the syndic of the Paris stockbrokers, de Verneuil, went to St Petersburg to negotiate with the Russian government on the conditions for a huge annual loan of 400–500 million francs to be raised on the Paris stock exchange.[13] From the available sources it is not clear whether the initiative for these negotiations came from Russian or French financial circles. In any case the French government stepped in when it realised that the loan could be used to give weight to its military demands on Russia. De Verneuil was therefore informed that authorisation for the transaction of the loan would be granted on the condition that Russia immediately set to work on the strategic railway line on its western border and, in addition, considerably increased her peacetime effective strength.[14]

In view of the strategic demands at this time—prior to the general staff's conference at the end of August 1913—the Russian Finance Minister, Kokovcov, accepted these conditions and asked the French government to give the go-ahead to the arrangements made with de Verneuil as soon as possible. This request was granted at once.[15] So at the end of July 1913 it seemed that the agreements made by the general staffs in 1912 would finally be put into effect, and Delcassé and Joffre were therefore confident that the bulk of the Russian army would be able to launch its offensive on the thirteenth day after mobilisation.[16]

Under these auspices the conference of the allied general staffs at the end of August 1913 ran much more smoothly than that of the previous year, in particular because at this stage the *Loi de Trois Ans* had already been passed.[17] The representations of both general staffs testified to their determination to launch an 'energetic and, as far as possible, simultaneous' joint offensive in the event of war. Joffre stated that France would concentrate the bulk of her troops—200,000 men more than stipulated in the 1892 military convention—on the north-east Franco-German border. These troops would be fully mobilised on the tenth day, so that France could launch her offensive on the eleventh day after mobilisation. On this point, however, the Russians could still only confirm the 1912 agreements that their army would be ready to launch an attack on the fifteenth day after mobilisation, although the Russian Commander-in-Chief, Zilinsky, assured his allies that from the end of 1914 the concentration of Russian troops could take place two days earlier, which would enable the Russian offensive to be launched on the thirteenth day after mobilisation. The Russian general staff was indeed prepared to make every effort to ensure that the Franco-Russian offensive could be launched simultaneously. The French general staff's request for an extension of the scope of the 1912 arrangements, with regard to the modernisation and improvement of the strategic railway lines on the German-Russian border, was granted without reservation. The general staffs in fact drew up a vast railway project. Existing railway lines close to the western Russian border were to be expanded into double or four-track lines to guarantee swift troop movement, and additional lines were to be built. All in all a total of over 5,000 kilometres of new tracks were to be constructed and a large number of additional heavy locomotives and wagons procured.[18]

However, this comprehensive railway project was given a cool reception by the Russian government. The Finance Minister, Kokovcov, informed the French *chargé d'affaires* in St Petersburg that to build completely new railway lines would not only overstrain the Russian budget but was in any case not 'of direct interest'.[19] Furthermore, on account of these fresh demands from the general staffs, the Tsar's government was no longer prepared to accept the conditions of the loan negotiated with de Verneuil, and at the end of September Kokovcov submitted a new draft contract which was considerably more imprecise than de Verneuil's original version. The Russian government would 'take account' of the French government's requests concerning the strategic railway lines, but no reference was made to the further plans of the general staffs. The French government's demand that the work on the new railway lines should be started 'immediately' was not complied with either. Although a representative of the Russian government politely stated that the new agreements between the general staffs had not been taken into consideration for the simple reason that there had been no official communication on the outcome of the talks, the French government's suspicions that the Russians did not intend to respect the general staffs' agreements were not dispelled—especially since these agreements were not even mentioned in a Russian *aide-mémoire* of 10 October.[20]

The French *chargé d'affaires* in St Petersburg interpreted this reticence as a reflection of Russian general opinion, which at that time was that there was no immediate likelihood of further complications on the international scene. He added that Kokovcov, whose position was in any case already precarious, had had to bow to this opinion. Russia's wait-and-see attitude was also facilitated, he reported, by the fact that since the end of the Balkan wars offers of supply of capital had been more forthcoming, so that the government saw no need to subject itself to France's conditions for the granting of a loan.[21]

So, since the French government continued to insist on concrete promises from Russia on the strategic railway lines in accordance with the general staffs' agreements before the loan from the Paris stock exchange was approved, the negotiations remained in the air, for the time being at least.[22]

In mid-November 1913, five months after the beginning of the negotiations, Kokovcov came to Paris on an official visit. The 'main aim' of his consultation with the French government was to 'find out whether France was prepared to support us in extending our railway network'.[23] During these talks Kokovcov gave a straight answer to a straight question from the French Foreign Minister as to whether the Russian government was willing to go beyond the planned infrastructural measures and build the strategic railway line. Kokovcov did not share the opinion of the general staffs that there was a fundamental difference between railway lines of economic and strategic importance. Both aspects, he believed, had to be seen as an integral part of the railway network Russia required. If it were really necessary to build certain lines for purely strategical reasons, it would never occur to Russia to raise the necessary funds by loans. Such expenditure would have to be covered by the regular budget, since it would be impossible to raise capital for unproductive purposes.[24]

Faced with Kokovcov's resistance, the French were prepared to climb down to a certain extent. A new agreement was suggested, this time with no link between the loan and strategic demands. The main points of this draft agreement were as follows:

1. The Russian government was to be given authorisation over a period of five years to raise an annual sum of not exceeding 500 million francs on the Paris market to cover the costs of its railway line project.
2. The railway network demanded by the Russian and French general staffs in August 1913 was to be completed within four years. It was up to the Russian government as to whether this project was financed by the loan or through the regular budget.[25]

Despite this flexibility shown by the French government, it still proved impossible to reconcile the interests of both parties. Kokovcov returned home without having signed the agreement. His report to the Tsar did not reflect the actual facts; nevertheless, it illustrates that Kokovcov believed France would be prepared to make further concessions:

I suggested . . . to the French government that their concern with regard to the strategic railway lines should be replaced by a more general formula, i.e. recognition of the fact that the Russian railway network must be improved in accordance with both the economic and strategic requirements of the State . . . the formula I proposed gave rise to no objections.[26]

However, in his report to the Tsar Kokovkov made no reference to the additional French demand that Russia should commit herself to completing the strategic lines within four years.

The negotiations on the Russian railway loan remained in the air for another month, probably due to the fact that from mid-November 1913 France was faced with another domestic crisis, which was not resolved until early December when the Barthou government was overthrown and the new left-wing republican Doumergue/Caillaux cabinet was formed.[27] When the Russian ambassador in Paris, Izvolsky, asked the French government to give its immediate approval to the granting of the loan in mid-December 1913, his government's interest in this loan had been radically transformed. Presumably on the assumption that the new left-wing Doumergue/Caillaux government would be less concerned with the strategic demands of the French general staff, the Russian government again tried to get the loan approved without formally committing itself to completing the strategic lines within four years.[28] However, when Doumergue and Caillaux insisted that the loan would be authorised only if this condition were formally accepted,[29] the Russian government quickly relented:

Kokovcov is now asking me to inform [the government] that he would prefer his version of paragraph 2 [in the discussions on 10 November], but if serious disagreement or a delay should result he would be prepared to withdraw this version and accept the French proposal, unamended, with the proviso that the agreement is definitively concluded without delay.[30]

This sudden reversal of the position of the Russian government can be explained only by its concern and agitation with regard to the outbreak of the so-called Liman von Sanders affair which took place at exactly this time.[31]

The course of the Franco-Russian negotiations on the railway loan backs up the assumption that from this time on the Russian government and Russian public opinion were convinced that war with Germany was virtually imminent.[32] The change in the Russian government's position in regard to these negotiations with France reflects particularly the deep concern of the Russian government about the Sanders affair, which marks a turning-point in Russo-German relations. Whereas, at the time of the Paris negotiations, Kokovcov still believed that the crisis could be ironed out in friendly talks with Germany,[33] the sudden decision to accept the French conditions for the loan was undoubtedly due to the announcement a few days earlier that Germany and Turkey had signed an agreement on the German military mission in Turkey.[34] Russia feared that her vital interests would be encroached upon by an increase of German influence in Turkey and therefore ascribed greater importance than before to the military agreements with France. Henceforth the alliance was no longer held together by political and military concessions granted by France to a reluctant ally, as had been the case since early 1912 under the Poincaré and Barthou goverments—even the *Loi de Trois Ans* was to a certain extent an offshoot of the precarious relations with Russia. The successful conclusion of the negotiations on the Russian loan in 1913 was of great political importance. Russia now also had an interest in the strategic agreements with France, and this consolidated the alliance decisively.

This new dimension to the alliance with Russia also left its mark on further developments in French internal politics. Following the fall of Barthou and the formation of the left-wing Doumergue/Caillaux cabinet in December 1913, the tone of Franco-Russian relations may have changed fundamentally if the previous dynamics of the alliance—based on Poincaré's policy—had prevailed. It can be assumed that the new government would not simply have continued in the footsteps of Poincaré and Barthou, consolidating the alliance on the basis of advance military concessions. A departure from this Poincaristic line of French foreign policy would certainly soon have led to the repeal of the three-year law which most left-wing Republicans had accepted only as a provisional line of defence against an *attaque brusquée*. However, in the wake of the Liman von Sanders affair, Russia now demanded—for the first time!—that France maintain the three-year law.[35] Russia's new concern to uphold the military agreements with France tied the hands of the Doumergue/Caillaux left-wing government and was an essential reason, if not the only one, why the change on the domestic front after the passing of the *Loi de Trois Ans* did not lead to an amendment of the new conscription law.

CHAPTER 7

Changes on the Domestic Front after the Adoption of the Three-Year Law

The Revisionistic Change in CGT Policy

Following the soldiers' 'riots' in May 1913 and the subsequent police action against the CGT, various militant syndicates and advocates of direct action, for example Yvetot, became convinced that a fresh wave of unrest would break out in the barracks if the government were to carry out its plans to retain the class of 1910. The CGT leaders were urged from various sources to take the initiative if this occurred and back the striking soldiers by calling a general strike which might spark off the 'social revolution'. The union headquarters, however, refused to adopt such Blanquistic plans and followed a very moderate line. The demonstrations in protest against the application of the 1905 emergency paragraph which had been planned to follow up the soldiers' unrest were called off and, for the first time in the history of revolutionary syndicalism, syndicalist action had openly become subordinated to that of the Socialists.

Despite this remarkable swing in policy, the government stepped up its campaign against the CGT at the beginning of July. Leaders of revolutionary syndicates were arrested on false charges of having instigated the 'mutinies'. One reason for these arrests may of course have been to eliminate the potential initiators of revolutionary agitation in the autumn of 1913. In any case, their underlying purpose was to woo the votes of the left-wing republican lobby which was sceptical about the three-year law but had no wish to be associated with 'anti-patriots' and alleged saboteurs. The defeat of the Paul-Boncour/Messimy counter-proposal is indicative of the success of this red herring.[1]

Apart from its immediate success, the government's action also had a long-term effect: it accelerated the revisionistic change in CGT policy which, although under way for some time, had been temporarily halted by the campaign against the three-year law.

On the basis of a report from an informer in the upper echelons of the CGT, the Prefect of Police gave the following account of the leading Syndicalists' reaction to the surprise arrests on 1/2 July:

> Jouhaux admits that the government's repeated attacks on militant workers —to which the only response have been manifestos, since in fact no more than this can be done—are of the greatest detriment to syndicalism, since they illustrate that the strength of syndicalism amounts to no more than verbal violence and impotence. And that the prestige of the CGT is gradually subsiding. But he will admit these bitter facts only to his friends.[2]

The CGT leaders were in fact extremely reserved towards the plans of action of various militant syndicates.[3] For instance, the plan to launch mass demonstrations and call for a general strike to coincide with the CGT annual congress in mid-June in Paris was turned down point-blank. At the construction workers' congress on 3 July Jouhaux reminded his audience of the failure of the great anti-war strike on 16 December 1912.[4] He maintained that the majority of the working class had not considered recent events serious enough to warrant a great strike, so that this step would have little hope of success. Jouhaux nevertheless conceded that it might be possible to launch a general strike at a later stage.[5] But this statement was hardly to be taken seriously, since at virtually the same time he had remarked to other members of the *Comité Confédéral* that the CGT was not in a position to launch any large-scale action. According to information Jouhaux had received, even some of the most militant organisations were not prepared for a new *tour de force*, and the large metal-workers', railwaymen's and printers' unions were no longer willing to 'march on the streets to no avail'.[6]

Jouhaux's assessment of grass-roots opinion was evidently shared by most of his colleagues on the *Comité Confédéral*. As a result, the only reaction to the arrests was a proclamation of protest in the form of a manifesto entitled 'The CGT Stands Firm'. This defiant title did not hide the fact that recent events had put the CGT into a very tight corner. The manifesto began by stating that the soldiers' unrest had been absolutely spontaneous and that it was up to the government to produce evidence that the 'mutinies' had been orchestrated by syndicalist organisations.

However, fear of further action cannot have been the only reason for the reticence of the CGT leaders. In June 1913—that is, before the arrests—the positions of activists such as Yvetot, who had originally hoped that the campaign against the *Trois Ans* would be the first stage of a renaissance of revolutionary syndicalism, were no longer reflected in the official *Voix du Peuple* or in the generally pro-activist *Bataille Syndicaliste*. Instead, attempts were now made to formulate an independent syndicalist position on the three-year issue, an exercise which had been neglected at the beginning of the debate.[7] Particular reference was made to the catastrophic socio-economic consequences of the law. In a number of statements from leading Syndicalists the original key issue—namely, the opportunity of using political propaganda to increase the public appeal of syndicalism—was no longer mentioned. Reference was now made only to the responsibility of syndicalism for French economic development. There was no allusion to the political reasons behind the objectively reactionary character of the three-year law. It was argued instead that 320 million working hours had been forfeited on account of the law. This in turn implied not only an increase in the cost of living but a strengthening of the position of the employers. Furthermore, since more and more foreign workers would be brought into the country who would hardly become members of the unions, the position of the capitalists would become even more firm.[8]

The first public confrontation between activists and revisionists since the beginning of the three-year debate occurred at the 'Conférence ordinaire des Fédérations nationales et des Bourses du Travail ou Unions de Syndicats'[9] from 13 to 15 July 1913. The apple of discord at this conference was the question, would it be possible—or expedient—to organise a general strike in the autumn of 1913? At the very beginning of the debate Jouhaux tabled a motion obviously aimed at appeasing the advocates of direct action and at the same time opening the door to revisionism. This long and involved resolution, sarcastically described by some of the delegates as a 'fine literary monument', laid down the CGT position along the lines of the manifesto issued at the beginning of July. However, it avoided the decisive question of whether or not a general strike should be organised against the three-year law, simply calling on the syndicates and labour exchanges to give the CGT the mandate 'to take advantage of every situation which might coordinate an outburst of indignation among the workers, the only victims of militarism!'[10]

In contrast with Jouhaux's vague and non-committal resolution, a number of delegates demanded a public statement that the CGT was prepared to call a general strike. This demand sparked off a heated debate. It was mainly representatives of the smaller syndicates and labour exchanges who were in favour of this step, since it was at this level that the anarcho-syndicalist tradition of direct action had its roots and still survived. A motion tabled by the delegate of the coopers' federation, Marchand, and a representative of the Cognac labour exchange, was backed by Constant, representing both the large federation of cartwrights and the Saumur labour exchange. Jouhaux's reaction was the ironic remark that Constant had not received a mandate on this issue from the cartwrights and was therefore entitled to vote for a general strike only on behalf of the Saumur labour exchange 'which has 50 syndicate members'.[11] Among the large syndicate federations, only Péricat, representing the construction workers, and Broutchoux, on behalf of the Pas de Calais miners, spoke out in favour of the resolution.[12] Péricat declared that the *Trois Ans* issue must remain the cornerstone of syndicalist action: 'The day the CGT gives up its action it will cease to exist!'[13]

The most famous of the revisionists within the CGT, Merrheim, protested against these 'castles in the air'. He was convinced that the CGT must now finally put an end to the 'clenched fist policy' outside the syndicalist framework which ignored the real problems of labour organisation. The CGT must now turn its attention, he maintained, to winning over non-organised workers methodically. To do so, it must prove itself as the legitimate spokesman of the proletariat on corporate and social issues. To bite continually at the bait of political provocation could only be detrimental to the CGT's real task of organising workers' action. The vast majority of the delegates at the congress were in favour of Merrheim's proposal for a new strategy of revolutionary syndicalism. Jouhaux's motion (outlined above) was adopted, with only four votes against. Although this motion was couched in relatively ambiguous terms, the course of the discussion had left no doubt that it was to be interpreted as a rejection of the idea of organising a general strike in protest against the three-year law.

This 'remarkable and sudden swing' was described by the bourgeois press as either a victory of the opportunists within the CGT or a direct result of the government's intimidation tactics.[14] *L'Humanité* commented that the CGT would have no alternative in future but to abandon all forms of 'general action' and to restrict itself to matters of pure corporatism.[15] Following the congress, prominent CGT members issued statements on these commentaries in an attempt to define the new path of syndicalism which, to quote Jouhaux, would be 'more silent and more effective'. Merrheim affirmed that serious efforts would now be made to improve syndicate organisation, among both the leaders and the rank and file. Particular efforts would be made to recruit new members by more committed action on purely social and economic questions. The priority for the future was to establish an effective syndicalist counterweight to the fortified strength of the employers' organisations, a phenomenon which Merrheim and *La Vie Ouvrière* had already been analysing for some years.[16] Jouhaux tried to win over supporters to direct action for the new CGT line by affirming that the efforts to tighten syndicalist organisation would not only strengthen the position of the CGT in day-to-day labour disputes but would be beneficial in promoting the struggle against militarism and nationalism.[17] There was very little substance to this concession, which did not hide the fact that recent events could indeed be regarded as a turning-point in the history of syndicalism. The revisionists' relief at the defeat of political activism is reflected in a statement by Pierre Monatte, originally an anarchist and now one of Merrheim's closest associates and founder of the revisionistic *La Vie Ouvrière*.

According to Monatte, the Conference of the Federations and Labour Exchanges had demonstrated that the CGT was weary of those who imagined a new revolutionary situation 'every two weeks'. Today, following the adoption of the three-year law, the CGT had come to the conclusion that resistance against the 'ultra-revolutionary clamour' and the Blanquistic conception of revolution could serve only a truly revolutionary form of syndicalism completely orientated towards the economic sector.[18] Rejection of the political line should therefore not be equated with the adoption of reformist practice. It was repeatedly stressed that the new stance of the CGT did not imply the renunciation of revolutionary objectives.[19]

An official CGT declaration on 27 August illustrated that this line was no longer the position just of individual revolutionaries and organisations but in fact met with general approval at union headquarters. This declaration affirmed that the resolution of the Conference of Federations and Labour Exchanges on the three-year law had marked a reformist swing in CGT policy. It was not the intention of the CGT, it continued, to restrict itself to reformist practice and hide behind state bureaucracy. On the contrary, it would preserve its independence—which included independence from the Socialist Party—and remain a revolutionary movement. Nevertheless, the practice of revolutionary syndicalism could not continue to follow the past forms of action. It was the right and the duty of the CGT, read the declaration, to adapt its propaganda and organisation, both in form and substance, to the structural changes of the industrial world in accordance with the 'opportunities of the times and circumstances'.[20]

The failure of political syndicalism and its ineffective intervention in the 'three-year' debate led to a radical realignment of CGT policy, owing to which syndicalism was to remain politically insignificant up to the outbreak of the war. While domestic politics remained dominated by the *Trois Ans* and the question of tax reform until July 1914, the CGT was almost completely forgotten. In fact the impression left by the anti-political swing, following the failure of its campaign against the three-year law, was so deep that the syndicalist movement paid virtually no attention to the bitter struggle over tax reform in the first few months of 1914. Its contribution to this debate was an ironic disparagement of the 'clowning' inherent in any attempts at reform the left-wing bourgeois and Socialist parties might make.[21] And although the CGT continued to oppose the three-year law, it nevertheless refused to support the intensive SFIO campaign against the law in the 1914 election campaign.[22]

Historical research has often raised the question why the Syndicalists offered such little resistance to the *Union Sacrée* in July 1914. The turn of events in the years 1913/14 offers at least a partial answer. The renunciation of direct action and the revisionistic swing of syndicalism meant that the movement now shied away from the political issues of the time to such an extent that at the critical moment it lacked the sufficient organisational and ideological strength even to plan an anti-war demonstration.

The Unification of the Radicals at the Congress of Pau

Throughout the public and parliamentary debate on the three-year law both the leaders and the rank and file of the Radical Party had been divided on the defence issue. Realising that a split on this important issue, on top of the party's traditional organisational deficiencies, could lead to a fiasco and the routing of the party in the 1914 elections, the Radicals concluded that a comprehensive overhaul of the party programme and structures was necessary.[23] At their annual congress in Pau in October 1913 the party's organisational committee called for the implementation of the resolution passed at the 1910 congress in Rouen, so that the various radical groups in Parliament would be amalgamated and represented by the party and the party alone.[24] There was considerable interest among the public as to whether the representatives of the departmental federations, local committees, lodges and parliamentarians[25] assembled at Pau would succeed in agreeing on a common programme and how the Radical Party would distinguish its aims from those of the parties of the Left and Centre. It was generally expected that the conclusions of the

congress on the three-year law and its financial implications would set
the pace for the future development of the party. A point of particular
speculation was whether the Radicals would aim at a revival of the
parliamentary bloc of the Left of the pre-1905 Combes area, or
whether they would define their political stance so as to be able to
continue to represent a substantial part of the Centre.[26]

Both options as to the future direction of the Radical Party were
voiced before the congress by Combes and his rival, Caillaux.
Combes, still party chairman but on the verge of retirement, advised
the congress not to be too specific about the Radicals' long-term
political strategy. Since it was the aim of the conference to find a
common platform for a wide range of very progressive and more
moderate elements for the remainder of the legislatory period, and
with a view to the 1914 election campaign, it was essential to lay down
no more than a minimum programme. Combes called for the re-
establishment of the radical/socialist bloc to fight against the revival of
'clericalism' and 'nationalist reaction'.[27]

Basically these statements, on the political combinations which were
to provide a platform for a policy of the Left in the future, were
extremely vague. Although the struggle against clericalism and reaction remained the very heart of radical ideology, in view of the issues
of the day, both at home and abroad, this did not provide an adequate
basis for a greater degree of party unity, as had already become clear
during the *Trois Ans* debate. Combes failed to explain how radical
policy for the future would view the three-year law and its financial
implications. He simply advised the radical deputies not to 'step on the
Senators' toes', the Senate being an institution which had proved itself
as a bulwark of the Republic against the attacks from clericalism and
nationalism.[28] This warning could have been directed only against the
lobby (which included Caillaux) in favour of incorporating the 1909
tax reforms—progressive taxation and compulsory declaration of
income—in the 1914 budget, a measure designed to use budgetary
legislation as a means of forcing the Senate finally to implement these
principles.[29] Combes's opposition to the tactics of the tax reformers
highlights the socially conservative implications of Combistic ideology, the expression of a whole era of radical domination of French
politics.

On the question of how the Radical Party should distinguish itself
from other political formations, Caillaux's position was diametrically
opposed to that of the party chairman. In a declaration of principle
published prior to the Pau congress,[30] Caillaux described the party as
the only legitimate democratic French party, equally opposed to
revolutionary agitation and the intrigues of reaction. The minimum

programme would have to respect this position and be both sufficiently precise and sufficiently moderate. As a result, he continued, anyone who rejected the programme could not justifiably call himself a loyal Republican. In practical terms this meant that the Radical Party and its parliamentary groups intended to uphold the strategy applied during the *Trois Ans* debate and keep the doors of the party open to moderate Republicans.[31]

The minimum programme which Caillaux proposed illustrated the true extent of republican unity. Apart from its reaffirmation of the traditional republican commitment to the principles of anti-clericalism, the programme consisted of no more than references to the three-year law and tax reform. On the latter issue Caillaux demanded that the Senate adopt the guide-lines of the 1909 Chamber bill once and for all, adding that the introduction of a capital tax would be necessary to cover the costs of rearmament. Moreover, since defence of *la patrie* was *the* absolute priority for the Radical Party, it was obliged, he declared, to ensure that national defence was organised more comprehensively and methodically than before. The necessary reorganisation would have to be based to a greater extent on the principle of the nation in arms, eliminating superfluous costs and above all avoiding all unnecessary use of men. Although these words naturally implied criticism of the three-year law, Caillaux was careful not to qualify the defence bill as completely superfluous or even as reactionary. His approach therefore appealed to many of the Republicans who, to quote the Army Committee spokesman, regarded the three-year law as no more than a 'solid backbone', imperative in view of the *attaque brusquée*, and who nevertheless believed that a thorough reorganisation of the army would be necessary at a later stage.

The Socialists followed the Caillaux-Combes debate with great interest. Jaurès's assessment of the positions of the two leading spokesmen of the Radical Party gave an indication of the scope of future cooperation between Socialists and Radicals in Parliament and in the 1914 elections. With reference to Combes's proposals, Jaurès flatly turned down any idea of a formal revival of the parliamentary bloc. Such a step, he argued, would involve an intolerable 'confusion of programmes'. He nevertheless offered the Radicals his loyal cooperation if they seriously attempted to implement a progressive programme; 'seriously' being understood by the SFIO as all the party's deputies being obliged to 'reject, break and castigate' the three-year law.[32] However, a few days later when Caillaux's declaration of principle had been published, Jaurès moderated his position on a number of important points. For example, he now conceded that if the Radical Party were to come to power, the SFIO would be satisfied if the new government immediately passed new legislation on army reorganisation with the express purpose of reducing military service to two years 'at a given point in time'. The Socialists would continue to support the principle of a militia but would not expect the Radical Party to follow their example.[33] In justification of his concession to the Radicals, Jaurès stated that the internal unity of the Radical Party was in the interest of all true democrats, since the SFIO alone was not strong enough to block the path of reaction, and carry through social and political progress.[34] Like Caillaux, the socialist leader was evidently intent not to let the *Trois Ans* stand in the way of a greater degree of internal unity within the Radical Party. This compromise on the defence issue was to play a significant role in later internal French developments, since it provided the Radicals with the opportunity of uniting on the basis of Caillaux's proposals without having to cut off their links with the far Left.

The Pau congress (16–19 October 1913) was initially dominated by the dispute between the supporters of Combes and Caillaux. However, from the very first session, it was clear that the defeat of the pro-Combes faction was in the offing when the party's vice-chairman, Debierre, spoke out against the anti-republican right-wing Barthou government and called for a return to the old radical slogan, 'No enemies on the Left!', and a revival of the bloc. The delegates' reaction to this speech illustrated that the idea of a left-wing bloc along with the Socialists was supported only by a minority, though a vociferous one.[35] Combes's approach, which laid full emphasis on organisational matters and failed to come up with a definite programme for left-wing policy, had misfired. Combes underestimated the fact that, in view of the current problems on the domestic scene, there was great demand within the party for a redefinition of its ideological standpoint. Realising this, Debierre withdrew as a candidate for the party chairmanship. A heated debate between the supporters of an out-and-out left-wing republican programme and the pro-Caillaux faction, in favour of mild reforms, now followed.

Camille Pelletan,[36] chairman of the party executive committee and a prominent supporter of doctrinaire radicalism, now stood against Caillaux for the party chairmanship. With regard to party organisation and strict party discipline, Pelletan believed that only politicians who were actually party members and followed the party whip should be fielded as official party candidates. Members would have to endorse the minimum programme, including the following points: no cooperation whatsoever with the Right, defence of the anti-clerical Republic, the restoration of the 1905 conscription law, progressive income tax with obligatory declaration of income, and a capital tax to cover the costs of rearmament.

Whereas Pelletan's points on anti-clericalism and tax reform were uncontroversial, the question of finding a definition for the Right led to such a heated debate that at one point the congress was in danger of breaking up. What Pelletan actually meant by urging the Radicals to disassociate themselves from the Right became clear when he supported a motion in favour of an emphatic rejection of Poincaré's nationalistic and anti-parliamentary 'personal policy'. Caillaux, however, succeeded in blocking the motion, thus warding off an even deeper rift within the party.[37]

The most important item on the Pau agenda was the position of the Radical Party on the three-year law. Pelletan and the left wing rather drastically demanded a return to the two-year law. No vote was taken on this extreme demand—it was submitted for further examination to a specially convened committee, where it was completely reformulated. The text finally passed by the plenary assembly without debate (!) ran as follows: 'Congress, firmly attached to the principle of the 1905 law, declares the following priorities of its programme: organisation of the reserves, military preparation of the young and a return to the two-year law.'

Although this was undoubtedly a clear-cut statement in favour of the principle of a republican conscription law and a nation in arms, care was taken not to classify the three-year law as reactionary or to demand that it should be instantly repealed. Even radical deputies convinced of the momentary need to extend military service could subscribe to this formula with a clear conscience, since it could be interpreted—as was in fact later the case—that the 1905 law would be reintroduced only after the implementation of a series of preparatory and fundamental reforms in the organisation of the army. The majority of the delegates were evidently anxious that the public might interpret this resolution as a rejection of the three-year law. How else can it be explained why this resolution was not included in the minimum programme? In accordance with Caillaux's statement before the congress, it was simply stated in the programme that the defence of the Republic and the security of national defence were both of equal importance. The Radical Party would ensure that the army would be organised so that 'at the first sign' the whole nation could rise to defend *la patrie*. Alongside Caillaux's general statements—repeated virtually word for word—the minimum programme also outlined the short-term army reforms the Radicals deemed necessary. The most important of these were as follows:

1. Military preparation for the young.

2. A bill on the role of the reserve units in the event of a war (this point had not been clarified in the three-year law).
3. Reform of the high command.
4. Reorganisation of the officer corps.

All these reforms were aimed at finally applying the principle of the nation in arms in order to reduce the length of regular military service. It is interesting that, unlike the congress resolution, the minimum programme was not committed to a return to the two-year law. The following explanatory note was added to the programme in order to prevent the resumption of the inner-party debate on the *Trois Ans*: 'All Republicans, whether for or against the new law, had agreed that German rearmament had forced France into making an "equivalent sacrifice". All honourable Republicans who had voted for the *Loi de Trois Ans* had done so only in the belief that this law was merely a stopgap measure necessary to ward off the acute danger from Germany. [The note concluded] that they were nevertheless convinced that this additional strain on the population would have to be reduced as soon as possible by the implementation of fundamental military reforms.' The Radical Party had therefore succeeded in maintaining a certain leeway for the future. A radical government would not have its hands completely tied.

The 'offensive' dimensions of the party manifesto and the 'minimum programme' lay in their insistence on the wide-ranging income tax reforms stipulated in Caillaux's bill passed by the Chamber in 1909, naturally an essential point of Caillaux's speeches at the congress. A resolution drafted by Malvy, then chairman of the parliamentary committee on financial legislation, was unanimously adopted and added to the minimum programme without amendment. This resolution demanded the introduction of a general income tax, the essential principles of which were progressive taxation and compulsory declaration of income. In addition to this 'promise of great reform which had not been kept', the introduction of a capital tax was demanded, based on the same principles, to cover annual military expenditure estimated at 400 million francs. It was also decided that in future each deputy of the party would not only have to commit himself to the party line by signing the minimum programme, but would have to be a member of one of the party's grass-roots organisations. A resolution passed in accordance with Combes's express wishes went even further. All the party's deputies were to register in one exclusively authorised parliamentary group to be established in the form of a Radical Party *groupe unique* or a *groupe unifié* by 31 December 1913.

These organisational reforms were unprecedented in the history of the French bourgeois parties. Hitherto the principle of the parliamentary parties strictly adhering to the party whip had been applied only on the far Left and to a certain extent by the Catholic Right (ALP). It was only after Caillaux had succeeded in bringing down the Barthou government a month after the congress that the public became aware of this new dimension to radicalism. Directly after the conference it was generally assumed that the unification would not survive for very long, since latent tension on the three-year question persisted and it was generally felt that radicalism stood to forfeit its parliamentary strength on account of the new organisational constraints.[38]

In which direction was the French political scene now to move? This basically depended on the social consequences of the suspension of internal politics as a result of the pre-eminence of national defence. Statements from conservative groups (in Parliament, economic circles and public opinion) showed no readiness to grant social reforms to compensate for the 'three-year' sacrifice demanded of the people.[39] On the other hand, there could be no doubt that the SFIO was determined to concentrate the 1914 election campaign on the *Trois Ans* and to project the Conservatives' intransigence as evidence that the law was inherently reactionary.

In contrast to the Socialists, the majority of the Radicals assembled at Pau did not link the new defence bill directly with reaction in domestic policy. The final resolution of the congress reaffirmed the Radicals' determination to ensure that the consensus on defence policy could not in future be used as an obstacle to social reforms on the basis of the conservative formula of the unity of all Frenchmen. Caillaux had already warned the government of this at the conclusion of the three-year debate in the Chamber. The opposition, he had stated, would prevent the reactionary domestic trends of recent years— above all the permanent cooperation between the government and the anti-republican Right—from taking root in the field of budgetary and credit policy. The congress ended with Caillaux's election as chairman of the party. The great majority in his favour (170 to 58) naturally strengthened his position as leader of the opposition. Therefore, despite the judicious formulae of the congress resolutions on the defence issue, the three-year law was still not out of danger. A police report at the time of the parliamentary financial debate expressed concern about the wave of public support for socialist agitation which might lead the Radicals to adopt a profile based on 'very progressive ideas'.[40]

The Financing of Rearmament and the Fall of Barthou

Late in May 1913, under pressure from the Left, Barthou had proposed a national tax to be levied on incomes above the 10,000 francs mark intended to cover the interest rates and redemption costs of the planned loan of around 1 billion francs.[41] At the end of June Barthou had told Parliament that, according to the government's plans, only 'the rich' would have to cover the costs of rearmament: 'If the government and Parliament demand this great sacrifice from the country and prolong military service, the ineluctable consequence of this sacrifice must be a tax on acquired wealth, a tax levied not on the poor classes of society . . . but on the comfortably off and rich taxpayers.'[42] This pledge, greeted by the Left with such tremendous applause that even Jaurès declared himself completely satisfied, failed to be followed up by a concrete bill. On 4 July all the Finance Minister could tell the budgetary committee was that the government intended to use the national tax to cover the costs of the loan which had to be raised to finance the construction of new barracks and army equipment. Similar measures were to be applied to cover the annual costs accruing from the three-year law.[43]

The budgetary committee was not satisfied with these vague comments. By a substantial majority (17 to 5), it demanded of the government to introduce a tax bill based on the supplementary tax approved by the Chamber in 1909 to cover the costs of the *Trois Ans*.[44] The government refused and on 15 July informed the budgetary committee that the principle of a national tax would be maintained, since it had not yet been stipulated which income brackets would be liable to the supplementary tax.[45] However, the total of about 100 million francs, the financial authorities' estimate of the maximum return from the national tax, would not nearly cover the total annual costs of some 220 million francs (70 million francs for interest and redemption of the loan, and a further 150 million francs for permanent expenditure accruing from the three-year law).[46] The government had extremely vague ideas on how the annual deficit of around 120 million francs could be covered. It had proposed an increase in the existing estate duty (43 million francs), hoping that the Senate would soon adopt the new income tax law passed by the Chamber in 1909, which would increase the returns from taxes on movable assets.[47]

The budgetary committee's response to these unsatisfactory proposals was rather unorthodox. Its spokesman, Noulens, was entrusted with drafting a bill based on the supplementary tax passed in 1909, to be levied on income over 10,000 francs, which along with a capital tax would yield a total of 200–220 million francs per year. Noulens's proposal, submitted only a few days later, contained a relatively high rate of progression—1 per cent to 7 per cent—on annual income of 10,000–500,000 francs.[48] Apart from this, the most significant element of Noulens's proposal was that compulsory declaration of income, stipulated in the 1909 Chamber bill, was introduced for the first time into French tax legislation.

On 22 July the committee on financial legislation, which had been asked for its expert opinion, came out in favour of the budgetary committee's proposals. This committee even went a step further and—against the wishes of the government, which continued to insist on a fundamental separation between its 'national' tax and income tax in general—supported a motion presented by Jacquier and Javal (Radicals), stipulating that the budgetary committee's bill should be incorporated into the financial bill for the 1914 budget.[49]

Thus the stage was set for a conflict between the government and the Chamber committees. Even the right-wing radical *La France* was convinced that the conflict would inevitably lead to the government's downfall. On account of the defence debate, deputies who were dubious about the rash introduction of the new tax system could not possibly fight against the 'currents of democratic trends'.[50] Jaurès pointed out to the Radicals that the outcome of this debate would leave its mark on French domestic politics for years to come. In particular, Radicals who had supported the government on the defence issue would now have to show whether 'their heart was still with the Left' or whether they wanted to help Barthou establish a socially conservative parliamentary majority.[51] Jaurès's warning was superfluous. Both radical parliamentary groups voted in favour of the proposals of the budgetary and financial committees by an overwhelming majority.[52]

Faced with this situation, the government's only alternative was to give in or sign its own death warrant. When Malvy, chairman of the committee on financial legislation, presented the Jacquier/Javal motion to Parliament on 24 July in the form of an interpellation, Barthou finally bowed before the storm. He not only accepted the principle of the budgetary committee's proposals, including compulsory declaration of income, but committed himself to presenting the Chamber with a bill to this effect directly after the autumn recess. If at the time of the debate on the 1914 budget the Senate had not yet adopted the general income tax pending since 1909, Barthou intended to include the governmental bill in the 1914 finance bill, providing that the Chamber gave him the go-ahead to do so.[53]

However, when the government presented the 1914 draft budget at the beginning of the special parliamentary session early in November, it transpired that Barthou was not seriously intending to keep his promise. The draft budget stipulated that the 'exceptional' expenditure for the construction of barracks, and so forth, and for the new army equipment, should be transferred to the regular budget. This expenditure, estimated at some 900 million francs, was to be financed by a loan, the terms of which were to be presented a few days later. A rough estimate of expected state returns in the financial year 1914 left the overall budget of 5.4 billion francs with an initial deficit of 794 million francs, 327 million of which resulted from the permanent annual costs accruing from the three-year law. The shortfall in the budget was to be offset as follows: 100 million francs were to be taken from the reserves from the 1912 budgetary surplus; a further 403 million francs, originally earmarked for the appeasement of Morocco, were to be transferred; this heading was to be carried over to the planned loan which was now to be increased to a total of 1.3 billion francs. The remaining deficit was to be covered by an increase of taxes and duties amounting to a total of 288 million francs.

These measures were evidently not in accordance with the repeated promise that 'the rich' would have to bear the financial brunt of the three-year law, even if the property-owning classes would also have to contribute to the covering of the outstanding deficit of 288 million francs. The sum of 158 million francs was to be raised on the basis of a minor increase in direct taxation and an increase of duties (e.g. on stock exchange transactions), but a further 128 million francs were to be raised from additional excise (above all on wine, beer, and domestic lighting).[54] Although the draft budget contained a series of minor concessions, this did not hide the fact that it was fundamentally conservative. Moreover, a few days later the government published details of the proposed loan of 1.3 billion francs which, as we have already seen, was to cover the 'exceptional' expenditure resulting from the *Loi de Trois Ans* and the costs for the appeasement of Morocco which had been deleted from the budget. Open confrontation between the government and Caillaux at the head of the Radicals who supported the Pau programme was now inevitable: the proposed loan went completely against the grain of the 1909 tax reform package, not yet ratified by the Senate. Article 3 of the draft loan stipulated that, henceforth, all French state loans must include a clause whereby the bonds would retain the same immunities (especially exemption from tax and seizure) applicable under present tax legislation.[55] It had been known since mid-May that, if a loan were raised, the government was planning to guarantee the immunity of the bonds by contract;[56] but there had never been any question of this loan on behalf of national defence being used to block a key aspect of the 1909 tax reform—that is, the taxation of all movable assets.

Caillaux's reaction was clear and logical, as *Le Temps* observed.[57] He immediately demanded the deletion of Article 3 and announced an interpellation.[58] The debate on the loan thus led to the first major confrontation between the government and the Radicals, whose position had been strengthened following the congress of Pau. It now remained to be seen whether the unification of the Radicals had really changed fundamentally the balance of power within Parliament. Caillaux could be sure of the Socialists' support in his fight against the government's 'provocation'.[59] And, strangely enough, he was also supported by the 'rallied' Catholics, who were absolutely opposed to a loan for national defence being used to relieve the budget.[60] The principle of tax exemption for state loans was also rejected by a great number of moderate deputies. Speaking on behalf of a group of deputies to the left of centre who had not joined the united Radicals, the well-known financial expert Théodore Reinach declared that his group would not tolerate a 'canonisation' of government loans. Even the centrist *Entente démocratique et sociale*, formed in June, was against the government on this issue.[61]

It is interesting to note that Poincaré, whom historians have frequently classified as extremely conservative in financial matters,[62] showed no sympathy for Barthou's insistence on tax exemption for state loans. When this question was discussed in cabinet and the principle of exemption adopted, despite Poincaré's objections (!), Poincaré pointed out to Barthou that there was no justification for this decision and that the government was moreover in danger of losing its majority in Parliament.[63] The only reason Poincaré could find to explain why Barthou was seeking confrontation in this way was that the Premier was deliberately trying to provoke his own downfall so that he could then withdraw from politics after a 'happy ministry' and devote his efforts to his candidature for the *Académie Française*.[64] Poincaré's assumption was in fact proved wrong. In the coming months Barthou, along with Briand, became the leader of an anti-Caillaux *rassemblement* of moderates and conservatives under the banner of the three-year law.[65]

Barthou's draft loan and the principle of tax exemption, both inseparably linked, can be seen as an attempt to create a basis for a new majority following the collapse of the heterogeneous majority for national defence, which had been provoked by the efforts of leading Centre groups not to break off links with the Radical Party, whose appeal to moderate Republicans had increased since the congress of Pau. This was due to the fact that the Pau resolution on the three-year law had not cut off the Radicals from the Centre. At the same time it was to be expected that the reorganisation of the Radical Party—the formation of a *groupe unifié*, the drafting of a minimum programme and the nomination and support only of candidates who had signed this programme—would leave its mark on the results of the 1914 elections. The emergence of the party as a power factor in its own right could also be of great significance to deputies who had not joined the unified Radicals but nevertheless wanted to campaign with the left-wing republican ticket. Particularly in the second ballot, support from a large and well-organised party was bound to offer a candidate a greater prospect of success than the then predominant system of arrangements made among the local electoral committees.

An important sign that moderate Republicans were veering towards the Left was the rebuff received by the *Alliance République Démocratique* from the *Entente démocratique et sociale*, a parliamentary group comprising some 100 deputies from mainly Centre groups who supported Barthou and the three-year law. A letter from Maginot, chairman of the *Entente*, to the chairman of the ARD, was published in all the leading newspapers. In his letter Maginot refuted any attempt to use patriotism and the *Loi de Trois Ans* as a basis for an amalgamation of republican and reactionary elements in an amorphous and anti-radical coalition. The ARD was gradually drifting into a policy along these lines and, 'in the interests of political perspicuity', this trend had to be countered by the preservation of the old 'party classification'.[66] Briand's *La Petite République* adopted Maginot's statement.[67] Even Dupuy, proprietor and editor of the largest Paris daily, *Le Petit Parisien*, generally politically neutral, published a largely acclaimed manifesto calling for a return to the concentration of left-wing and moderate republican groups under the old slogan of resistance to revolution and reaction.[68]

Barthou now tried to steer against this new undercurrent in domestic politics. He increased the loan for the relief of the budget to 1.3 billion francs, linked it to tax immunity for all future government loans, and called for a vote of confidence on the whole package. The first part of this overall strategy could lead to a new split within the ranks of the left-wing Republicans, since opinion was divided on this point. On the one hand, it was felt that the crisis of public finances as a result of rearmament should be exploited in order to push through the new taxation system. On the other hand, liberal Republicans who advocated the reorganisation of the tax system in principle nevertheless hoped that the Senate would delete a number of the provisions of the 1909 Chamber bill regarded as too rigorous, 'statist' or inquisitional. This liberal lobby also hoped that the planned loan would give fresh impetus to trade and industry without strengthening state bureaucracy.[69] The second part of the proposal—immunity—clearly reflected the demands of the extreme conservative groups which welcomed the clause on immunity as a decisive incursion into the whole of the new tax system. These groups advanced the 'national' argument that the loan for national defence would be doomed to failure if subject to taxation, and would be sure to induce an even greater flight of capital. The commentary of the progressive *La Liberté* was exemplary of this line of thought. If the loan project were to fail, France would be humiliated in the eyes of the whole world, since financial power had always been an essential factor of her strength and influence on the international scene: 'To prejudice this power ... would be to weaken national defence while there is a threat of invasion.'[70]

Barthou's attempt to choose a formula to appeal to both liberal and conservative interests, thereby setting up a new parliamentary majority distinct from the Left on the basis of social issues, came to grief. Article 3 of the government's proposal, stipulating the immunity of future state loans, failed to gain a majority in Parliament, and Barthou resigned. The result of the ballot—263 votes to 290 [71]—was all the more significant in that the Catholic Right had been solidly behind the government, so that the 290 votes cast against Barthou represented a united majority of the Left. Almost seventy deputies from the Centre, led by Théodore Reinach, who wanted to voice their basic approval of tax reform, voted along with the SFIO and the *radicaux unifiés*.[72] This means that within the Centre there was substantial support for Caillaux when, as undisputed leader of the Left in the debate, he accused the government of having become 'the accomplice of the egoism and fears of the bourgeoisie' and retorted:

I profoundly hope that the bourgeoisie which for one hundred and fifty years has played such a useful role in the great days of our history, knowing when it was time to make the necessary concessions, will not be overcome by the spell of dizziness which swept over the privileged classes at the end of the 18th century. The inertia of the satisfied is no formula for democratic government.[73]

According to the constitution, the President had sole responsibility for the choice of Premier. This put Poincaré in a quandary after the fall of the Barthou government. Poincaré's own premiership in 1912, his election as President of the Republic and the formation of the Briand and Barthou cabinets in the spring of 1913[74] had been possible only because of the disintegration of the traditional parliamentary majorities which resulted from the pre-eminence given to foreign policy since the Agadir crisis. Now the tables had been turned. A parliamentary majority, with the United Radicals led by Caillaux at its core, and to all appearances relatively homogeneous, had now been formed on a purely domestic issue. Moreover, this majority posed a threat to the continuity of Poincaré's foreign policy. Although it had been formed on the specific issue of the tax question and lacked a common stance on the three-year law, it could nevertheless be assumed that the vast majority of the deputies in this group regarded the defence bill as at best a provisional shelter against a German attack and not as an essential element of French alliance policy.

Poincaré was in principle prepared to take account of the left-wing orientation of the Chamber in forming a new cabinet.[75] But he bluntly refused to entrust Caillaux with the reins of government, although, as Poincaré himself later admitted, this would have been quite warranted on account of the key role Caillaux had played in the tax debate.[76] However, since Caillaux had emerged as the spokesman of the opposition to the three-year law, Poincaré considered it impossible to appoint him as Premier, believing that such a step would jeopardise French relations with her allies and other friendly powers.[77] In a private discussion with the President, Caillaux protested against this assumption, which Poincaré had candidly admitted, but went on to declare with temporising irony that he would respect the President's decision and was prepared to support any left-wing cabinet Poincaré cared to choose.[78]

What was the real significance of the President's traditional prerogative in the wake of recent events? What was the real scope of a president faced with a Chamber tending towards the Left, undoubtedly as the result of the unification of the Radicals? The conservative press openly urged Poincaré to steer against the Radicals, arguing that the Chamber's decision against Barthou jeopardised the future of the three-year law and represented an attack on the credit of France. All the achievements of recent years, the moral and national revival of France after a period of radical domination, had been called into question by the latest developments.[79] However, these prophecies of doom offered no solution to Poincaré's dilemma—how to form a stable cabinet in open opposition to the Radicals.

Poincaré's first attempt to get the better of the situation was to set up a cabinet of republican 'concentration'. This was aimed at taking account of the Chamber's tendency towards the Left while at the same time guaranteeing the continuity of French foreign policy and the three-year law. At first it seemed that this combination would work. The chairmen of the Chamber and Senate budgetary and finance committees advised the President that there would be a parliamentary majority in favour of a moderate government if it were to guarantee the principle of taxation of future loans.[80]

Under this proviso Poincaré entrusted the moderate Senator Ribot with the task of forming a cabinet. However, Ribot's endeavours to win the support of leading Radicals were thwarted by their 'excessive' demands,[81] and so the Senator stood down. Poincaré now tried to form a cabinet with a broad republican union, this time without the help of a leading member of the Radical Party. His choice fell on Senator Jean Dupuy, editor of *Le Petit Parisien*, who had just published a manifesto endorsing the idea of a concentration of radical and moderate Republicans 'against revolution and reaction'.[82] However, like his predecessor Ribot, Dupuy also had to admit defeat when all the influential radical politicians made it quite clear that, regardless of a possible agreement on individual issues, they would agree to accept portfolios only in a cabinet chaired by a member of their own party.[83]

Poincaré's hands were now tied and he was compelled to give in, at least partly, to a political force which was no longer purely inter-parliamentary in origin but sprang from a hitherto unknown degree of party discipline. Persevering in his running fight, he refused to put the reins of government into Caillaux's hands and instead turned to another radical politician, Gaston Doumergue. But in the final analysis Poincaré could not prevent Doumergue from appointing Caillaux as Finance Minister, and of filling six out of ten cabinet posts with members of the Radical Party and the remaining seats with politicians from the left of centre.[84] To the contemporary observer it was obvious that the *éminence grise* in this government would be Caillaux, the champion of a tax policy which had led to the fall of Barthou and chairman of both the United Radical Party and its parliamentary group.

The formation of a cabinet with a radical majority, with Caillaux as its real leader, was certainly a shattering defeat for Poincaré. Apart from being a blow to his personal pride,[85] this new situation could have long-term structural consequences. This first manifestation of party discipline among the Radicals was not only unprecedented in the history of French parliamentarianism; it was a phenomenon which could restrict the freedom the President had enjoyed so far—and this applied in particular to the Poincaristic independence of the executive from Parliament—and make government on the basis of hetero-geneous majorities of 'national defence' impossible. The nationalist Right was most concerned about this new phenomenon, described by Jaurès as a 'new fact' and by *Le Radical* as a 'political renaissance'.[86] *Le Gaulois* bluntly compared Poincaré's acquiescence to the Radicals with the 'desecration of a temple with the help of the priest',[87] an interpretation which largely reflected Poincaré's own assessment of the situation. On the anniversary of his election as President he noted bitterly in his diary: 'A year has passed! . . . the latest cabinet crisis has broken the charm and shattered the national movement.'[88] Another comment recorded in his diary a month later shows that this was more than a moment's vexation: 'And what about today? The national movement has been partially halted, disappointment upon disappointment with clouds hanging over the future.'[89]

Poincaré blamed this turn of the tide on 'persistent subversion' against the three-year law and governmental authority.[90] This pessimistic and realistic assessment of the new domestic scenario explains Poincaré's cool and essentially hostile attitude towards the new government, above all towards Caillaux.[91] Nevertheless, this new informal, but *de facto* restriction of Poincaré's authority, did not mean that the Doumergue/Caillaux government enjoyed the support of a coherent parliamentary majority. Apart from the support of the united group of Radicals, Caillaux was dependent on the backing, not only of the SFIO, but of at least a number of the left-wing Republicans who had not signed the Pau programme.[92] And even this majority of the Left had only one objective in common: the implementation of tax reforms. Moreover, attempts to consolidate this majority any further would come up against the brick wall of the three-year law, for Poincaré had encumbered the new cabinet with a heavy burden. Extending his constitutional prerogatives as far as he could, the President had entrusted Doumergue with the task of forming a cabinet on the condition that the defence bill would remain unaltered: 'The condition I've put to him [Doumergue] is the maintenance of the three-year law and our foreign policy.'[93] Doumergue had had 'no difficulty'[94] in accepting this condition, for, although originally he had been opposed to the 'nationalistic dogma' of the *Trois Ans* during the defence debate,[95] he was nevertheless one of the many radical deputies who had finally voted in favour of the governmental bill.

In these circumstances, could the Pau programme be adopted as the programme of the new government? In a certain sense the fall of the Barthou government had taken place too soon for the Radical Party. Although the Pau resolution and minimum programme on the three-year law had served as a compromise to secure the inner cohesion of the party, the united Radicals had not yet become the obviously predominant force within Parliament. The Socialists had openly declared their readiness to support the government—on one condition: that the Pau resolution on the *Trois Ans* be part and parcel of the government's programme. Jaurès interpreted this as the duty of the government to announce clearly a return to the two-year law and make energetic if gradual steps in this direction.[96] Had the government respected this wish and given such a wide interpretation to the content of the Pau programme, the unification of the Radicals would have been promptly nipped in the bud.

In the light of these problems it was in Caillaux's interest to avoid a fresh outbreak of the *Trois Ans* controversy and at the same time to pursue a consistent left-wing tax policy. By so doing he hoped that the Socialists would continue to support the government despite the bypassing of the three-year law. But since parliamentary elections were imminent, his main concern was to steer republicanism clear of internal wrangling and lead the burgeoning Radical Party into the 1914 elections as the governmental party.[97]

Doumergue's governmental declaration to the Chamber on 11 December[98] reflected this wait-and-see attitude. The new Premier declared that it was not his intention to implement a wide-ranging programme so soon before the elections, but rather to let the electorate decide on the issue of electoral reform which had caused a split in the republican ranks before the debate on the three-year law.[99] Doumergue's statement on the *Trois Ans*, awaited with some suspense, was in a similar vein:

> Gentlemen, none of you expects us to reopen the debate on the military bill adopted recently. It is the law and we intend to apply it loyally. It is also our intention to devote our attention to a series of measures in order to bring the defensive strength of the nation to a maximum, regardless of the length of military service.

This statement had the desired effect: applause from the Left and the Centre. Despite a number of interpellations from both the Socialist and non-Radical Republican benches, Doumergue obstinately evaded the fundamental issue of whether or not the government would adopt the Pau resolution.[100] In fact the governmental declaration gave no indication of what the 'loyal application' of the three-year law actually meant. Was the law now simply regarded as a provisional measure along the lines of the Pau resolution? Objectively there was only one contradiction between the governmental declaration and the Pau resolution: the statement that measures to improve the defensive strength of the army were to be applied regardless of the length of regular military service. Following a series of interpellations, Doumergue added the following nuance: 'What I said . . . was that the length of military service is not a dogma. But the law is the law.' The only 'dogma' the government accepted unconditionally was the 'necessity to defend *la patrie*'.[101]

Doumergue was in contrast much more precise on matters of financial policy. The government, he said, would completely revise the draft budget of its predecessors and present new bills to cover the exceptional expenditure for national defence.[102] Caillaux continued that Barthou's idea of a 1.3 billion francs' loan had been abandoned. The new government would distribute the costs of national defence over a very limited number of annual budgets. He added that the government could not yet be absolutely precise with regard to the financial transactions to be carried out. Only following examinations of Barthou's estimates on the level of 'exceptional expenditure' for the three-year law could it be decided whether it would be appropriate to raise a loan or earmark the total under this heading. In any case, continued the new Finance Minister, the government was determined to cover either all the costs accruing from the three-year law, or at least the interest and redemption costs of a potential loan, with a tax on acquired wealth.[103] Caillaux's speech was applauded by the far Left and the Left, while a mood of discontent hung over the Centre on account of the withdrawal of the loan. Nevertheless, this did not prevent a substantial majority of 302 votes to 141 in support of the governmental declaration. This represented a particularly strong majority, since, dissatisfied with Doumergue's vagueness on the *Trois Ans* issue, the Socialists had abstained, although they were prepared to accept Caillaux's finance policy. Despite the uncertainty surrounding the future of the three-year law, there was no direct threat to the Doumergue/Caillaux government. In the United Radical Party the government had a degree of organisational and propagandist support beyond the framework of Parliament which could prove to be crucial so soon before elections. This was a new and impressive phenomenon. As long as there was no counterbalance to this force, even left-wing deputies who had not joined the group would be advised to tread with caution.

The liberal Centre was surprised and mistrustful of this new phenomenon. Briand's *La Petite République* bemoaned the fact that under Caillaux's leadership the Radical Party had become a 'congregation of the Index', sabotaging all efforts towards a reconciliation between left-wing and moderate Republicans in Parliament and therefore undermining 'the normal functioning of the parliamentary system'. If the bourgeois Centre was not to be crushed by this new force it, too, would have to set up a party structure to meet the challenge from the Radical Party. This anti-radical 'catch-all' movement began to take shape at the end of 1913 when Briand initiated the foundation of the *Fédération des Gauches* (FDG).

The Foundation of the *Fédération des Gauches* and the Front against Caillaux

Briand's famous policy speech at St Étienne on 21 December 1913 marks the birth of the *Fédération des Gauches*. This was Briand's first public appearance since the fall of his government in March 1913 and his speech attracted great public interest. At the time of Doumergue's governmental declaration Briand had already announced his intention to create a counterbalance to the United Radicals whose sole *raison d'être*, he had maintained, was will to power.[104] It became apparent that a new party was in fact to be founded when a number of leading deputies of the non-radical Centre, including members of Barthou's cabinet, announced an inaugural meeting of a new organisation 'with a view to the forthcoming legislative elections' on 22 December.[105] Briand described the political stance and aims of this organisation in an interview: 'We want to set up a new party, a federation of Republicans covering a broader spectrum than the *Alliance Démocratique*. . . . The aim of this party will be the implementation of the political ideas I outlined . . . in my speech at St Étienne.'[106]

La Petite République, presumably assisted by Briand himself, expounded on this very general statement on the position of the new formation within the party political spectrum. Briand was addressing all the Republicans who had not joined forces with the United Radicals and aimed at the creation of a united front, ranging from the *républicain-socialistes* to the *progressistes*. The common objective of this new formation was to be the realignment of the Republic in accordance with 'social progress'.[107] The question was how to draw up a programme acceptable to both the *républicain-socialistes*, to the Left of the Radicals on specific social issues, and the extremely conservative *progressistes*. Briand's St Étienne speech, regarded as the 'statutes' of the new party, seemed to provide the answer.[108]

The leitmotiv of Briand's speech was his concern about the structural repercussions the unification of the Radical Party was liable to have on French politics. The principle of the party whip and the commitment of all radical deputies to the minimum programme were likely to burst the seams of the established bourgeois and liberal parliamentary system and posed a particular threat to government by an inner-parliamentary oligarchy.[109] Briand saw the Radicals' demand for party discipline as an attack on the entire republican system. The United Radicals, he said, wanted to replace the representative system, based on the 'freedom' of the individual deputy, by the 'anonymous tyranny' of demagogically controlled 'powerless citizens without a mandate'. It was essential, Briand went on, to organise the resistance of all clear-sighted Republicans to this movement without making the same mistake of introducing 'tight excommunicative' discipline. This was the only way Parliament could uphold its political sovereignty, imperative for the peaceful development of the Republic. In view in particular of the forthcoming elections, the aim of the union of responsible Republicans, he said, was to present the electorate with a programme of 'decided republicanism' to prevent 'certain petty ideals' from being exploited for party political purposes by cynical demagogues.

In Briand's eyes the Pau resolution on the three-year law was typical of this demagogic ideology which endangered both the interests of *la patrie* and the stability of republican institutions. Even the Doumergue government which relied on this group had not been able to comply with the United Radicals' demagogic insistence on the 1905 conscription law in its governmental declaration. The pressure of governmental responsibility, he maintained, had shown that this demand, appealing only to the egoism of the electorate, was absolutely unwarranted— which would nevertheless not prevent the demagogues from making the repeal of the three-year law the linchpin of their 1914 election manifesto. As an organisation of 'authentic Republicans', the FDG must keep the electorate aware of the 'lasting' and 'sanctified' interests of *la patrie*, and expected no more from its deputies than the implementation of these interests.

Briand's comments on the three-year law reflect a weakness which characterised the dilemma of the political doctrine of the *Fédération des Gauches* from the very outset. In this case the anti-radical *rassemblement* could not simply fall back on the traditional and demagogic *attaque brusquée* ideology, since the Pau resolutions on military policy were based on the assumption that German armament posed a real threat to French security. Following the long public and inner-party debate, a peremptory identification of the three-year law with national defence could hardly be substantiated from the point of view of domestic politics. If Briand were to avoid shutting the door of the FDG to left-wing Republicans who had rejected the Pau compromise formula from the very outset on the grounds that it concentrated excessively on home affairs, he would have to come up with more than the original simplistic justification for the *Trois Ans*. But if the *attaque brusquée* ideology was not a sufficient platform for a decided anti-radical front, what exactly were the 'lasting' and 'sanctified' interests of *la patrie* which, according to Briand, were threatened by the United Radicals' aspirations to power? Briand's St Étienne speech introduced

a new element into the three-year debate. The international aspect of
the arms race was brought before the public for the first time, albeit to
only a limited degree. Briand did not justify the *Loi de Trois Ans* with
the traditional argument that German rearmament was an indication of
aggressive intentions, but maintained that the real reason for the arms
race in recent years had been the Caillaux government's abortive
policy on Morocco in 1911:

> Agadir was one of the consequences of this policy; another was the military
> conquest of Morocco; others were to follow. The military conquest of
> Morocco involved Italy in Tripolitania. With Italy in Tripolitania and
> Turkey weakened, the war in the Balkans was unleashed. New international
> battle formations were created and Germany strengthened her military
> force. Meanwhile we were forced to reduce our own [military capacity] by
> sending fresh troops to Morocco to sustain the conquest. Thus danger is
> growing, the European horizon is overshadowed with clouds, everyone is
> anxious. And to sustain this conquest we have to hold back 60,000 soldiers
> there while our army at home is weakened accordingly.

It is striking that this general account of the overall international
background to the three-year law included no reference to the immediate reason for the introduction of the bill—that is, the efforts to
strengthen the Franco-Russian alliance. This shows that the function
of the defence bill within the framework of Poincaré's foreign policy
of strength remained taboo. On these grounds Briand's reasoning was
inconsistent, since it shed no light whatsoever on the 'sanctified' and
'lasting' interests of France. His assessment of Caillaux's foreign policy
in 1911 and its alleged consequences was extremely critical, yet he
could not offer any suggestions as to a positive doctrine for French
foreign policy.

The fact that Briand's line of argument finally ended up with the
stereotype of national defence is indicative of the pitfalls inherent in
the government's policy of constantly reducing the implications of the
three-year law in the fields of foreign and military policy to the
attaque brusquée. Briand therefore had to retract somewhat on his
anti-demagogic approach. Following his initial assertation that only
the *Trois Ans* could guarantee French independence and security, he
now conceded that it was no one's intention to perpetuate the law and
that it would have to be maintained only 'for as long as the conditions
obtain which made it indispensable'.

Objectively there is certainly a fundamental difference between this
statement and the position of the Radicals. At the Pau congress the
Radicals had agreed, and this was reflected in Doumergue's governmental declaration, that the 1905 law could be reintroduced only if a

series of reorganisational measures were implemented in order to strengthen the army's defensive capacity to eliminate the threat of an *attaque brusquée*. While the Radicals ignored the overall framework of foreign policy, strong diplomacy and the standing army, Briand apparently wanted to detach the *Loi de Trois Ans* from domestic policy by referring to the 'circumstances' in foreign policy. However, as we have seen, he was not in a position to expound on these circumstances in greater detail. But, given that the public debate had been almost exclusively based on the threat of an *attaque brusquée*, Briand and the Radicals seemed to be following virtually the same line of argument. Owing to this ambiguity with regard to the actual meaning of the word 'circumstances', the dividing line between the Radicals and Briand's supporters was often blurred in the course of the 1914 election campaign. As a result of this confusion, on the one hand, and the organisation's anti-radical stance, on the other, the public tended to regard the FDG as an anti-Pau movement based purely on considerations of domestic policy.[110]

This impression is substantiated by Briand's St Étienne speech, which was absolutely anti-radical from the social point of view, despite the fact that his political ideas were not inherently conservative. Briand's sympathies lay in the direction of a Republic guided by national and liberal values, with a degree of social progressiveness far removed from demagogic and collectivist ideas. He was in favour of promoting labour organisations—for example, by giving legal status to collective agreements and extending the syndicates' property rights so as to establish 'social appeasement' in France as a basis for confidence in the future. The organisation of labour would enable modern-day republicanism to bury the ideological hatchet of the past. No longer requiring hate as a criterion for its purity, it could be endowed with the spirit of national solidarity beyond the dividing lines between confronting political ideas. This would augment the readiness of all Frenchmen to stand together in their country's hour of need on a firmer, more positive, basis.

It is difficult to assess whether Briand's vision of a Republic blessed with internal peace at home, and therefore in a position to conduct a dynamic foreign policy, meant more than an attempt to prolong the consensus of national defence which had become rather fragile in view of the tax debate. In any case, this ideological aspect of social democracy was predominant. On the question of tax reform, at this time the only real touchstone of national solidarity and social justice, Briand evaded the issue by hurling criticism at Caillaux and accusing him of having only one aim in mind: to divide the country. Briand claimed that Caillaux's demagogic commitment to an absolute reorganisation of the tax system was in reality superfluous and unfeasible and aimed only at diverting the people's attention from realistic reforms: 'He shakes his fist at wealth but does so in such a threatening, confused and exaggerated manner that we have the right to ask whether it is really clenched against wealth or not rather to protect it.'

Briand's remarks, which culminated with the accusation that Caillaux was a 'demagogic plutocrat', marked the early stages of a smear campaign against Caillaux which was to become the main issue in the moderate and conservative press in the months to come. Barthou and Briand were the instigators of this campaign, which was to climax in the murder of the editor of *Le Figaro*, Calmette, by Caillaux's wife, and Caillaux's subsequent resignation.

So Briand's speech itself failed to provide a positive political programme as a basis for the foundation of a movement in support of the 'reconstruction of the Republic within the Republic'[111] beyond the narrow context of a handful of—albeit influential—deputies. At the inaugural meeting of the *Fédération des Gauches* on 26 December 1913 a resolution was passed calling for the establishment of party committees all over the country. Since in actual fact the 'founding fathers' were able to do no more than outline a party programme,[112] it was difficult to imagine this party becoming an organisational alternative to the United Radicals in the near future.

The large Paris newspapers gave an enthusiastic welcome to the foundation of the FDG. *Le Temps* declared its firm intention to back Briand 'with all our strength' and to defend the Republic from the assault of the demagogues. *La Petite République* encouraged its readers to take out a subscription to increase the newspaper's circulation to 300,000, so that it could really become a 'major propaganda instrument' on behalf of the *Fédération des Gauches* throughout France.[113] The proprietor and editor of *Le Petit Parisien*, Dupuy, was one of the founders of the party. Even *Le Matin*, the second largest Paris daily with a circulation of over a million, originally sympathetic towards Caillaux, changed sides.[114] Thus the newspapers which were the main representatives of moderate and conservative public opinion were behind Briand and his party. Although undoubtedly an advantage for the spreading of FDG propaganda, the support of the press was of limited value, since at this time there were virtually no national newspapers in France carrying public opinion beyond Paris. Therefore this factor did not provide a real substitute for local committees or similar structures.

The *Fédération des Gauches* was therefore initially characterised by an unclear political programme and inadequate organisational structures. This implied that Briand could not hope to gain a parliamentary majority and topple the 'hateful' Doumergue/Caillaux government, for the time being at least. Briand himself informed Poincaré that he did not intend to overthrow the government in the immediate future, a statement which the President interpreted as an indication that Briand was aware of the parliamentary difficulties this would have involved in the present situation.[115] Ribot, President of the Senate and one of the main opponents of Caillaux's tax reform, remarked to Poincaré with some concern that Briand would not be in a position to overthrow the cabinet, since his St Étienne speech had been 'too personal and too cutting'.[116]

Ribot's hope that the Doumergue/Caillaux government was exposing itself to 'converging fire' with its budgetary proposals was a precise interpretation of the newly emerging scenario. Regardless of Briand's political intentions, the FDG was becoming the partner and political spokesman of trade associations and lobbies whose antipathy towards Caillaux had a firmer basis[117] than Briand's personal dislike of Caillaux or concern for the stability of the traditional political institutions.

In its first commentary on the foundation of the *Fédération des Gauches*, *Le Temps*, correctly assessing the party's weak organisational basis, stated that these 'true Republicans' would have a chance of success in the 1914 elections only if they managed to secure strongholds in the provinces—for example, business associations with an organisational framework throughout the country, but still politically chaste.[118] The *Alliance Républicaine Démocratique*, hitherto the only extra-parliamentary reservoir for moderate Republicans and therefore to a certain extent the rival of the FDG, took *Le Temps*'s proposal a little further and declared that the *Fédération* should not set itself up as a new political party as such, but should instead work hand in hand with the legitimate political representatives of moderate republicanism— the ARD—in order to coordinate the propaganda and action of extra-parliamentary factions in the 1914 election campaign.[119]

The major business associations did indeed offer massive resistance to the government's tax proposals. On 12 December 1913 the largest of the French business associations' umbrella organisations, the *Comité Central d'Études et de Défense Fiscale* (CCEDF),[120] held a conference to examine the problems of the budgetary deficit. The *Comité* was convinced, in accordance with the general conservative doctrine, that statist mismanagement (nationalisation of the western railways, the excessively large civil service) was at the root of this problem, not the costs of national defence. The final resolution of this conference rejected new taxes violating citizens' equality as arbitrary and inquisitional and evoked the dangers of state monopolies as the expropriation of free enterprise. Even more significant than this usual conservative *cri de coeur* was the second part of the resolution in which the associations declared their intent 'to combat in any circumstances and in particular in the coming elections any programme liable to prejudice public credit and compromise the economic and financial strength of France'.[121]

Immediately after Caillaux's statement to Parliament that the new government had dropped its predecessors' plans for a loan, the CCEDF protested in an open letter to Caillaux, demanding that the loan be raised at once.[122] Soon afterwards the business associations backed up their decision actively to enter the election campaign by publishing an 'Economic Programme for the 1914 Elections' signed by forty business associations under the aegis of the CCEDF, the *Union des Intérêts Économiques* (UIE) and the *Confédération des Groupes Commerciaux et Industriels de France*.[123] This economic programme, which largely coincided with the CCEDF's demands, was to be presented to all the candidates in the 1914 elections, and only candidates who signed and publicly supported the manifesto were to be given propagandistic and financial support.[124]

This movement was an open declaration of war against Caillaux's government. It regarded itself as a 'rebellion' against a government about to push through an 'abhorrent' tax system which would endanger the life and soul of 'small and medium-sized property-owners'.[125] *Le Temps* heartily welcomed this merger of economic interests, which it heralded as the birth of a new party outside the framework of the traditional political formations, a party representing 'work and savings' which, beyond the confines of purely political bickering, understood the 'laws of the modern world' as follows:

> Employers, employees, wage-payers and wage-earners are aware of the common interests which bind them in the world economic order, as each is concerned with the other's prosperity, and the guarantee of everyone's prosperity is in the interests of all and will secure the freedom of everyone. Fiscal defence, social defence and national defence are organised for the wealth of our citizens and the power of *la patrie*.[126]

A comparison between this socially conservative concept of the political order and the content of Briand's speech at St Étienne highlights the latter's more liberal and national line of argument. Briand, for example, did not directly link national defence with the ideological harmonisation of antagonistic social interests. In fact this merger of extra-parliamentary interest groups contradicted his endeavours to stabilise the traditional parliamentary system and maintain the deputies' freedom from demagogic aspirations.

However, in the winter of 1913/14 the boundaries between conservative and liberal/anti-radical groups were obscured by the common front against Caillaux. On the same day as the publication of the
trade associations' economic programme, the *Fédération des Gauches*
also presented its party programme.[127] In an obvious attempt to woo
the support of the trade associations, the main point in the FDG programme now was that tax reforms should not contain any 'vexing'
measures liable to hinder the development of the 'nation's productive
forces'.[128] In a vein similar to the statements of conservatives during
the debate on the financing of the three-year law, the FDG manifesto
presented the free development of the productive forces, the military
strength of France and the *Loi de Trois Ans* as a whole, and maintained
that only the combination of these three elements was representative of
the nation's real strength. For this reason (!), it stated, the country
could not allow the defence law to be applied 'hesitantly, as would be
the case of a provisional measure'.

Briand's group had now given a positive interpretation to the
three-year law within the context of conservative financial policy. Its
initial postulate of a link between national strength and social appeasement, on the basis of a progressive social programme, had disappeared.

Thus, despite all Briand's assurances to the contrary, the *Fédération
des Gauches* had adopted a conservative image. In this light it could
hardly emerge as a reservoir for the liberal Centre and the non-united
Radicals and challenge the parliamentary strength of the Radicals. A
few months later, in the 1914 elections, it transpired that this interpretation of the three-year law as an integral part of a general concept of
power and social policy was not shared by either the electorate or the
deputies of the left-wing Republicans. The FDG was therefore later
forced to adjust its line and to readopt more or less the position
outlined by Briand at St Étienne—but only after successive parliamentary defeats. In the winter of 1913/14 Briand's catch-all movement seemed to have formed a united, socially conservative pro-three
years' front against Caillaux. Ironically, perhaps the main result of this
was that the Socialists, assuming that the Centre and the Right had
gained momentum, began to give greater support to the Doumergue/
Caillaux government than they would otherwise have considered
objectively expedient.[129]

CHAPTER 8

The Policy of the Doumergue/Caillaux Government and the Fall of Caillaux

The Struggle over Tax Reform

In the course of the parliamentary debate on Doumergue's governmental declaration in December 1913, Caillaux, in his capacity as Finance Minister, had announced that the new government had dropped Barthou's plans to raise a loan and would present its own draft bill as soon as Barthou's estimates on the 'permanent' and 'exceptional' costs of the *Loi de Trois Ans* had been reviewed.[1] This exercise was concluded in mid-January 1914. To everyone's surprise the new figures submitted by the War Minister, Noulens,[2] and Commander-in-Chief, Joffre, were considerably higher than the Barthou government's estimates. The 'exceptional' expenses were now estimated at 650 million francs—170 million francs more than the previous government's estimates.[3] On top of this came the enormous sum of 1.8 billion francs for a new armament programme (modernisation of the army, technical equipment for the navy and new fortifications).[4]

The tremendous increase in 'exceptional' costs was an ingenious political move, for it demonstrated beyond any doubt that the new government was seriously concerned with the strengthening of national defence. Without having had publicly to disown the three-year law, the government had conceded to the left-wing Republicans' demands that army reorganisation should not be limited to just the regular army. Moreover, the Socialists' protest against the new govern-

157

ment's unexpected militarism totally refuted the claim of the anti-radical Centre that the government was prepared to betray the inter-ests of national defence in favour of a coalition with the SFIO.[5] A further advantage of this voluntary increase in the overall rearmament costs was that Caillaux could carry out his plan to avoid taking any steps prior to the elections which might split his left-wing majority.[6] The total of 1.8 billion francs was so immense that the demands of many Radicals that the 'exceptional' expenditure be financed by special levies, as opposed to a loan, were now completely illusory. Caillaux could therefore give in to the demands of the Centre without exposing himself to opposition from the Left. On 15 January he informed the Chamber of his decision to cover the exceptional costs accruing from the defence bill by the raising of a loan. Caillaux's plans differed essentially from those of Barthou; it had in fact been this issue which had led to the fall of the Barthou government. Barthou had intended to use the loan not only to cover the costs of rearmament but to bridge the gap in the budget so as to avoid substantial increases in taxation.

Both the new government's policy on the question of the loan and the overall draft budget for the financial year 1914, submitted to the Chamber on 15 January, reflected its wish to steer clear of any fundamental disagreements between the left-wing and relatively mod-erate elements of the majority. With virtually no recourse to new taxation, Caillaux succeeded in reducing the initial deficit of 794 million francs in the Barthou government's draft budget to 168 million francs. The shortfall was to be covered by the issuing of short-term treasury bonds.[7] Caillaux won the support of the Left for his pragma-tic financial policy by making it clear that in future the capital market would not be used to balance the budget. Root-and-branch tax re-forms were to be prepared to bridge this gap in the future. The government's priority would be to introduce a capital tax which could boost state returns by a total of around 190 million francs per annum. If the tax reform package, pending in the Senate since 1909, could finally be implemented in 1915, the budget would be permanently balanced.

The government's determination to reform the tax system became apparent when, only a week later, Caillaux presented the Chamber with a draft bill on a capital tax to take effect from 1 January 1915.[8] Apart from bolstering the budget, the purpose of this tax was to sell the package of tax reform to its conservative opponents in public and in the Senate. Caillaux himself admitted that this tax would produce an 'unequal distribution of burdens'. Confirming that this was unavoid-able owing to the present tax system, he added ironically that the 'injustice' of capital incomes' being liable to much higher tax brackets than other forms of income would soon be eliminated. Once the Senate had adopted the tax reform package, which was imminent, this disparity would be removed and a uniform level of taxation be applied to all incomes.[9]

The proposal on capital tax linked to the package of tax reforms represented an open challenge to the Senate from the Doumergue/ Caillaux government. At the end of 1913 it had already become clear that the Senate was not going to adopt the tax reform passed by the Chamber in 1909 when, after five years of debate, the responsible Senate committee had presented an alternative proposal. Therefore the basis for the Senate discussions, when they reopened at the end of February 1914, would no longer be the text of the Chamber resolution of 1909 but the new proposal, named, after the spokesman of the Senate committee, the 'Aimond proposal'.[10]

The main stipulation of the 1909 Chamber bill had been that the four traditional forms of direct taxation—*les quatre vieilles*—applicable since the French Revolution, would be replaced by seven *cédules* covering the various forms of income on a uniform basis.[11] The bill had also stipulated a supplementary tax on overall incomes above 5,000 francs per annum. This supplementary tax which, according to Caillaux's estimates, would be applicable only to approximately 500,000 taxpayers, was the cornerstone of the entire reform. However, the Aimond proposal replaced this supplementary tax by a general income tax, with the purpose of spreading the burden as 'equally and justly' as possible over all 5 million taxpayers. The justification given for this fundamental amendment was that it would be unjust and detrimental to 'national unity' to make a small class of citizens the 'hostages' of a form of progress couched in 'abstract and absolute' terms. Instead, the Senate committee wanted to achieve the 'close solidarity' of all citizens as regards taxation.

Although a number of prominent public voices rejected the Aimond proposal on the grounds that it authorised the principle of obligatory declaration of income,[12] it was nevertheless first and foremost a 'direct challenge to Caillaux's tax policy'. [13] Caillaux accordingly called on the Senate to respect the essential guide-lines of the original 1909 Chamber bill, threatening to use the financial bill for the 1914 budget as a vehicle for reform if the Senate failed to do so.[14] Caillaux's demand, criticised by a number of senators as excessively authoritarian (and not without reason), illustrates that he believed he had a strong enough majority in the Chamber to use the finance bill in order to break the Senate's resistance to his concept of tax reform. This was a realistic assumption, as a rough analysis of the strength of support in Parliament for the government on at least financial matters shows. By the end of January 1914 a total of 168 deputies had joined the ranks of the United Radicals. The SFIO had seventy deputies who would undoubtedly be prepared to support a progressive line of domestic policy, and at least twenty *républicain-socialistes*, traditionally to the Left of the *radicaux-socialistes*, also backed the government on this issue.[15] Thus more than 250 deputies could be counted on to support Caillaux's finance policy. The government therefore required only the support of a handful of non-United Radicals or moderate Republicans to achieve a stable majority. The fact that part of the bourgeois Centre had helped in toppling the Barthou government made this seem feasible. In view of Caillaux's cautious and conciliatory policy on the budgetary issue and the imminence of parliamentary elections, support within the Centre was likely to grow.

The Senate discussed the addendum demanded by Caillaux to Article 1 of the Senate committee proposal—the so-called 'Perchot amendment'[16]—on 25 February 1914. This amendment was to make the inclusion of the essential guide-lines of the 1909 Chamber bill in the Senate committee draft legally binding. Despite the personal intervention of the Premier, Doumergue, the Senate turned down the Perchot amendment by 140 votes to 134. Since the majority against the government was so slim, this could hardly be regarded as a real defeat of the tax reform, especially as not all the senators who voted against this amendment were opposed to the tax reform as a whole. The opinion of the Left that this vote of the Senate could not be viewed as a preliminary decision against the tax reform was therefore bitterly echoed by the conservative press: 'What a warning to the country! . . . the adversaries of fiscal inquisition must increase their vigilance and their efforts more than ever!'[17]

Only two days after this defeat of Caillaux in the Senate, the government and the opposition had the opportunity of finding out exactly how much support there was in Parliament on their respective sides. On 27 February the deputy Dubois, backed by Briand, Miller-and and other leading FDG politicians, entered an interpellation calling on the government to adopt the 1.4 billion francs' loan proposed by the Barthou government,[18] on the grounds that it was even more indispensable now that the Senate was obviously not prepared to approve Caillaux's tax proposals. Dubois's motion was politically ingenious, in that it was not explicitly levelled against the tax reform and was therefore attractive to the large group of deputies in the Centre who were not basically conservative in matters of finance policy but had nevertheless supported Barthou's proposed loan.[19] Briand, taking the floor in the debate in the Chamber for the first time as leader of the FDG, supported Dubois's motion with the characteristic argument that this initiative had been necessary only because Caillaux had failed to push through the tax reform with sufficient *élan*. In fact, continued Briand, Caillaux had no intention of implementing the reform and was deliberately procrastinating so as to be able to capitalise on this issue in election campaigns, and so forth, for years to come.[20] Caillaux reacted to Briand's attempt to discredit his personal integrity, and thus disconcert his followers in Parliament, with a self-assured appeal to party discipline: 'I may make mistakes like anyone else. But I'm sticking to my party.'

Caillaux had meanwhile asked for a vote of confidence, against Dubois's interpellation. The result was a 'Sedan of the *Briandistes*'[21]—the Chamber declared its confidence in the government by a substantial majority of 329 votes to 214. Moreover, in its resolution,[22] the Chamber declared its readiness to support the government's struggle for 'reforms of fiscal justice'. This statement, with the backing of such a substantial Chamber majority, lent considerable political weight to Caillaux's threat to the Senate to make the finance bill a vehicle for reform. The adoption of the package of tax reforms had now become a real possibility.

Domestic and Foreign Policy and the Preservation of the Three-Year Law

The dispute on tax reform illustrated that at the beginning of 1914 the Doumergue/Caillaux government had the support of a firm majority in Parliament. However, at the same time there was a danger that the *Trois Ans* might lead to a schism within this left-wing majority. On the one hand, the Socialists and a number of Radicals were pushing for the abolition of the reactionary conscription law; whereas, on the other, most Radicals advocated the maintenance of the law, at least as a provisional measure, as a means of securing national defence.[23] Moreover, the members of the non-radical Centre who supported the government in financial affairs (as the division on the Dubois interpellation showed), presumably shared the *Fédération des Gauches'* view that the conscription law must be upheld as the 'organic charter' of national defence.

The FDG tried to take advantage of this virtual dissent. The liberal/conservative, anti-radical alliance was particularly fragile on domestic issues and the FDG concentrated its agitation on the three-year law. With the backing of most of the moderate and conservative press, a persistent campaign was launched against the 'anti-patriotic' Socialist–

United Radical pact, held together, it was maintained, by the pledge to abandon the three-year law. These attacks culminated at the height of the debate on tax reform with the accusation that the government was 'ignominiously' collaborating with the Socialists and jeopardising the law of national security. In their first joint public appearance at an FDG meeting in Le Havre on 15 February 1914, Briand and Barthou brought the *Trois Ans* into the centre-stage of political dispute 'with a hitherto unknown degree of bitterness'.[24] Barthou accused the Radicals of deliberately gambling with the 'life of *la patrie*' for the sole purpose of strengthening their own position. Briand declared that, although his own party was comprised of groups with varying political aims, they were all inspired by one common duty, to 'protect the life of France', and they would not tolerate the sacrifice of the *Loi de Trois Ans* to the 'lower instincts of the masses' and the dragging of the sacred interests of *la patrie* 'into the dirt of the election campaign'.[25] Several days later the FDG steering committee stipulated the conditions in which it would give its support to republican candidates: 'The *Fédération des Gauches* . . . resolves that in the coming general elections it shall give its support only to the various parties of the Left determined to support the laws of anti-clericalism and social democracy and to uphold the law of national defence.'[26]

Faced, as were Doumergue and Caillaux, with a campaign aimed at reopening the debate on the *Trois Ans* in order to split the government's majority, it was absolutely indispensable for them to uphold the ambiguous formula used in the governmental declaration that the law was to be applied 'loyally'.

The government soon had an opportunity to prove how committed it really was to national defence and the three-year law. In mid-February 1914 the Socialists presented an interpellation on the alarming increase in epidemic diseases and deaths in the barracks, over-crowded with the third class of conscripts.[27] Without trying to play down this problem, the government was able to provide Parliament with evidence that, since the beginning of its term of office, a whole series of measures had been taken to prevent the epidemics from spreading further.[28] The Socialists demanded that a parliamentary committee of inquiry be set up to prove that the increase in deaths in the barracks was the direct result of the impetuous introduction of three-year military service. The Socialists' interpellation was opposed by a motion presented by an FDG deputy, supported by the government(!), to the effect that the Chamber committee on health should be given the mandate of examining the possibility of taking further steps to improve hygiene in the barracks. Greeted by resounding applause from both the Centre and the radical Left, the Under

Secretary, Maginot, declared that the government abhorred attempts to exploit the deaths in the barracks as a means of turning public opinion against measures passed by Parliament in the interests of national defence. The adoption of the latter motion by an overwhelming majority of 385 votes to 25, the SFIO abstaining (!), proved that the attacks of the *fédérés* were not a real threat to the government.

One reason for the government's position of strength was that, by emphasising its loyalty to the *Trois Ans*, it had the backing of part of the parliamentary Centre, without losing the support of the SFIO. The Socialists frequently gave vent to their dissatisfaction with the unexpected 'militarism' of the Doumergue/Caillaux government, but were not prepared to 'play the game of the *Briandistes*'. Marcel Sembat's proclamation, 'Rather a lame duck than a blind one!', and his warning to the members of his party not to oppose the *Trois Ans* in Parliament 'through and through', reflected the position of Jaurès and the CAP.[29] Although the election campaign was to reveal the considerable opposition to this policy within the party as a whole,[30] this tactic was nevertheless followed by the entire SFIO parliamentary group throughout Doumergue's ministry.

The socialist group's abstention in the division on the debate on sanitary conditions in the barracks was a first sign that the SFIO was prepared to compromise. Another was the adoption of the cadre law for the implementation of the three-year bill,[31] presented by the government on 16 February at the height of the FDG campaign, without any serious opposition from the socialist benches.[32]

While the firm line of the government on financial reform provided the essential basis for the backing of a sound left-wing majority, its cautious treatment of the *Trois Ans* issue formed the second pillar of its parliamentary strength. In view of the formation of the liberal/conservative opposition, the preservation of the three-year law had become the necessary correlate to a progressive form of domestic policy.

The careful tactics of the Doumergue/Caillaux government had significant domestic motivations, which do not however imply a 'primacy of domestic policy'. Considerations of foreign affairs also made the preservation of the three-year law indispensable, despite the fact that the government's foreign policy was by no means strictly Poincaristic. On the contrary, Doumergue's promise to 'apply loyally' the defence bill, and assurance that his government also considered the Russian alliance as a keystone to French foreign policy,[33] were to a certain extent the necessary correlate to the implementation of a new type of diplomacy. The new government had abandoned the Poincaristic approach of using every issue in foreign policy to demonstrate the stability of the French alliance system to the Triple Alliance powers.

This new policy also explains why the Doumergue/Caillaux government was viewed with such scepsis and, in certain cases, was openly opposed by leading French and allied diplomats. For example, the French ambassador in London, Paul Cambon, wrote to his brother Jules, ambassador in Berlin: 'It is true that the new French cabinet suits Germany, since it is anti-militarist and impotent abroad.'[34]

The Russian ambassador in Paris, Isvolsky, complained that the new government was neither capable of nor willing to conduct an effective foreign policy. Doumergue, he said, lacked both initiative and diplomatic experience and was therefore in no position to take 'quick, independent' decisions. Unlike Poincaré, the new head of government submitted all matters of foreign policy to the cabinet; questions from the Russian ambassadors were always answered in the form of *aides-mémoire*, and so forth.[35] Even the King of Spain asked Poincaré how long the new cabinet was likely to survive.[36] Poincaré himself also expressed his dissatisfaction with the new government's approach to foreign policy: 'In cabinet I try in vain to get Doumergue to discuss the key questions of foreign policy before his colleagues.'[37]

Poincaré was not so much concerned about the government's apparent lack of interest in foreign affairs as about the new line of foreign policy itself, fearing that his entire policy might collapse and that he himself would be faced with a personal fiasco: 'I have not quite reached the Tarpeian rock. But the policy of Caillaux's ministry of megalomania is bringing me closer and there's nothing I can do.'[38] Two examples of what Poincaré described as 'megalomania' are provided by French policy towards the Anglo-German talks on the partition of Portuguese colonies, and the Turkish loan of 1914.[39]

Since 1912 Germany and Britain had been negotiating on the possibility of partitioning the Portuguese colonies in Africa, particularly Angola and Mozambique. These negotiations aimed at a renewal of the secret Anglo-German Angola Treaty of 1898 and a definition of the spheres of influence of the two powers in preparation for the bankruptcy of the young ·Portuguese republic, which was generally expected. The Anglo-German agreement on the Portuguese colonies, initialled on 13 August 1913, stipulated that Germany and Britain would take joint action, if necessary 'repelling possible intervention from other powers', to 'secure their rights by treaty in these territories by granting appropriate loans'.[40]

The Barthou government was extremely concerned about these negotiations, especially because at the end of October 1913 France had not yet received any precise information as to the contents of the treaty. Grey's assurances that the new agreement with Germany was merely the continuation of the 1898 Angola agreement[41] could not allay the suspicions of French diplomats. Reporting from London and Berlin, Paul and Jules Cambon were convinced that for the Germans the negotiations had the general political purpose of undermining the Anglo-French *Entente Cordiale*.[42]

The Anglo-German agreement also involved far-reaching consequences for French colonial policy. After a series of enquiries from the French ambassador, Whitehall had finally informed France of the essential elements of the initialled agreement in December 1913. This information seemed to confirm French suspicions that Germany was using the same tactic as during the Agadir crisis of 1911 and was trying to encircle the French Congo as a preliminary step towards repartitioning the territories in the area. According to the Anglo-German agreement, the coastal regions of Angola and Cabinda were to be ceded to Germany if and when the Portuguese colonial administration collapsed. This meant that French possessions would be encircled by German colonies, both to the north and south.[43] Both the Barthou and Doumergue governments were absolutely opposed to this principle, which was totally incongruous with French interests.[44]

Although the two governments were essentially of the same opinion as to the overall assessment of the colonial question, the Barthou government decided to protect French interests by using methods which differed completely from those of its successor. Paléologue, the leading Foreign Ministry official and a close friend of Poincaré, demanded that French diplomats should take official steps to block the Anglo-German negotiations and preserve the *status quo* in Africa. He proposed that the French government should officially request the convening of a conference of the signatories to the Congo Act subscribed in Berlin in 1885. According to Article 16 of the Franco-German convention on Equatorial Africa (1911),[45] France had the right to demand the convening of an international conference, since the now disputed territories lay within the scope of the 1885 Act of Berlin. Pichon, Barthou's Foreign Minister, and Lebrun, Doumergue's Minister for Colonial Affairs,[46] agreed. Paul Cambon also believed that French intervention through official diplomatic channels was the appropriate means of preventing the Anglo-German agreement from being definitively signed.[47]

Regardless of the potential wide-reaching international complications this might involve, the responsible politicians in Barthou's government endorsed a 'demonstrative' approach to this issue. Faithful to Poincaristic foreign policy, they were prepared to use the Anglo-German negotiations to test Britain's solidarity towards the *Entente*, despite the danger that this could lead to further confrontation between the diplomatic blocs.

In contrast, the approach of Doumergue, when he took office in mid-December 1913, was more informal. To the despair of the 'hawks', the new Premier believed that bilateral negotiations between individual members of the Triple Alliance and the *Entente* powers were not necessarily to be regarded with suspicion. France, in Doumergue's opinion, had no general political interest in officially intervening in Anglo-German negotiations and should therefore do no more than inform Whitehall 'frankly and clearly'—but through unofficial channels—that French interests in Africa must be duly observed in Britain's negotiations with Germany. In any case, the Premier maintained, given the friendly relations between the two powers, France would trust Britain not to do anything which might jeopardise either French interests in Africa or the stability of the *Entente Cordiale*. Doumergue sent a circular to the French embassies in Berlin, London, Madrid, Lisbon and Brussels outlining his approach and expressly instructed the ambassadors to follow these guide-lines.[48] Paul Cambon refused to accept these orders, believing that France's chief concern on this issue was to prevent publication of the Anglo-German agreement.[49] He therefore advocated that his government should officially inform Britain that publication of the treaty would lead to the issuing by France of a public statement.[50] The Colonial Minister, Lebrun, who like Paléologue also agreed with Cambon, complained to Poincaré on several occasions that Doumergue's colonial policy was 'weak and indecisive'.[51] Of even greater significance was the fact that Poincaré himself supported the opposition within the cabinet to the new Premier's policies. In the cabinet meeting on 10 February 1914 the President insisted that the French government must finally confront Britain with an 'official document'.[52] Soon afterwards Poincaré took a personal initiative which quite clearly went beyond the scope of his constitutional rights as President, informing the British ambassador Bertie that France would not recognise any treaty 'negotiated by two European nations between themselves without regard to the Act of Berlin and the treaty of 4 November [1911]'.[53] In his memoirs Poincaré maintains that he made this statement to Bertie with the agreement of the entire cabinet.[54] This is a fallacy fabricated by Poincaré to justify his act. In despatches to Cambon immediately after the cabinet meeting, Doumergue repeated his demands for 'clear and frank talks' with the British government and reiterated the principle of non-intervention in Anglo-German negotiations.[55]

The rejection by Doumergue of a policy of permanent confrontation between the two diplomatic blocs in Europe led to a new concrete political approach. Irrespective of the outcome of the Anglo-German negotiations, he conducted a policy of economic cooperation with Portugal. The young republic was to be strengthened financially and bound to France as a means of securing French interests in Africa. Doumergue wanted to save Portugal from bankruptcy, because for Portugal to be faced with financial disaster would imply the implementation of an Anglo-German agreement which might be detrimental to French interests.[56]

The first obstacle to this plan to combine economic and political interests, thus giving France greater scope in terms of general politics than had been possible under Poincaristic policy, was that, despite Portugal's appeal for assistance, the Doumergue government could not persuade French financial circles and industrialists to enter into cooperation with the Portuguese colonies.[57]

Apart from this concrete problem, given the international scenario of the time, it is difficult to assess how realistic this new approach to French foreign policy really was, since the Anglo-German negotiations came to an almost complete standstill in the spring of 1914. The theory that this standstill was 'not least' due to 'French energetic intervention in London'[58] has so far not been sufficiently substantiated. It seems much more likely that the German government itself held up the negotiations on account of the difficulties in finding sources of private investment for a German policy of pacific penetration in Africa.[59] Moreover, if Jagow wanted to dispel French doubts with the assurance that territorial changes in the Congo basin would be carried out only with French approval,[60] the German government would have been obliged in consequence to avoid publication of the treaty for domestic reasons. This gave Poincaré and Cambon the hope that Whitehall would break off the negotiations with Germany,[61] although Poincaré remained concerned that Britain would put her own colonial interests before the guarding of French interests and the *Entente Cordiale*.[62] It was not until the outbreak of the First World War that the Anglo-German negotiations at last ground to a halt. When the German government finally announced that it was prepared to publish the treaty at the end of July 1914,[63] the new French approach to European politics had already been nipped in the bud.

While the question of the Portuguese colonies remained a major issue in the foreign policy of several great European powers up until the spring of 1914, the 'Liman von Sanders affair' early that year posed a real trial of strength to the European power system. 'The concrete issue concerning the German military mission was linked . . . with the fundamental problem of the preservation and fortification of the *Entente* alliance system.'[64] The Russian government feared that the

German military mission would strengthen German influence in Turkey and threaten vital Russian interests.[65] So great was the apprehension of Russia that she now began to prepare for a war with Germany which seemed inevitable in the long term. The first signs of this became apparent when the Tsar's government confirmed the agreements concluded between the Franco-Russian general staffs in the autumn of 1913 and announced that it was prepared to step up the construction of strategic railway lines with the aid of the French loan.

However, consolidation of the military agreements did not suffice to stabilise the Franco-Russian alliance as a whole. The Liman von Sanders affair was not only the breaking-point of Russo-German relations but revealed conflicting interests, mostly of an economic nature, among the *Entente* powers themselves. Even the Russian suggestion that the *Entente* powers should address a 'friendly enquiry' to Berlin[66] was rejected by both London and Paris. The reasons for Britain's reluctance need not be examined here.[67] The French government informed Sazonov that intervention of this kind would be likely to have a detrimental effect on the Russo-German negotiations under way at the time.[68] The French government's caution can be seen as a further indication of the Doumergue/Caillaux government's new approach to French diplomacy,[69] although in this case Poincaré fully endorsed Doumergue's caution. On 5 January 1914 the President pointed out to Izvolsky that *Entente* intervention in Berlin would make it impossible for Germany to cover up and settle the affair.[70]

The reserve of the entire French government was due to the fact that Russia was not only pressing for joint action by the *Entente* powers but was trying to persuade France to break off negotiations on a loan to Turkey. In Sazonov's opinion, financial pressure would be the most effective means of persuading Turkey to withdraw Liman von Sanders's appointment as commander of the first Turkish army corps.[71] In a meeting with Izvolsky, Poincaré flatly refused. All decision-making in Turkey, he said, was dependent on the whims of the German government. Moreover, the Russian proposal that France should 'starve' Turkey into acquiesence would imply a 'great sacrifice' in view of the considerable French economic interests in the country. Poincaré concluded that financial pressure would have little hope of success in this case, since if she were really on the verge of bankruptcy, Turkey could always count on Germany to provide the necessary credit.[72] On 13 January 1914 Poincaré explained to the cabinet that a further weakening of Turkey's financial position would be extremely harmful to the Franco-German negotiations on an extension of the Baghdad railway. To give in to the Russians on this point would soon involve a 'new Baghdad affair'.[73] The French ambassador in St Petersburg,

Delcassé, had argued that France must prevent the revival of Turkey at all costs. The re-emergence of Turkey, he claimed, would infringe upon Russia's vital interests and could jeopardise the whole of the French alliance.[74] Poincaré refuted this argument: 'To have followed these proposals would have been to sacrifice all our intentions and all our interests in Asia to comply with Russia, and once again the alliance would have worked only to the benefit of our allies.'[75]

The Liman crisis highlighted the dilemma of Poincaré's entire alliance policy since 1912—namely, the problem of strengthening the Russian alliance despite the conflicting interests of the two allies. Poincaré's political strategy to overcome these difficulties finally led to the attempt to resolve the latent conflict between Russia and Turkey by including Turkey in the Franco-Russian alliance (!). With Poincaré's approval, Pichon, Foreign Minister in the Barthou cabinet overthrown in 1913, tried to convince the Russian ambassador, Izvolsky, at private meetings towards the end of January 1914, that it would be advantageous if Turkey joined the alliance.[76] Despite Izvolsky's extremely cool reaction to this idea, Poincaré took his plans a stage further. Following a report from Constantinople that Turkish government circles were disposed to the 'entry of the Ottoman Empire into the Triple Alliance system',[77] the President advised Doumergue to take initiatives in this direction and to give the French ambassadors in London and St Petersburg instructions to sound out this possibility.[78]

In open opposition to Poincaré, Doumergue failed to pass on these instructions to the ambassadors in the British and Russian capitals. Poincaré's bitter complaint that Doumergue obviously no longer intended to follow his advice on matters of foreign policy[79] is an indication that this disobedience was not limited to individual issues, but reflected the will of the Doumergue/Caillaux government to conduct its own foreign policy.

Unlike Poincaré, Doumergue and Caillaux were not prepared to consider the question of the Turkish loan solely in terms of direct French economic interests and dispel Russia's apprehension of the revival of Turkey by the hazardous venture of including Turkey in the Franco-Russian alliance. Even Poincaré must have realised that the German government would not have stood idly by while such a sweeping political change took place on the Bosphorus. Doumergue and Caillaux nevertheless wanted to avoid an open confrontation of the European alliance systems over the Turkish question. For this reason they took an important initiative to implement Grey's idea of a collective memorandum from the Great Powers in Europe to Turkey and Greece. Originally this memorandum was not directly connected with the problem of the Turkish loan and the Liman von Sanders crisis, but concerned the Treaty of London of 30 May 1913 between the states involved in the First Balkan War. Article 5 of this treaty stipulated that the Great Powers in Europe were to be responsible for the partition of the Aegean Islands between Turkey and Greece. In mid-December 1913 Grey had submitted to the European powers concrete proposals on this matter, with the suggestion that his plans should be backed up by a joint memorandum to Greece and Turkey. The Triple Alliance powers and Russia were basically in favour of this joint approach. [80] And despite his deep scepticism about the intentions of the Triple Alliance, even Paul Cambon in London believed that the question of the Aegean Islands could be settled on this basis, although he rightly pointed out that the agreement could be thwarted if Turkey took it upon herself to annex a number of the contentious islands before the memorandum was handed over.[81] As a precautionary measure, Doumergue and Caillaux decided from mid-January 1914 that Turkey would be granted a loan only if she cooperated in a peaceful settlement of the Aegean Islands' question along the lines of Grey's proposal. When in mid-January 1914 the Turkish Premier asked France for an immediate 700-million-franc loan, Caillaux replied 'that the whole matter was dominated by the political question, that Turkey would have to demonstrate her will for peace, without which we could do nothing'.[82] In a series of statements to Turkey, the Doumergue/ Caillaux government left no doubt that it was determined to subject the Turkish loan to the 'imperatives of general policy' and'to use it as a means of achieving a peace settlement in the Balkans.[83]

Despite the failure of Doumergue in his last attempt before the Great War to conduct a policy based on the 'Concert of Europe', the significance of the new line in foreign policy should not be underestimated. In his memoirs Poincaré considers the fact that the French government subjected the Turkish loan to the dictates of general politics as proof that French policy prior to the First World War was geared towards keeping the peace. This comment, a total contradiction of his opposition to the policy of the Doumergue/Caillaux government in 1913/14, is perhaps the best indication that the government's policy was in fact innovative and guided by the conviction that the preservation of peace in Europe was to be considered as the supreme good.[84]

Nevertheless, in view of the opposition at home and the scepsis of France's allies, the new government's unrelenting devotion to the Russian alliance remained the necessary correlate to this new approach to foreign policy. During the first few months of 1914 Doumergue had a number of opportunities of illustrating to the public exactly how seriously this point in his governmental declaration had been meant.

As a direct result of the Liman von Sanders crisis—and from this point only—the Russians began to show great interest in carrying out the strategic agreements concluded between the Russian and French general staffs. The first sign that the Russians were stepping up their armament projects was the definitive adoption of the results of the negotiations on the Russian railway loan in the form of an exchange of memoranda between Delcassé and Sazonov on 30 December 1913.[85] Russia's efforts in preparation for a conflict with Germany, considered as inevitable since the Liman crisis,[86] culminated in the famous 'special conferences' in St Petersburg on 13 January and 21 February 1914.[87]

Doumergue and Caillaux were even more conscious than Poincaré that the fulfilment of the strategic agreement was now of the utmost importance to Russia. Although on the purely political level they tried to settle the international crisis sparked off by the Liman affair, they were nevertheless aware that Russia regarded the application, to the letter, of all military agreements as *the* criterion for the overall political alliance.[88] Caillaux was therefore almost demonstrative in accepting a request from Russia that the first instalment of the railway loan be raised from 500 to 600 million francs to enable Russia to press ahead with the extension of the strategic lines. This concession did in fact dispel Russian doubts about the new French government's loyalty to the alliance.[89]

Given the Russians' efforts to boost their defence potential, it now became imperative for the Doumergue/Caillaux government to maintain the three-year law, not only because of domestic circumstances but on account of foreign policy. At this point the Tsar referred to the three-year law as an integral part of the alliance and demanded that it be maintained.[90] This was the first time his government had made such a statement! When the French general staff submitted a new cadre law in February 1914, Doumergue proved his intention of 'loyally' applying the three-year law, not only at home but to Russia. The purpose of this cadre bill was to reinforce the regular French army by establishing additional army units, changing the strength of existing units and supplementing the weaponry of individual formations. The bill, regarded by the public as a purely technical complement to the conscription law,[91] was soon adopted by Parliament on 12 March 1914, following the government's request (upon Poincaré's initiative) that the bill be passed immediately.[92]

However, at this stage Parliament was unaware that the new cadre law was not in fact a merely technical follow-up to the three-year law, but, like the conscription law itself, directly linked with the unconditional offensive strategy of Plan XVII. Without this cadre law, Joffre's now famous army instructions issued at the end of 1913 and early 1914—the keystone to his offensive planning[93]—would have remained pure theory. Joffre himself pointed out this link to the President: 'Joffre outlined the new organisation of the armed forces [= cadre law] and the instructions to be issued in the event of mobilisation . . . fortunately the plan established henceforth contains a rapid offensive.'[94]

It is unlikely that the general staff also informed the head of government about this link, which was not so much as mentioned in the course of the parliamentary debate. The fact that Poincaré later tried to obliterate all traces of the link [95] is further conclusive evidence that both politicians and army officers responsible for the *Trois Ans* persisted in hiding the law's real function within the framework of the general staff's offensive strategy from the public. Even if Joffre or Poincaré had enlightened Doumergue and Caillaux as to the offensive function of the cadre law, the Premier and his Finance Minister could hardly have blocked its enactment. To disclose the real implications behind three-year military service would definitely have sparked off a campaign of the Left frcm which the law would certainly not have emerged intact. However, the international dimension to the three-year law from the time of the Liman crisis—but *only* from this point onwards—meant that to repeal the law would be to renounce the Russian alliance. Russia's new vigour gave Poincaristic alliance policy a rationality which even a government embarked on a new direction in both domestic and foreign affairs could not refute as long as it accepted the alliance with Russia as the cornerstone of French foreign policy. And there is not the slightest indication that either Doumergue or Caillaux were not absolutely convinced of the necessity of this alliance.

The Campaign against Caillaux

The Doumergue/Caillaux government had a relatively stable parliamentary majority on account of its persistent efforts to push through the tax reform package, on the one hand, and its caution on the *Trois Ans*, on the other. *Le Temps* concluded from the obvious defeat of the *Fédération des Gauches* in the parliamentary finance debate[96] that the future of France now depended upon whether the economic lobby, as the representative of the 'world of labour', would succeed in defeating the government's 'anti-French' policy on tax reform.[97]

Since the presentation of the proposals on capital tax a storm of protest from the major trade associations had in fact been raging against the government's proposals. In an open letter to the Premier the *Comité Central d'Études et de Défense Fiscale* demanded the withdrawal of all income and capital tax proposals on the grounds that these measures would ruin trade and industry. The budget, it suggested, could also be balanced by slightly increasing existing taxes, a measure which would offer the additional advantage of strengthening the solidarity of all Frenchmen. Moreover, the raising of a large national loan would help to curtail the imminent tax increases for a period and would also encourage an upswing of industrial and commercial activity.[98] At a meeting of the chairmen of all the chambers of commerce, convened to discuss the tax proposals on 26 January 1914, a virtual ultimatum was passed calling upon Parliament to reject the capital tax. If Caillaux's proposals were adopted, it was argued, a wave of panic would inevitably break out in trade and industry which would paralyse private enterprise. Compulsory declaration of income was also rejected on the grounds that it could lead to the establishment of a register of incomes and all sorts of incursions into private income. Along the lines of the CCEDF resolutions, the chairmen of the chambers of commerce also recommended a national loan to balance the budget. At the same time some of the traditional direct taxes and consumer taxes could also be increased.[99] This resolution was endorsed by the *Association de l'Industrie et de l'Agriculture Françaises* and the *Union des Intérêts Économiques*.[100] Even more than these extremely conservative financial opinions, a resolution of the *Comité Républicain du Commerce et de l'Industrie* (*Comité Mascuraud*), by tradition closely linked with the Radical Party, received considerable public attention. Although endorsing the principle of tax reform, the *Comité* demanded that it should be introduced gradually and cautiously. Furthermore, it totally rejected Caillaux's tactics of using the present budgetary difficulties as a vehicle for reform, and condemned the principle of declaration of income and the supervision of the tax authorities as incompatible with 'national feeling'.[101]

These statements reflected an inflexible attitude. It is none the less interesting that these associations restricted themselves to economic and financial arguments, carefully avoiding any reference to problems of a general political nature. This approach was in sharp contrast with the invidious campaign of almost the entire moderate and conservative press and the nationalist Right, launched at the beginning of January 1914 against Caillaux, 'the demagogue'.[102] In the wake of the unification of the Radicals, Caillaux's 'seizure of power' against the will of Poincaré and the imminent introduction of the new tax systems as an expression of social levelling, the bourgeoisie was filled with fear at the prospect of root-and-branch political reforms to come. A comment by the conservative *Gaulois* in January 1914 is typical of the tone of this campaign. Caillaux's assertion, it stated, that public opinion demanded a new and more just taxation system, was only superficially wrong because, under the present government, the opinion of the upper and middle classes was no longer considered as public opinion and had been replaced by the will of the 'masses', who were purely concerned with improving their own living standards regardless of the welfare of the state. Caillaux was finally accused of exploiting the problems of national defence in order to use this sheer greed as a means of extending his own personal power.[103]

The platform for the campaign against Caillaux was Briand's policy speech in St Étienne in December 1913, in which he had described Caillaux as a 'demagogic plutocrat'. The foundation of the *Fédération des Gauches* was also regarded by Briand's supporters as a 'movement against Caillaux's demagogy'.[104] It is true that not only personal interests but general political concern had been at the root of this movement. However, since Caillaux was pushing ahead with tax reforms and trying to avoid controversy on other domestic issues, his opponents were forced to concentrate their campaign on the tax question. The problem was that a reform of the tax system was endorsed far into the Centre, so that Caillaux's influence in Parliament remained virtually unchallenged. The hopes of *La Petite République* that the country would soon rid itself of its 'bad shepherd'[105] were wishful thinking, as even Caillaux's diehard opponents must have realised. The main reasons for the campaign against Caillaux were in fact apprehension as to the outcome of the parliamentary elections in April 1914 and the fear that Caillaux would capitalise on the unreflected will of the masses. In the final analysis this agitation, described by Caillaux's socialist and radical supporters as a 'capitalist crusade' and as an attempt to rally fundamentally disparate interests against Caillaux,[106] remained politically impotent. *Le Figaro*'s press campaign—with a dramatic climax in Caillaux's resignation—was linked only vaguely with political agitation.

At the beginning of 1914 *Le Figaro*, fundamentally conservative but without any clear-cut political stance,[107] began publication of a series of reports claiming that Caillaux was involved in a number of political and financial scandals. The newspaper's editor, Gaston Calmette, declared that it was his aim to prove Briand's accusation that Caillaux was a 'demagogic plutocrat'. Caillaux's policy, wrote *Le Figaro*, was not only 'objectively' harmful to the good of the nation. Caillaux himself had 'infamous' personal intentions, too. Cynical misuse of political power through vanity and greed had made him the 'true enemy of the nation', a 'public criminal who must not only be fought on a political level but brought before the courts.[108]

Calmette backed up his accusations by publishing a number of episodes from Caillaux's political past—which will not be examined here in detail. At first there was little public interest in this campaign, especially since Calmette generally failed to provide any proof of his accusations.[109] It was not until 10 March 1914, when Calmette revived the notorious 'Rochette affair', that Caillaux was really in danger. From 1910–12 the Rochette affair had already been the subject of a parliamentary inquiry. In the first decade of the century, a banker named Rochette had gathered a huge fortune by obscure speculations on the stock exchange, founded a number of stockholding companies, and had ultimately attempted to gain the controlling interest of *Le Petit Journal* and the *Compagnie des Omnibus*. In 1908, during Clemenceau's ministry, Rochette was suddenly arrested on charges of suspected fraud. It had later transpired that Rochette had been arrested not on the basis of conclusive evidence, but because leading politicians (Clemenceau, Briand) had advised the judicial authorities to do so. It was suspected that these politicians wanted to rid the previous owner of the *Compagnie des Omnibus* of an unpleasant rival. However, the accusations against Rochette were confirmed in the course of the inquiry. Finally, immediately before Rochette's trial was due to open in the spring of 1911 under the Monis/Caillaux cabinet, the proceedings were postponed, again for obscure reasons. When the case was to be eventually resumed at the beginning of 1912—Poincaré was now Premier—Rochette escaped and fled to South America. In 1912 a parliamentary committee on inquiry chaired by Jaurès had voiced the suspicion that both Rochette's arrest and the sudden postponement of his trial could be traced back to illegal pressure by various governments on the judicial authorities. However, no absolutely conclusive evidence had been found.

When Calmette turned his attention to this affair on 10 March 1914, he was concerned only with Caillaux's role in the sudden postponement of Rochette's trial. Calmette's version of the events was based on a previously unknown document, from which he quoted liberally without actually disclosing its origin. The incriminating document, later to become famous as the 'Fabre document', was a protocol drafted by the state prosecutor Fabre in the spring of 1911 giving an account of his talks with Premier Monis and submitted to Briand in his capacity as Minister of Justice in Poincaré's cabinet. In this protocol Fabre had stated that he had been given express instructions from Premier Monis to postpone the proceedings against Rochette, apparently following a request from Caillaux.[110]

This allegation against Caillaux was a severe threat to his position in

Parliament and in public. On account of the close ties between the bourgeois political oligarchy and financial and capitalist interests, financial scandals were not exactly infrequent throughout the Third Republic. The Rochette affair was nevertheless a challenge not only to Caillaux's personal integrity but to his position as the leader of a democratic and socially progressive movement. The reopening of the debate on the Rochette issue now linked Calmette's hitherto isolated campaign with the forces of the entire anti-Caillaux movement. In fact, with hindsight, it can be proved that the leaders of the political opposition to Caillaux—primarily Briand and Barthou—had supported Calmette's campaign by giving the editor of *Le Figaro* a copy of the Fabre document.[111] This fact is a clear illustration of the weakness of the political opposition. Faced with the unthwarted political success of Caillaux, his opponents now resorted to desperate means. Apart from the fact that recourse to intrigue could hardly be beneficial to either Briand's or Barthou's reputations, both these politicians were also incriminated by the Fabre document. Briand had received Fabre's report on the events of 1911 in his capacity as Minister of Justice in 1912 but had not submitted the document to the parliamentary committee of inquiry on the matter. Moreover, he had not added the document to the official files of the Ministry of Justice, but had passed it on personally to his successor and political disciple, Barthou. For the public to discover that Calmette had received this document from Barthou personally would obviously lead to the impression that Briand and Barthou had deceived Parliament and deliberately withheld evidence from the judicial authorities in order to use it at the appropriate moment as a means of eliminating a political adversary.

Caillaux, who of course had the greatest interest in preventing the Fabre document from being published, tried to take advantage of this fact. In a series of conversations with Poincaré he asked the President to prevent Barthou and Briand from publishing the Fabre document on the grounds that it would be equally harmful to the reputation of both leaders of the rival republican parliamentary groups—Briand and Caillaux. Poincaré realised that this was a valid argument[112] and made it clear to Barthou and Briand that he strongly disapproved of their illegal appropriation of a document providing legal evidence. The President ordered Barthou to try to prevent an escalation of the scandal by ensuring that Calmette did not publish the Fabre document. Briand and Barthou promised to do so but at the same time failed to admit to Poincaré that Calmette had received the document from them and not, like other journalists (e.g. Jouvenel of *Le Matin* and Berthoulat of *La Liberté*), directly from Fabre himself.[113]

A few days later, it transpired that Briand and Barthou were not prepared to follow Poincaré's instructions, obviously seeing publication of the Fabre document as the final opportunity to discredit Caillaux before the April 1914 parliamentary elections and thereby initiating a turn-about on the domestic scene. On 14 March Briand's *La Petite République* called for the publication of the incriminating document. Hoping that the Socialists would henceforth cease to collaborate with the Caillaux government, it continued that Jaurès, chairman of the parliamentary committee of inquiry on the Rochette affair in 1911/12, would now be forced to press charges against his friend Caillaux.[114] Buneau-Varilla, editor of *Le Matin*, had a conversation with Poincaré on 14 March, which the President described in his diary as follows:

> On the subject of Caillaux, he said to me with unaccustomed vehemence, 'We've finally got him!' . . . He added, 'I told him that he was done for and I'll tell him again. This document [the Fabre document] will be published, it must be. That man is leading France into disaster. He's trying to treat us the Prussian way. That income tax is a monstrosity. I'm going to rally all the traders and all the grocers in France against him. We must get rid of this madman at all costs.'[115]

However, as the plot against Caillaux thickened, there was an unexpected turn of events. On the afternoon of 16 March Caillaux's wife broke into *Le Figaro*'s office and shot Calmette. This act was not, however, directly linked with the imminent publication of the Fabre document. In the course of her trial before the court of assizes, Mme Caillaux succeeded in convincing the jury that it had been a question of honour that had led her to this act of despair, and on 31 July 1914 she was acquitted. Calmette, not content with digging into Caillaux's political past, had in fact announced on 10 March that at this time, so decisive for the 'salvation of *la patrie*', he would not shrink from using 'any means, no matter how painful to our customs or unsavoury to our manners and tastes'.

What this strange threat[116] actually involved was revealed in a 'comical interlude' three days later when *Le Figaro* published a letter written by Caillaux in 1901 to his then mistress and later wife. In this letter Caillaux had implied that, as Finance Minister in the Waldeck-Rousseau cabinet, he had stifled a proposal on income tax, despite his pretence to Parliament that he was in favour of the proposal.[117] In retaliation for this attempt of Calmette to prove once and for all that Caillaux was a 'demagogic plutocrat', Caillaux stated that in 1901 he had in fact been compelled to block a left-wing proposal on income tax which was basically progressive, but incoherent and technically inapplicable.[118] To make matters worse, Calmette was evidently planning to publish further extracts from Caillaux's private correspondence. It had been known for some time that personal letters written by Caillaux were circulating among Paris journalists.[119] When Calmette threatened to use 'distasteful' methods, Caillaux feared that Calmette had got hold of other personal letters he had written and intended to challenge Calmette to a duel.[120] His wife's act of despair had made this superfluous.

Caillaux's downfall had now become inevitable and on 17 March he resigned from office. Yet the 'comical interlude' which had taken such a dramatic turn continued, although even the press opposed to Caillaux was at first extremely reserved in its comments. 'Let us content ourselves with saluting the tomb of the victim', wrote *La Revue des Deux Mondes. Le Temps* went no further than publishing a moralising discussion on the unleashing of uncontrolled personal passion as a result of political disputes being brought down to a personal level. This caution probably resulted from the consideration that, as *La Petite République* commented, Caillaux's resignation had made a *rapprochement* between moderate and progressive Republicans possible, so that hysteria and political polarisation were to be avoided.[121]

Poincaré was also intent on reducing public excitement so far as possible. Following the murder of Calmette, he again warned Barthou to prevent the document from being published, else public order would be endangered. This conversation between the President and Barthou on 17 March proves that Briand and Barthou were responsible for the escalation of the Calmette campaign. On the other hand, it disproves Caillaux's later suspicion that Poincaré himself had at least been sympathetic with, if not jointly responsible for, the persistence of the campaign:[122]

> Barthou asked to speak to me. He came, he told me, to confide something in me which was on his conscience. He admitted that it was he, along with Briand, who had let Calmette copy Fabre's protocol. Calmette had all the elements for the campaign [against Caillaux] except the text of the document. Barthou gave it to him in his office in the presence of Briand but made him promise not to publish it and only to refer to it. Calmette had agreed and had apparently kept his promise, but had nevertheless read out the document to a number of persons. . . . Today in the Chamber, Delahaye [a nationalist Right deputy] is going to raise the incident. A committee of inquiry may be appointed. Barthou may be called upon to account for his action. . . .
>
> I replied to Barthou, first that it had been a most serious mistake to have given the document to Calmette, even under the seal of secrecy; second, that I agree with him that it is necessary to tell the absolute truth before a committee of inquiry or the court of assizes; third, that in view of Caillaux's resignation, Delahaye's point will probably be dropped and brought up

again only if *Le Figaro* publishes the document, and that for the sake of public order the best thing to do would be to prevent the publication of this document which should never have been passed on to anyone.[123]

Barthou did in fact promise Poincaré to try to prevent the document from being published, but Poincaré was wrong in assuming that Barthou had confided in him because it was on his conscience.[124] The very next day Barthou himself read out the Fabre document to Parliament and moved that the committee of inquiry on the Rochette affair be reconvened in the light of this fresh evidence.[125] This shows that Barthou's 'confession' to Poincaré was not made because the question was preying on his mind; rather, it was no more than an attempt to gain the President's support and pursue the campaign against Caillaux. Poincaré later remarked that Barthou had given him no indication of his intention to publish the document.[126] Knowledge of his conversation with Barthou on 17 March implies that this comment was a bitter criticism, since, against Poincaré's advice, Barthou made the Fabre document public in a final attempt to discredit Caillaux politically: 'The document has now been made public other than by publication in *Le Figaro*, and M. Caillaux's enemies will try to use it against him.'[127]

Parliament granted Barthou's request and set up a committee of inquiry, which was even delegated judicial powers.[128] Without going into detail on the work of the committee chaired by Jaurès, let us enumerate the politically relevant aspects, which were as follows. The committee's final report concluded with proof that Monis and Caillaux had put pressure on the public prosecutor, Fabre, in 1911. Although suspicions that the motives of Caillaux had been dishonourable had not been proved, he was nevertheless guilty of the 'most deplorable abuse of influence'. However, not only Caillaux, but Briand and Barthou, were guilty of this disrespect of jurisdictive sovereignty, since they had failed to submit a document providing legal evidence to the competent authorities and had instead subjected the 'interests of truth' to 'group or party contrivances'. This criticism was true of Barthou in particular, since he had appropriated the Fabre document in order to use it against a political opponent. The committee was nevertheless not in a position to clarify this accusation any further, because Barthou had sworn under oath (!) that he had not shown the document to anyone. The committee concluded its report by stating that Barthou's action implied that Caillaux would not have been subjected to *Le Figaro*'s 'campaign of morality' if he had not been so adamant in his attempts to push through the tax reform.[129]

Caillaux's opponents had hoped that by removing the champion of tax reform from the centre of the political stage, and at the same time halting the trend towards the Left, they would be killing two birds with one stone. They were wrong. The Rochette scandal certainly stirred up some excitement, but the question of tax reform remained the focal point of parliamentary and public interest. This became clear several days later when, on 20 March, Caillaux's successor, Renoult, requested the Chamber to include both the taxation of the bonds and the general and progressive income tax, rejected by the Senate only a month before, in the 1914 budgetary finance bill.[130] Although the former proposal was rejected, despite protest action from many trade associations, the Chamber adopted the latter proposal on 29 March —the penultimate day of the legislatory period—by a substantial majority of 370 votes to 125. The keystone of Caillaux's tax reform package—the general and progressive supplementary tax on all incomes—was therefore included in the finance bill. The surprisingly large majority in favour of this measure was undoubtedly due to the fact that the elections were only two weeks away, so that the electorate would be able to assess the behaviour of the individual deputies. Before the decisive vote, Doumergue had again reminded the deputies that tax reform was the price to be paid for the three-year law: 'The republican majority is bound to this inclusion because it solemnly committed itself to it when the military law was adopted. . . . At the time of the vote on the military law there was much talk of fiscal patriotism!'[131]

CHAPTER 9

The 1914 Elections and their Political Consequences

The Election Campaign

After the fall of the Barthou government at the beginning of December 1913, the fronts in French domestic politics hardened once again, this time on account of the struggle over tax reform and the campaign against the 'demagogic' policy of Caillaux. Although the Doumergue/Caillaux government was obviously willing to implement the new conscription law 'loyally', the anti-Caillaux opposition accused the cabinet and the left-wing Republicans of aiming at an electoral alliance with the SFIO at the expense of national defence.[1] Moreover, the *Fédération des Gauches*, led by Briand and Barthou, readily supported the conservative campaign against Caillaux's fiscal policy. Thus the differences between the moderate and extreme conservative groups on social issues were pushed into the background in favour of the 'joint front against demagogy'.

Regardless of these circumstances, there is little substantiation for the opinion, widely held among historians, that the key issue—the *Loi de Trois Ans*—led to an extreme polarisation betweeen Right and Left in the 1914 elections.[2] This is a rather uncritical theory. It sticks too closely to the propaganda and ideology of both the far Left and the extreme conservative and nationalist Right which, in contrast with the radical Left, regarded the *Trois Ans* as a symbol of a general reorientation of society—that is, of reaction. A statement in the right-wing republican/conservative *Liberté* directly after the 1914 elections may be considered typical of this synthetic approach:

181

It is evident . . . that the three-year law is like the cornerstone of a policy of French harmony without which this policy is bound to collapse. To advocate the integral maintenance of the forces of national defence is of no purpose unless one also rallies to a domestic policy of conciliation opposed to the *néo-combisme* advocated by the coalition of the far Left. If one is for the *Trois Ans*, one must also oppose fiscal inquisition and support electoral reform. The one follows on from the other.[3]

Had the emphasis been a different one, every Socialist would have endorsed the principle of an overall social dimension to the *Trois Ans* issue. But even the vast majority of the left-wing Republicans opposed to the law had always differentiated between the technical issue—was reinforcement of the army necessary?—and the nationalist and reactionary campaign in support of the bill.[4]

The Radicals largely maintained this position throughout the election campaign, one factor which prevented the establishment of a left-wing republican/SFIO bloc. Moreover, following the failure of their campaign against Caillaux, the *Fédération des Gauches* swung towards the Left. Throughout the election campaign this group tried to play down their differences from the Radicals on social policy, mainly justifying their front against the United Radicals with the argument that the latter were not taking a firm enough stand to defend the 'law of national salvation' against the attacks from the Socialists. However, since the FDG did not succeed in formulating a clear-cut alternative to the position of the Radicals on the military issue, it cannot be maintained that the three-year law was the catalyst for a head-on confrontation between Left and Right during and following the 1914 elections. On the contrary, in view of the persistent refusal of many of the left-wing Republicans to take a firm stand against the new military law, no blocs of antagonism were established, even after the elections, and the links between the republican Left and Centre were not broken.

The Socialists' campaign leading up to the first ballot on 26 April 1914 followed the guide-lines laid down in the resolution adopted at the Amiens party conference. During the first phase of the election campaign, action was to be concentrated on underlining specific socialist ideals and demonstrating the political presence of the Socialist Party throughout the country. No tactical pacts on the nomination of candidates in the individual constituencies were concluded between the SFIO and left-wing bourgeois groups prior to the first ballot. The party fielded its own candidate in more than 420 out of 600 constituencies, regardless of whether the opposition's candidate was considered progressive or reactionary. The demarcation line between the SFIO and left-wing Republicans was highlighted by the Socialists' campaign against the *Trois Ans* on internationalist and pacifist grounds. Accordingly, the main weapon of the socialist campaign was a pamphlet circulated by SFIO headquarters entitled *Socialism Means Peace. Against the Three Years.* Another leaflet, a report of *Socialist Activity in Parliament*, also underlined the international reasons for the Socialists' struggle against militarism, chauvinism and war. It was stressed that the SFIO had organised the 'attack of the working class and democracy on the murderous law', along with the German Social Democrats, in order to halt the arms race and to keep the rising wave of chauvinism in Germany and France at bay. This socialist campaign in Parliament even enjoyed the support of the anti-parliamentary Syndicalists.[5] Apart from these two pamphlets, the SFIO also distributed leaflets pressing for tax reforms and again expounding its arguments against chauvinism and the arms race.[6] A final manifesto on election day summarised the party's political principles as follows:

> ... against the three-year law which is enchaining France to ... militarism; ... in favour of tax reform, dreaded and spurned by the privileged classes with their fortunes; ... in favour of a firmly and actively pacifist foreign policy based on a *rapprochement* with Germany; ... in favour of the expansion of labour and social legislation ... the first seed of liberation; ... in favour of a social Republic which shall liberate humanity by abolishing the property-owning capitalist classes.[7]

This emphasis of international motives was a rather peculiar swing in socialist policy, because since the early summer of 1913 socialist agitation had almost completely concentrated on domestic issues, with a view to the formation of a common front with the left-wing Republicans. This new approach is surprising. In March 1914 international tension had not yet come to a head, so that the Socialists had little reason to mobilise public opinion against a war looming ahead. The SFIO presumably focused on the international dimensions of the three-year law—the arms race and the danger of war—in order to provide the rank and file with well-known and long-familiar slogans as a basis for their action and so as not to 'tread on the toes' of the Radical Party. For the Socialists to have over-emphasised the reactionary domestic motives behind the military bill would have been an obstacle to future cooperation with the Radicals, the majority of whom were not convinced that the law was reactionary and had accepted it as at least a transitional measure to safeguard national defence. This assumption on the reasons for the new SFIO line is backed up by the fact that one of the Socialists' traditional political platforms, electoral reform (proportional representation), was not even mentioned in their election manifesto. Since 1910 the Socialists had frequently cooperated with moderate and conservative groups in Parliament to push through this reform, and it was in fact the essential reason why they had supported Poincaré's 1912 cabinet, although this policy had at times led to estrangement between the SFIO and the Radicals. [8] The fact that the SFIO dropped this traditional demand in the 1914 election campaign suggests that the party was trying to cover up its ideological differences with the Radicals, even though electoral pacts were not concluded between the two parties prior to the first ballot.

Throughout the election campaign the Radical Party was obviously trying to ignore the defence question so far as possible. Just as the vague compromise formula adopted at the Pau congress had been the price paid for the sake of party unity, the 'loyal application' of the new defence bill by the Doumergue/Caillaux government made extreme caution the order of the day. On account of the ambiguous Pau formula and the seizure of power shortly afterwards, the domestic and international significance of the three-year law had never really been clarified within the Radical Party. This was even truer now that domestic fronts were being determined on the issue of tax reform, as opposed to the *Trois Ans* issue. The Radical Party executive committee accordingly declared in its manifesto that the real significance of the elections lay in the struggle between two antagonistic political concepts—that is, republicanism versus reaction. The republican side was comprised of all those who subscribed not only to the expansion of the anti-clerical achievements of the Republic but to the introduction of tax reform as a means of achieving a greater degree of social justice. Meanwhile, continued the manifesto, the opposing camp was no longer made up simply of the traditional reactionary groups. A heterogeneous coalition had now gathered behind the *Trois Ans*; these 'two-faced candidates' were aiming at halting social progress by branding the Radical Party as anti-patriotic. To combat this discrediting of the party, it had to be stressed again and again that the Radical Party was on the contrary deeply patriotic. At the same time—and this was the only reference to the defence issue in the radical manifesto—it had to be pointed out that the Radicals would ensure that the necessary national defence measures would be implemented without wasting either men or money. They respected the demand that the nation should be strong, but this could be achieved only if army organisation were subject to constant and methodological improvement. Therefore the Radical Party would carry out reforms facilitating a gradual reduction(!) of military service.[9]

These words provided no direct statement on the importance of the three-year law for national defence, a tactic which was reflected in the statements of policy of many leading radical politicians. Caillaux did not even mention the *Trois Ans* in his manifesto. The War Minister, Noulens, went no further than declaring to his electorate that the three-year law might be the only means of preserving peace. If and when circumstances were such that French territory was no longer in danger, military service could certainly be reduced again. F. David, Minister for Public Works, tried to draw a synthesis between domestic and international arguments: the extension of military service had been necessary to maintain the balance of power in Europe and to protect French territory. French preparedness would in future have to be increased by a 'better organisation of the reserves'. Following root-and-branch army reform, the *Loi de Trois Ans* could be repealed, in so far as this was compatible with the international situation (*sic*).[10] Even the head of government's statement, given great public attention, provided no direct answer to the question of the domestic and international importance of the *Trois Ans*. Doumergue simply stated that his government had loyally enforced the military bill in accordance with majority opinion in the Chamber, which considered the bill necessary as a provisional shelter. Nevertheless, he continued, further improvements with regard to army organisation had to be envisaged and the door kept open for reform. The demand from the opponents of the government and the Radical Party that the *Trois Ans* should be 'categorically perpetuated' was not only technically inexpedient but detrimental to the continued development of national defence. In future the government and the Radical Party would therefore make particular efforts to improve the training of the reservists, extend strategic railway lines and supplement the technical equipment of the army. Doumergue avoided committing himself as to whether these technical improvements could lead to the reintroduction of the 1905 conscription law. France, he said, could not weaken her national defence by hasty improvisations while other states rearmed. Alongside the executive committee manifesto, Doumergue only touched upon the domestic aspects of the *Trois Ans*. He accused the forces opposed to the government and the Radical Party of having made the defence question the central issue in the elections for purely ideological reasons, of wanting to make the electorate forget that they themselves had had little time in the past for national solidarity and had doggedly opposed the 'financial cover' of national defence.[11]

All the leading radical politicians were therefore careful not to brand the three-year law as reactionary. Although this reflected the spirit of the Pau manifesto, it is nevertheless striking that it was always stated—in rather imprecise terms—that an amendment of the law depended on a relaxation of international tensions. The Pau manifesto had made no reference to foreign policy and had made a reduction of military service conditional on army reorganisation. Later, when the Radicals attempted to form a government following the 1914 elections, these statements made by prominent party members were to pose a serious problem, and many Radical deputies refused to accept this concession to foreign policy arising from the pressure of governmental responsibility. During the election campaign this ill-feeling could already be observed in the comments of *Le Radical*, which had advised the Doumergue/Caillaux government not to lay too much emphasis on its loyalty to the defence bill. It was the Radicals' duty, it stated, to enlighten the people about the reactionary character of the 'ill-fated law'.[12] A few days after publication of the executive committee's election manifesto, the editors of *Le Radical* again published a dissenting opinion and urged the party leaders to respect the spirit of the Pau manifesto and pronounce a determined *non* to 'militarist and Caesarean reaction, symbolised by the *Loi de Trois Ans*'.[13]

Le Temps described this dissent as proof that the Radicals' endeavours to unite on this issue had 'gone bankrupt'.[14] Doumergue's statement in particular was, strangely enough, given a mixed reception by the Socialists. The *Guesdistes* saw this as further evidence that the Radical Party, without a uniform doctrine, was being crushed between the two blocs on either side of the *Trois Ans* divide: socialism and reaction. The SFIO would therefore be able to round up all the 'healthy' elements in the Radical Party.[15] The *Jaurèsiste* Marcel Sembat, in contrast, maintained that the obvious incoherence of the Radical Party's line was of political advantage, since it had prevented an extreme confrontation within the republican camp. Doumergue's ambiguity with regard to the three-year law, he wrote, would prevent 'Briandistic reaction' from turning the elections into a 'torchlight procession on behalf of nationalism' on the basis of a 'tremolo' on the international scene and thus diverting attention from potential domestic reform.[16]

As was to be expected, the *Loi de Trois Ans* was the linchpin of the election campaign of the *Fédération des Gauches*. The following resolution was drafted by the FDG steering committee at the end of February 1914: 'The FDG . . . resolves that its support in the forthcoming general elections shall be given only to Republicans from the various parties of the Left resolved to uphold the laws of anticlericalism and social democracy and who come out in favour of the maintenance of the law of national defence.'[17] This resolution is of interest, since it shows that despite Briand's original intentions of setting up a new political party, the FDG did not intend to stand as an independent party in the election campaign.[18] The reasons for this change of mind seem to have been, first, the Briandistes' lack of success in the parliamentary dispute with the Doumergue/Caillaux govern-ment,[19] and second, the fact that the political agitation of the trade associations, earmarked as the backbone of the new party, had not come up to expectations.[20] Only the *Union des Intérêts Économiques* was actively involved in the election campaign, but even its warnings against 'collectivism and revolution' alluded only to tax reform and not to the *Loi de Trois Ans*. No particular political party was recommended,[21] and the assembly of the chairmen of the chambers of commerce, which had spoken out in the struggle against Caillaux's fiscal policy on a number of occasions, even expressly instructed its members not to come out in favour of any particular party in the election campaign.[22]

The FDG was therefore intent on re-establishing links with the republican Left. Emphasis on the determined left-wing stand of this group and exclusive concentration of its election campaign on the *Trois Ans* were to thwart the Radical Party's tactic of evading this issue so far as possible and instead focusing on social antagonism. The FDG election manifesto[23] therefore stressed that there was no significant link between socially conservative aspirations and the emphatic de-mand for the maintenance of the conscription law. All 'anti-clerical and democratic Republicans among all the groups of our great party'[24] were to guard the bill against 'unworthy demagogy'. On financial policy the manifesto advocated the immediate raising of a large loan, with the proviso that the budget would subsequently be balanced by the introduction of a capital yield tax levied on the affluent classes of society 'in accordance with their capacities'. The FDG also endorsed a general rehauling of the tax system, but this was to be enforced only step by step and 'inquisitional' penalties were to be avoided.

As for the *Loi de Trois Ans*, in the FDG election manifesto the general international background to the extension of military service came to light with more clarity and precision than had so far been the case in the public debate. According to the manifesto, the 'integral and loyal' application of the law—that is, continued reinforcement of French troops—was a prerequisite for the voice of France to continue to be heard in international politics and so that France, along with her allies, could preserve international peace.

This endorsement of the principles of Poincaré's foreign policy was somewhat watered down by the manifesto's pathetic description of the extension of military service as a question of life or death for France. This inherent contradiction is another expression of the dilemma apparent in Briand's statement of policy in his speech at St Étienne:[25] after the fear of God had been put into the French public with the threat of an *attaque brusquée*, the international dimension of the *Loi de Trois Ans* did not seem so momentous to the French Republic.

When Millerand, War Minister in Poincaré's 1912 cabinet and a leading FDG member, declared at an election rally, without alluding to the *attaque brusquée*, that the *Trois Ans* would have to be maintained in the long term if the balance of power were not to be upset, *L'Humanité* expressed suspicions that Millerand was now trying to play down the defence issue.[26] Other leading FDG politicians had followed the now predominant trend from the very outset. In his statement of policy Barthou again reduced international and military problems to the stereotype of the *attaque brusquée*: 'For France, threatened by foreign armaments, the three-year law was a matter of life or death. We wanted France to live.'[27]

Moreover, Briand's claim at an election rally, that leading Radical Party members had meanwhile adopted the FDG's arguments, did not help to clarify the fronts or the real international significance of the three-year law.[28] The fact that the FDG's unconditional support for the new conscription law was not considered as a real alternative to the Radical Party manifesto is reflected in comments by both *La Petite République* (Centre) and the moderately radical *France*. In the midst of the election campaign both newspapers called for cooperation between the FDG and the Radical Party on the grounds that both groups saw eye-to-eye on the key issue—the *Loi de Trois Ans*—and, unlike the SFIO, intended to amend the law only in the distant future.[29]

Thus the FDG's claim that, unlike the Radical Party, it was unconditionally committed to the *Trois Ans*, was purely ideological. The Radicals' accusation that the FDG wanted to turn the bill into an election issue just to divert attention away from its campaign against Caillaux's taxation policy, was objectively untrue, but not completely unfounded. The elections were to prove that the electorate did not accept the FDG as an alternative to the Radical Party. Nevertheless, the FDG played an historically important role in internal affairs immediately before the war. First, prior to the elections, it was owing to the FDG's organisation and action against Caillaux that the Socialists continued to support the Doumergue/Caillaux government, despite their discontent with regard to the defence issue. Second, following the elections, the alleged similarity between the FDG and Radical Party stance on the defence question, and the FDG's efforts to project itself as a left-wing movement, combined to prevent the formation of a joint parliamentary bloc of Socialists and Radicals, the consequence of which would certainly have been fundamental amendments to the bill.

Unlike the FDG, the *Alliance Républicaine Démocratique*, the traditional party of the moderate and 'national' bourgeoisie, did not concentrate its election campaign exclusively on the *Trois Ans* issue. The paradigma of the conservative bloc theory, quoted at the beginning of this chapter, can be applied to this formation. During the public and parliamentary debate before and immediately after the adoption of the *Loi de Trois Ans*, the ARD had interlaced its commitment to national defence with conservative social principles to such an extent that the centrist, anti-radical *Entente démocratique et sociale* had seen fit publicly to disassociate itself from the ARD on account of this swing to the Right.[30] Following the SFIO congress in Amiens, the ARD had called on all 'patriots' to join forces against the 'shameful pact' between the SFIO and the Radicals: 'In three months' time, faced with problems from abroad, the sabotage of our public fortune and national humiliation, we'll see the partisans of insurrection marching hand in hand with the candidates of the government.' [31]

A little later the ARD stipulated with which groups it intended to cooperate in the campaign against the 'unpopular governmental coalition' of Socialists and Radicals. To a certain extent it held itself aloof from the Right, but only in so far as it rejected any form of cooperation with the 'right-wing cliques', which in contemporary usage referred to only extreme nationalist and anti-parliamentarian groups— for example, the *Action Française*, the *Ligue des Patriotes* or the *Oeuvre* group. The possibility was therefore not ruled out of links between moderate Republicans and the *Progressistes* (the far Right of the bourgeois parties, traditionally outside the *majorité républicaine*), and cooperation with the 'rallied' ALP Catholics and the monarchist Conservatives. According to the ARD, it was necessary for all 'patriotic' elements to cooperate, because the supposedly united socialist-radical front was cynically jeopardising national defence and intent on undermining public property by tampering with fiscal legislation.[32]

By the beginning of March 1914 it had become clear that the movement against Caillaux had not succeeded. The ARD now quickly changed its strategy: the party executive's first official statement of the election campaign concentrated wholly on the *Loi de Trois Ans*. The party appealed to 'all patriots' to ensure that the conscription bill could be 'ceremoniously ratified' by the electorate. Candidates in each constituency had to be confronted with the clear-cut question, 'Are you for or against the *Loi de Trois Ans*?' To counteract criticism that this polarisation for or against the bill was a means of pursuing socially conservative objectives, the party offered to negotiate with the left-wing Republicans on their tax demands.[33] An explanatory statement on this official declaration pointed out that the decision in favour of the *Trois Ans* was a symbolic one. Regardless of whether they had voted for the bill or for an extension of military service to thirty months, all left-wing Republicans were now faced with the alternative of either entering an electoral alliance with the SFIO, detrimental to the interests of the Republic and *la patrie*, or recognising that the three-year law had created an 'insurmountable trench' between the revolutionary Socialists and all the bourgeois parties.[34]

When the official ARD election manifesto was published a month later,[35] there were no longer any traces of this openness towards the left-wing Republicans. In obvious opposition to the strategy of the FDG, and aware that the differentiated arguments of the Radicals excluded left-wing bourgeois groups from the 'patriotic' bloc, conservative arguments were pushed more and more to the fore. The ARD now declared that it would 'irreconcilably' pursue all candidates who refused to follow the 'national feeling' and agree to the conscription law as the only 'guarantee for peace'. The nation would have to refuse to vote for any candidate who denied France 'the weapons she needs to defend herself'.

Despite the fact that the nationalistic dogma of the *Trois Ans* had lost much of its significance in the course of the parliamentary debate in the summer of 1913,[36] this represented a revival of the original campaign of fear on behalf of national defence in extremely nationalistic and chauvinistic terms. Since the ARD was equally energetic in its opposition to the alleged plans of the United Radicals to turn tax reform into a vehicle for social revolution, it appeared right-wing and reactionary in the contemporary perspective. This was confirmed by a warning to the electorate that the election concerned more than individual issues and involved an option between two diametrically opposed political ideologies. However, in view of the failure of the anti-Caillaux *rassemblement* in Parliament, it was doubtful from the very outset whether the electorate would go along with this determined swing towards the Right of the traditional representative of moderate Republicans. It was not just by pure chance that the FDG, whose members and policy had been traditionally linked with the ARD in the past, was now trying to separate the defence issue from overall social ideology.

Significantly enough, this tactic of explicitly linking the three-year law with conservative financial principles was not even supported by the *Fédération Républicaine* (FR), an extremely conservative group which was not traditionally regarded as a republican party. This party of *Progressistes* originally drew up an election manifesto at the beginning of February 1914,[37] which was replaced two months later by a revised version, in which in particular the party's stance on the defence issue had been redrafted.[38] Shortly afterwards, the FR brought out its election manifesto in the form of a poster,[39] which was different yet again. In its original manifesto in February 1914, the FR had stated that, in retaliation for the expansion of the German army, the defence of the country would be safeguarded only by an increase in the effective strength of the regular French army. In the manifesto published on 8 April, the *Trois Ans* were no longer justified only on the basis of the need to defend *la patrie*. This time the extension of military service was to give France a strong army as a basis for 'peaceful but proud' diplomacy with which she could consolidate her colonial possessions. Despite this allusion to the international dimension of the *Trois Ans*, the FR election manifesto poster simply stated that the bill would have to be maintained as long as circumstances required. This fluctuation clearly shows that the bourgeois Right failed adequately to interpret the new military bill—or that it felt it inadvisable to expose the electorate to the real significance of the *Trois Ans* in terms of power politics. It too finally opted for the stereotype argument of the *attaque brusquée* and the danger to the nation, for the purposes of the election campaign.

The FR's policy on tax reform obviously aimed at backing up the impression that the party's one and only concern in these elections was the defence of France. Although it believed that the budget could be adequately balanced within the framework of the existing tax system, the FR was nevertheless prepared to agree to tax reforms for the sake of national defence, provided that these reforms were combined with an increase of the burden on the property-owning classes. The party's main concern in this respect was that tax reform should not be used as an instrument of social revolution.

Early in February 1914, the 'rallied' *Alliance Libérale Populaire* Catholics, whose leader, Albert de Mun, had played a key role in the original campaign on behalf of the *Trois Ans*, drafted their election manifesto.[40] The ALP's principal demand was the maintenance and loyal application of the three-year law on the grounds that the security of France could no longer be guaranteed in any other way. The supporters of the party were urged to make it clear to the people in the election campaign that the German 'enemy', which had already 'grabbed' a piece of French territory, had introduced its recent rearmament measures to launch an attack on France. The 'patriotic *élan*' which had enabled France to introduce three-year military service and ward off this danger must continue to guarantee the lasting triumph of a policy of national unity over hate and dogmatic anti-clericalism. The financing of the additional military expenditure, the manifesto continued, would pose no problems on the basis of a sustained national consensus. As long as the 'Prussian example' was not followed and a 'parade-ground tone' adopted in tax policy, every reasonable citizen would agree that the national budget could be stabilised only by measures such as tax increases, additional levies and cut-backs.

It is interesting to note that in the ALP manifesto the traditional and specifically Catholic/conservative demands—for example, the re-establishment of diplomatic relations with the Vatican, the reauthor-isation of schools run by the religious orders, and administrative decentralisation—were only an afterthought to the *Trois Ans* issue. This was reflected in public statements made by the party leaders. A. de Mun urged the party supporters to sacrifice the particular prefer-ences of a Catholic party to the overriding objective of transforming the patriotic *élan* of the previous years into a lasting policy of national unity. The party's advice to Catholics in constituencies without an ALP candidate was in the same vein: the local *comités* and party supporters were encouraged to vote for the candidate who, regardless of his political colour, was a supporter of the *Trois Ans* and offered 'the greatest guarantees' for the stabilisation of the national consensus. The representatives of political Catholicism even offered to cooperate with left-wing Republicans! The Archbishop of Paris supported this policy and urged all Catholics who were not committed to a particular party not to abstain from voting (as was the usual practice), but to back the ARD or the FDG in constituencies where there was no ALP candi-date. The Catholics, he said, had to help prevent a victory of the United Radicals and the SFIO.[41]

This offer of cooperation from the Catholic Right was an attractive prospect for the moderate Republicans because the ALP had local branches and youth organisations in nearly every department which could be used for electoral propaganda.[42] The party executives of the ARD and the FR—but not the FDG!—were also prepared to enter into electoral alliances with the ALP for the second ballot, although it was always stressed that these pacts were aimed only at protecting the three-year law from a stormy attack by the Left and did not imply agreement on social issues. In actual fact very few electoral alliances between the Centre and Right were concluded before the second ballot. Despite all the propaganda from the party leaders, the members and supporters of the Centre groups were evidently not prepared to set aside their deep-rooted prejudices against 'clerical reaction' for the sake of the three-year law.

All in all, the 1914 election campaign ran along very moderate lines, at least so far as organisation and propaganda at party headquarters were concerned. There are various reasons why public agitation during the election campaign seldom reached the excesses of the *Trois Ans* campaign in the spring of 1913.[43] In the first place, the edge was taken off the campaign by the adoption of an electoral law at the end of March 1914 permitting the circulation of election posters only two weeks before election day. The same law further stipulated that election posters were to be displayed only on the official election notice-boards. This served also to dampen the ardour of the campaign.[44] Moreover, the government did its best to clamp down on chauvinistic abuses. For example, the police authorities were ordered to remove a poster of a certain 'Union of Commerce and Industry for Social Defence' denouncing all the opponents of the three-year law as accomplices of Prussian militarism.[45] Finally, even more significant than these administrative measures, the extreme militant organisations on both sides—for instance, the *Jeunesses Syndicalistes* on the far Left or the *Action Française* and the *Ligue des Patriotes* on the nationalist and anti-republican Right—kept a low profile throughout the election campaign.[46]

However, the main reason for the relative calm throughout the election campaign was that, although the key issue—the three-year law—was a subject of controversy, the positions of the various republican parties on national defence did not diverge to such an extent that ideological differences were fundamentally accentuated. For this reason there was no extreme political confrontation which could have led to a polarisation of the political fronts. Above all, there still remained the possibility of a *rapprochement* between left-wing and moderate Republicans.

The Failure of the 'Bloc' Concepts and the Victory of the SFIO in the Elections

On 26 April 1914 a total of almost 2,500 candidates, of whom only some 2,000 were regarded as serious,[47] ran for the 602 seats in Parliament. After 349 deputies were elected with the required absolute majority in the first ballot, a second ballot on 10 May was to determine the allocation of the remaining seats.

It is not possible to classify the newly elected deputies according to their precise party political colours, since many candidates, especially those who regarded themselves as left-wing Republicans, had not been officially nominated by one of the national parties. The Radical Party, for example, had nominated official party candidates in only 248 out of 602 constituencies, all members who had at least signed the Pau manifesto. The party explained that for reasons of 'republican discipline' it had not put forward a candidate in constituencies where there was either no suitable party member or a candidate representing similar policies who had a reasonable chance of being elected.[48] Since the absence of the Radical Party had contributed to the victory of the

SFIO in a number of constituencies, the anti-radical press concluded that the Radical Party was the servant of the Socialists.[49] This accusation, however, was totally unfounded: in the first ballot forty-three Radical Party candidates were elected against an SFIO representative, while twenty Socialists defeated officially nominated radical candidates. Of even greater interest is the fact that, in seventy-six further constituencies, neither left-wing candidate gained an absolute majority.[50] A decisive factor explaining the reluctance of the Radical Party to nominate official party candidates was therefore probably the fear of losing deputies and voters, who were traditionally sympathetic towards the party but sceptical about the Pau manifesto and its stance on the *Trois Ans* issue, to the Briandistes.

The Radical Party's tactic provided a welter of left-wing and relatively moderate candidates with a welcome opportunity to run for Parliament without having to commit themselves fully to one of the competing republican parties. In fact almost 400 left-wing republican candidates who had not been officially nominated stood in the elections. These candidates fell back on the support of the traditional local committees and adopted the vague political labels with which the electorate was well acquainted: *radical, radical-socialiste, républicain de gauche, gauche démocratique.*

The FDG and the ARD, also hit by the reluctance of candidates formally to commit themselves to the national parties, generally recruited their candidates from the two latter groups, *républicains de gauche* and *gauche démocratique*. According to *Le Temps*'s statistics, only twenty-eight candidates (!) ran on the FDG ticket, most of these being founding members of the group from the previous Parliament. Of the 193 candidates who officially endorsed the ARD manifesto, only sixty-three expressly defined themselves as *républicain de gauche* or *gauche démocratique*, although these two groups were the traditional rallying-points for the parliamentary non-radical Centre. The vast majority of candidates who signed the ARD manifesto did not specify their political background, either meaninglessly declaring themselves as *républicain* or simply quoting their profession—for instance, 'doctor' or 'lawyer'. It can therefore be concluded that among the upper-middle classes the *Loi de Trois Ans* and tax reform were regarded as socially relevant issues which encouraged members of the notability, otherwise not engaged in politics, to stand in the elections. This, however, left little impact on the general allocation of seats in the new parliament.

As a rule, traditional party orientation and party nomination seem to have coincided only within the SFIO, the extreme right-wing republican/conservative *Fédération Républicaine* and the Catholic 'rallied' ALP. Sixty-one of the eighty-seven candidates backed by the FR described themselves as *Progressistes* or supporters of the *Union Républicaine*, and virtually all the 130 ALP candidates declared themselves as 'Liberal' or 'Catholic'. The SFIO fielded candidates in 421 of the 602 constituencies, regardless of their prospects of success.

The nomination problems of the national groups of the bourgeois Left and Centre show that the political antagonism which had evolved at parliamentary level since the fall of the Barthou government had no direct analogy outside Parliament. As a result, there were considerable discrepancies in the statistics published after the elections giving a breakdown of the political allegiances of the candidates who had polled most votes in the first ballot. The official Ministry of the Interior statistics interpreted the results of the first ballot as follows:[51]

Réactionnaires (including ALP)	66
Progressistes	47
Fédération des Gauches	20
Républicains de gauche	38
Radicaux et radicaux-socialistes	118
Républicain-socialistes	11
SFIO	40

In contrast the liberal/conservative *Le Temps* published the following table:[52]

SFIO	40
Socialistes indépendants et républicain-socialistes	12
Radicaux unifiés	72
ARD	66
Radicaux indépendants et républicains de gauche	50
Progressistes	77
FR	35
ALP	30
Droite	19
Indépendants	13

The FDG's estimates ran as follows:[53]

SFIO	38
Socialistes indépendants (nuance Augagneur)	8
Socialistes indépendants (nuance Briand), Radicaux non unifiés, républicains de gauche, ARD, FDG, Union Républicaine	125
Radicaux unifiés	77
Progressistes	26
Droite et ALP	61

All sources, regardless of their political leaning, agreed that the SFIO had substantially increased its share of the vote and could expect to have approximately 100 deputies following the second ballot.[54] The defeat of the anti-radical FDG was also evident. Significantly this group is not even mentioned in *Le Temps*'s statistics. In its own statistics the FDG combined all the non-united groups of the bourgeois Centre and Right under one heading. This too was an admission of defeat. For the Socialists and the Radicals this was the most significant result of the election analysis. The anti-radical groups, in contrast, concentrated on the 'failure of the radical union'.[55] Even the Radical Party conceded that its results did not meet the expectations aroused, following the reorganisational efforts after the Pau conference. There were conflicting views on the reasons for this defeat. *Le Radical* was of the opinion that many of the party's candidates had lost votes because they had not opposed the unpopular conscription bill with sufficient firmness.[56] The moderately radical *France*, on the other hand, considered that the party's defeat was due to the fact that many of its candidates had not supported the three-year law, whereas the vast majority of the population was convinced of its necessity.[57]

In view of these diverging interpretations, the Radical Party preferred not to come out either for or against the *Trois Ans*, and did not change its tactics in the campaign leading up to the second ballot. The party executive called on the electorate to form a left-wing bloc against the forces of social reaction, but did not even mention the defence question![58]

SFIO headquarters supported the Radical Party tactics. Sembat advised the SFIO departmental federations (according to a resolution passed at the Amiens party conference in January 1914, they themselves had the responsibility to decide on possible alliances in the second ballot) not to make the *Trois Ans* issue the only criterion for withdrawing their candidates. This degree of intransigence, he warned, would serve the interests only of the allied groups of political and social reaction. The SFIO should, rather, apply the principle of 'republican discipline', withdrawing a candidate in constituencies where a left-wing Republican had polled more votes in the first ballot.[59] Jaurès agreed with Sembat and reminded the party organisations that, unlike the Briandistes, the vast majority of the Radicals who had come out in favour of the three-year law regarded it as a mere 'provisional shelter'.[60] The CAP's advice to the federations was equally cautious. The Amiens resolution[61] was relaxed and the federations were advised not only to support left-wing republican candidates who were firm opponents of the conscription law. Since it was the SFIO's task to ward off the 'wave of militarism', it had to stand in the way of the re-election of all those who were 'particularly guilty' of establishing the act.[62]

Nevertheless, there is evidence that by no means all the SFIO regional branches towed the party line. In seventy-one out of a total of 253 constituencies where a second ballot was to be held, the SFIO candidate stepped down in favour of a United Radical, whereas twenty-five candidatures were upheld against Radicals. In a further twenty-five constituencies, socialist candidates were withdrawn on the grounds that they had little chance of success, but the electorate was not advised to vote for an alternative candidate.[63]

The reason for this reluctance to respect 'republican discipline' probably lay in the fact that many federations had concentrated their political activity against the *Loi de Trois Ans* over the past year and were not prepared to follow the sudden turn-about in the party line, especially since, as mentioned above, the party CAP had not referred to the international dimension of the *Trois Ans* in any great detail except at the beginning of the election campaign. The attitude of many federations suggests that a large proportion of the socialist rank and file was not prepared to go along with this change of policy and disregard the problems of foreign policy and international under-standing for the sake of considerations of home politics.

Although the bloc concept of the leaders of the Socialist and Radical Parties met with concrete difficulties at grass-roots level, the campaign of the ALP, FR and ARD for the second ballot was almost exclusively directed against the alleged plans of 'anti-French sabotage'.[64] The Radical Party was accused of aiming at a pact with the Socialists, despite the fact that the SFIO was not prepared to take the necessary steps to defend the nation. In its revised manifesto before the second ballot, the FR appealed to all 'good Frenchmen' to unite against this 'ungodly pact'. Despite the allegations of the Radicals, it continued, the republican institutions of the country were not being attacked by reaction. All that was important at the moment was to safeguard national defence—but the Left bloc supporters were deliberately exposing the country to danger: 'Away with the criminal disputes on the doorstep of the burning house! Help, all good Frenchmen, help!'[65]

This was wholly endorsed by the ALP in the form of a proclamation from its leader, A. de Mun.[66] In another election manifesto the ARD leaders protested against the secret pact between Socialists and Rad-icals which was endangering the 'vital interests' of France in such a scandalous way. In the face of this danger the electorate's decision should no longer be guided by the traditional demarcation line be-tween the Republic and reaction.[67]

Given the overall development of the debate, it was impossible entirely to reduce politics to a decision for or against the *Loi de Trois Ans*, and these attempts to bring the debate on national defence to an ideological climax ended in wasted effort. All the manifestos calling on Frenchmen to unite to quench the flames of 'the burning house' were virtually ignored by the candidates and local committee members of the anti-radical Centre and the Right, who on account of their day-to-day contact with the electorate were better acquainted with the real options open to the population. In the second ballot there were in fact very few cases of electoral alliances between moderate Republicans, on the one hand, and *Progressistes* and the 'rallied' and anti-republican Right, on the other. Candidates from the Centre and the Right who had stood in the first ballot officially withdrew in the second ballot in only eighteen constituencies. In nine further constituencies the final poll would seem to suggest the conclusion of unofficial agreements. In contrast, in the second ballot, candidates of the ARD and other bourgeois Centre groups stood against the anti-republican and *progressiste* Right in twenty-six constituencies—despite the fact that these groups saw eye-to-eye on the *Trois Ans* and tax reform. In a further forty-one constituencies, agreements were made between left-wing bourgeois candidates and supporters of the anti-radical groups of the Centre to field a joint candidate against a far Left or Right candidate. And in ten constituencies, alliances were even concluded between the SFIO and non-radical candidates. All this is an indication that the bloc theory of the leaders of the ARD, FR and ALP did not reflect this general mood among the electorate.

In fact, all in all, there was considerable opposition to the bloc concept of the main national party formations on the Right and the Left from candidates, local election committees and the electorate. Confronted with this, the FDG tried to make amends. It began by disassociating itself from the ARD. The FDG steering committee stated that the latter's attitude was incompatible with the joint front against anti-republican reaction, to which moderate Republicans must be committed.[68] In a revised version of its election manifesto, the FDG's advice to Republicans was to vote only for candidates 'who do not separate the interests of the Republic from those of *la patrie*'. Thus, continued the FDG, citizens should pronounce a clear *oui* to national defence, the only guarantee of which 'at present' (!) was the *Trois Ans*. However, votes should be given only to candidates with a socially progressive platform, prepared to approve considerable tax increases on behalf of national defence.[69] Although the FDG rejected an 'inquisitional' tax policy—again differing on this point from the Radical Party—it was more concerned with maintaining the image of the unity of the republican forces as an alternative to the bloc theories of the Left and the Right.

It is difficult to define the overall results of both ballots in terms of the distribution of seats in the new Parliament. Since the electorate voted for a candidate, as opposed to a party, and the candidates were frequently only loosely linked with the national party formations, it is often impossible to pinpoint the political affiliation of the newly elected deputies, as can be seen from the following selection of statistics published after the elections. According to *Le Temps*, which may be regarded as relatively neutral on this point,[70] the allocation of seats in the new Parliament was as follows:

Socialistes unifiés	102
Socialistes indépendants et Republicain-socialistes	30
Radicaux unifiés	136
Alliance Démocratique	100
Radicaux indépendants et républicains de gauche	103
Progressistes et Fédération Républicaine	54
Action Libérale	34
Droite	26
Indépendants	16

These statistics were corrected the next day—presumably owing to the potential formation of parliamentary coalitions:

SFIO	101
Socialistes (parti ouvrier)	2
Republicain-socialistes (nuance Augagneur)	13
Radicaux unifiés	134
Radicaux non unifiés, partisans du programme de Pau	25
Républicain-socialistes et Radicaux douteux	7
Républicain-socialistes et Radicaux non partisans du programme de Pau; FDG et ARD	187
Progressistes et Fédération Républicaine	54
ALP	34
Droite	26
Indépendants	18

This table was obviously drawn up according to the conservative bloc theory, with the intention of illustrating a demarcation line running through the new Parliament approximately situated between the *républicain-socialistes et radicaux douteux* and the *républicain-socialistes non partisans du programme de Pau*, the latter being unrealistically allocated to the camp of the moderates. *Le Radical*'s[71] statistics are equally revealing:

Radicaux et radicaux-socialistes (dont 189 radicaux unifiés)	236
Républicain-socialistes	30
Socialistes unifiés	102
Républicains de gauche	30
FDG	31
Progressistes	59
Réactionnaires (ALP compris)	81
Parti ouvrier	1

This table more or less reflected the distribution of seats among the political groups in the previous Chamber. It is particularly striking that the number of United Radicals is quoted in brackets only and that in the republican-socialist group no differentiation is drawn between Briandistes and anti-Briandistes. This shows that the party leaders were no longer aiming exclusively at the establishment of a left-wing bloc, but were now trying to steer the majority in the Chamber towards the Centre, which presumably meant that it was no longer appropriate to differentiate between *Troisannistes* and *Anti-trois-sanistes*.

Finally, a reference to the statistics of the socialist *L'Humanité*: here a demarcation line was drawn between the United Radicals and the Radicals and they were all placed in the political Centre:

Groupe socialiste au Parlament	101
Socialistes en dehors du parti	2
Républicain-socialistes	
(nuance Augagneur)	29
(nuance Briand)	8
Radicaux unifiés	174
Radicaux et républicains de gauche	149
Progressistes	69
Action Libérale	34
Droitiers	34

All these statistics had only one common denominator: the SFIO had clearly won the election. For the conservative press this success represented the deluge of the 'red floods', and was largely to be ascribed to the radical campaign against the policy of national unity. The Socialists themselves rated this victory as proof of the people's rejection of the three-year law. Although these interpretaions of the results of the election may seem understandable, it nevertheless remains questionable whether the results represented a 'bursting of the dam' in comparison with previous elections, implying that the majority of the population was opposed to the *Loi de Trois Ans*. The number of seats gained by the SFIO was not in fact substantially larger than in previous elections. In the 1902 elections the Socialist Party had gained forty-one seats, followed by fifty-four in 1906 and seventy-four in 1910.[72] However, the peculiarities of French majority suffrage make it necessary to consider the percentage gains or losses of the SFIO in each individual department, since this factor is reflected only indirectly in the overall results shown in the Table below (pp. 202–3).[73]

The discrepancy between gains in terms of percentage and gains in terms of seats is particularly evident in the following cases. In the department of Isère, the SFIO's poll fell from 15 per cent (in 1910) to about 10 per cent in 1914, but the number of SFIO deputies representing this department increased from three to five. In the department of Nord, although the SFIO's share of the vote remained constant at about 25 per cent, its number of seats increased from six to ten. In Seine-et-Marne the SFIO increased its poll from 5 per cent to about 15 per cent but nevertheless lost its seat. One of the few departments where percentage increases directly correspond with the number of seats gained was the department of Haute-Vienne, where the SFIO increased its poll from about 15 per cent to about 30 per cent, and its number of seats from one to three. All in all, it can be concluded that the SFIO poll remained more or less constant in forty-nine out of eighty-seven departments. It fell by about 5 per cent in seven departments, and increased by 5 per cent in twenty-two. Thus gains of about 10 per cent applied to only five departments. Apart from this, a 15 per cent increase was achieved in three departments, and in Haute-Saône the SFIO poll fell from 15 per cent to zero. These statistics demonstrate that the 1914 elections took place within the framework of a political system in which there was very little voter fluctuation. The increase of the Socialists' influence was not so much due to their position on an *ad hoc* political issue—the *Loi de Trois Ans*—but a reflection of the continued process of industrialisation. Nevertheless, the outcome of the 1914 elections naturally appeared to the Socialists as a confirmation of their political struggle against 'military reaction'. It had at least become clear that, despite all the defamatory allegations that the SFIO were anti-patriots and 'the Prussians of the interior', the continued rise of socialism had not been halted.[74]

The Domestic Crisis on the Eve of the First World War

The socialist victory in the elections represented the *de facto* end of the informal governmental coalition between the extreme

Department	Percentage bracket 1910–1914	Seats 1910–1914
Ain	1 – 2	0 – 0
Aisne	3 – 3	1 – 2
Allier	7 – 7	4 – 3
Alpes, Basses	2 – 2	0 – 0
Alpes, Hautes	2 – 1	0 – 0
Alpes Maritimes	2 – 1	0 – 0
Ardèche	1 – 1	0 – 0
Ardennes	6 – 6	2 – 4
Ariège	1 – 2	0 – 0
Aube	3 – 4	1 – 1
Aveyron	2 – 2	1 – 1
Belfort	× – 2	0 – 0
Bouches-du-Rhône	5 – 6	3 – 3
Calvados	× – 1	0 – 0
Cantal	2 – 1	0 – 0
Charente	1 – 2	0 – 0
Charente, Inf.	1 – 2	0 – 1
Cher	5 – 6	2 – 2
Corrèze	1 – 2	0 – 0
Corse	1 – 1	0 – 0
Côte-d'Or	1 – 1	0 – 1
Côtes du Nord	1 – 1	0 – 0
Creuse	1 – 2	0 – 0
Dordogne	1 – 1	0 – 0
Doubs	1 – 1	0 – 0
Drôme	3 – 2	0 – 1
Eure	1 – 1	0 – 0
Eure-et-Loire	1 – 1	0 – 0
Finistère	2 – 2	1 – 1
Gard	6 – 5	2 – 4
Garonne, Haute	4 – 4	2 – 3
Gers	1 – 1	0 – 0
Gironde	3 – 3	1 – 1
Hérault	4 – 4	2 – 2
Ille-et-Vilaine	1 – 1	0 – 0
Indre	2 – 2	0 – 0
Inde-et-Loire	3 – 3	0 – 1
Isère	4 – 3	3 – 5
Jura	2 – 2	0 – 1
Landes	1 – 1	0 – 0
Loir-et-Cher	1 – 2	0 – 0
Loire	2 – 3	0 – 1
Loire, Haute	1 – ×	0 – 0
Loire, Inf.	× – 2	0 – 0
Loiret	1 – 1	0 – 0

Department	Percentage bracket 1910–1914	Seats 1910–1914
Lot	1 – 2	0 – 0
Lot-et-Garonne	1 – 1	0 – 0
Lozère	1 – 2	0 – 0
Maine-et-Loire	1 – 1	0 – 0
Manche	1 – 1	0 – 0
Marne	1 – 2	0 – 0
Marne, Haute	1 – 1	0 – 0
Mayenne	× – ×	0 – 0
Meurthe-et-Moselle	1 – 1	0 – 0
Meuse	× – ×	0 – 0
Morbihan	1 – 1	0 – 0
Nièvre	3 – 6	1 – 3
Nord	6 – 6	6 – 10
Oise	2 – 2	0 – 0
Orne	1 – 1	0 – 0
Pas-de-Calais	5 – 5	4 – 6
Puy-de-Dôme	2 – 3	1 – 2
Pyrénées, Basses	1 – 1	0 – 0
Pyrénées, Hautes	1 – 1	0 – 0
Rhône	3 – 4	3 – 4
Saône, Haute	4 – ×	0 – 0
Saône-et-Loire	1 – 4	2 – 3
Sarthe	1 – 1	0 – 0
Savoie	1 – 1	0 – 0
Savoie, Haute	1 – 1	0 – 0
Seine (Paris et Banlieue)	5 – 6	17 – 22
Seine, Inf.	1 – 2	0 – 0
Seine-et-Marne	1 – 3	1 – 0
Seine-et-Oise	1 – 3	0 – 1
Sèvres (Deux)	2 – 2	1 – 1
Somme	3 – 3	1 – 1
Tarn	4 – 4	2 – 2
Tarn-et-Garonne	1 – 1	0 – 0
Var	6 – 7	3 – 3
Vaucluse	4 – 3	0 – 1
Vendée	1 – 1	0 – 0
Vienne	1 – 2	0 – 0
Vienne, Haute	4 – 7	1 – 4
Vosges	1 – 2	0 – 0
Yonne	2 – 4	0 – 1

Left, the United Radicals and part of the left of Centre, established following the fall of the Barthou government in December 1913. The crack in the surface of this left-wing majority—the *Loi de Trois*

Ans—could no longer be held together by Doumergue's compromise formula that the defence bill was not a 'dogma' but would nevertheless have to be 'loyally executed'. In view of their success in the elections, the Socialists now made it clear that they were no longer prepared to go along with such a vague formula. In his first commentary following the elections, Jaurès declared that the Socialists now had the opportunity to achieve a 'precise and great task' in Parliament and to ensure that the first step of the new Parliament would be the abolition of the three-year law.[75] Jaurès's statement also met with the approval of the *Guesdistes*. Although they stressed that the SFIO had to act independently of all the bourgeois parties, this principle tended to be pushed aside in view of the real possibility of the SFIO's becoming the decisive element in the parliamentary majority. Compère-Morel, for example, clearly indicated that, in view of the increased number of SFIO deputies, the *Guesdistes* would also share the Socialists' 'new responsibility' for the fate of the Republic. The SFIO, affirmed *L'Humanité*, would not hesitate to support a progressive cabinet along with the Radicals, provided that the government's policy included the implementation of tax reform and a return to the 1905 conscription law.[76] Immediately before the beginning of the new legislative period the SFIO parliamentary group drafted a resolution of principle. The group, it stated, would guard its independence, but at the same time support all serious attempts of the republican Left to implement reforms. It would not support any government which was not prepared to take the necessary energetic steps to reintroduce the 1905 conscription law.[77] The small *républicain-socialiste* group also declared that it would only support a government which immediately announced measures to reintroduce the 1905 law.[78]

The Radical Party, in contrast, initially tried to evade the *Trois Ans* issue, which was a threat to the unity of the party. When the SFIO and the *républicain-socialistes* issued their resolutions, the United Radicals were still busy forming their parliamentary group and there was reason to assume that a large number of hitherto non-United Radicals would join the official party formation before the beginning of the new legislatory period.[79] Therefore in their first statement of policy after the elections on 1 June the United Radicals avoided associating themselves with the Socialists' statements, despite the fact that the socialist demand for the immediate reintroduction of the 1905 conscription law corresponded exactly with the resolution passed at the congress of Pau in October 1913.[80] The Radical Party executive committee supported the parliamentary group's tactics of caution and issued a resolution on 3 June urging the party's deputies 'immediately to take the necessary measures to implement the concept of the nation in arms, which implies not only a reduction of regular service but an increase in the defensive power of the country'.[81]

The wording of this resolution did not completely rule out the possibility of other compromise solutions, such as a revival of the Paul-Boncour/Messimy counter-proposal. From the point of view of French internal politics, the Radicals' caution was significant. The Radicals had not committed themselves to the Socialists and so the door leading to a coalition with the non-United Left and moderate Republicans had not been closed, provided that these groups agreed with the Radicals that the defence law should not be regarded as a 'dogma' and were prepared to accept tax reform. In contrast, these considerations of internal opportunism were totally irrelevant to considerations of strategics in foreign policy. Since it was imperative to maintain the three-year law as part and parcel of both the Russian alliance and French strategic planning, it was immaterial which alternative the Socialists, United Radicals and moderate Republicans could agree upon. From this angle the only aspect of importance was that, following the 1914 elections, the amendment of the conscription law had become a real possibility.

These developments explain why, to everyone's surprise, the Doumergue cabinet (formed in December 1913) suddenly resigned on 1 June 1914, shortly before the beginning of the new legislatory period. The reason Doumergue gave for this step was that the government's only objective had been to achieve a 'union of the Left' after a period of 'ambiguous' policy. The election results had proved that this policy had been a success.[82] These words, although by no means discourteous, were interpreted by the left-wing press as the rejection of a bloc of the United Radicals and Socialists, and were greeted with great surprise. The fact that there might be a link between Doumergue's resignation and the possibility of the conscription law being amended, evidently occurred to no one.[83] Indeed, there was no direct contradiction between the Premier's repeated public statements on the defence issue and the apparent determination of the Left to introduce some kind of amendment to the three-year law. Apart from his pledge to apply 'loyally' the *Loi de Trois Ans*, Doumergue had always stated that he did not regard the law as a 'dogma'. *Le Temps* nevertheless hit the nail on the head by surmising that Doumergue had resigned because he could not accept the Left's demand for an immediate reorganisation of the army.[84] A few days earlier Doumergue had explained the reasons for his resignation to the President of the Republic. Poincaré noted in his diary: 'He [Doumergue] does not want to promise to repeal the three-year law and of course I encouraged him to stand firm on this point. But he fears the demands of his friends and prefers to withdraw for the time being'.[85]

Doumergue was indeed in a quandary. On the one hand, his period of office as Premier and Foreign Minister had convinced him of the necessity to maintain the conscription law as a prerequisite for the stability of the Russian alliance. On the other hand, he could not give enough weight to this conviction in the public debate for fear of being branded a newly converted *Troisanniste*, which would undoubtedly have led to a split with the Radicals and the imminent downfall of his government. But Doumergue was not prepared to break with the Radicals. After over a year's public debate on national defence, fresh in everyone's minds again just after the election campaign, to change fundamentally the arguments in favour of three-year military service would certainly have sparked off a domestic crisis and led to a loss of governmental authority, which would have forced Doumergue to step down anyway. Even the emphatic advice of the French ambassador in Berlin, Jules Cambon, to disclose the real reasons for French rearmament to the French public, offered Doumergue no way out of his dilemma. At the time of the election campaign Cambon had already sent the following despatch to Doumergue outlining the entire dialectics of the demagogic campaign in favour of the *Trois Ans*:

> There are illusions in France about the character of these laws [the German armament bill of 1913]. It has been regarded as an indication of a German design to strike us, an immediate and one-off danger. This is mistaken . . . reading the newspapers and speeches of the candidates in support of three-year service during the election campaign, I have noticed that this reform is frequently presented as a reform intended to protect us from a momentary danger. This is the profound error . . . and I believe it is necessary not to let public opinion in France grow accustomed to the idea that the three-year law is a law of circumstance.[86]

Doumergue's resignation faced the President of the Republic with a predicament. Poincaré had just given a widely acclaimed speech in Lyons on the constitutional role of the head of state. In this speech he had emphasised that, as 'President of all Frenchmen', he did not intend to intervene in purely domestic issues and would intercede only in political questions of 'great national interest'.[87] Although Poincaré undoubtedly considered the *Loi de Trois Ans* as of the utmost national interest, he had avoided making any reference whatsoever to the defence question in this speech. Although criticised on this score by *Le Temps*, Jaurès had drawn the correct conclusion from the President's reticence—that Poincaré did not want to adopt a stance against the left-wing majority in Parliament.[88] His Lyons speech was therefore clearly a rejection of the frequent demands made by the anti-republican and conservative press since the elections that he should step in and oppose the new Parliament in order to save France.[89]

But how could these two conflicting imperatives—the formation of a clearly left-wing cabinet, on the one hand, and the maintenance of the three-year law, on the other—be reconciled? The question to which Doumergue could find no answer also represented an *impasse* to the President.[90] He too was unable to untie the Gordian knot of national defence ideology—for example, in the manner suggested by Cambon. Although this would have unleashed a domestic crisis, it was presumably the only opportunity of distinctly separating national defence from general foreign policy which would allow a political reorientation of the parties in Parliament. Thus it might have been possible to confront the Radicals with the defence issue and force them to come up with a more concrete stance than the vague formula passed at the congress of Pau. But this was not what Poincaré decided to do. The day after Doumergue's resignation he made a speech in Rennes in Brittany which reflected the pattern of the 'campaign of fear' in the spring of the previous year: 'France does not wish to be exposed to laws from abroad. . . . To defend ['her independence, her rights and her honour', she needs] an army on a grand scale which can be swiftly mobilised; she also needs well instructed, exercised and trained troops.'[91]

This speech was quite obviously an endorsement of the *Trois Ans*. Jaurès immediately condemned it as both unconstitutional and an attempt to challenge the left-wing majority in Parliament.[92] This was in fact not at all Poincaré's intention. He was prepared to accept the fact that the Left would play the key role in the new Parliament but hoped, as his diary shows, that the disagreement between the Socialists and the United Radicals on the demand for an immediate return to the 1905 conscription law would at least protect the three-year law for the time being.[93]

Poincaré accordingly followed Doumergue's advice and entrusted the *républicain-socialiste* Viviani, Minister for Education in Doumergue's cabinet, with the task of forming a government. Although, unlike the former Premier, Poincaré was by no means convinced that Viviani was totally committed to the three-year law,[94] Viviani nevertheless seemed a suitable premier, since his position on the defence issue had so far more or less corresponded with that of most of the Radicals. Viviani had voted against the government's bill and in favour of the 'thirty months' in July 1913. In his statement of policy prior to the 1914 elections he had declared his staunch conviction that the conscription law must be applied 'correctly and loyally' to give France the opportunity of 'warding off aggression'. As to when the law might be amended, he, like other members of the government, had gone no further than stating that military service had had to be extended because of given 'circumstances', and could therefore be reduced again on the basis of 'other circumstances'.[95]

In forming his cabinet, Viviani did his best to take account of the Radicals as the predominant element of the governmental majority. Most of Doumergue's ministers retained their post, and two further leading members of the United Radicals were given portfolios. This fundamentally homogeneous radical cabinet was nevertheless doomed to failure, since the two new cabinet members, Godard and Ponsot, refused to accept the new Premier's statement on the three-year law in his governmental declaration. The controversial passage of Viviani's speech ran as follows:

> The government confirms its intention to apply correctly and loyally the law voted by Parliament. However, the new cabinet intends to examine proposals concerning the military preparation of the young and a better utilisation of our reserves. When these proposals have been adopted and experience has proved their merit, we could then envisage reducing the military burden, the situation abroad permitting.[96]

The only stumbling-block was the clause 'the situation abroad permitting'. These—presumably intentionally eclectic—words were, without doubt, intended to pad out Doumergue's vague assurance that the conscription law would be applied 'loyally'. They were also an indication that, despite the Premier's openness to radical and socialist demands, the dictates of foreign policy also had to be considered. What these dictates actually were, Viviani left relatively vague: within the contemporary context the reference to the 'situation abroad' automatically implied an *attaque brusquée*. To announce a change in 'circumstances' abroad as a prerequisite for an amendment of the conscription law was more in line with the arguments of the FDG than the demands of the United Radicals.

Following talks with leading members of the Radical Party, Viviani came to the conclusion that the intransigence of the two new cabinet members was a true reflection of the mood of the majority of their supporters in Parliament. As a result, he decided not to attempt a cabinet reshuffle and stood down.[97]

After Viviani's admission of defeat, Poincaré first of all tried to appoint a politician of some repute from the left of Centre as Premier. However, recent events had shown that the Radical Party was still not prepared to accept foreign policy as a basis for the three-year law and neither Deschanel, just elected as President of the Chamber, nor Jean Dupuy, publicist and founding member of the FDG, felt in a position to accept the President's call to office.[98]

Poincaré then took a step assessed by the whole of public opinion as an open challenge from the President of the Republic of the United Radicals. A moderate Republican, Senator Ribot, was given the task of forming a cabinet. Within a few days Ribot had actually managed to achieve this goal—without a single member of the Radical Party. But, contrary to the fears of the Left and the hopes of the Right, the Ribot government did not represent the President's intention to adopt a socially conservative line against the will of the left-wing majority in the Chamber.[99] The very fact that Léon Bourgeois, one of the Third Republic's leading left-wing politicians, accepted the post of Foreign Minister, indicated that the only task of Ribot's government was to protect the conscription law. Bourgeois, whose name had been linked with social progress for decades, had left the Radical Party in the Spring of 1914 in protest against the party's ambiguous attitude towards the *Loi de Trois Ans*. Moreover, the fact that Delcassé, ambassador in St Petersburg until early 1914 and well known as a resolute *Troisanniste*, was appointed as War Minister in the new cabinet, stressed the determination of both Ribot and Poincaré to force the Radicals into stating a definitive 'yes' or 'no' to the law.[100]

Ribot's governmental declaration on 13 June referred to the *Loi de Trois Ans* law in categorical terms:

> The law on the length of military service . . . cannot be called into question today. . . . To make the mistake of relaxing the law while nothing has changed with regard to the balance of military forces in Europe, would be to forfeit not only the security we require but the moral effect produced by the adoption of the law and its acceptance by the country.[101]

It was therefore clear that Ribot had no intention of getting involved in negotiations on the defence question nor of entertaining the vague compromise formulae so far used by nearly all politicians. To make it easier for the Radicals to give their approval to his governmental declaration, he also tried to relieve suspicions that he was hiding socially conservative aims up his sleeve. In the financial part of his governmental declaration, Ribot announced that he was willing to give in to the Left on the main domestic issue of previous months, tax policy and public borrowing, and introduce legislation to this end. The loan to cover the 'exceptional expenditure' for national defence was to be reduced to 800 million francs, and the bonds in connection with the loan were to be liable to the tax on movable assets. Ribot also promised that the government would do all it could to persuade the Senate to adopt the Chamber's resolution of March 1914[102] and include general income tax in the 1914 budgetary finance bill. The government's olive-branch policy was even more surprising, since only a few months previously Ribot had sharply criticised Caillaux's tax plans in the Senate. As Premier he was obviously now trying to make it clear that the *Trois Ans* could and had to be kept out of internal wrangling.

Ribot's attempt to induce a split in the Radical Party, or an estrangement between the Radicals and the SFIO over the defence issue, was to no avail. The United Radicals followed the advice from the party executive not to support a Ribot cabinet, because its political profile was diametrically opposed to the electorate's mandate.[103] Immediately after Ribot's governmental declaration, the radical parliamentary group tabled a resolution demanding that it remain the core of the governmental majority. This motion was again devoid of any reference to the three-year law: 'The Chamber, respecting the will recently expressed by universal suffrage, resolves that it shall put its confidence only in a government capable of uniting the forces of the Left. . . .'[104]

This was quite evidently a motion for a vote of no confidence. A group of moderate deputies now put forward a resolution calling on the Chamber to express its confidence in the new government, determined both to apply progressive financial measures and maintain the *Loi de Trois Ans* 'for as long as circumstances abroad have not changed'.[105] According to traditional parliamentary practice, Ribot asked for a vote of confidence on the priority of the second motion. When, by a majority of 306 votes to 262, the Chamber decided to accord priority to the United Radicals' motion, Ribot resigned, even before the Chamber had decided on the substance of the opposing motions. Since the 306 votes against Ribot were mainly from the parliamentary groups of the three organised parties of the Left,[106] it appeared that a bloc of the Left had in fact been established. The unity of this bloc came as a surprise even to its supporters, and led to gloomy forecasts from its opponents about the fate of France.[107]

Nevertheless, Goguel's theory that this division was paradigmatic of the polarisation in French politics on the eve of the First World War, is very questionable. It cannot be stated that all the deputies who voted in favour of Ribot's cabinet were right wing 'in the sense this term had assumed in 1914'. Nor can it be maintained that the establishment of a firm bloc of the Left had prompted the merger of the Centre and Right in complete unity.[108] Only a few hours after this first division, a second division took place in Parliament, this time 'on the substance' of the United Radicals' resolution. This time there were 395 votes in favour of the Dalimier/Puech motion. This meant that virtually the entire non-United left of Centre had changed sides, presumably so as not to be cut off from the overwhelming left-wing majority. This swing was undoubtedly facilitated—if not indeed made possible—by the fact that the anti-Ribot resolution did not expressly mention the defence issue. Without going into the left-wing republican deputies' individual motives for this swing, it must nevertheless be stated that, contrary to the claim made by Goguel, they by no means saw themselves 'amalgamated into a single political tendency with the Right'. The links between the Left and the Centre were maintained.

In general, the fall of the Ribot government was rightly assessed as a personal defeat for the President. The headline in *L'Humanité* the next day was 'Give in or resign'.[109] Jaurès, who had been attacking Poincaré's 'unconstitutional behaviour' since the formation of the Ribot government,[110] saw this defeat as evidence that the majority in Parliament would no longer let itself be intimidated by 'M. Poincaré's cunning and insolent inclinations toward dictatorship'.[111] Nevertheless, strange as it may seem, the 395 votes cast by the 'Union of the Left' offered Poincaré, personally extremely depressed after the defeat of Ribot and considering resignation,[112] an answer to this dilemma. The result of this first vote of the new Parliament on an issue of substance proved that a left-wing republican majority could be achieved without the participation of the SFIO. The United Radicals were therefore faced with having to decide whether to maximise the Pau programme and work hand in hand with the Socialists alone, or to pursue their ambiguous policy on the defence question and remain the core of a left-wing majority without the help of the Socialists. The second option seemed more expedient: this tactic was, after all, the price which had had to be paid for the unity of the Radical Party for some time. Moreover, at this time (the governmental crisis lasted two weeks) a greater willingness to compromise seemed to have emerged within the party. In view of this new mood, the President of the Chamber, Deschanel, informed Poincaré that a new Viviani cabinet would now stand a good chance of gaining a left-wing republican majority. Viviani himself was prepared to try again.[113]

Poincaré was mistrustful of Viviani's intentions but had little other option but to accept.[114] He now had to stand back and watch Viviani form a government almost entirely comprised of United Radicals. In his government declaration of 16 June, Viviani largely reflected the Radicals' demands on the *Trois Ans*. This time Viviani avoided the provocative words 'circumstances' and the situation 'abroad' and simply stated that a reform of military service was on the agenda. He nevertheless endorsed the interpretation given by so many left-wing Republicans to the three-year law—namely, that it was a transitional measure which could not be dispensed with for the time being—and turned down the possibility of an immediate reduction of military service: 'Only when these proposals [military preparation of the young, utilisation of the reserves] have been adopted and applied in consideration of both the results of the experience thereof and the demands of national defence, will the government be in a position to propose a reduction of the military burden.'[115]

In the division on the governmental declaration, Viviani gained a substantial majority of 362 votes to 139. This majority was comprised as follows: 142 *radicaux unifiés*, twenty-two *républicain-socialistes*, 168 deputies from the various Centre and left-wing groups which did not belong to the Radical Party (*gauche radicale, républicains de gauche, gauche démocratique*), and thirty members of the *progressiste* and 'rallied' Right.[116] Ninety-eight deputies, mainly from the ranks of the monarchist and 'rallied' Right and the *Progressistes*, abstained. As A. de Mun explained, despite their scepticism towards Viviani, they were satisfied 'for the time being' because the conscription law had emerged victorious from the debate.[117] It was also for this reason that all the SFIO deputies (along with eighteen United Radicals and ten members of the Right) voted against the new cabinet. In an interpellation Jaurès explained the SFIO's position on the grounds that the party could not sanction any formula which did not stipulate precisely when the envisaged reforms were to take effect. The SFIO, he assured, was not asking for the *Trois Ans* to be repealed 'from one day to the next' (*sic*), but on the other hand the Socialists could not allow an amendment of the defence law to be subjected to the 'imperatives of national defence', because in this way the introduction of the 'regressive' law could be justified retroactively.[118]

The significant fact that the Viviani government had gained a left-wing republican majority without the backing of the Socialists did not, however, imply that the bloc concept had given way to a stable coalition of the Centre or that there was no prospect of future cooperation between the United Radicals and the Socialists. The *Loi de Trois Ans* remained a potential snake in the grass in this new constellation which had only come about due to the fact that not all left-wing groups were capable of adopting a clear-cut stance either for or against the defence bill.[119]

The snake was soon to raise its head. Only two days after the new Premier's governmental declaration, the Radical Party executive stated that its approval of Viviani's declaration did not mean that the party had given up its fight for an amendment of the law.[120] Jaurès suspected that the 'Briandistic ambiguity' of the governmental programme would not survive for very long. Viviani's intention both to preserve the three-year law and to improve military preparation and the training of the reserves was doomed to failure, he asserted, if only because of the practical impossibility of financing this programme.[121] Indeed, a re-

newed outbreak of the antagonisms over financial and social policy of
the pre-election period in the forthcoming Chamber and Senate debates on the loan to cover the *Loi de Trois Ans* and the inclusion of the
general tax in the 1914 finance bill might bring the Socialists and
United Radicals together again.

It was on account of this threat that the Briandiste and conservative
groups in Parliament and public now offered no substantial resistance
to the tax reform. In his governmental declaration, Ribot had manifested that he was prepared to make considerable concessions to the
Radicals' demands, and Viviani now kept this promise with amazing
haste. Directly after his governmental declaration, taking up Caillaux's
proposals of the previous January,[122] Viviani presented to Parliament
his plan to raise a loan of 800 million francs to cover the immediate
'exceptional expenditure' for national defence. The returns from the
bonds issued for this purpose were to be liable to the tax on movable
assets. On 19 June Parliament adopted this bill by 459 votes to 108.
This finally concluded the long controversy over the taxation of state
bonds, an issue which had led, *inter alia*, to the fall of the Barthou
government in December 1913.[123] The second financial bone of con-
tention, of greater long-term significance, was also swiftly digested.
On 17 June the Senate opened its debate on the draft budget proposed
by the Chamber at the end of March which introduced the general and
progressive income tax as the cornerstone of the entire tax reform.[124]
On 22 June, after the Viviani government had announced its intention
to ask for a vote of confidence on the issue,[125] the Senate budgetary
committee gave the go-ahead for the inclusion of this provision in the
finance bill. The Senate itself adopted this measure on 2 July, which
took effect as from 18 July with its publication in the *Journal Officiel*.
The dispute on tax reform which had been going on since 1907 had
now been settled with a triumph for Caillaux's principles. The three-
year law had thus been sold to the Left for the price of social
concessions. Its preservation provisionally secure, it still remained to
be seen whether and how the defence bill could be maintained in its
present form.

The Russian government had had every reason for concern when at
the height of the June 1914 governmental crisis it had reminded
France, through unofficial channels, that the repeal of the three-year
law would jeopardise the necessary degree of coordination of Franco-
Russian military planning.[126] This warning confirmed the words of
advice from Joffre and Paléologue, who had both already intervened
personally, and caused quite a stir. Early in June Joffre had threatened
to resign if the three-year law were amended.[127] Paléologue, ambassador in St Petersburg, had left his post and come to Paris to tell Viviani

that an amendment of the law would put such a strain on Franco-Russian relations that it would be impossible for him to continue his mission at the court of the Tsar.[128] Viviani and his War Minister Messimy seem to have been unruffled by these warnings, which were regarded by the left-wing press as purely internal manoeuvring on the part of the reactionary forces.[129] Directly after the formation of Viviani's second cabinet, Poincaré was forced to inform the new Premier of the activities of the War Minister Messimy who, Poincaré had been informed, was already working on a draft amendment to the conscription law.[130] These rumours were confirmed at a cabinet meeting on 4 July when Messimy announced, without however going into details, that he would soon be submitting a new defence bill to the cabinet.[131] Since Viviani also insinuated to the President that in his opinion the lid had not been put on the military issue once and for all,[132] Poincaré decided himself to put pressure on the War Minister to dissuade him from his plans.[133] However, since he was neither able nor willing to put the new War Minister in the picture with regard to the inseparable link between French alliance policy, strategic planning and the conscription law, he could do no more than warn Messimy 'in cryptic terms' not to lay a finger on the *Loi de Trois Ans*.[134] But vague hints that the tension in international politics had become so great that a war 'might be closer than the public assumes' could not dampen Messimy's determination to present an amendment to the three-year law following the parliamentary autumn recess.[135]

A further blow to the *Trois Ans* came with the radical Senator Humbert's disclosures on the state of the army. On 13 July Humbert, spokesman for the Army Committee of the Senate, presented the plenary with the results of his inquiry into the material equipment and supplies of the army. Humbert complained that interest in military affairs had been concentrated on the 'three-years' problem in the course of the previous year to such an extent that reforms to do with the army's technical equipment and supplies had been neglected. Above all, a decision had still to be taken on the proposal made on 13 February 1913 to earmark 420 million francs for the improvement of defence installations (fortifications, heavy artillery, etc.).[136] The Senator's charges against army and political leaders caused quite a public commotion,[137] and not only politicians and publicists known as *Antitroisannistes* now began to reiterate their doubts about the law. Even Clemenceau, leader of the Radicals in the Senate who had always been a resolute supporter of the *Trois Ans*, gave a speech equal in vehemence and rhetorical effect to Zola's *J'accuse!* Clemenceau condemned the policy of national unity and the forces of domestic reaction rallied around the *Loi de Trois Ans*, as a result of which France could 'be neither governed nor defended'.[138]

In these circumstances it is hardly surprising that the debate on the *Trois Ans* continued right up to 31 July 1914, especially since the French public took very little notice of the storm gathering in international politics.[139] Jaurès's forecast that the law was bound to be amended fundamentally in the autumn of 1914 was a realistic assumption.[140] Poincaré, afraid of this prospect, had no opportunity of exerting influence on the policy of the new government and Parliament. He was well aware that renewed personal intervention in the debate would lead to a governmental crisis and to his own downfall, as the following entry in his diary shows:

> Simond [proprietor of the nationalist *Echo de Paris*] came to talk to me. He spoke ... of my popularity, the hopes put in me; he is aware that neither the course of events nor the constitution allowed me to fulfil popular expectations, but he believes that a great crisis is looming ahead and that sooner or later I shall have to give the order for the dissolution [of the Chamber], using my powers as President to safeguard the national defence laws and French foreign policy. I replied that I did not rule this out as impossible and that it would mean little to me to be immediately deprived of the presidency but that before taking any action whatsoever one had to be sure of the country's support. Moreover, I stated that I would neither violate nor bend the constitution.[141]

Highly resentful, Poincaré was forced to accept the advice of the Prefect of the department of the Loire and cancel a visit to St Étienne already scheduled for some time. According to the Prefect, Poincaré's appearance in public could spark off demonstrations against the three-year law which the public were likely to support.[142]

Thus in July 1914, on the eve of the international crisis, it was evident that the policy of national unity as a means of backing up an energetic foreign policy had failed. This element of home politics left its mark on the decision-making of the French government in the course of the July crisis.

The July Crisis

On 16 July 1914, Poincaré, accompanied by the Premier, Viviani, left Paris for his long-scheduled state visit to St Petersburg. In the debate on the July crisis of 1914 considerable importance has always been attached by historians to this visit and it has given rise to great speculation, especially since very little reliable information is

available on the content of Poincaré's talks with the Tsar and his
government. Luigi Albertini, who has compiled the widely scattered
sources with admirable precision, has concluded that Poincaré and
Paléologue, the French ambassador in St Petersburg, made no attempt
to settle the crisis. Albertini believes that Paléologue in particular
poured 'oil on the flames' of Russia's anger; his repeated assurances to
Sazonov that France was prepared to respect fully her obligations
under the alliance led the Russian Premier 'to take the fatal course of
mobilisation'.[143] Albertini continues that after the President and Viviani left St Petersburg for Stockholm on 23 July, Paléologue, entrusted with the decisive role of coordinator, failed to keep the Foreign
Ministry correctly informed as to the stages of Russian mobilisation,
fearing that if it had been completely *au fait*, the Foreign Ministry,
provisionally in the hands of the Justice Minister, Bienvenu-Martin,
would have intervened to prevent Russia from further escalating the
crisis. Albertini concludes that for this reason he had not followed
Viviani's instructions to try to restrain the Russians.[144]

Jules Isaac, whose analysis of the research of B. Schmitt, Fay and
Barnes in the 1930s still surpasses all other works on the July crisis,[145]
also devotes particular attention to the activities of Poincaré and
Paléologue. Despite his criticism of the behaviour of the 'pseudo-
traitor', Paléologue, Isaac sees no grounds for the assumption that
Paléologue's secret diplomacy was incongruous with Viviani's aims.
Isaac is of the opinion that Paléologue informed the Quai d'Orsay
'more or less quickly and clearly' about Russian mobilisation plans. In
his opinion the decisive factor was that Paris failed to react to these
reports and made no attempt to restrain her ally.[146] In Isaac's view this
was an even greater mistake, in that it was Russian general mobilisation
which made war inevitable: 'Would war have been avoided if the order
for general mobilisation had not been issued on 30 July? *Most probably
not*. Did Russian general mobilisation make war inevitable? *It certainly
did*.'[147]

Isaac explains the French government's reluctance to try to restrain
the Russians with the fear, deeply rooted 'in all French hearts', of
German aggression, the consequence of which was a 'secret complacency' with regard to the military preparation of their Russian ally.[148]
French diplomacy, he writes, did not fulfil its duty and exercise
restraint on Russia's 'risky initiatives' and 'impulsive gestures', but was
dominated by the thought of 'attacking from the rear, the enemy,
assumed, suspected . . . in advance: Germany'.[149]

It is not possible at this point to give a comprehensive interpretation
of the July crisis and to weigh up the degree of responsibility of the
powers involved. The following examination of the behaviour of the

French government during the July crisis has been inspired by the fact that research to date had tended to neglect internal developments in France on the eve of the European crisis, although these developments had a considerable influence on decision-making in foreign policy. Poincaré's diary, which has become available only recently, sheds considerable light on this problem and gives an indication as to how not only Poincaré, but the entire French government, assessed and reacted to the crisis.[150]

As we have already seen, despite all the President's efforts, there was still no long-term guarantee for the three-year law as Poincaré left for St Petersburg. On the contrary, it seemed very likely that the law would be amended immediately after Parliament's summer recess. From the point of view of foreign policy this was of great significance, since the three-year law was the very core of the Franco-Russian military agreements and therefore a key aspect of the political alliance.[151] This means that when Poincaré and Viviani left Paris for St Petersburg on 16 July, the future of the Russian alliance was in fact in doubt. For Poincaré this was evidently a very critical state of affairs, and on a number of occasions in the course of the journey and the official visit he tried to acquaint Viviani, obviously little versed in matters of foreign policy, with the principles of his foreign and military policy:

> I spoke to him about the military law and the various questions which I felt he should know about before his arrival in Russia. Details on the alliance, on the subjects discussed in St Petersburg in 1912. . . . I informed him of my concern with regard to Messimy's plans;[152] he promised me to keep on the look-out. I insisted on the imperative of preserving the military bill. He agreed in principle. I related the difficulties I have had to settle with Germany. . . . I showed him that I have never had serious problems with Germany because I have always been extremely firm in my dealings with her. He seems to have been impressed by my comments.[153]

It is interesting that Poincaré did not so much as mention the current tension between Austria-Hungary and Serbia, and its potential consequences for European politics. This suggests that at this stage he did not realise that the crisis might come to such a dramatic head.

This impression is reinforced by Poincaré's talks with the Tsar directly after his arrival in St Petersburg on 20 July. The notes on these talks in Poincaré's diary more or less coincide with what he wrote in his memoirs.[154] This implies that Albertini's assumption that the Serbian problem played an essential role in the talks is unfounded.[155] The talks were in fact focused on the tension between Britain and Russia on account of the Anatolian railway line and the danger that this tension could permanently jeopardise the Anglo-Russian talks on a navy convention which had come to a standstill the previous month. A further point, not mentioned in Poincaré's memoirs, was the Tsar's concern about rumours that Caillaux and the former Russian Premier, Witte, were trying to open up French and Russian policy towards Germany.

This point—only to be mentioned in passing, since there are no further sources on the subject—is of interest in that the Tsar made it clear to Poincaré that he was concerned about the recent swing to the Left in French politics, which posed a threat to the three-year law. Immediately after the welcoming ceremony on board the imperial yacht (20 July), the Tsar stated 'with great firmness' that it was necessary to strengthen the Franco-Russian alliance and 'clearly and emphatically' expressed the wish 'that the *Loi de Trois Ans* should not be touched'.[156] Poincaré's reply can hardly have set the Tsar's mind at rest. The French President had no choice but evasively to assure the Tsar that the newly elected French Parliament was not opposed to the *Trois Ans in extenso*, and that in any case an amendment to the bill would not get through the Senate. Viviani, he continued, who had rejected the bill in the parliamentary debate in July 1913, had now changed his mind and was convinced that the preservation of the law was indispensable.

In view of these difficulties, the Tsar's subsequent conclusion that in the present circumstances 'full agreement between both our governments . . . is more necessary than ever'[157] does not seem to be a reflection of unconditional Franco-Russian agreement, as the after-dinner speeches in St Petersburg and Poincaré's memoirs would suggest, but rather a frank and candid warning arising from the deep concern about the future of the Franco-Russian alliance.

This leads us to the conclusion that Poincaré's famous words to the Austro-Hungarian ambassador in St Petersburg, Szápáry, on the evening of 21 July were not in fact offensive or a flippant escalation of the conflict.[158] In commenting to the ambassador 'that Serbia has friends in Europe who might be surprised by a move of this kind'[159] Poincaré was probably intending to make a gesture of goodwill to Russia, a personal contribution to assure the Russian government of France's loyalty to the alliance. It is significant that Poincaré immediately hastened to inform Sazonov of this statement.[160] This demonstration of French firmness seemed to Poincaré all the more indispensable, given that at this very time news was arriving from Berlin and Paris that Germany had no intention of restraining Austria. The perspective that the powers of the Triple Alliance might exploit the Austro-Serbian conflict to divide the *entente*—presumably precisely Germany's intention at this point—obviously gave rise to great concern. The Franco-Russian alliance was already under some strain owing to internal developments in France. Poincaré, moreover, was by no means convinced that Sazonov was determined to give Serbia diplomatic support despite the latter's warning to the contrary on 21 July.[161]

For this reason Grey's initial compromise proposal of 21 July to settle the conflict within the framework of a *conversation à deux*— talks between Austro-Hungary and Russia—did not suit Poincaré.[162] Grey's proposal went against the grain of his overall political concept that negotiations between individual members of both alliance systems should be avoided at all costs.[163] However, his rejection of Grey's proposal as 'dangerous' was not only on these grounds. Given the recent Russian doubts about French loyalty to the alliance, for Poincaré to have agreed to Grey's proposal would indeed have tried the alliance to breaking-point.[164] It was presumably on the basis of these doubts about individual action on the part of members of the alliance—fostered by recent events—that Poincaré was completely opposed to a joint Sazonov-Viviani initiative. Even before receiving news of the Austrian ultimatum to Serbia on 23 July, immediately prior to the French statesmen's departure from St Petersburg, Viviani and Sazonov had instructed their respective ambassadors in Vienna to take cautious steps 'in separate visits' in order to exert restraint on Austria-Hungary. In Poincaré's diary there is not the slightest reference to an agreement of this kind between Viviani and Sazonov, and his memoirs reveal that Poincaré considered this form of discreet and separate action as inappropriate: 'Messrs Sazonov and Viviani still imagine that this attempt could still be in time.'[165]

On 24 July, on their way from St Petersburg to Stockholm, Viviani and Poincaré received news of Austria-Hungary's ultimatum to Serbia. Their initial reaction was to send a telegram to the French ambassadors in St Petersburg and London specifying the French position as follows: Serbia should yield to Austria-Hungary's wishes as far as her honour and independence would permit, and first of all ask for an extension of the 48-hour deadline. France herself would not only support this request but do her best to launch a joint British, French and Russian initiative to replace the Austro-Serbian inquiry, which might appear humiliating to Serbia, by an international inquiry. So far, the only reference to this telegram was in Poincaré's memoirs,[166] which led Albertini to the conclusion that it was probably a forgery.[167] This is improbable, as the entire content of the telegram is recorded in Poincaré's diary under 24 July—with one interesting variation. Instead of the clause 'which may seem humiliating to Serbia', Poincaré quotes the much more forceful 'which Serbia cannot accept without being humiliated'. These words, which seem more typical of Poincaré than the latter diluted version, represent an emphatic demand to Russia to back Serbia. As we shall soon see, Poincaré was highly sceptical at this point as to whether Russia would continue to back the Serbs. Although Viviani signed this telegram, he was totally unaware of the implications that these endeavours to internationalise the dispute between Austria-Hungary and Serbia involved for the alliance.[168]

Poincaré's concern that Russia was not prepared to back the Serbs was confirmed by dispatches from Paléologue in St Petersburg. On 25 July, shortly after Poincaré and Viviani had received the first reports about the German 'localisation' demand, Paléologue reported that Sazonov was 'very eager to keep the peace' and intended to advise Serbia against putting up any resistance if she were invaded by Austria. In Sazonov's opinion, continued Paléologue, Serbia should do no more than protest and call for the 'judgement of the world'. The Russian cabinet was to meet on the afternoon of 25 July, when Sazonov intended to obtain the seal of approval for this position. Poincaré was extremely angry at Paléologue's report and described Sazonov's reticence in harsh terms as the abdication of Russia to Austria-Hungary. But he saw no opportunity of influencing the course of events this 'sinister day' had triggered off: 'We can assuredly not be more Slav than the Russians. Poor Serbia thus stands a good chance of being humiliated.'[169]

Sazonov's famous reaction to the Austrian ultimatum to Serbia— 'This means European war!'—and his decision to ask the Tsar and the cabinet to approve mobilisation of part of the Russian army against Austria-Hungary, illustrate that there can be no question of a Russian 'abdication' to Austria. How then can Paléologue's false report to Poincaré and Viviani be explained? Albertini claims that on this very day, 24 July, Paléologue 'poured oil on the flames' by indicating to Sazonov that France would, if necessary, not only support Russia diplomatically but respect all her obligations under the alliance. This assurance was made although Paléologue had already been informed of the Russian mobilisation plans.[170] It was not until the evening of 27 July that Poincaré and Viviani received full information about Russia's initial mobilisation plans, news which was of considerable importance for their subsequent action. It can only be assumed that Paléologue's false report was the result of his concern that Viviani might take retaliatory steps. Paléologue had known, at the latest since the St Petersburg meeting on 20–22 July, that Viviani did not rate the Franco-Russian alliance very highly and that he certainly would not have accepted Russia's 'energetic' stance unconditionally. For

Paléologue, the problem of not being able fully to inform Poincaré without also leaking the news to Viviani while the two statesmen were at sea and means of communication were limited, was not such a serious one. The ambassador had always agreed with the basic assumptions of Poincaré's foreign policy and could invariably be sure of acting according to the President's wishes.

This assumption that Poincaré and Viviani were not fully informed of Russia's military decisions sheds a different light on one of the most famous documents of the July crisis, Viviani's telegram to Paléologue at noon on 27 July with instructions to inform the Russian government 'that France, appreciating, as does Russia, the great importance for the two countries to affirm their perfect *entente* to other Powers and to undertake every possible effort to settle the conflicts, is prepared, in the interests of general peace, to back fully the action of the imperial government'.[171] Albertini claims that Viviani knew at this point that the Russians had decided 'on principle' to mobilise thirteen army corps against Austria-Hungary, and he therefore interprets the telegram as evidence of a 'level-headed, pacific attitude on the part of Viviani'. This is in fact unfounded. Paléologue, according to Albertini, deliberately failed to pass on these pacific words of advice—or warning—to the Russian government and, on the contrary, again assured Russia of unconditional French support when Sazonov decided on general mobilisation on 28 July.[172] Albertini's conclusions, however, do not hold good: Viviani and Poincaré did not receive the—very fragmentary—information from Paléologue on Russian mobilisation plans until the evening of 27 July—after the telegram had been despatched. Poincaré's diary sheds sufficient light on the real meaning of the telegram:

> We have again received telegrams. Germany has told both London and Paris that if the matter is not [solved?] the situation will worsen. Sir Edw. Grey gave a firm reply that if war breaks out in the east, no nation could avoid being implicated.
> I quoted this firmness as an example to Viviani, who is becoming more and more anxious and worried and is full of the most contradictory ideas. I told him to maintain contact with St Petersburg and to tell the Russian g[overnment] that in the general interests of peace France will support her action.... After further hesitation Viviani decided to despatch [the message].[173]

It would be most interesting to know exactly what these 'most contradictory ideas' were. In any case, Poincaré's concession to Viviani's scruples—the insertion of 'in the general interests of peace'—was of little significance. The telegram was despatched at a time when Poincaré was still extremely anxious about the alleged 'abdication' of

Russia and worried that Europe would not intervene in the Austro-Serbian conflict. At the first vague indication that Britain was adopting a firm stance *vis-à-vis* Germany, Poincaré immediately began to put pressure on the Russian government which, in his opinion, had so far been over-cautious. Without mincing his words, he urged Russia to act, at the same time promising France's unconditional support. So when Paléologue assured Sazonov on 28 July that Russia had France's unconditional support, he was not distorting completely the instructions he had received.

It was not until the evening of 27 July that the French statesmen on their way from Copenhagen to Stockholm on board the *France* received Paléologue's report of 25 July stating that the Russian cabinet chaired by the Tsar had that day decided 'on principle' on the mobilisation of the thirteen army corps to be deployed against Austria-Hungary in the event of war. Preparations were being carried out in secret, so that these troops could be immediately concentrated on the border upon mobilisation.[174] Paléologue had reported on only a fraction of the decisions actually taken. Above all, he had failed to mention that the Tsar had adopted a cabinet resolution stipulating the commencement of the period of pre-mobilisation during the night of 25/26 July, a measure which involved the call-in of the reservists and which, in certain areas—not only on the Austro-Russian border—was paramount to general mobilisation. Moreover, although he was aware of the serious consequences of his step, Paléologue made no reference to his words of reassurance to Sazonov regarding unconditional French support.[175]

In these circumstances it is hardly surprising that Poincaré mentioned Paléologue's report only in passing in his diary.[176] Poincaré tries to make out in his memoirs that on 27 July he had a very incomplete picture of the situation and was therefore anxious on two counts that evening. Apparently he was worried not only that Europe might tolerate an Austrian attack on Serbia; he claims also to have been equally anxious that Russian intervention on behalf of Serbia might have incalculable effects on both Britain's and Germany's stance.[177] In actual fact he was not concerned about the second possibility at all. When on the evening of 27 July, in all probability shortly after having received Paléologue's report, Poincaré found out about Grey's proposal that the powers not involved in the issue should act as mediators between Austria-Hungary and Russia, he retorted angrily: 'Why [mediation] between Austria and Russia? Russia has not yet said anything and hasn't budged. So far she is in no way involved in the conflict. On the other hand, are we going to leave Austria alone with Serbia?'[178]

We shall not discuss here whether Poincaré's assessment of the situation was more realistic than Grey's or whether, as Albertini claims, the British proposal for mediation was tantamount to a localis- ation of the conflict in accordance with German demands.[179] In an attempt to interpret the key French politicians' perception of and reaction to the crisis, it is important to note that Poincaré told Viviani to inform London of the French doubts about Grey's proposal. Viviani, however, refused to do so.[180] This first open conflict between the two leading French statesmen came to a head the same evening when a series of despatches arrived with news of a number of meetings between the acting French Premier, Bienvenu-Martin, and the German ambassador in Paris, von Schoen. Poincaré's résumé of these de- spatches was that Bienvenu-Martin and von Schoen had been trying to find means of keeping the peace. Viviani apparently did not share the President's concern that Bienvenu-Martin, in his eagerness for peace, had not been firm enough. Poincaré again seemed very apprehensive about Viviani's state of mind and tried once again to explain the principles of French foreign policy to the Premier: ' . . . [to show] weakness towards Germany has always been a source of complica- tions. The only way to ward off danger has been to show persevering strength and callous cold-bloodedness'.

But Viviani remained sceptical about this doctrine, which Poincaré again considered as a lack of insight into the dictates of foreign policy.[181] There is no doubt that, in accordance with his general concept of foreign policy, Poincaré considered a hard line *vis-à-vis* Germany on this question as a guarantee of the preservation of peace. It is equally true that in these times of crisis this doctrine degenerated into no more than a confrontation tactic which objectively triumphed over Viviani's doubts. Paléologue's line, which basically corresponded with that of Poincaré, was confirmed by warnings sent to Russia from the Commander-in-Chief, Joffre, and the War Minister, Messimy. The responsible army officers were at first alarmed at Paléologue's reports of 25 and 26 July, according to which Russia had decided 'on principle' to mobilise against Austria-Hungary and to avoid any measures which might seem to be levelled directly against Germany. They were even more alarmed when the Russians announced their determination to leave the initiative to Germany to attack Russia. This strategy was quite obviously a contradiction of the agreements concluded by the Franco-Russian general staffs in 1912 which posed a considerable threat to the French operational plan, based on a coordinated offensive of the allied powers against Germany. Joffre was in any case doubtful as to whether Russia would be prepared or be in a position to launch an offensive against Germany with the sufficient 'diligence' in the event of war.[182] Paléologue's reports on 25 and 26 July seemed to confirm these doubts and led to strong protests from Messimy and Joffre to the Russian military attachés in Paris.[183] Given the French strategic plan, the protests were quite justified and cannot be interpreted as war-mongering. These words of warning to Russia, although motivated by considerations of pure strategics, nevertheless reinforced the political initiatives of Paléologue—and, indirectly, those of Poincaré—and were a more convincing expression of the determination of France to stand by her ally at all costs than were the assurances of Paléologue.[184]

The extent to which the insistence of leading French politicians and soldiers that Russia should take energetic action actually prompted Russia's decision on general mobilisation—which, according to Isaac, made war inevitable—cannot be examined here. In this context the only point of interest to note is that the majority of French decision-makers were neither prepared nor in a position to make what might have been a decisive contribution towards peace in Europe by warning Russia that other Great Powers would inevitably follow her example. Even Isaac deplored the fact that French diplomacy made no more than 'a few faint, faithless gestures' and that France had levelled her gaze only on the 'aggressor suspected in advance'—namely, Germany. Basically this holds true, although it is not fully applicable to Viviani, Bienvenu-Martin and other members of the cabinet.

Moralising explanations and accusations against individuals, refer-ences to, for example, Poincaré's policy of revenge or Paléologue's warmongering,[185] ignore the dictates to which French diplomacy was subject, or rather to which it thought it was subject, at the time. During the first phase of the July crisis (up until the Austrian declara-tion of war on Serbia), the efforts of Poincaré and Paléologue were concentrated on preserving the stability of the Russian alliance. They were both concerned about the recent tension and rightly suspected that the Germans' intention was to split the *entente* over the Serbian question. At the very latest, after Austria had declared war on Serbia and Germany had announced her 'bogus acceptance' (Albertini) of the British mediating proposals, Poincaré and Paléologue became con-vinced that Germany was on a war footing. In these circumstances they were not alone in believing that to warn Russia of the risk of bringing the crisis to a head by stepping up pre-mobilisation, or to force her into preliminary consultations with France in accordance with the military convention, would be incompatible with the interests of French security.[186]

The conclusion that Poincaré's concept of the crisis and the policy of unconditional support for Russia prevailed over Viviani's doubts seems to contradict the fact that, on 30 July, Viviani warned Russia not to aggravate the crisis any further:

> France is resolved to fulfil all the obligations of the alliance. But, in the very
> interest of general peace and since a conversation is being conducted
> between the less involved Powers, I believe it would be appropriate, in the
> measures of precaution and defence Russia deems necessary, that no provi-
> sion should be immediately applied which could provide Germany with a
> pretext for a total or partial mobilisation of her forces.[187]

Close analysis of the background leading to this telegram shows that
this warning was not absolutely unambiguous and that, faced with
Poincaré's policy, the efforts by Viviani to hold back his country's ally
at the eleventh hour were futile. Viviani in fact sent this telegram on
the morning of 30 July because he had received an urgent appeal for
help from Sazonov the previous night. Sazonov had informed him of
Germany's demands that Russia cancel her mobilisation against
Austria-Hungary, threatening German mobilisation if she failed to do
so. It was impossible, Sazonov continued, for him to comply with this
demand and, so far as he was concerned, the only option was to
'accelerate armament and face the imminence of war'. For this reason,
he wrote, an official French statement that Russia could count on her
unconditional support was of particular importance.[188] Poincaré later
retorted that this famous telegram had been an over-interpretation of
Viviani's assurances of 27 July, made before Austria's declaration of
war on Serbia when the French government had not the slightest
suspicion that Russia was planning mobilisation.[189] However, Albertini points out that Poincaré's 'correction' had 'skimmed over' the fact
that Paléologue had made such a clear pledge of assistance to Sazonov
in their various conversations.[190] Given the background to Viviani's
instructions to Paléologue on 27 July, it must be added that
Paléologue's one-sided report in fact mirrored Poincaré's intentions.
Therefore it is hardly surprising that there is no trace of a rejection of
or indignation at Sazonov's apparently excessive interpretation of
Paléologue's report in Poincaré's diary, although the President was
well aware of the fact that Sazonov's decision to accelerate armament
implied a further escalation of the crisis. On 30 July Poincaré wrote in
his diary:

> Things seem to be taking a critical turn [followed by a report that Izvolsky
> had delivered Sazonov's urgent message in the night of 29/30 July]. *Because
> of Britain's ambiguous attitude*, we have told St Petersburg that we shall
> naturally fulfil our obligations as allies, but that we recommend that in its
> defence preparations the imperial government should not take any steps

which could be regarded by Germany as a pretext for aggression. At the same time, we shall take the necessary measures to establish the frontier-covering troops in the east.[191]

Although this entry is a faithful reflection of Poincaré's doctrine of strength and his overriding concern to preserve the alliance, it is highly questionable whether Poincaré's résumé reflected the intention behind Viviani's warning to Sazonov. Viviani's action had certainly not been guided by Britain's 'ambiguous attitude' but by the general interest in avoiding any escalation of the crisis in the 'interest of general peace'. Following Sazonov's message, which specifically referred to Viviani's instructions to Paléologue on 27 July, it may have dawned on Viviani, who so far could not really pinpoint why he felt so uneasy about Poincaré's line, what the real implications of the 'policy of strength' were. The obvious discrepancy between the entry in Poincaré's diary and the contents of the dispatched telegram implies that Viviani's report to Sazonov on 30 July was not only a warning to Russia but represented a step away from Poincaré's approach. What would have happened if, instead of his vague statement that Russia would have to 'accelerate armament', Sazonov had reported that general mobilisation had at this point already been decided—which was then in fact cancelled by the Tsar at the last minute?[192] What would have happened if Paléologue had not kept the dramatic turn of events in Russia from his government? These questions may at first seem purely hypothetical, but they gain in significance when we consider that disagreement between Poincaré and Viviani had been latent since the very beginning of the July crisis. In these circumstances it can be taken as probable that clearer information on developments in Russia would have led to an open conflict between the two politicians. And it can by no means be taken for granted that Poincaré's line would have come out on top.

Further evidence for this assumption is that Viviani and other members of the government had still not given up hope of settling the conflict peacefully. When the German ambassador in Paris, von Schoen, reported on the afternoon of 31 July that Germany had declared *Kriegsgefahrzustand* on account of the general Russian mobilisation and enquired whether France would remain neutral in a war between Germany and Russia, Viviani, ignorant of Russian mobilisation, announced that there was as yet no question of this and that he still hoped that the crisis could be settled peacefully.[193] Viviani's reticence is even more striking, since Poincaré had advised him to inform the German ambassador that France would 'act according to her own interests'. Viviani's reply to von Schoen therefore did not meet with the President's approval. Directly after the visit of the

German ambassador, Poincaré noted in his diary that he was extremely concerned about Viviani's behaviour: 'Viviani is getting carried away with the most contradictory of impressions with alarming ease. At times he is very morose and then suddenly dreams up a miracle to solve everything.'[194] This indecision apparently reflected majority opinion in the cabinet, for, in the late afternoon of 31 July, the decision on Joffre's request for the immediate mobilisation of all French troops was postponed until the next day.[195]

The following morning—1 August—Viviani seemed so relieved after further talks with von Schoen that Poincaré seriously feared that the cabinet would again postpone its decision on general mobilisation, despite Joffre's threat of resignation. It was not until Poincaré had 'very firmly' told the cabinet that he would not tolerate further delay that general mobilisation was finally ordered.[196] The basis of this consensus was extremely fragile, as is illustrated by the fact that Viviani tried to revoke the decision only a few minutes after the mobilisation machinery had been set in motion.[197]

These facts seem to provide sufficient proof of the above assumption that, if the Viviani government had got wind of Russian mobilisation in time, it would have put considerable pressure on Russia to prevent an escalation of the crisis.

Poincaré was naturally not better informed of developments in Russia than for example Viviani, Messimy and Joffre. Although it cannot be said for certain how he would have reacted if Paléologue's reports on decisions in Russia up to the point of general mobilisation had been more precise, it is nevertheless unlikely that Poincaré would have had the power or the will to hold Russia back. For years the thoughts and policy of Poincaré had been determined by his concern to strengthen the political and military alliance with Russia at all costs, since he regarded this alliance as the only means of offsetting German expansionism and aggression. Apprehension that the *Loi de Trois Ans*, an integral part of his foreign policy, might soon be repealed on account of recent developments at home, had prompted him into even more determined action at St Petersburg. The absolutely justified impression that, during the July crisis Germany had deliberately run the risk of war to weaken the alliance, reaffirmed his overall political concept. This apparent confirmation of all his long-held fears and assumptions (was it too apparent?) gave the President an extremely narrow view of events during these decisive days, and Paléologue's deliberate misinformation of course did not help matters. The already narrow scope of his policy, which had for years been following a single track, now vanished completely, as is illustrated by the notes in Poincaré's diary between 29 July and 3 August 1914. Poincaré was highly sceptical about a report from the French ambassador in Berlin on 30 July that Jagow was concerned and intended to accept the proposal of the mediation of non-involved powers between Austria-Hungary and Russia in the event of an Austrian annexation of Serbia. He did not regard this as a 'vague shimmer of hope', as he wrote in his memoirs, but indignantly noted in his diary that Cambon was 'easily contented,' and that if Germany were really concerned about preventing a war she would adopt a more emphatic line towards Austria-Hungary.[198] A report from Paléologue in St Petersburg, which arrived shortly afterwards, that the German ambassador had demanded of Sazonov to suspend Russian mobilisation against Austria-Hungary, since the latter was not intending to violate Serbia's territorial integrity, was considered by Poincaré as further evidence that Germany was giving more and more support to her ally while expecting Russia to 'lay down her weapons'. Furthermore, there is no record by Poincaré in his diary of his deepest regret at the—incomplete—news from Paléologue on the evening of 30 July that Russia had 'secretly taken the first steps of general mobilisation'.[199] On the contrary, in Poincaré's opinion, Russian general mobilisation on the afternoon of 30 July—news of which did not reach Paris until the following evening, owing to Paléologue's incomplete reports—was a fully justified counter-manoeuvre:

> Russia has given orders for general mobilisation, having learned that Germany had begun mobilisation. Germany immediately demanded that Russia suspend mobilisation, which means that war is now more or less inevitable.
>
> Germany obviously does not want to negotiate on equal terms. She claims to be ready to negotiate, but she doesn't [. . . ? . . .] Russia and France to be in a position to defend ourselves in negotiations.
>
> Austria has given orders for general mobilisation. Germany is mobilising behind the *Kriegszustand* (*sic*), but when Russia takes the same precautions there are cries of 'Halt!'[200]

This entry in Poincarés' diary can indeed be regarded as an illustration of Isaac's criticism, mentioned at the beginning of this section, (p. 218ff.) of the French government's attitude towards Russia's 'impulsive gestures'. Poincaré, Paléologue, Joffre and possibly also the War Minister were 'secretly complacent . . . with regard to Russia'. A point stressed by Isaac which cannot be over-emphasised is that the ultimate reason for this was not irresponsible 'playing with fire' or 'warmongering', but years of fear of Germany's world-wide aspirations and aggression.

On the other hand, Isaac's theory that this 'secret complacency' with regard to Russian policy was deeply rooted in 'the hearts of all

Frenchmen' is not conclusive. Paléologue's personal secret diplomacy and Poincaré's excessive compliance with Russia in the July crisis arose from the desperate attempt to maintain the basis of both French power policy and French military policy—the alliance with Russia—which was in great danger owing to domestic developments of recent months and the possibility of an imminent amendment of the conscription bill.

These calculations remained jeopardised up to the outbreak of war. Poincaré, just as Paléologue, was well aware of the fact that his policy of stabilising the alliance had little domestic substantiation at the climax of the European crisis. When the Russian ambassador in Paris, Izvolsky, formally enquired of France what steps she intended to take following the German declaration of war on Russia, Poincaré pointed out that France would have to wait and see, since a French declaration of war on Germany might lead to a public dispute on the Franco-Russian alliance.[201]

In view of these obstacles in domestic politics, Poincaré was greatly relieved when Germany declared war on France:

France had done all that was expected of her to [. . . ? . . .] peace but war has nevertheless become inevitable. It is a hundred times better that we were not led to declare war ourselves, even on account of repeated violations of our frontier. It was imperative that Germany, fully responsible for the aggression, should be induced to admit her interests publicly. If we had been forced to declare war ourselves, the Russian alliance would have become a subject of controversy in France, national [*élan*?] would have been broken, and Italy may have been forced by the provisions of the Triple Alliance to take sides against us. . . .[202]

This entry in Poincaré's diary elucidates France's entire policy on the eve of the First World War and highlights not only its obstacles but its dynamics. The clash between developments on the domestic scene and the system of alliances in foreign policy had greatly reduced the scope of Poincaristic policy and was conducive to crisis. However, France did not enter the war because of her commitments within the alliance. The *Union Sacrée* was not so much a result of spontaneous, chauvinistic excitement as, above all, a consequence of the fear of a German assault which had dominated the domestic scene in France since early 1913 at the latest. Even the most determined opponents of the *Trois Ans* had never disputed the necessity of guaranteeing French preparedness against the aggression of Germany. Now all Frenchmen, irrespective of their political stance, regarded Germany's declaration of war as the confirmation of an 'unspoken assumption' (Joll). The debate on national defence had at times been characterised by very sharp antagonism. The nation had nevertheless not been polarised into two blocs. Beyond the sphere of internal dissent, all the political parties agreed that in one way or another it was essential to strengthen French preparedness as far as possible. Even the Socialists could join the 'Government of National Defence', especially since the failure of the *offensive à outrance* in the frontier battles of August 1914 proved that their concept of a nation in arms was a realistic one: 'The whole nation . . . must rise to defend its territory and its freedom. . . . The head of government . . . knew that in all its times of need, in 1793 as in 1870, the nation put its trust in these men, these Socialists, these revolutionaries. . . . He has appealed to our Party. Our Party has replied: Present!'[203]

Summary

The aim of this study has been to trace developments in French politics and illustrate the interdependence of domestic, foreign and military politics in France on the eve of the First World War. It begins at the time of the second Moroccan crisis in 1911, since 'Agadir' set in motion a series of wide-ranging changes in the French military and alliance system as well as a number of upheavals at domestic level which, in turn, were to leave their mark on foreign policy.

With regard to the context of military and foreign policy, the reorganisation of the French high command and the appointment of Joffre as Chief of General Staff were probably the most significant direct effects of the Agadir crisis. Joffre and his military aides drafted a new operational plan, based on the principle of an unconditional offensive strategy, which finally emerged as the famous, or infamous, Plan XVII in 1914. The virtually axiomatic belief of the French army officers, later described by Joffre himself as dogmatic, that only a strictly offensive approach to warfare and deployment of the regular troops could lead to victory, reflected a constriction of strategic thought which was a result of the isolation of military society from civil society in the wake of the Dreyfus affair. This offensive approach to strategics did not in fact became fully implemented until 1911 when Caillaux's left-wing republican government, faced with the threat of a war with Germany and the obvious inadequacies of French army organisation, had no option but to give the military a free hand. However, Joffre's offensive planning from the autumn of 1911 was confined by a number of restrictions in the field of foreign policy. Fearful of losing the support of Britain, both Caillaux and his successor Poincaré (1912) vetoed Joffre's original plan to violate the neutrality of Belgium in the event of a war in order to launch an out-and-out offensive on strategically favourable terrain.

Since the French general staff could not conceive of fully renouncing their offensive strategy, the decisive initial offensive would now have to be launched on the highly fortified Franco-German border in Lorraine. This meant that, since the offensive would be carried out in less favourable conditions, it would be essential for France's ally, Russia, to launch a simultaneous assault on Germany's eastern border. However, the Agadir crisis had shown that Russia was neither militarily nor politically prepared to support France in the event of a war and to respect the terms of the 1892 Franco-Russian military convention, which stipulated a full, simultaneous Franco-Russian attack on Germany.

As a result, the alliance policy of Poincaré's 1912 cabinet and of the subsequent Briand and Barthou governments (1913) was dominated by one overriding objective: to strengthen the political alliance with Russia as a means of ensuring Russian observance of the military agreements upon which the French operational plan was dependent. This was also the main aim of the St Petersburg agreements in the autumn of 1912.

The Agadir crisis was not the only source of change for French foreign and military policy in this period. The impression that Germany was blackmailing France with the threat of war in order to achieve her imperialist goals led to a nationalist revival in France (Eugen Weber) coupled with domestic structural change. Although these elements were not as lasting as the changes in foreign and military policy, they were nevertheless of a long-term effect in these fields. The domestic policy of the Poincaré government had a twofold objective. The first was to conduct a policy of moral unity as a pillar at domestic level to support Poincaré's 'foreign policy of strength'. Steps taken to achieve this aim included measures to promote the public prestige of the army (e.g. the reintroduction of public military retreats, prohibited since the time of the Dreyfus crisis, and the introduction of national holidays). Poincaré's second objective—of considerably more importance than the kindling of nationalism which has been emphasised by so many historians—was to strengthen the position of the executive *vis-à-vis* Parliament. Electoral reform was introduced to this end; it was an appropriate means of reviving the latent tensions between the various groups of the republican Left, increasing the influence of the Centre and the conservatives and above all severing the Socialists—who were in favour of the reform—from the left-wing Republicans. This strategy of 'divide and rule' proved even more effective, since, following the Agadir crisis, the left-wing Republicans were not able to offer serious opposition to Poincaré's cabinet. Although many of them (Clemenceau!) were concerned about the swing French politics had taken to the Right and the anti-radical implications of the 'policy of national unity', they were not in a position to form a bloc of the Left against Poincarisme, since they supported Poincaré's line of foreign policy. This was also true of the Socialists, who had basically no doubt that Poincaré's foreign policy had purely defensive motives and was aimed at preserving the peace in Europe. In fact in the presidential elections of January 1913 Poincaré was elected only because the Socialists refused to support the left-wing republican candidate. This, and not the open support of the nationalist Right for a 'national' President, so often advanced in historical research, was the key factor in Poincaré's election to the presidency.

Domestic politics in 1912 were therefore 'under the spell' of the Agadir crisis. The basis for the increased strength of the executive and the stability of Poincaré's government was the fact that all the parties were convinced of the need for a resolute foreign policy. However, the implications this policy of strength might have for military and alliance policy were never discussed in the public arena.

This relative consensus within French society, based on considerations of foreign policy, was suddenly called into question at the beginning of March 1913 when, following Poincaré's election to the presidency, the Briand government introduced a bill to Parliament stipulating an increase of regular military service from two to three years. To political and military leaders the *Loi de Trois Ans* had become an imperative: since January 1913 the Germans had been drafting a major arms bill. Although at this time French decision-makers had no precise information as to the actual extent of German military expansion, it was nevertheless evident that the only hope of survival for the French offensive strategy was an increase in the regular army. However, both the government and the general staff were aware that neither public opinion nor the left-wing Republicans, the key group in Parliament, would accept the law if it were presented on the basis of long-term considerations and constraints of strategics and alliance policy. For this reason, backed up by nationalist street agitation and a determined press campaign, the three-year law was projected to Parliament and the public as a measure indispensable for protecting national territory from the threat of a German 'assault'. One of the government's repeated arguments in this context was that the extension of conscription was aimed only at securing France with a 'solid dyke' without which aggressive Germany could 'flood' the country within a matter of hours.

The discrepancy between the real motives for the expansion of the army and its ideological justification led to a crisis in French domestic politics which lasted until July 1914. The argument that only the three-year law—that is, the reinforcement of the regular army alone—

could secure national defence against the *attaque brusquée* from Germany implied a certain contradiction of the traditional left-wing republican theory of the nation in arms. According to this theory the army was to be organised in such a way that, in the event of war, all able-bodied citizens could be called to arms to defend their country. It was therefore not the striking power of the standing army that was decisive, but the possibility of keeping a large number of fully trained men in reserve. Although this principle had not been applied to the letter in the 1905 conscription law, since the original left-wing republican militia concept had been alien to many Radicals, the introduction of two-year military service without exemption, in the face of opposition from the conservative parties and army officers, had been one of the most important—and, accordingly, most symbolical—achievements of the 'Radical Republic'. Therefore the demand for the introduction of three-year conscription aroused the suspicions of many left-wing Republicans that the planned increase of only the regular forces was an instrument of domestic reaction. This added fuel to the resentment of many left-wingers at the anti-radical implications of Poincaré's domestic policy—which in turn was further aggravated by the smear campaign of the nationalist Right, which qualified anyone who raised any doubts whatsoever about the government bill as anti-patriots or the accomplices of Germany. However, most of the Radicals in Parliament and in public, including the provinces, were not of the opinon that the bill had been introduced for reactionary reasons. In view of the apparent threat of an *attaque brusquée*, most of them were prepared to accept amendments to the 1905 conscription law provided that the government could prove that this policy was the only means of securing the defence of the nation.

However, the government was neither in a position to provide this proof nor prepared to consider the possibility of any alternatives to the three-year law. Although its categorical insistence on the bill was justified from the points of view of military and foreign policy, this intransigence nevertheless seemed to confirm the suspicions of the Left that the government was motivated not only by considerations of defence but intended to exploit the *crise des armaments* as a means of further repressing left-wing republican policy. As the criticism mounted against the authoritarianism of the powers that be, above all against Barthou, Premier since April 1913, the government was suddenly forced to amend its original proposals in April 1913 when news of the actual scope of the German arms bill reached Paris. Using highly nationalistic slogans, and in particular with recourse to the emergency paragraph of the 1905 conscription law, the government tried to stir up hysteria and fear of an *attaque brusquée* and to nip all opposition to its defence policy in the bud—but in vain. In the course of the public debate it became increasingly clear that, although the French people basically agreed with the principle of reinforcing national defence, the criticism of the left-wing Republicans also met with popular support. Counter-proposals providing for a short-term increase in the effective strength of the standing army, in particular the Paul-Boncour/Messimy counter-proposal initiated by Caillaux, were greeted with considerable support both in Parliament and among left-wing republican public opinion all over the country.

This prompted the Socialists to abandon their intransigent position in order to prepare the way for a Left bloc opposed to the *Loi de Trois Ans*. *Section Française de l'Internationale Ouvrière* (SFIO) had originally opposed the defence bill on internationalist and pacifist grounds, hoping to be able to use the wave of popular protest to attract left-wing bourgeois elements into its ranks. However, these arguments had been of little appeal. Despite the vehement protest of the *Guesdiste* faction, the party now began to adjust its campaign to the slogan 'Pour la Défense Nationale'. Moreover, to reassure the Radicals, it increasingly focused on the reactionary domestic implications behind the *Trois Ans*.

This *rapprochement* between the Socialists and the Radicals was facilitated by the fact that in the course of the campaign against the bill the revolutionary syndicalists, the *Confédération Générale du Travail* (CGT), had been forced to subordinate itself to the SFIO. The revolutionary syndicates and the protagonists of the old anarcho-syndicalism had initially tried to exploit the latent discontent with the government's policy in order to propagate their ideas among the working classes as a means of overcoming the crisis in revolutionary syndicalism which had been evident since 1909, especially since Agadir. However, there had been virtually no response to the CGT campaign, which had in any case been weakened by the fact that the Syndicalists were incapable of defining a coherent anti-militarist position. Therefore the struggle against the three-year law did not lead to the revival of anarcho-syndicalism, as it was hoped. On the contrary, the struggle against the defence bill clearly illustrated the conflict within the CGT between reformist and revisionist groups, on the one hand, and the advocates of revolutionary, anti-patriotic and anti-militarist *action directe*, on the other. Along with exogenous factors— above all, governmental repression following the soldiers' unrest in May 1913—this split within the CGT and the failure of *action directe* against the conscription law led to a marked revisionist swing within the CGT. From the autumn of 1913 revolutionary syndicalism became increasingly devoid of significance—which explains why this group undertook no action against the policy of the *Union Sacrée* in August 1914.

Despite the judicious Paul-Boncour/Messimy counter-proposal, which was extremely attractive to the Left, and after weeks of heated parliamentary debate, the three-year law was passed on 19 July 1913. The main reason for the majority in favour of the bill was the fact that the Socialists had not succeeded in convincing an adequate number of left-wing republican deputies that the governmental bill sought only to serve reactionary domestic purposes. The government endeavoured to dispel these doubts by changing tactics and doing all it could to prevent any trace of nationalistic and reactionary intrigues. Backed by the military authorities, it insisted that the three-year law was the only means of warding off an *attaque brusquée*, but, unlike before, now insinuated that the bill could be amended if and when the danger from abroad subsided. The government's second new tactic was its willingness now to consider tax reform (a new capital tax) as a means of covering the costs of the expansion of the army. This was in fact the first step towards a general reform of the French tax system which the left-wing Republicans, Socialists and elements of the bourgeois Centre had been advocating for years. This olive branch convinced many sceptics on the Left that their original concern about the domestic reactionary trends of *Poincarisme* was unfounded and that there was therefore no reason not to support the government. In addition, the government also succeeded in temporarily thwarting the tactics of the Socialists. Despite evidence to the contrary, the soldiers' unrest, a spontaneous expression of protest in a number of barracks at the extension of conscription, was attributed to CGT agitation. The Socialists were accused of having incited the rancour of the recruits by their extreme campaign against 'domestic reaction'. For a number of wavering left-wing Republicans this criticism was undoubtedly a further reason for them to support the government and to dissociate themselves from anti-patriotic intrigues and 'revolutionary agitation'. The *Loi de Trois Ans* was therefore pushed through on the basis of political diversionary tactics and arguments actually unrelated to the issue. For this reason the fate of the bill was to remain precarious.

As the July crisis of 1914 was to show, the shaky domestic foundations of the new military constitution were to have serious consequences on overall calculations of French foreign policy and strategics. However, following the adoption of the three-year law, Joffre was now in a position, for the time being at least, to implement the provisions of the new offensive Plan XVII, the guide-lines of which had been approved by the *Conseil Supérieur de la Guerre* (CSG) in April 1913. This work was concluded in February 1914. However, it still remained uncertain as to whether Russia would really be prepared to launch a 'full and simultaneous attack' on the German eastern front—imperative to prevent Germany from concentrating the bulk of her forces on the border with France, which would be a severe handicap to the initial French offensive. The doubts of the French government and general staff with regard to Russia's allegiance to the alliance were not dispelled at the conference of the general staffs in the autumn of 1913. On the contrary, it transpired that Russia's network of strategic railway lines would not permit the full striking power of Russian forces to be deployed on the German eastern border in the event of war.

For this reason the Barthou government tried to use Russia's financial requirements as a means of exerting pressure on the Tsar's government to extend the strategic railway lines, and declared that it would agree to the raising of a major loan for Russia on the Paris stock exchange only if St Petersburg complied with French military demands. However, negotiations dragged on for some time, since Russia was not prepared to make these concessions. It was not until the deterioration of Russo-German relations in the wake of the Liman von Sanders crisis at the beginning of 1914 that the Russian government showed a sudden interest in the implementation of the military agreements with France.

Meanwhile, in the French domestic scene, changes had taken place which posed a threat to the survival of the three-year law and, in consequence, the essentials of military planning. The congress of the Radical Party in Pau in October 1913 failed to heal the latent split between those left-wing Republicans who, like the Socialists, rated the military bill as superfluous and reactionary, and the large group of Radicals who considered the bill as an essential provisional shelter. However, the adoption of the Radical Party's minimum programme, which stipulated that all the left-wing Republicans who had voted in favour of the law were of the opinion that conscription must be reduced again as soon as possible, showed that the republican Left, ignorant of the real strategic significance of the expansion of the army, was not prepared to tolerate the bill in the long term. At the same time the Radicals, under Caillaux, made it clear that they intended to link the financing of the expansion of the army with the long-planned tax reforms (including, above all, the introduction of progressive income tax), a tactic which prevented a split with the Socialists—despite the latter's continued opposition to the reactionary defence policy and criticism of the Radicals' undecided stand on the defence issue—since tax reform was one of the Socialists' main demands. Turning their backs on the *Guesdiste* faction, the majority of the Socialist Party endorsed Jaurès's policy of provisionally putting the defence issue on ice to join forces with the Radicals in order to push through the tax reform package.

However, this strategy by no means implied that the Socialists had abandoned their struggle against the three-year law. The consensus of the Left on tax reform could be preserved in the long term only if the Radicals adopted concrete measures to re-introduce a progressive army constitution. And since the majority of left-wing Republicans had accepted the *Trois Ans* only as a stop-gap measure, it was evident that an amendment of the defence bill would be put before Parliament as soon as the spell of the *attaque brusquée* ideology began to lose its charm.

The Barthou government attempted to contain these tendencies, apparent since the congress of the Radicals in Pau in October 1913. However, Barthou did not succeed in forming a liberal and conservative counterbalance to the burgeoning union of the Left. His hope of using the tax issue to drive a wedge between the determined left-wingers and the more moderate elements within the Radical Party was unrealistic. Moreover, he was wrong to assume that the entire moderately liberal bourgeoisie would oppose the tax reform, which conservatives denounced as 'un-French' and 'demagogic'. Of course there were also dissenting voices within the Radical Party on the scope of the tax reform, and many centrist and liberal deputies certainly rejected some of the proposed reforms (e.g. compulsory declaration of income), as excessively statist. However, many of these moderate Republicans also realised that, in view of the difficulties the financing of the new defence bill posed, substantial concessions would have to be made to the Left if the consensus on defence policy were not to fall apart. The Barthou government was therefore forced to resign at the beginning of December 1913 when the draft loan for the financing of rearmament, which included the traditional tax exemption for state loans, failed to obtain a parliamentary majority. Taxation of the bonds had been a key aspect of the tax reforms proposed by the Radical Party, led by Caillaux.

After the fall of Barthou and the formation of the exclusively left-wing republican Doumergue/Caillaux ministry in December 1913, Briand, Barthou and other leading figures of the bourgeois Centre founded a new party, the *Fédération des Gauches* (FDG) as a counterbalance to the 'demagogical' aspirations of the Radical Party, which, it was maintained, was prepared to abandon the defence bill for the sake of an alliance with the SFIO. However, despite the vehement support of the trade associations and the moderate and conservative press, this liberal and conservative catch-all movement failed to gain momentum. Briand and his followers did not manage to break through the traditional identification of the *Loi de Trois Ans* with the protection of the nation from an *attaque brusquée*. Although Briand and other FDG politicians made several attempts to explain the real significance of the defence bill in terms of military and alliance policy, this was never done with sufficient perspicuity and, in the final analysis, the FDG was also forced to fall back on the *attaque brusquée* stereotype so as not to alienate the relatively moderate elements on the bourgeois Left. Briand's arguments that the *Loi de Trois Ans*, as the 'organic' charter of national defence, must be preserved in the long term, but that it had been necessary only because of the present demands of national defence, largely seemed to coincide with those of the Radicals. Although from an objective point of view this was not in fact the case, the FDG therefore appeared as no more than a *rassemblement* with purely domestic motives, levelled against the policy of tax reform. These suspicions seemed to be confirmed by the famous campaign of *Le Figaro* denouncing Caillaux as a traitor and a demagogue, which was initiated by Barthou and Briand and culminated in the murder of the newspaper's editor, Calmette, by Caillaux's wife.

As a result the liberal and conservative *rassemblement* remained politically sterile. The Doumergue/Caillaux government, with the support of a parliamentary majority of Socialists, radical Republicans and elements of the non-radical bourgeois Centre, was able to carry through the tax reform in March 1914 without having to repeal the defence bill. This was even more significant, since, despite serious attempts to adopt a new line in French foreign policy (on the partitioning of the Portuguese colonies and the Turkish loan at the beginning of 1914), the left-wing republican government was forced to uphold the 'Poincaristic' policy of strengthening the Russian alliance. As we have seen, following the Liman von Sanders crisis it was now in Russia's own interests to respect the military agreements with France. To repeal the three-year law at this stage would be to abandon the alliance with Russia.

However, the French public and Parliament were still not enlightened as to the real context of military and foreign policy in which the three-year law had been introduced. The 1914 election campaign was dominated by the stereotypical identification of the *Trois Ans* with the protection of French territory and the vague promise that an amendment of the law might be feasible in the near future. The following dispatch from the French ambassador in Berlin, Jules Cambon, to Doumergue, at the height of the election campaign, is an excellent illustration of the dilemma inherent in the year-long demagogic campaign on behalf of the *Trois Ans*:

There are illusions in France about the character of these laws (the German armament bill of 1913). It has been regarded as an indication of a German design to strike us, an immediate and one-off danger. This is mistaken . . . reading the newspapers and speeches of the candidates in support of three-year service during the election campaign, I have noticed that this reform is frequently presented as a reform intended to protect us from a momentary danger. This is the profound error . . . and I believe it is necessary not to let public opinion in France grow accustomed to the idea that the three-year law is a law of circumstance.*

Following the 1914 elections it was clear that the three-year defence bill could not be maintained any more in the long term. Although close analysis of the election results shows that this was not fully justified, the sweeping victory of the SFIO in the 1914 elections was interpreted as an indication that the population flatly rejected the reactionary defence bill. This naturally encouraged the Socialists to push for the immediate reintroduction of two-year conscription. Although the majority of the Radicals still had doubts, it was nevertheless a foregone conclusion that concrete steps towards an amendment of the *Loi de Trois Ans* would soon have to be taken; even more so, since the socially conservative *rassemblement* in defence of the law had strengthened the suspicions of the left-wing Republicans that the *Trois Ans* was in fact an expression of domestic reaction.

The Doumergue government, aware that an amendment of the defence bill, which it too considered as an imperative, was now imminent, resigned directly after the elections in May 1914. President Poincaré now endeavoured to install a ministry diametrically opposed to the *antitroisanniste* tendency of the new majority in Parliament, but in vain. The Ribot government (June 1914) was short-lived and defeated on the defence issue in the division on its governmental declaration—despite the fact that Ribot was prepared to make concessions to the Radicals on the question of tax reform.

The policy of the French government during the July crisis was determined by these developments in internal politics. The irrefutable prospect of the *Loi de Trois Ans* being amended in the autumn of 1914 made the Russians highly sceptical as to the future of the strategic agreements with France. In his talks with the Tsar's government in St Petersburg (20–22 July 1914) Poincaré therefore tried to reassure his allies by demonstratively declaring France's unconditional support. Thus, on account of the fear that the imminent amendment of the three-year law would weaken the Russian alliance, a keystone of

---

* Documents Diplomatiques Français (DDF), III série (1911-14), vol. 10, no. 194 (3 May 1914).

French security policy since the second Moroccan crisis, the French government uncritically subordinated itself to the 'impulsive gestures' of Russian policy up to general Russian mobilisation—which were paving the way for war (Isaac). The new left-wing republican Premier, Viviani, was prevented from taking any steps in the opposite direction because of Paléologue's deliberate tactic of not keeping him sufficiently informed. Whether a more flexible and critical attitude on the part of Poincaré and Paléologue could have settled the crisis peacefully cannot be said. For domestic reasons—that is, owing to the rising conflict between developments in internal French politics and French foreign policy—the French government in the July crisis was unable to develop initiatives which might have prevented the aggressive test of German policy against the constellation of the powers in Europe.

The *Union Sacrée* was independent of these problems and considerations of foreign and alliance policy. Despite the years of struggle about rearmament and despite social antagonisms, the 'sacred truce' was established spontaneously because the public dispute had always been dominated by national defence. The attacks against 'revolutionary anti-patriots' and domestic reaction, which had characterised the armament campaign, had not led to a clear-cut polarisation of French society. Despite the dispute on the technical means of defending *la patrie*, the basic inter-party consensus on defence had been preserved, and in fact to a certain extent implicitly reinforced, by the armament debate. It had never been seriously called into question that French preparedness must be secured against an *attaque brusquée*. The German declaration of war on France therefore seemed to confirm the year-long basic assumption of the Left in particular, including the Socialists. As a result, the real reasons for French armament and the full concentration of French foreign policy on the Russian alliance had never been open to discussion, much less confronted with alternative concepts of foreign policy.

Abbreviations

AD	Archives Départementales
AF	Action Française
ALP	Alliance Libérale Populaire
AN	Archives Nationales
APP	Archives de la Préfecture de Police (Paris)
ARD	Alliance Républicaine Démocratique
BdT	Bourse du Travail
BEF	British Expeditionary Force
BN	Bibliothèque Nationale (Paris)
BS	*La Bataille Syndicaliste*
CAP	Commission Administrative Permanente (of the Socialist Party)
CC	Comité Confédéral (of the CGT)
CCEDF	Comité Central d'Etudes et de Défense Fiscale
CE	Comité Exécutif (of the Radical Party)
CG	Conseil Général
CGT	Confédération Générale du Travail
CP	Contre-Projet
CSG	Conseil Supérieur de la Guerre
DDF	Documents Diplomatiques Français
d.n.	'dernières nouvelles' (stop press)
Echo	*L'Echo de Paris*
FDG	Fédération des Gauches
FR	Fédération Républicaine
IISG	Internationaal Instituut voor Sociale Geschiedenis (Amsterdam)
ISB	Internationales Sozialistisches Büro
JOC	*Journal Officiel de la Chambre des Députés, Débats parlementaires*
JOS	*Journal Officiel du Sénat, Débats parlementaires*
NJ	'Notes Journalières' (Poincaré diaries)
PP	Préfecture de Police, Préfet de Police
PSU	Parti Socialiste Unifié (identical with SFIO)
RP	Représentation Proportionnelle (Proportional Representation)
SFIO	Section Française de l'Internationale Ouvrière (most usual name of the PSU)
SG	Sûreté Générale (Security Police)
UIE	Union des Intérêts Economiques

Notes

Introduction

1. F. Fischer, *Krieg der Illusionen: Die Deutsche Politik von 1911 bis 1914* (Düsseldorf, 1969), especially pp. 622–7. Published in English as *War of Illusions* (London, 1975)
2. A summary of this research and its essential aspects in W.J. Mommsen, 'Domestic Factors in German Foreign Policy before 1914', in *Central European History*, 6 (1973), pp. 3–43.
3. A.J. Mayer, 'Causes and Purposes of War in Europe, 1870–1956: A Research Assignment', in *Journal of Modern History*, 41 (1969), pp. 291–303; idem, 'Domestic Causes of the First World War', in L. Krieger and F. Stern (eds), *The Responsibility of Power* (New York, 1967), pp. 286–300.
4. Mayer, 'Causes and Purposes', op. cit., pp. 295, 298–9; see also 'Domestic Causes', op. cit., p. 291.
5. Mayer, 'Causes and Purposes', p. 299.
6. Mayer, 'Domestic Causes', pp. 292–3.
7. Ibid., p. 302.
8. Ibid., p. 289.
9. An interesting—but equally problematic—counter-position has been adopted by James Joll, who concludes from the defeat of the Right in the 1914 elections that France had gone into war under a government based on the Left which for this reason was hardly in a position to pursue an aggressive foreign policy. Cf. J. Joll, 'War Guilt 1914: a Continuing Controversy', in P. Kluke and P. Alter (eds), *Aspects of Anglo-German Relations through the Centuries* (Stuttgart, 1978), pp. 60–80, here: p. 75. For a criticism of Mayer's approach, see also M. Trachtenberg, 'The Social Interpretation of Foreign Policy', in *Review of Politics*, 40 (1978), pp. 328–50.
10. C. Seignobos, *L'Évolution de la IIIe République (1875–1914)* (Paris, 1921) (*Histoire de la France contemporaine* ed. E. Lavisse, vol. 8).
11. Ibid., pp. 252–74, 284–6.
12. G. Bourgin, J. Carrère and A. Guérin, *Manuel des partis politiques en France* (Paris, 1928), 2nd ed., p. 13; similarly P. Boujou and H. Dubois, *La Troisième République* (Paris, 1967), p. 80; F. Goguel, *La Politique des Partis sous la IIIe République* (Paris, 1973), 2nd ed., pp. 153–4; D. Thomson, *Democracy in France since 1870* (Oxford, 1969), 5th ed., p. 179; R.D. Anderson, *France 1870–1914: Politics and Society* (London, 1977), p. 29.
13. See note 12 above and J.-J. Chevallier, *Histoire des institutions politiques de la France moderne* (Paris, 1958), pp. 528–30.
14. J. Chastenet, *Histoire de la Troisième République*, vol. 4: 'Jours inquiets et jours

sanglants, 1906–1918' (Paris, 1955), chaps. VII, VIII; similarly, Joll, 'War Guilt 1914', op. cit., p. 78.
15. S. Hoffmann, *Sur la France*, (Paris, 1976), esp. pp. 171–179, quotation p. 178; similarly: M. Agulhon/A. Nouschi, *La France de 1914 à 1940*, (Paris, 1971), p. 7. The latest account of domestic developments, J.-J. Becker, *1914: Comment les Français sont entrés dans la guerre*, (Paris, 1977) also puts forward the consensus theory. Becker's meticulous analysis of the formation of the blocs pro and contra rearmament leads him to the conclusion that '. . . in 1914 the French appeared as a people . . . in a pacifism which did not exclude patriotism, rejecting the excesses of both nationalism and anti-patriotism' (ibid., p. 119).
16. G. Michon, *La Préparation à la Guerre: La Loi de Trois Ans (1911–1914)*, (Paris, 1935); E. Weber, *The Nationalist Revival in France, 1905–1914*, (Berkeley, 1959) (reprinted 1968).
17. M. Rebérioux, *La Republique Radicale? 1898–1914* (Paris, 1975). This book has been translated into English as J.-M. Mayeur and M. Réberioux, *The Third Republic from its Origins to the Great War, 1871–1914* (Cambridge, 1984). The following quotations are from this edition.
18. Cf. Ibid., pp. 271, 278–83, 341–4.
19. Ibid., pp. 280–1, 323–4.
20. Ibid., p. 345.
21. Ibid., p. 348.
22. Michon's study (see note 16 above) need not be expounded on at this point, since his main theories have been presented in a much more subtle way by Rebérioux (e.g. virtually no personalisations).
23. Cf. note 16 above.
24. Weber, *Nationalist Revival*, pp. 15–16.
25. Ibid., p. 6.
26. Ibid., p. 25.
27. Quoted from Weber, op. cit., p. 9; similarly Becker, *1914: Comment les Français sont entrés dans la guerre*, p. 52; Becker, however, unlike Weber, regards the new nationalism as a minority phenomenon which, in his opinion, explains why it remained without influence (cf. ibid., pp. 52, 80, 83, 118).
28. Weber, *Nationalist Revival*, p. 156.
29. Ibid., p. 124.
30. Ibid., p. 134.
31. Ibid., pp. 14, 160.
32. Eugen Weber refers to this dispute as 'the debate'; J.-B. Duroselle concludes that 'There have been few debates of greater importance in the history of France than that on the Lois de Trois Ans', cf. J.-B. Duroselle, *La France et les Français, 1900–1914* (Paris, 1972), p. 372.
   Michon's *La Préparation à la Guerre* is the only monograph so far published on this subject; his sources, however, are extremely limited. Moreover, following in the footsteps of the innocentistic criticism of the warmongering of Poincaré, Paléologue and Izvolsky, he gives an uncritical account of the contemporary arguments of the SFIO. In an excellent dissertation, which has unfortunately not been published, G.W. Chapman, a pupil of Arno Mayer, has substantiated Mayer's theories: G.W. Chapman, 'Decision for War. The Domestic Political Context of French Diplomacy, 1911–1914', diss. (Princeton, 1971). Unfortunately I have not been able to read the dissertation of yet another pupil of A. Mayer, David Sumler. See D.E. Sumler, 'National Union versus Social Reform: Polarization in French Politics, 1906–1914' (Princeton, 1968); cf. Sumler's essays mentioned in the bibliography. In his new book, *The Persistence of the Old Regime: Europe to the Great War* (New York, 1981), A. Mayer has fallen back behind the results of his pupils Chapman and Sumler: cf. for instance his assessment of Poincaré (ibid., pp. 135–6) and of the significance of the *Trois Ans*, the only function of which, according to

Mayer, was 'to integrate and subdue the workers by forcing them into the army, the school of the conservative nation . . .' (ibid., p. 309)—rather flippant statements, given the level of research already carried out on these points.
D. Porch, in *The March to the Marne. The French Army, (1871–1914)* (Cambridge, 1981), devotes a whole chapter (pp. 191–212) to this question. Porch, however, views the question from the military angle and fails to enter into matters of domestic and foreign policy or the link between German and French armament.
33. Quoted from *Le Procès de l'assassin de Jaurès* (Paris, 1919), p. 8.
34. Detailed documentation on agitation against the SFIO and the smear campaign against Jaurès in: *Le Procès de l'assassin de Jaurès*; H. Guillemin, 'Péguy et Jaurès', in *Les Temps Modernes*, 18 (1962), no. 194, pp. 78–108; J. Rabaut, *Jaurès et son assassin* (Paris, 1967).
35. Poincaré's diaries (1912–1914) are also referred to in the recent work by F.V. Keiger, *France and the Origins of the First World War* (London, 1983)—however, with no reference to my evaluation of the diaries, published in 1980. Keiger's quotations of Poincaré are only referred to in the following if given a different interpretation. The original French texts of the extracts from these diaries can be found in the German edition of the present book.
36. J. Touchard, *La Gauche en France depuis 1900* (Paris, 1977), pp. 47–8; similarly, Weber, *The Nationalist Revival in France*, pp. 150–1.

CHAPTER 1. After Agadir

1. Fischer, *Krieg der Illusionen*, pp. 117–25. Increased interest has been shown in the Agadir Crisis in recent years, cf. esp. J.C. Allain, *Agadir 1911* (Paris, 1975); G. Barraclough, *From Agadir to Armageddon* (London, 1982), a most stimulating and innovative interpretation, based essentially on Allain's research. On the reasons for and problems surrounding the German *coup* see E. Oncken, *Panthersprung nach Agadir* (Düsseldorf, 1981).
2. G. Ziebura, *Die deutsche Frage in der öffentlichen Meinung Frankreichs von 1911–1914* (Berlin, 1955), p. 118; Weber, *Nationalist Revival*, pp. 94–9.
3. Joffre and Caillaux gave concurrent reports on this discussion. Cf. J. Joffre, *Mémoires du Maréchal Joffre*, vol. 1 (Paris, 1932), pp. 15–16; J. Caillaux, *Mes Mémoires*, vols 1–3 (Paris, 1942–7), here: vol. 2, p. 145.
4. W. Serman, *Les officiers français dans la nation, 1848–1914* (Paris, 1982), pinpoints the link between the military's relative social isolation and their loyalty to the respective governments; see R. Girardet, *La société militaire dans la France contemporaine, 1815–1939* (Paris, 1953) especially p. 199; also F. Engerand, *Le Secret de la Frontière* (Paris, 1918), pp. 7, 221–6, 133–45. Engerand's observations on the links between the offensive hysteria, the cult of heroic leadership and increasing bureaucracy within the military apparatus have unfortunately never been adequately followed up.
5. On the development of the Supreme War Council, originally under the military authorities and, following the Dreyfus affair, strictly subordinated to the civil authorities, see in particular R. d'Ornano, *Gouvernement et Haut-Commandement en régime parlementaire français* (Aix-en-Provence, 1958), pp. 138–46.
6. Cf. H. Contamine, *La Revanche* (Paris, 1957), pp. 116–17; and *Les Armées Françaises dans la Grande Guerre*, I, 1, ed. Ministère de la Guerre, Etat-Major de l'Armée, Service Historique (Paris, 1923), p. 13.
7. J.D. Wallach, *Kriegstheorien: Ihre Entwicklung im 19. und 20. Jahrhundert* (Frankfurt, 1972), pp. 137–49; and Sir B. Liddell Hart, 'French Military Ideas before the First World War', in M. Gilbert (ed.), *A Century of Conflict, 1850–1950: Essays for A.J.P. Taylor* (London, 1966), pp. 136–44, here: pp. 136–40;

S.T. Possony and E. Mantoux, 'Du Picq and Foch: The French School', in E.M. Earle (ed.), *Makers of Modern Strategy: Military Thought from Machiavelli to Hitler* (Princeton, 1943), pp. 206–33, esp. p. 228. An excellent summary of all these theories and an attempt to explain their social derivation can be found in a study by the Dutch historian, H.L. Wesseling, *Soldaat en Krijger: Franse opvattingen over leger en oorlog, 1905–1914* (Assen, 1969).

8. Quotation from Contamine, *La Revanche*, p. 167; cf. R.D. Challener, *The French Theory of the Nation in Arms* (New York, 1955), p. 82; E. Carrias, *La Pensée militaire française* (Paris, 1960), pp. 296–7; Liddell Hart, 'French Military Ideas', op. cit., p. 136; and S.R. Williamson, *The Politics of Grand Strategy; Britain and France Prepare for War, 1904–1914*, (Cambridge, Mass., 1969), p. 206. For a criticism of the militarily stagnative dimension of this revival movement, see also C. de Gaulle, *La France et son armée* (Paris, 1945), p. 133; Général F. Gascouin, *Le Triomphe de l'Idée* (Paris, 1931), pp. 19–31, 53–4; see also J.-B. Duroselle, *La France et les Français*, pp. 48, 77. Duroselle defends Grandmaison from the later reduction of his theories; in a similar vein: M.G. Merlier, 'De Grandmaison, Penseur et Ecrivain militaire' in *Actes du 87ᵉ Congrès National des Sociétés Savantes* (Poitiers, 1962; Paris, 1963), pp. 529–41.

9. R. d' Ornano, *Gouvernement et Haut-Commandement*, pp. 143–46; A. Messimy, *Mes Souvenirs* (Paris, 1937), pp. 71–2, 74–82.

10. S.R. Williamson, *Grand Strategy*, p. 205—a pertinent criticism of the previously held opinion that Messimy's measures had made the army virtually independent of the state, cf. Porch. *The March to the Marne*, pp. 172ff.

11. Joffre, *Mémoires*, p. 32.

12. Joffre rejected the 1908 operational Plan XVI with the argument that it did not correspond with the traditions of warfare or the national temperament of France, and with its defensive approach reflected the defeat of 1870 (Joffre, *Mémoires*, p. 23). For Joffre war is an act of force; battle must be desired with all one's energy (*culte de l'énergie*) (ibid., pp. 29–33). A defensive strategy would entail the danger of invasion which has a demoralising effect (ibid., p. 143).

13. Cf. Williamson, *Grand Strategy*, p. 224; see sources quoted in ibid., note 62; Gascouin, *Le Triomphe de l'Idée*, passim; Caillaux, *Mémoires*, vol. 2, pp. 127, 211–12; Messimy, *Souvenirs*, pp. 78–9.

14. Joffre, *Mémoires*, p.39

15. Williamson, *Grand Strategy* p. 220. Cf. ibid., p. 226: 'In the first place Plan XVII represented a fundamentally unsound compromise between the realities of France's military situation and the desires of its military leaders.' Cf. the lengthy discussion of this problem in Porch, *The March to the Marne*, chap. 11. However, Porch's interesting comments on the compensatory nature of the *offensive à outrance* are rather spoiled by his absurd identification of the offensive theory with the philosophy of the left-wing Republicans(!). For purposes of comparison, it is interesting to note that very similar thought patterns were evident within the British general staff at the time, see T.H.E. Travers, 'The Offensive and the Problem of Innovation in British Military Thought, 1870–1914', in *The Journal of Contemporary History*, 13 (1978), pp. 531–53.

16. Caillaux, *Mémoires*, vol. 2, pp. 211–15.

17. See the detailed description of this point in Joffre, *Mémoires*, p. 102.

18. Caillaux, *Mémoires*, vol. 2, pp. 127, 211–12.

19. See Joffre at an informal discussion between high-ranking politicians and military on 21 February 1912. For his exposé at this meeting, see Joffre, *Mémoires*, pp. 119–22; cf. Williamson, *Grand Strategy*, p. 212. At the general staff conference in August 1911 Dubail had stated 'that the first major clashes will probably come about in Lorraine, Luxembourg and Belgium between the fifteenth and eighteenth days'—quoted from F. Stieve (ed.), *Der diplomatische Schriftwechsel Iswolskis, 1911–1914*, 4 vols (Berlin, 1924), here: vol. 1, no. 117, p. 138.

20. On the discussions between the British and French general staffs, cf. Williamson, *Grand Strategy* pp. 207–8.
21. Joffre, *Mémoires*, pp. 119–26. Williamson, *Grand Strategy*, pp. 213–18, has clearly proved that in the spring of 1912, long before it had been officially pronounced on 26 November 1912, the British veto had been taken for granted. On the overall situation of French diplomacy and strategics at the time, see G. Pedroncini, 'Stratégie et relations internationales: La Séance du 9 janvier 1912 du Conseil Supérieur de la défense nationale', in *Revue d'Histoire Diplomatique*, 91 (1977), pp. 145–58. Pedroncini comes to mainly the same conclusions as the author. An interesting point is his reference to an alternative plan to Plan XVII, drafted by General Demange, which paid greater attention to the diplomatic and legal constraints, but was not taken into consideration by the competent bodies because it did not correspond with the *offensive à outrance* dogma (cf. ibid., pp. 155–7).
22. Joffre, *Mémoires*, p. 34.
23. *Les Armées françaises*, pp. 10–14; and Messimy, *Souvenirs*, p. 408.
24. Caillaux, *Mémoires*, vol. 2, p. 142.
25. Cf. General Dubail's memorandum, quoted and summarised in ibid., pp. 143–4, and the minutes of the general staffs' conference, 18–31 March 1911, in Stieve, *Iswolskis*, vol. 1, no. 117; see also Porch, *The March to the Marne*, p. 277, note 92, with a reference to the report of the *Deuxième Bureau* in December 1911; 'The Russians will launch no action of any kind against the Germans before the 30th day and this action will only become serious much later'.
26. See in particular Messimy, *Souvenirs* pp. 188–9.
27. Joffre's assertion (*Mémoires*, p. 26) that, owing to these agreements, his offensive plans had been realistic in 1911, is to be regarded as a retrospective euphemism in view of the general staffs' conferences of the following years, 1912 and 1913 (see chap. 6 above). J. Cairns, 'International Politics and the Military Mind: The Case of the French Republic, 1911–1914', in *Journal of Modern History*, 25 (1953), pp. 273–85 (here: p. 278), has illustrated that, on the contrary, in 1911 precisely the French generals were dubious about whether Russia was prepared or able to launch a simultaneous attack in the event of war. Williamson, *Grand Strategy*, p. 209, follows Joffre's account, but agrees with Cairns (ibid., p. 223).
28. See chaps 6 and 9 above.
29. Joffre, *Mémoires*, p. 130.
30. Quotation from *Documents Diplomatiques Français* (DDF), III série (1911–14), vol. 3, no. 200 (Paris, 1931): 'Procès-verbal de l'entretien du 13 juillet 1912 entre les chefs d'État-Major des Armées Française et Russe'. The following summary and quotations are also from this source.
31. R. Poincaré, *Au Service de la France*, vols 1–4 (Paris, 1962–7), here: vol. 2, pp. 81–2. Joffre, in his memoirs, makes no reference to these doubts, although they had by no means been eliminated following the 1913 talks (cf. Joffre, *Mémoires*, p. 134).
32. R. Poincaré, ibid., vol. 2, pp. 81–2; ibid., p. 99: 'There is something cracked in the alliance.'
33. On the domestic reasons and consequences of the formation of the Poincaré government, cf. chap. 1, pp. 30–43, above.
34. Cf. G. Wright, *Raymond Poincaré and the French Presidency* (Stanford, Calif. 1942; new ed., New York, 1967), p. 30.
35. These were the main points on foreign policy in Poincaré's governmental declaration. Cf. Poincaré, *Au Service*, vol. 1, pp. 23–5; and G. Bonnefous, *Histoire politique de la IIIᵉ République*, vols 1–2 (Paris, 1965/7), here: vol. 1, pp. 274–5. J.F. Keiger, *France and the Origins of the First World War*, pp. 55–6, gives the following appropriate description of Poincaré's alliance policy: 'Poincaré . . . wanted the balance of powers observed to the letter—a total separation of the two blocs and a strict refusal to allow any penetration of the alliance systems'.
36. Cf. L. Albertini, *The Origins of the War of 1914*, vols 1–2 (Oxford, 1952), here:

vol. 1, pp. 372–3; A.J.P. Taylor, *The Struggle for Mastery in Europe* (London, 1954), p. 488; Fischer, *Krieg der Illusionen*, p. 220; and E. Thaden, *Russia and the Balkan Alliance of 1912* (University Park, Pa., 1965), pp. 115–18. Poincaré's insistence that these commitments were defensive and in the interests of peace (*Au Service*, vol. 2, p. 202) does not change the facts.

37. Poincaré, *Au Service*, vol. 1, p. 302; vol. 2, pp. 26–60. See also Poincaré's detailed report to P. Cambon on his state visit to St Petersburg, DDF III/4, no. 170 (15 Oct. 1912). Taylor, *Struggle* pp. 186, 492–3, describes this policy as an attempt to find 'the quadrature of the circle': 'he [Poincaré] wanted her [Russia] to be firm towards Germany, while keeping a free hand himself'.

38. Poincaré, *Au Service*, vol. 2, pp. 32–42; and DDF III/4, no. 170.

39. DDF III/4, no. 170; and DDF III/3, no. 264, here: p. 340.

40. Poincaré, *Au Servicé*, vol. 1, pp. 137, 293.

41. Ibid., p. 202.

42. Conversation with Kokovcov on 13 August 1912: DDF III/3, no. 264, here: p. 344.

43. Ibid., here: p. 342. Sazonov's reluctance is even more obvious in his report to the Tsar on his talks with Poincaré: cf. Stieve, *Iswolski*, vol. 2, no. 401, here: p. 220.

44. DDF III/3, no. 264, here: p. 344.

45. Cf. Sazonov's report to the Tsar: Stieve, op. cit., vol. 2, no. 401; here: p. 223.

46. This was the opinion of P. Cambon in particular: DDF III/4, no. 627. B.E. Schmitt, *The Coming of the War, 1914*, vol. 1 (New York, 1930); new ed., 1966), p. 21, refers to a new attitude in French policy towards Russia after the First Balkan War. Albertini, in *The Origins*, vol. 1, p. 415, however, regards this as a linear continuation of Poincaré's policy since he entered office. Weber, *Nationalist Revival*, p. 112, also perceives a new interest in the Balkans among the French public at the end of 1912: 'The tone of the press was not unconnected with the changed tone of the Quai d'Orsay.'

47. Cf. Stieve, *Iswolski*, vol. 2, no. 639 (Izvolsky to Sazonov, 5/18 Dec. 1912), and F. Stieve, *Iswolski und der Weltkrieg* (Berlin, 1924), p. 118 (conversation between the War Minister, Millerand, and the Russian military attaché in Paris, Ignatiev, on 18 Dec. 1912).

48. For further details see chap. 2.

49. DDF III/6, no. 72, Pichon to Delcassé, 27 March 1913; ibid., no. 39, letter from Poincaré to the Tsar, 20 March 1913.

50. Weber, *Nationalist Revival*, p. 100.

51. Ibid., pp. 96–7, with many examples from the left-wing republican press: cf. Ziebura, *Die deutsche Frage*, pp. 117–19; and Anderson, *France 1870–1914*, p. 26.

52. On the Socialists' stance towards Poincaré, cf. p. 42, below.

53. Cf. Poincaré, *Au Service*, vol. 1, pp.24–5.

54. 'Discours de Dunkerque'. Cf. Poincaré, *Au Service*, vol. 2, pp. 168–9; and in a similar vein, the '*discours de Nantes*' (26 October 1912), ibid., pp. 278–9.

55. These were the express words of Poincaré; cf. ibid., p. 78.

56. Millerand, *Pour la Défense Nationale* (1913), quoted here from ibid., p. 76. Cf. Joffre, *Mémoires*, p. 28; and R. Persil, *Alexandre Millerand* (Paris, 1949), p. 74 Millerand's activities in 1912 are outlined in: M.M. Farrar, 'Politics versus Patriotism: Alexandre Millerand as French Minister of War', in *French Historical Studies*, 11 (1980), pp. 577–609. Millerand's uncritical submission to the demands of the military, which became so evident later, were already ascertainable in 1912.

57. Cf. L. Thile, *Pouvoir civil et pouvoir militaire* (Paris, 1914), pp. 77–84.

58. Bonnefous, *Histoire politique*, vol. 1, p. 309. On the tightening of military discipline in 1912–13, see also Th. Zeldin, *France 1848–1945*, vol. 2, pp. 881, 888–90.

59. Poincaré, *Au Service*, vol. 2, pp. 78–80, 68–9.

60. Cf., in particular, Weber, *Nationalist Revival*, pp. 101–3 (this also gives details on the reaction abroad); Contamine, *La Revanche* p. 132; Bonnefous, *Histoire*

Politique, vol. 1, p. 314; and Caillaux, *Mémoires*, vol. 3, pp. 19–24.

61. Maurras later described Poincaré and the 'national' Republicans as 'new Royalists' who had rediscovered the 'traditional public spirit of the monarchy . . . and love for France' *La Contre-Révolution spontanée* (Lyons, 1943), p. 148. Cf. Weber, *Nationalist Revival* p. 111.

62. See D.E. Sumler, 'Domestic Influences on the Nationalist Revival in France, 1909–1914, in *French Historical Studies*, 6 (1970), pp. 517–37, here: p. 527. Cf. ibid., for further examples of the planned reinforcement of the prestige of 'military society'. Sumler, a pupil of Arno Mayer, attempted to express these general theories (cf. Introduction, above) in concrete terms.

63. See Archives Nationales (AN), F 7/12811: 'Sociétés de préparation militaire (1909–1913)'. Number of applications: 1909, 3,058; 1910, 1,004; 1911, 854; 1912, 748; (Jan.–March) 1913, 257. On the origins of these *sociétés* and how they developed into the reservoir for nationalist and anti-Republican elements, cf. AN, F 9/1433: 'Préparation militaire obligatoire (–1917)'.

64. See AN, BB 18/2508, doss. 128 A 13, carton 51b, 'Sou du Soldat: Chambre syndicale de la Maçonnerie': Minister of the Interior Monis to the Minister of Justice, 14 June 1911. Cf. Caillaux, *Mémoires*, vol. 2, pp. 83–5. Caillaux's energetic containment of syndicalism earned him the nickname of 'Caillaux-de-Sang' in these circles.

65. See Sumler, 'Domestic Influences', op. cit., p. 526.

66. See AN, C 7419, doss. 185–92; in the SFIO report for the 1914 elections (= A. Dunois, *L'Action socialiste au Parlement*, Paris, 1914) the fight against the 'Loi Millerand' was not even mentioned!

67. See J. Julliard, 'La CGT devant la guerre', in *Le Mouvement Social*, no. 49 (1964), pp. 47, 62, here: pp. 48–53.

68. See H. Dubief (ed.), *Le Syndicalisme révolutionnaire* (Paris, 1969), p. 154; J.-J. Becker, *Le Carnet B. L'anti-militarisme vu par les pouvoirs publics*. (Paris, 1973), p. 188.

69. For further details, see E. Dolléans, *Histoire du mouvement ouvrier*, vol. 2 (1871–1920), (Paris, 1957), p. 192. On the anarcho-syndicalist theory of 'direct action' and 'proletarian violence', cf., more recently, Z. Sternhell, *La Droite révolutionnaire: Les Origines françaises du fascisme* (Paris, 1978), pp. 338–47.

70. Quoted from a police report on this CGT annual assembly, held between the regular, two-yearly congresses, from Julliard, 'La CGT', op. cit., p. 68.

71. The *Encyclique syndicaliste* is printed in Dubief, *Le Syndicalisme révolutionnaire*, pp. 216–19.

72. Cf. Dolléans, *mouvement ouvrier*, pp. 194–5; and G. Lefranc, *Le Mouvement syndical sous la Troisième République* (Paris, 1967), p. 195.

73. Cf. B. Georges and D. Tintant, *Léon Jouhaux. Cinquante ans de syndicalisme*, I (Paris, 1962), pp. 165–6; Julliard, 'La CGT', op. cit., p. 52; and Lefranc, *Mouvement Syndical*, p. 191.

74. C. Rappoport, 'Der Gewerkschaftskongress von Havre', in *Die Neue Zeit*, 31 (1913), vol. 1, pp. 22–30; here: p. 27. F.F. Ridley, *Revolutionary Syndicalism in France: The Direct Action of Its Time* (Cambridge, 1970), pp. 135–9, draws the—hardly tenable—conclusion from this development that anti-militarism in the CGT was fundamentally of an economic nature and could never be identified with true anti-patriotism. :

75. This body of 'workers' solidarity', founded in 1900, was one of the few organised union support funds of the time. The task of the member federations and syndicates was to support their members engaged in military service by sending them a sum of 5 francs every quarter and constantly to remind them to 'remain workers' (e.g. urging them not to shoot at their worker comrades in strike action). In line with the anarchistic and anti-patriotic tendencies in the CGT, the *adjonction Péricat (sic)* at the congress of Toulouse (1910) gave the *Sou du Soldat* the task of

organising the 'general revolutionary strike' in the event of war. For documentation on the *Sou du Soldat*, cf. AN, F 7/12911, report 'M/6347', 3 January, 1912; and Becker, *1914: Comment les Français sont entrés dans la guerre*, p. 85 note 62.

76. See *Confédération Générale du Travail: Le Congrés du Havre (16–23.9.1912)* (Le Havre, 1912), pp. 185–92. In a communication from the Minister of the Interior to the Minister of Justice, on 7 August 1912, it was remarked that the *Sou du Soldat* had of late been distributing the money among its members 'without comments on the army'. See AN, BB 18/2508, doss. 128 A 13, carton 51a, 'Sou du Soldat' (1909–1914): 'Création de la caisse fédérale'.

77. See A. Kriegel, 'Patrie ou révolution: Le Mouvement ouvrier français devant la guerre', in *Revue d'Histoire Économique et Sociale*, 43 (1965), pp. 363–85, here: p. 369. Georges and Tintant, *Léon Jouhaux*, p. 120, point out that the wording of the resolution, 'if, by folly or by calculation, the country we are in entered into a wager of war', contains *in nuce* a differentiation between an offensive and a defensive war.

78. In AN, F 1a/3518, no. 164, a confidential circular to the prefects (10 December 1912) instructing them to use the means at their disposal (dispersion of demonstrations and assemblies, confiscation of red and black flags, and above all strict orders to all workers employed in the public sector not to absent themselves from work on 16 December without due reason). See also Lefranc, *Mouvement Syndical*, p. 191, and Chapman, *Decision for War*, pp. 240–3, with further information from the files of the political police. An account of the preparation and course of the strike on 16 December 1912, based on police reports, can be found, in J.-J. Becker, *Le Carnet B.*, pp. 57ff.

79. *La Bataille Syndicaliste* (BS), 23 January 1913 (Griffuelhes), and *Voix du Peuple*, 10/17 March 1913 (Yvetot).

80. See in general P. Campbell, *French Electoral Systems and Elections since 1789* (London, 1969), 2nd ed., pp. 70–90.

81. Cf. above all the Duverger/Lavau discussion: M. Duverger, *Les Partis politiques* (Paris, 1951), especially pp. 268–85, 405; and J. Lavau, *Partis politiques et réalités sociales* (Paris, 1953).

82. F. Goguel, 'L'Influence des systèmes électoraux sur la vie politique d'après l'expérience française', in idem, (ed.), *Nouvelles études de sociologie électorale* (Paris, 1954), pp. 74–81; and idem, *La Politique des partis*, p. 135.

83. Chevallier, *institutions politiques*, pp. 501–2.

84. On the number of seats of the individual groups in Parliament, see A. Bomier-Landowski, 'Les Groupes parlementaires de l'Assemblée Nationale et de la Chambre des Députés de 1871–1940', in F. Goguel and G. Dupeux (eds), *Socilogoie électorale* (Paris, 1951), pp. 75–89, here: p. 80. Cf. Bonnefous, *Histoire politique*, vol. 1, p. 185.

85. Chevallier, *Institutions politiques*, p. 524, rightly describes the system as a *véritable majorité de dislocation du Bloc*.

86. Cf. Goguel, *La Politique des partis*, p. 142.

87. Cf. Chevallier, *Institutions politiques*, p. 524; Bonnefous, *Histoire politique*, vol. 1, pp. 145–50.

88. This included in particular the right of dissolution, i.e. the power to dissolve the Chamber before the end of the legislatory period with the approval of the Senate.

89. See R. Escaich, 'L'Influence des présidents de la République', in *Ecrits de Paris*, no. 237 (1965), pp. 64–76. On the function of the Supreme War Council, see p. 254 (note 28) below; cf. the recent overview by L. Derfler, *President and Parliament: a short History of the French Presidency* (Boca Raton, 1983).

90. Poincaré, *Au Service*, vol. 3, p. 35.

91. Ibid., p. 61.

92. Stieve, *Iswolski*, vol. 3, no. 705.

93. Ibid.; cf. Poincaré, *Au Service*, vol. 3, p. 94.

94. For example, *Action Française* (AF) (13 January 1913); *Echo de Paris*

(17 January 1913). Cf. Weber, *Nationalist Revival* pp. 110–14.

95. *La Liberté* (19 January 1913); *Revue des deux Mondes* (RddM) (1 February 1913).

96. Cf. F. Payen, *Raymond Poincaré* (Paris, 1936), p. 387; Contamine, *La Revanche*, pp. 132–3.

97. Cf. J.J. Fiechter, *Le Socialisme français: de l'Affaire Dreyfus à la Grande Guerre*, (Geneva, 1965), pp. 175–6; L. Derfler, *President and Parliament*, p. 71.

98. A. Compère-Morel, 'Die Präsidentenwahl in Frankreich', in *Die Neue Zeit*, 31 (1913), vol. 1, pp. 617–21, here: p. 621. Eduard Vaillant, a leading French Socialist, also wrote in a letter to Huysmans in September 1912 that Poincaré was obviously striving for peace in Europe; see Vaillant to Huysmans, September 1912, in G. Haupt and J. Howorth, 'Edouard Vaillant, délégué au Bureau Socialiste International', in *Annali della Fondazione G. Feltrinelli*, 17 (1976), pp. 209–305. The editors' commentary which is aimed at 'correcting' Vaillant, is completely out of place.

99. *La Lanterne*, 16 January 1913: Weber, *The Nationalist Revival in France*, p. 203, writes that *La Lanterne* was always a decided opponent of Poincarisme; the left-wing Republican *L'Aurore* also supported Poincaré's election to the presidency on account of his foreign policy (6 January 1913).

100. *Le Républicain Socialiste* (*Le Rép. Soc.*), 12 January 1913.

101. Poincaré, *Notes Journalières* (NJ) in B.N., n.a.f. 16024–16027 (1 January 1913).

102. The official Radical Party newspaper, *Le Radical*, stated on 16 January that Poincaré had been brought to power by an anti-parliamentarian 'bastard plebiscite' staged by the Right. See D.R. Watson, *Georges Clemenceau: a Political Biography* (London, 1974), p. 244: in July 1912 Combes and Clemenceau founded a Committee for the Defence of Universal Suffrage, against Poincaré.

103. C. Paix-Séailles, *Jaurès et Caillaux* (Paris, 1920), p. 80. Paix-Séailles was one of Caillaux's close assistants; see Caillaux, *Mémoires*, vol. 3, p. 25. Weber, *Nationalist Revival*, p. 112, uncritically adopts Caillaux's memoires.

104. Cf. J.T. Nordmann, *Histoire des Radicaux 1820–1973* (Paris, 1974), p. 182. A. Mayer's characterisation of Poincaré (idem, *The Persistence of the Old Regime*, p. 135) repeats every stereotype of postwar anti-Poincaré literature; in contrast is Duroselle's precise and well-balanced judgement in *La France et les Français*, p. 363. See also G. Krumeich, 'Poincaré und der "Poincarismus"' in *Francia*, 8 (1980), pp. 427–54 (with a summary in French), which looks at the problem as a whole.

105. Letter from Clemenceau to Poincaré, 31 December 1912; see Payen, *Raymond Poincaré*, pp. 393–5.

106. Cf. Poincaré, NJ (17 January 1913).

107. Compère-Morel (see note 98) above. The contemporary press concentrated almost exclusively on the anti-radical character of Poincaré's election: cf. *Le Siècle* (17 January); *L'Aurore* (17 January), *Le Radical* (16 and 23 January); *Le Gaulois* (18 January); *Le Temps* (10 January): Cf. Michon, *La Préparation à la Guerre*, p. 126, for further appraisals of Poincaré's election as the 'defeat of the Left'.

108. This stalemate within the Republican camp is highlighted in the famous preparatory meeting of the leftist groups of the Chamber and the Senate in which Pams was elected by 323 votes to 309 as the candidate of the Left against Poincaré. Cf. *inter alia* the detailed account in Bonnefous, *Histoire politique*, vol. 1, pp. 318–20.

109. Michon, *La Préparation à la guerre*, p. 126.

110. See the letters of protest from Albert de Mun, leader of the Catholic Right, to Poincaré in 1912 in BN, n.a.f. 16010, fos 322–6 (letters of 23 June and 4 July 1912). Further examples of the impossibility of closing the divide between moderate Republicans and the Catholic Right with the help of the two groups of joint nationalism, in B.F. Martin, *Count Albert de Mun, Paladin of the Third Republic* (Chapel Hill (NC), 1978), pp. 554–5. Martin's account of the continuation of the closure of religious schools under Poincaré's 1912 government is an absolute

contradiction of the theory adopted by Martin from Sumler, 'Domestic Influences', that nationalism had established a lasting link between these two groups.

111. Weber, *Nationalist Revival*, p. 111, explains this support on the basis of Poincaré's promise to the Right to introduce three-year military service. He bases this assertion on a conversation in 1916 between Caillaux and the leader of the ALP, Piou, mentioned in the former's *Mémoires* (vol. 3, p. 24). However, the inter-ministerial discussions on the three-year law in February 1913 show that in January 1913—before news of the German arms bill had reached France—there could be no question of concrete plans to introduce this bill. Cf. chap. 2 above. Martin, *Albert de Mun*, quotes a new source which may give some substance to the long-standing rumour of the link between the three-year law and a *rapprochement* between Poincaré and the nationalist Right. According to Martin (p. 261), the estate of A. de Mun's confessor contains a document in which de Mun gives an account of secret meetings with Poincaré on the subject of support from the Catholic Right for Poincaré's candidature. Unfortunately Martin does not make it clear whether this source shows that the three-year law was the price for this support. According to Martin this estate is not normally available to research, so it would be difficult to examine this document. The author therefore upholds his opinion that such a link did not exist.

112. Cf. letter from de Mun to Poincaré, 11 January 1913, in Payen, *Raymond Poincaré*, pp. 389–90.

113. See Poincaré, NJ (10 Jan.).

114. Letter from de Mun to Poincaré, 12 January, in BN n.a.f. 161010, fo. 338. In *L'Écho de Paris* (3 Feb.), de Mun deplored the fact that the 'pack of wolves' in Parliament—in particular Jaurès—had succeeded in sacrificing Millerand, a 'good servant of France', to party wrangling: Paléologue, Poincaré's closest confidant, described his behaviour towards Millerand as 'inexcusable weakness' (M. Paléologue, *Au Quai d'Orsay: À la veille de la tourmente: Journal 1913–1914*, Paris, 1947, p. 6), Paul Cambon, French ambassador in London, wrote to his brother Jules, ambassador in Berlin: 'It's an absolute mess. Millerand's resignation is lamentable. Poincaré, concerned above all about his candidature, has dropped his War Minister' (P. Cambon, *Correspondance 1870–1924*, vol. 3 [1912–1924], Paris, 1946, p. 34, letter dated 15 January 1913).

115. *Alliance Républicaine Démocratique* (ARD) (2 March 1913).

116. Weber, *Nationalist Revival*, pp. 15–16. Idem, 'Un demi-siècle de glissement à droite', in *International Review of Social History*, 5 (1960), pp. 165–201, here: p. 170, takes this theory a step further by concentrating almost exclusively on the socially conservative aspect of this link. However, he does so under the misapprehension that Poincaré and other politicians of the 'national Centre' were *progressistes*, i.e., supporters of the extremely conservative group of Republicans.

117. This is how M. Duverger, 'L'Éternel Marais: Essai sur le centrisme français', in *Revue Française de Science Politique*, 14 (1964), pp. 33–51, describes the real dynamics of French domestic politics in contrast with the pattern of a constant polarisation of political forces between Right and Left predominant since Goguel's analyses; See also Z. Sternhell, *Maurice Barrès et le nationalisme français* (Paris, 1972), p. 76, n. 4.

118. See Payen, *Raymond Poincaré*, p. 393; and cf. ARD (26 Jan., 9 Feb.); *Siècle* (18 Jan.); and *La Petite République* (22 Jan.).

CHAPTER 2 The Origins of the Three-Year Law

1. See in detail chaps 3, pp. 53–8 and 5, pp. 110–17, above. See also *inter alia* Poincaré, *Au Service*, vol. 3, pp. 144–9; Paléologue, *Au Quai d'Orsay*, pp. 54–5; Bonnefous, *Histoire politique*, vol. 1, p. 337; Goguel, *La Politique des partis*,

pp. 143–4; P. Renouvin, *La Crise européenne et la première guerre mondiale* (Paris, 1969) (*Peuples et civilisations*, vol. 19), pp. 189–190; and Fischer, *Krieg der Illusionen*, pp. 622–4.

2. Cf. H. Herzfeld, *Die deutsche Rüstungspolitik vor dem Weltkriege* (Bonn, Leipzig, 1923), in particular pp. 129–43; F. Stieve, *Iswolski und der Weltkrieg* (Berlin, 1924), pp. 135–7; Michon, *La Préparation à la guerre*, pp. 128–35; J. Monteilhet, *Les Institutions militaires de la France* (Paris, 1926), p. 275; and A. Kovacs, 'French Military Legislation in the Third Republic', in *Military Affairs*, 13 (1949), pp. 1–12; here: p. 9. R. Poidevin and J. Bariéty, *Les Relations franco-allemandes 1815–1975* (Paris, 1977), p. 209, go no further than the statement that both positions are scarcely tenable.

3. See W.J. Mommsen, 'Domestic Factors in German Foreign Policy before 1914', in *Central European History*, 6 (1973), p. 28.

4. The main new sources evaluated in this context are the minutes of the *Conseil Supérieur de la Guerre*, Poincaré's diary, and the minutes of the Chamber Army Committee. To the present author's knowledge, no minutes of cabinet meetings or inter-ministerial correspondence on the subject of the introduction of the three-year law have survived.

5. Herzfeld, *Rüstungspolitik*, p. 94; and *Le Temps* (26 January 1913).

6. DDF III/5, nos 239, 253: reports from the military attaché and the ambassador in Berlin dated 20 and 24 January 1913, respectively.

7. On the dispute between the German government and general staff on the scope of the new defence bill, cf. Herzfeld, *Rüstungspolitik*, pp. 47–77; *Der Weltkrieg 1914 bis 1918* (ed. in the Reichsarchiv), *Kriegsrüstung und Kriegswirtschaft*, vol. 1 (Berlin, 1930), pp. 117–89; Fischer, *Krieg der Illusionen*, pp. 251–6.

8. According to Joffre, *Mémoires*, pp. 162–9, the infantry cadre bill (23 Dec. 1912) was an integral part of Plan XVII, at this point almost ready for adoption. This bill was to provide for the integration of certain reserve units into the front line forces; the expansion of the regular cadres was regarded as an essential factor for the improvement of the offensive spirit of the troops. See also *Les Armées françaises*, I, 1, p. 20, and ibid., annex no. 6: 'Instruction du 21 novembre 1913 sur l'encadrement des formations d'infanterie mobilisées'.

9. DDF III/5, no. 302 (31 Jan.); cf. ibid., no. 404 (15 Feb.).

10. Ibid., no. 494 (1 March). On the 'short war' theory, predominant at the time both in Germany and France, cf. *inter alia* J.D. Wallach, *Das Dogma der Vernichtungsschlacht* (Munich, 1970); L.L. Farrar, *The Short-War Illusion* (Oxford, 1973); Challener, *The French Theory*, especially pp. 102–3, 134–6; and Joffre, *Mémoires*, pp. 142–4.

11. Joffre, op. cit., pp. 87–90.

12. Ibid., p. 160. See also *Les Armées françaises*, I, 1, p. 19.

13. Ibid., I. 1, p. 26. The problem of the French *couverture* theories has not yet been examined adequately by military historians. A first attempt, with inadequate sources, is M.F. Weigold, 'National Security versus Collective Security: The Role of the Couverture in Shaping French Military and Foreign Policy (1905–1934)', Ph.D., St John's University, New York, 1970. See also G. Krumeich, 'L'offensive à outrance et la crainte de "l'attaque brusquée"', in *Forces armées et systèmes d'alliance. Colloque international d'histoire militaire* (Montpellier, 1981), 1984, pp. 447–54.

14. Report of these meetings, *Le Temps* (18 Feb.—no further details); names of participants, ibid.

15. Poincaré, *Au Service*, vol. 3, p. 146. Poincaré's diary makes no reference to these conferences.

16. Poincaré, NJ (15 and 17 Feb. 1913).

17. *Le Temps* (18 Feb.) (d.n.).

18. Poincaré, NJ (17 Feb.).

19. *La Petite République*, (18 Feb.). This publication was generally regarded as Briand's newspaper; cf. C. Bellanger, *Histoire Générale de la presse française*, vol. 3 (Paris, 1972), p. 374.
20. Poincaré, NJ (17 Feb.).
21. Poincaré, NJ (27 Feb.). In his memoirs (*Au Service*, vol. 3, p. 147), Poincaré also mentions Klotz's project but with no reference to it as a counter-proposal to the three-year law.
22. *Le Temps* (26 Feb.). *Le Figaro* (26 Feb.) reported from 'reliable sources' that the War Minister had instructed the general staff to draft an arms bill on the basis of an extension of military service to three years.
23. See in detail chap. 3, pp. 53–8, 70–6 above.
24. See especially General Legrand-Girarde, *Un Quart de siècle au service de la France* (Paris, 1954), pp. 189–9. Millerand, War Minister until January 1913, stated in *Le Matin* (26 Feb.), that the strict maintenance of the principle of *égalité* was superfluous from the purely military point of view. Poincaré also considered affirmation of this principle as a step which went far beyond what was necessary (NJ, 24 Feb.).
25. See the discussions in the *Conseil Supérieur de la Guerre*, 4 March 1913, note 35 below.
26. In a press release on 27 February, Premier Briand stated that all the reports made hitherto were either 'inexact or premature'. Cf. Poincaré, *Au Service*, vol. 3, p. 147.
27. Poincaré, NJ (1 March).
28. *Le Temps* (2 March). The *Conseil Supérieur de la Guerre* (CSG) was established by a law of 27 July 1872. All the commanders of an army corps, the Premier and the War Minister were members. According to a decree in January 1912, the President of the Republic chaired meetings he wished to attend. The CSG was to be the link between military and political leaders. It was asked for its opinion 'on all matters of concern to the army, on the subject of which the minister deemed it appropriate that it be consulted'. Cf. Thile, *Pouvoir civil et pouvoir militaire*, pp. 124–7; and Ornano, *Gouvernement et Haut-Commandement*, pp. 138–46.
29. Poincaré, NJ (3 March).
30. The War Ministry's *note de présentation* of 3 March, which provided the guidelines for the CSG discussions on 4 March, included these problems, examined at length below. See Archives du Ministère de la Guerre, État-Major de l'Armée, CSG, 1 N 11, doss. CXLII, no. 839. fo. 82.
31. P. Cambon, *Correspondance*, vol. 3, p. 53 (letter dated Oct. 1913).
32. DDF III/5, no. 475 (27 Feb.); ibid., no. 494, Serret's reports (1 March).
33. *Note de présentation* (see note 30); author's italics.
34. The statements by Joffre, Pau, Poincaré and Briand are quoted and resumed from 'Conseil Supérieur de la Guerre, Procès-verbal de la Séance du 4 mars 1913', in Archives du Ministère de la Guerre, État-Major de l'Armée, CSG, 1 N 11, doss. CXLII, no. 840, fos 9–17. In his *Mémoires* (pp. 92–5), Joffre quotes his comments at the CSG almost word for word, with the exception of the passages in (the present author's) italics, i.e. he deletes the references to the offensive strategy. Joffre fails to mention either Poincaré's comments or Pau's demagogic 'precise definition'. Briand's statement is also mentioned by D. Ralston, *The Army of the Republic* (Cambridge, Mass., 1967), p. 360. Ralston's source is meanwhile not absolutely clear and does not seem to include the statements of Poincaré and Pau. Ralston wrongly assumes that politicians, army officers and public opinion all accepted the principle of the offensive strategy, and as a result overlooks the actual discrepancy between the 'technical' and the 'political' arguments.
35. 'Conseil Supérieur de la Guerre, Procès-verbal de la Séance du 4 Mars 1913' (see note 34 above), fos 12–13.
36. Cf. *note de présentation* (see note 30 above), fo. 79, and the statement of the CSG spokesman, General Legrand, at the meeting on 3 March: CSG, Procès-verbal (see note 34 above), fo. 12.

37. Statement by Briand, ibid., fos 16–17.
38. Cf. Izvolsky's detailed report of 13 March (Stieve, *Iswolski*, vol. 3 no. 760). See p. 71 on the impression the CSG decisions left on radical politicians.
39. In the *note de présentation* (see note 30 above), fo. 84, reference is made to company strengths of approximately 140–160!
40. Communiqué published in *Le Temps* (6 March).
41. See Poincaré, *Au Service*, vol. 3, pp. 148–9. *Le Figaro* (6 March) reported on this meeting and stressed that Poincaré had again reiterated the arguments of the CSG experts, following which the cabinet had approved the draft without further discussion.
42. JOC, pp. 815–17 (6 March).
43. See chap. 3, pp. 53–8, 58–70, below.
44. For further details, see p. 88, below.
45. *Le Matin* (6 March).
46. As opposed to Weber, *Nationalist Revival*, p. 14, who regards the three-year law as the 'apex of the nationalist revival'.

CHAPTER 3. The Early Stages of the Public Debate on the Defence Bill

1. *Le Temps* (17, 18 and 20 Feb., 6 March); *L'Écho* (19 and 22 Feb., 3 March); *Le Figaro* (2 March); *La Patrie* (5 March); *Le Gaulois* (17 Feb., 7 March); *La Liberté* (25 Feb.); ARD (2 and 9 March). See also Michon, *La Préparation à la guerre*, pp. 136–48. However, his more far-reaching identification of the campaigns of both groups is highly problematic.
2. In particular, *Le Temps* (18, 21, 24 and 27 Feb.) See also Carroll, *French Public Opinion and Foreign Affairs*, p. 278: *Le Temps*, writes Carroll, was originally of the opinion that the *Loi de Trois Ans* would not necessarily be detrimental to Franco-German relations. But these 'recommendable purposes [were] promptly forgotten in the need of convincing a reluctant public opinion'.
3. Whether and to what extent the campaign—of *Le Temps* in particular—had been coordinated with the supporters of rearmament within the government, cannot be precisely determined owing to a lack of sources. There is nevertheless an interesting reference in Joffre, *Mémoires*, p. 96: 'Once the government took the decision to demand three-year service . . . an energetic campaign was begun in the press to channel opinion in this direction.'
4. For further details see pp. 70–6.
5. See especially *Le Matin* (18 Feb.). Further examples of this 'numbers campaign' in Michon, *La Préparation à la guerre*, pp. 137–8.
6. The poll entitled 'Le Pays et les Trois Ans' in *Le Temps* (daily from 28 Feb. to 15 Apr.).
7. For further details, see chap. 3, pp. 58–70 below.
8. *Le Temps* (27 Feb.).
9. Cf. *inter alia*, *Le Gaulois* (24 Feb.); A.F. (17 and 18 Feb., 3 March); RddM (15 March); *Le Figaro* (16 Feb., 1 and 2 March); *L'Écho* (15, 19 and 26 Feb.); *La Patrie* (23. Feb.); and *La Liberté* (18 Feb., 2 March).
10. Cf. especially *La Patrie* (23 Feb.) (General Rebillot); *Le Gaulois* (20 Feb.) (General Zurlinden); *La Patrie* (18 Feb.); *L'Écho* (26 Feb.); and *Le Figaro* (2 March).
11. *La Patrie* (9 March) called for a party of the *ralliés de droite et de gauche*. *Le Figaro* (13 Jan.) commented that the fate of the 'national' Republic depended on whether it succeeded in assimilating Catholicism and nationalism.
12. *La Liberté* (25 Feb.).
13. M. Barrès, *Mes Cahiers* vol. 10 (1913–14), (Paris, 1936), p. 66. A description of these petitions and other actions of nationalist youth groups is given in detail by

Paul F. Lachance, 'French Youth and the Debate over the Three-Year Law', in *Proceedings of the 6th Annual Meeting of the Western Society for French History* (San Diego, 1978), pp. 363–70. See also chap. 4, pp. 77–88.

14. The position of the 'integral nationalism' of the *Action Française vis-à-vis* the 'national' Republic and Poincarisme was not so clear. Cf. C. Maurras *La Contre-Révolution spontanée* (Lyons, 1943), p. 148; and Weber, *The Nationalist Revival in France*, pp. 111–12. See also the heated discussion on the relationship between Maurras and Poincaré in *Centenaire de la Troisième République* (Paris, 1975), pp. 258–60.

15. Barrès, *Mes Cahiers*, p. 284: 'He [A. de Mun] seems to have played a great role in Poincaré's election and the voting of the three-year law. He was brought to the ministry, showed the documents (Briand); he was apparently being consulted or informed. Perhaps he abused this, he seems to have wanted to assume the role of a protector. In the summer of 1913 . . . he spoke of the *pact* of January. . . . That was the end. Clemenceau made this the subject of his campaign. At the Élysée, at the ministry, they became frightened. . . .' Cf. also *L'Echo* (3 March [A. de Mun] and 25 March); *Le Temps* (24 and 27 Feb., 6 March); and *La Petite République* (25 and 28 Feb., 30 May, 16 June).

16. This is the substance of the doctrine of appeasement advocated by Briand, in particular, since 1909 (*discours de Périgueux*), and · propagated by Briand's *Fédération des Gauches* from December 1913 (see chap. 7, pp. 149–56).

17. This comment is in contrast to Weber, *Nationalist Revival*, pp. 15–16, that the dispute over the three-year law was the 'apex of the nationalist revival' which had established a lasting link between the nationalist Right and the bourgeois Centre.

18. *L'Écho* (22 Feb.), *Oeuvre* (13 March); *Le Temps* (14 March) criticised this standpoint of the nationalists as 'demagogic', which is partly true. Cf. especially the amendment to the *Loi de Trois Ans* tabled by the monarchist deputy, Pugliesi-Conti, proposing that the costs of rearmament should be covered by a tax on all foreign workers from Germany (*La Patrie*, 9 and 13 March) and the opinion of the *Oeuvre* (12 June) that the 'Jew Rothschild' alone should pay the costs of rearmament.

19. *Information* (19 March): the minutes of the budgetary committee meetings for the period March–July are listed in the AN register but unfortunately are not to be found.

20. *Information* (21 and 26 Feb.); ibid. (27 Feb.): government denial; ibid. (28 Feb.): report that as a result of the expected panacea of rearmament the shares of the large metallurgical enterprises had risen several hundred points in the last few days. However, on the basis of an assessment of the minutes of meetings of many executive boards of large concerns, Becker, *1914: Comment les Français sont entrés dans la guerre*, pp. 46–52, comes to the conclusion that the arms campaign cannot be linked to *grands intérêts*.

21. Cf. *Information* (9 March) (Neymarck); *La Liberté* (25 and 27 Feb., 10 March); ARD (23. Feb., 30 March); *L'Économiste Français* (Leroy-Beaulieu), *passim*; *Journal des Économistes* (Apr. 1913) (Yves Guyot); *Le Temps* (14 March); ARD (16 March); statement from the ARD executive on 12 March); and *La Petite République* (8 and 16 March).

22. ARD (23 Feb., 30 March); *La Liberté* (17 March); *Journal des Économistes* (Apr. 1913).

23. Cf. *La Lanterne* (27 March); *Le Radical* (9 and 25 March, 15 Apr., etc); *La France* (14 and 26 July); *La Petite République* (25 and 30 May, 30 June); *L'Humanité* (18 Feb., 7 and 14 March, 2 May); and BS (17 Feb., 15 March, 17 Apr.).

24. Statist radicalism regarded nationalisation as a legitimation for bourgeois society, i.e. its ability to implement reforms and ease the class struggle. Cf. J. Caillaux, *Ma Doctrine* (Paris, 1926), and idem, preface to E. Cazalis, *Syndicalisme ouvrier et évolution sociale* (Paris, 1923); C. Debierre, *La Démocratie sociale* (Paris, 1910); and E. Desveaux, *Le Parti Radical et la question sociale* (Paris, 1910).

25. Cf. *Le Temps* (10 and 14 March); and *La Liberté* (25 and 27 Feb., 10 March).

26. Statement agreeing with the UIE in ARD (16 March). The UIE chairman, Forsans, was also vice-president of the ARD. Twenty-seven trade associations belonged to the *Union*; its official newspaper was *Le Reveil Économique*.
27. The names of all the associations in the CCEDF can be found in *Le Temps* (2 Nov. 1913). For the names of the chairmen of the individual associations who were also personal CCEDF members, see *Le Reveil Économique* (30 July 1913).
28. CCEDF statement in *Le Reveil Économique* (2 Apr.).
29. On the 1912 Basle congress of the International, see M. Drachkovitch, *Les Socialismes français et allemand et le problème de la guerre* (Geneva, 1953), pp. 338–43. This congress resolved *inter alia* that if there were a threat of war the proletariat of the countries involved would offer total resistance, 'supported by the integrating activity of the International Bureau'.
30. Vaillant to Huysmans (21 Feb. 1913), quoted from G. Haupt, *Le Congrès manqué* (Paris, 1965), p. 80. Haupt made the files of the International Socialist Bureau of the years 1913/14 accessible. The following considerations are based on this material.
31. Ibid., p. 82.
32. Vaillant to Huysmans (4 Feb. 1913), quoted from ibid., p. 79.
33. Cf. Fiechter, *Le Socialisme français*, pp. 160–4; G. Lefranc, *Le Mouvement socialiste sous la Troisième République* (Paris, 1963), pp. 161–2; M. Prélot, *L'Évolution politique du socialisme français* (Paris, 1939), pp. 178–204; D. Ligou, *Histoire du socialisme en France, 1871–1961* (Paris, 1962), pp. 232–7; and M. Rebérioux, 'Jaurès et l'unité ouvrière', in *Pensée*, n.s. no. 120 (1965), pp. 57–76.
34. *L'Humanité* (20 Feb.).
35. Allard's statement (*L'Humanité*, 17 March), went even further: German armament was because of the French and the wave of chauvinism in France. However, this argument soon ceased to be advanced within the SFIO.
36. Jaurès, *L'Humanité* (6 March).
37. See also *L'Humanité* (11 March): the aim of the public campaign must also be to confront radical deputies with the opposition of their electorate and therefore to give them 'cause for reflection' with a view to the forthcoming 1914 elections.
38. A. Dunois, *L'Action socialiste au Parlement, 1910–1914*, (Paris, 1914), p. 22.
39. See *L'Humanité* (30 March): in view of nationalist agitation on the streets, Jaurès recalled the analogies with the Dreyfus Affair in which the Republic had been saved by the cooperation between the Socialists and bourgeois Democrats. See also Albert-Thomas, 'Die politische Situation in Frankreich', in *Die Neue Zeit*, 31 (1913), vol. 2, pp. 329–33 (6 June 1913). Albert-Thomas, one of the leading Jaurèsistes, explained to the German socialists that it was the objective of the SFIO campaign to save the Republic from reaction and not only establish a parliamentary bloc of the Left but to 'gather the entire wavering masses of democracy around the SFIO'.
40. Lavigne to Guesde (30 May 1913), in IISG, Guesde archives 441/2 and Bonnier to Guesde (8 July 1913), ibid., 443/1.
41. *Le Temps* (26 March). In a similar vein C. Rappoport, 'Der Kampf gegen den Militarismus in Frankreich und der Kongress in Brest', in *Die Neue Zeit*, 31 (1913), vol. 2, pp. 47–52.
42. Fiechter, *Le Socialisme français*, p. 195, wrongly regards the Brest congress resolution as evidence of unity within the party.
43. This interpretation of the Compère-Morel motion is based on a statement of clarification in *L'Humanité* (29 March), which explicitly makes this demand.
44. Described and quoted from: Parti Socialiste (SFIO), *10ᵉ Congrès national tenu à Brest, 23–25 mars 1913, compte rendu sténographique* (Paris, 1913), pp. 238–311, especially pp. 234, 242, 245–6, 269–70.
45. Circular, no date (post 25 March, ante 10 Apr.), in AN, F 7/13337, doss. 3. Further details on p. 69, below.
46. Copies of these circulars drawn up by the police authorities, following the searches

in May 1913 (see pp. 94–102), can be found in AN, F7/13337, doss. 3. A copy can also be found in AN F 7/13340, doss. Meurthe-et-Moselle, file *Perquisitions.*

47. Circular dated 9 May in AN F7/13337, doss. 3. This is also published, with the exception of the paragraph quoted(!), in *L'Humanité* (9 May); ('signatories of the protest' referred to those who had signed the 'petitions against the *Loi de Trois Ans*' distributed by the SFIO throughout the country (see below).
48. Brunellière to Guesde (6 March 1913), in IISG, Guesde archives 439/1.
49. See BS (20 and 22 Feb.). A very different account of syndicalist agitation and the problems of cooperation with the SFIO is given by David E. Sumler, 'Opponents of War Preparedness in France, 1913–14, in Salomon Wank (ed.), *Doves and Diplomats: Foreign Offices and Peace Movements in Europe and America in the Twentieth Century* (Westport, Conn./London, 1978), pp. 109–26.
50. AN, F 7/10374, report 'M. 4046. U' (21 Feb.).
51. CC manifesto in BS (5 March).
52. Texts of the *ordres du jour* in BS (5 March). The forms for the collection of signatures were not delivered to the local syndicates until the second week in March. The manifesto was first published in BS (27 Feb.); the text—partly incorrect and excessively abbreviated—in Dolléans, *Mouvement ouvrier*, p. 208. A fine account differentiating between the socialist and syndicalist campaigns can be found in D.E. Sumler, 'Opponents of war preparedness in France, 1913-1914', in Salomon Wank (ed.), *Doves and Diplomats: Foreign Offices and Peace Movements in Europe and America in the Twentieth Century* (Westport (Conn.), 1978), pp. 109–26.
53. On the relations between French syndicalism and the Syndicalist International, cf. especially Dolléans, *Mouvement ouvrier*, pp. 209–14; and W. Westergard-Thorpe, 'Towards a Syndicalist International: The 1913 London Congress', in *International Review of Social History*, 23 (1978), pp. 33–78, here: pp. 37–9.
54. Dolléans, *Mouvement ouvrier*, p. 211.
55. See pp. 34–6, above.
56. AN, F 7/13337, doss. *Agitation contre la loi de trois ans (Dép. Seine)*, report of the Prefecture of Police (26 Feb.).
57. On the wish to use the campaign against the *Trois Ans* in terms of direct action to promote the syndicalist organisations, see *inter alia* BS (3, 13, 16 and 17 March, 5, 7 and 14 Apr., 11 May); and *La Voix du Peuple* (10/17 March).
58. BS (17 March); similarly ibid. (23 Feb.).
59. Georges and Tintant, *Léon Jouhaux*, pp. 118–22.
60. On the *Loi Millerand*, see p. 33, above.
61. Yvetot's statements in BS (6 March, 5 Apr.); and *La Voix du Peuple* (10/17 March).
62. The construction workers were the union closest to the direct action tradition of revolutionary syndicalism; over 30 per cent of the construction workers were affiliated to the CGT. The *Fédération Nationale du Bâtiment* was the largest individual union within the CGT (from Dolléans, *Mouvement ouvrier*, p. 208 note 2).
63. Published in BS (5 March) and *La Voix du Peuple* (10/17 March). *La Voix du Peuple* was the official CGT newspaper to which all affiliated unions had to subscribe.
64. AN F 7/13270, doss. 1, report 'M/7610': *A la CGT*, (29 March).
65. Ibid., report of the Prefecture of Police (PP) (10 Apr.).
66. Manifesto in BS (10 March).
67. *La Voix du Peuple* (16/23 March); not published in BS, which, as a 'revolutionary' newspaper, apparently refused to pay any attention whatsoever to cooperation with the SFIO.
68. Ibid.
69. AN, F 7/13270, doss. 1, PP report (10 Apr.).
70. AN, F 7/13337, doss. 1, official instructions from the *Sûreté Générale* (SG) (7 March).

71. AN, F 7/13337, doss. *Agitation contre la loi de trois ans (Dép. Seine)* and APP, B/a 752, 769.
72. Although the figures on the number of participants must of course be viewed with a certain degree of scepticism, since they are taken from PP reports, they are nevertheless of relevance in this comparison between SFIO and CGT action. The PP's statistics do not even distinguish between the SFIO- and CGT-organised demonstrations. Cf. APP, B/a 752, fo. 54.
73. AN, F 7/13337–13344, gives the reports on agitation against the three-year law (1913–1914) in all the departments (in alphabetical order). Since it was not possible to evaluate the extensive material covering ninety departments, analysis here has been limited to fifty-two departments. The criterion of selection was the existence or non-existence of syndicalist and socialist organisations in the individual departments (number and size of SFIO federations, labour exchanges and syndicates). The aim of the selection was to pinpoint the actual behaviour of Socialists and Syndicalists in a number of departments where their overall presence was unusually high, excessively low or average. The selection was carried out on the basis of: F. Goguel, *Géographie des élections françaises* (Paris, 1970), 2nd ed., pp. 70–3; P. Barral, 'Géographie de l'opinion sous la III. République', in *Information Historique*, 25 (1962), pp. 149–54; Kriegel and Becker, *1914*, pp. 200–24; and R. Rémond (ed.), *Atlas historique de la France contemporaine* (Paris, 1966). The dossiers of the following departments were evaluated: Ain, Aisne, Allier, Hautes-Alpes, Alpes-Maritimes, Ardèche, Ardennes, Ariège, Aude, Aveyron, Calvados, Cantal, Charente, Charente-Inférieure, Cher, Corse, Côte-d'Or, Côtes du Nord, Corrèze, Creuse, Ille-et-Vilaine, Indre, Indre-et-Loire, Jura, Loiret, Loir-et-Cher, Lot-et-Garonne, Maine-et-Loire, Haute-Loire, Haute-Marne, Marne, Mayenne, Meurthe-et-Moselle, Nièvre, Nord, Oise, Pas de Calais, Hautes-Pyrénées, Puy-de-Dôme, Rhône, Saône-et-Loire, Sarthe, Seine-et-Marne, Seine-et-Oise, Somme, Tarn, Tarn-et-Garonne, Var, Vendée, Haute-Vienne, Vosges.
74. Cf. the figures submitted at the Le Havre congress (1912), analysed in Rappoport, *Der Gewerkschaftskongress von Havre*, pp. 28–9.
75. Cf. *inter alia* A.N., F 7/13338, doss. Corrèze, no. 715; ibid., doss. Creuse, no. 744; 13340, doss. Ille-et-Vilaine (21 May); 13342, doss. Oise (14 June); ibid., doss. Puy-de-Dôme (24 May); and 13342, doss. Somme (12 March). The tearing down of the posters was clearly against the law (cf. F 7/13327, doss. 1, circular from the Minister of the Interior, 1 May 1910).
76. On Yvetot's propaganda campaign in the department of the Loire, cf. A.D. Loire, 10 M 158, nos 475–81. Eight hundred persons attended a rally where Yvetot appeared at the St Étienne labour exchange (29 March).
77. BS (19 Apr.). Briand had represented St Étienne for over twenty years.
78. This happened on 7 March, i.e. before the CGT *ordre du jour* had been sent out to the syndicates (see note 52 above).
79. Letter of protest in A.D. Loire, 10 M 158, no. 1. A further letter of protest from the metal-workers' union to the Prefect, ibid. (13 March).
80. According to the Prefect of the traditionally 'red' department of Var (see AN, F 7/13344, doss. Var, no. 117, report of 10 March).
81. Cf. A.N., F 7/13338, doss. Côte-d'Or, no. 656 (16 March); ibid., doss. Creuse, no. 732 (12 March); 13342, doss. Pas de Calais (28 March); and 13344, doss. Var (16 March).
82. Circular, no date (post 7 March, ante 15 March), in AN, F 7/13337, doss. 3; ibid., the *ordre du jour*.
83. Cf. A.N., F 7/13338, doss. Charente-Inf., nos 552–7, rally in La Rochelle (18 March), approximately 1,500 participants; 13341, doss. Nord, fo. 195, Valenciennes (30 March), 6,000 participants; and 13344, doss. Haute-Vienne, nos 259–62, Limoges (15 March), approximately 5,000 participants. It is striking that at these few real mass rallies the arguments against the 'regressive' governmental bill

were highlighted by the Socialists' fundamental commitment to patriotism and national defence.

84. AN, F 7/13344, doss. Tarn, *inter alia* nos 12, 40. On the evident failure of a number of large-scale SFIO demonstrations, see also 13338, doss. Hautes-Alpes, nos 153–5 (29 April); 13340, doss. Maine-et-Loire (report dated 27 Apr.); 13344, doss. Var. no. 124 (10 March). See also Y. Rinaudo, 'L'Opposition à la loi de trois ans dans le Var', in *Provence Historique*, 20 (1970), pp. 162–83, here: pp. 177–8.

85. According to the CAP circular (see note 82 above).

86. Circular, no date (post 25 March, ante 10 Apr.), in AN, F 7/13337, doss. 3.

87. AN, F 7/13338, doss. Ain (29 May); ibid., doss. Aisne, no. 53 (24 May); ibid., doss. Aveyron, no. 443 (19 March); 13340, doss. Indre (6 June).

88. According to the circular mentioned in note 86 above and *L'Humanité* (7 March): *Appel à l'action*.

89. See also AN, F 7/13344, doss. Tarn, no. 37, report (of 13 Apr.) on the great success of the petitions in this department whose population, according to the Prefect (see note 84 above), was not prepared to participate in the SFIO demonstrations. In Carmaux alone (10,000 inhabitants), 2,500 signatures were collected.

90. See AN, F 7/13338, doss. Cher (4 Apr.): the law had to be swiftly adopted by Parliament, otherwise the propaganda campaign against the bill might prove successful; 13340, doss. Loire-et-Cher (14 Apr.): there was latent discontent among the population which the SFIO was exploiting; 13342, doss. Pas de Calais (28 March, 1 May); 13344, doss. Tarn (1 Apr.), Rinaudo, *L'Opposition dans le Var*, p. 174 (report of the Prefecture of the Var, 29th. March); A.D. Côte-d'Or, 20 M 551 (reports of 28 and 30 March, 1 April. See also R. Andréani, 'L'Antimilitarisme en Languedoc Méditerranéen avant la Première Guerre Mondiale', in *Revue d'Histoire Moderne et Contemporaine*, 20 (1973), pp. 104–23, especially p. 120. Andréani interprets this rejection as the 'indifference' of a population which did not believe that war was possible. In view of the overall evidence, this interpretation is hardly valid.

91. See pp. 41–2, above.

92. *Le Radical* (19 Feb.) In a similar vein, *La Lanterne* (19 Feb.); *L'Aurore* (16 Feb., 2 March); and *Le Siècle* (9 March).

93. From 20 February to the end of March.

94. *embusqués*, as the recruits on non-combatant duty (cooks, batsmen, etc.) were called.

95. Cf. *inter alia La Lanterne* (21 and 28 Feb.), and *L'Aurore* (from 21 Feb.).

96. *Le Radical* (19, 26 and 27 Feb., 6 and 13 March). In a similar vein, *L'Aurore* (24 Feb.); and *La Lanterne* (26 and 28 Feb.).

97. *Le Radical* (5 March). This statement was published in almost the entire press. *Le Temps* (6 March), stated that all 'good Frenchmen' should follow Clemenceau's exemplary behaviour which implied that 'contact' with Jaurès and his comrades playing *le jeu de l'étranger* must be avoided.

98. *Le Temps* (4 March). Soon afterwards Dumont was appointed Finance Minister in Barthou's cabinet (see p. 77, below).

99. *Le Temps* (10 March). The examples given are only a selection; *Le Temps* published similar statements by leading Radicals almost every day.

100. *Le Radical* (7 March); *La Lanterne* (8 March).

101. *Le Temps* (9 March); *Le Matin* (11 March). The initial statement by the *Fédération de la Seine* was in a similar vein; cf. *Le Temps* (12 March).

102. Cf. *Le Temps* (8 March); and *Le Matin* (11 March).

103. This refers to the additional credit of 500 million francs requested by the government for the improvement of the technical equipment of the army (see p. 46, above). On 14 March the entire *gauche radicale* approved the Jacquier amendment (see *Le Matin*, 15 March).

104. *Information* (11 March).

105. *Le Radical* (13 March) published the resolutions of both the party propaganda and military reform committees, which diverged on essential points.
106. CE resolution in *Le Radical* (25 March).
107. *L'Humanité* (21 March). See also *Le Radical* (27 March), which welcomed the *sursaut d'opinion* against the *Trois Ans* but conceded that public opinion was not predominantly *antitroisanniste*. The radical deputies therefore had to account for the opinion of the people 'somehow' (*sic*).
108. The Peytral amendment on Article 1 of the electoral reform adopted by the Chamber on 10 July 1912 read as follows: 'The Members of the Chamber are elected by a list ballot. Following the majority rule no one can be elected if he has fewer votes than his rivals.' The Premier, Briand, had asked the Senate for a vote of confidence on 18 March 1913; the Peytral amendment was adopted by the Senate by 161 votes to 128. For details see Bonnefous, *Histoire politique*, vol. 1, pp. 329–33.
109. Poincaré, NJ (18 March).
110. JOS 1913, pp. 291–300 (18 March). The radical Senator Gervais declared to a large audience that the division in the Senate had been no more than a continuation of the radical opposition to Poincaré's election to the presidency (cf. *Information*, 20 March).
111. *Le Radical* (25 March). In a similar vein, *L'Aurore* (19 March).
112. Because of their exemplary significance, Étienne's comments have been quoted here in detail from the minutes of the discussions of the Army Committee. See AN, C 7421, doss. 365, fos 1–23 (meeting on 11 March).
113. The emergency paragraph of the 1905 conscription law stipulated that in certain circumstances the government could provisionally retain one class of recruits in the forces (further details on p. 88).
114. Compare these comments with War Minister Étienne's speech to the Chamber on 6 March in which he justified the government bill. Étienne stressed that this step was in actual fact no more than a perpetuation of Article 33/1905 (See p. 51, above). Several weeks following Étienne's comments to the Army Committee, the government in fact applied Article 33/1905 (see chap. 4, pp. 88–94).
115. See above, chaps. 1, pp. 21–30 and 3, pp. 53–76.
116. *La Lanterne* (14 March).
117. AN, C 7421, doss. 365, fo. 28 (meeting on 18 March).

CHAPTER 4. The Hardening of the Fronts Under the Barthou Government

1. Letter dated 18 March in BN, n.a.f. 16010, fo. 340. Similarly, *Le Gaulois* (20 March).
2. Louis Barthou (1862–1934): deputy (1889–1922); senator (1922–34). Barthou, regarded as a representative of the Right of Centre, became chairman of the *groupe progressiste*, a left-wing splinter group within the ranks of conservative republicanism following the Dreyfus affair. He held a number of ministerial posts from 1896 and was Minister of Justice in the Clemenceau (1907) and Briand (1909) cabinets. From 1922 to 1926 he was chairman of the Committee on Reparations.
3. Poincaré, NJ (19 March); cf. Poincaré, *Au Service*, vol. 3, pp. 156–7.
4. Ibid.
5. C. Dumont became Finance Minister and A. Massé Minister of Trade. Poincaré called this a 'pledge of conciliation' to the Radicals (ibid., p. 159).
6. Cf. Bonnefous, *Histoire politique*, vol. 1, p. 339.
7. *Le Temps* (22 March).
8. JOC, p. 1184 (25 March).
9. Cf. Bonnefous, *Histoire politique*, vol. 1, p. 338.

10. Figures from ibid., p. 340, and Chapman, *Decision for War*, pp. 84–5.
11. This meeting of the chairmen of the left-wing parliamentary groups was the famous *Délégation des Gauches* which had played a key role in the Combes era as an intermediary body between parliament and government. It was comprised of the *républicain-socialistes*, the *gauche radicale-socialiste*, the *gauche radicale* and the *gauche démocratique*. The PSF *Jaurèsistes* had also been members until 1905, when they left following the International's rejection of ministerialism. The *Délégation* had lost much of its authority as a result; cf. R.A. Winnacker, 'The Délégation des Gauches', in *Journal of Modern History*, 9 (1937), pp. 449–70.
12. *Information* (26 and 28 March).
13. Cf. Barral, *Géographie de l'opinion*, pp. 150–1.
14. Poincaré, *Au Service*, vol. 3, pp. 161–4.
15. Cf. Wright, *Raymond Poincaré*, pp. 81–5. See also Sumler, *Domestic Influences*, p. 531; and G. Tixier, 'Poincaré et le redressement français', in *Revue Politique et Parlementaire*, 57 (1955), pp. 185–91.
16. *L'Humanité* (31 March); *Le Radical* (31 March); and in a similar vein, *Le Siècle* (11 Apr.), which nevertheless asked the President to restrain his minister Étienne who was 'playing the same game' as the chauvinists.
17. Letter from de Mun to Étienne, 1 April 1913, Fonds Étienne, BN, n.a.f. 24327, fos 269–70.
18. See pp. 83–8.
19. Poincaré, *Au Service*, vol. 3, pp. 187–200. On the *Störenfried* article and the reaction of the French press and the Lunéville incident, cf. Ziebura, *Die deutsche Frage*, pp. 125–6; and Weber, *Nationalist Revival*, p. 122–3. On Bethmann Hollweg's speech to the Reichstag on 7 April 1913 and the fear of an imminent clash between the Slavonic and the Germanic worlds, cf. Mommsen, *Die latente Krise*, p. 61; Fischer, *Krieg der Illusionen*, p. 265; and Herzfeld, *Rüstungspolitik*, p. 103.
20. Joffre, *Mémoires*, p. 96.
21. DDF III/6, note on no. 210.
22. Michon, one of the sharpest critics of *Poincarisme* and the *Loi de Trois Ans*, believes (*La Préparation à la guerre*, p. 153) that the government had become the victim of a mystification of the general staff, since the principles evoked in the Ludendorf memorandum reflected the mentality of the French army officers but not the later facts of the German attack. The harder nationalist line of the government, he claims, was due to the fact that it believed in the authenticity of the memorandum.
23. For further details, see pp. 82–4.
24. DDF III/6, no. 210 (5 Apr.).
25. See p. 49, above.
26. See *Les Armées françaises*, I, 1, p. 20.
27. The most precise and detailed account of the Reinach/Montebello counter-proposal can be found in *La France Militaire* (3, 5 and 8 March 1913).
28. AN, C 7421, doss. 365 (meeting on 25 Apr.).
29. Joffre maintains in his *Mémoires* (p. 95) that the Reinach/Montebello counter-proposal was the proposal of the government as presented to the Chamber on 6 March. Although this statement is evidently false, it nevertheless proves that this counter-project corresponded with the plans of the general staff.
30. Ministère de la Guerre, État-Major de l'Armée, CSG, 1N 11, doss. CXLIII, no. 846 (CSG meeting on 18 Apr. 1913).
31. The original of the *Bases du Plan* (XVII) in ibid., no. 845; compare this with the 'corrected' version published following the war in *Les Armées françaises*, I, 1, pp. 18–40, especially pp. 20, 22.
32. Ministère de la Guerre, État-Major de l'Armée, CSG, 1 N 11, doss. CXLIV, no. 851 (*note de présentation* for the CSG meeting on 24 Apr. 1913).
33. AN, C 7421, doss. 365 (meeting on 25 Apr.). General Legrand explains in his

memoirs that no further details had been given to the Army Committee: for fear of
'indiscretions' the government had not wanted to divulge the true extent of the
rejection of the integration of reserve units into the regular army as a result of the
prejudices and errors of the general staff (Legrand-Girarde, *Un Quart de siècle au
service de la France*, pp. 491–6).

34. Circular from the SFIO *Conseil National* (no date, post 25 March, ante 12 Apr.), in
    AN, F 7/13337, doss. 3. See also *L'Humanité* (29 March, 4 Apr.).
35. Both circulars in AN, F 7/13270, doss. *Interpellation de M. Bouveri*.
36. AN, F 7/13270, doss. 2: letters from the Prefects of Pas de Calais (18 Apr.),
    Aveyron (20 Apr.), Jura (23 Apr.), Nord (25 Apr.), and Côte-d'Or (30 Apr.). On
    the above-mentioned interpellation (note 35) the Minister of the Interior, Klotz,
    expressly justified the instructions of 29 March with the argument that the govern-
    ment had acted only in accordance with the wishes of a number of prefects concerned
    about the public (JOC, p. 1533). These wishes are not to be found in the files.
37. AN, F 7/13270, doss. 2; exception: the Prefect of Côte-d'Or, cf. ibid., letter of
    30 April.
38. AN, F 7/13336, doss. 1: the Prefect of Aude, 11 April; approval from the Minister
    of the Interior, ibid. Further examples in *Le Temps* (15 Apr.); ibid., demand that
    the government should take more vigorous action.
39. AN, F 7/13336, doss. 4. See also the criticism in *Le Temps* (13 Apr.) that many of
    those educating the young generation were prepared to 'disarm France'.
40. *Le Temps* (2, 8 and 9 Apr.); *Le Matin* (7 Apr.).
41. *Discours des Jardies*, published in *Le Temps* (14 Apr.) and *La Patrie* (14 Apr). In a
    similar vein, a speech by Foreign Minister, Pichon, cf. ibid.
42. *Discours de Caen* published in *Le Temps* (5 May). In this speech Barthou also
    announced the application of Article 33 of the 1905 conscription law (see chap. 4,
    pp. 88–94).
43. Means of procedure put forward included deferred/advance call-up, which the
    government in fact reluctantly included in the bill several months later (see p. 112,
    below).
44. *Le Temps* (7 May). Several days later Barthou gave a speech on 'patriotic duty', and
    on why the three-year bill was necessary, at the *Fête Fédérale de Gymnastique* in
    Vichy. This speech was published in *Le Temps* (14 May). On the activities of the
    youth organisations of the nationalistic Right and the counter-action of the Left,
    see P.F. Lachance, 'French youth and the debate over the three-years law', loc. cit.
45. *L'Écho* (2 Apr.). It is impossible to determine the degree of the poster's circulation
    in the various departments, since the authorities had instructions to report only on
    the agitation of Socialists and Syndicalists (see p. 67, above). Its circulation was
    reported in ten of the fifty-two departments examined (AN, F 7/13338–44, doss.
    Ain, Hautes-Alpes, Charente-Inf., Ille-et-Vilaine, Indre-et-Loire, Meurthe-et-
    Moselle, Nord, Pas de Calais, Tarn). See also the report of the Prefect of Police, on
    28 June 1913 (APP, B/a 1463), that ALP agitation was being organised in particular
    by the *Fédération des Jeunesses Républicaines, Libérales et Patriotiques*, led by
    Barrès: 'The *Ligue d'Action Libérale* has numerous bodies which have taken
    advantage of the three-year campaign to gain good and serious customers'.
46. See *inter alia* AF (19 March, 28 Apr.).
47. Reports in AF (28 and 30 Apr., 5 and 11 May).
48. AF (5 May) naturally drew particular attention to the dispute between Barthou and
    Liard.
49. Statement by the *Ligue des Droits de l'Homme*, published in *Le Temps* (13 May).
50. *Le Radical* (10 Apr.; official bulletin). Cf. especially the daily complaints and
    warnings in *Le Siècle* (30 March–15 Apr.). See also *Le Radical* (3 and 10 Apr.);
    L'Humanité (1 Apr) and *L'Aurore* (7, 11 and 14 Apr.).
51. AN, F 7/13338, doss. Aude (4 Apr.); ibid., doss. Loir-et-Cher (15 Apr.); ibid.,
    13342, doss. Oise (7 Apr.); ibid., doss. Rhône (28 Apr.); ibid., 13344, doss. Var,

no. 114. See also Rinaudo, *L'Opposition dans le Var*, p. 167; P. Barral, *Le Département de l'Isère sous la III*ᵉ *République* (Paris, 1962), p. 366.

52. *L'Aurore* (7 Apr.): 'Appel au Parti!' published and supported by *Le Siècle* (7 Apr.).

53. *Le Radical* (9 Apr.).

54. The *Conseils Généraux* were comprised of the mayors and parliamentary deputies of a department and the *notables* elected in cantonal elections. The CG were not responsible for issues of general politics; if statements were made on such subjects, it was the prefect's duty to leave the meeting. The *Trois Ans* issue dominated public opinion to such an extent that most CGs passed resolutions on the bill, despite constant reminders from the prefects that they had no legal scope to do so.

55. Daily summary reports on the *Conseils Généraux* in *Le Temps* (16–22 Apr.); *Le Radical* (17 and 22 Apr.); and *Le Matin* (17 and 18 Apr.).

56. *Le Temps* (24 Apr.).

57. Quoted from *Le Radical* (15 Apr.). Also published in *Information* (15 Apr.) (d.n.).

58. Caillaux, *Mémoires*, vol. 3, especially pp. 52, 60. Caillaux's position is also reflected in a report by his friend Charles Paix-Séailles, *Jaurès et Caillaux* (Paris, 1920), especially p. 88.

59. See p. 109, below.

60. Quotation from P. Doumer, *La Loi militaire du 7 août 1913* (Paris, 1913), p. 177.

61. *Le Matin* (3 May); *Le Petit Parisien* (3 and 4 May).

62. JOC, p. 1413.

63. See chap. 4, pp. 94–102.

64. Joffre, *Mémoires*, p. 180.

65. Ibid., pp. 98, 182.

66. According to Reinach in a letter to Poincaré dated 16 May. Further details on p. 92, below.

67. *L'Humanité* (5 May).

68. Ibid. (6 May). This quotation shows implicitly the extent to which the rank-and-file SFIO organisations advocated 'reconciliation'.

69. Ibid. (9 May).

70. See chap. 3, note 47, on p. 258 above.

71. Because of domestic developments these demonstrations were not carried out; see p. 98, below.

72. *Le Temps* (8 and 17 May); *La Petite République* (16 May); *Le Figaro* (5 May); RddM (15 May); and *Le Gaulois* (6 May).

73. *La Lanterne* (5 May); *L'Aurore* (5 May); and *Le Radical* (5 and 7 May).

74. *Le Temps* (10 May). The 'amalgamation of the classes' (*soudure des classes*) included the demand that the precarious state of the regular army—which had only one reasonably trained class and a year of recruits when a class was dismissed—should be improved. In his memoirs, Caillaux refers to the *soudure* as the main reason why he was prepared to accept an extension of military service—but not to a period of three years (Caillaux, *Mémoires*, vol. 3, p. 51).

75. From *Le Radical* (18 May); ibid., the approval of the Radical Party CE. However, Caillaux stressed in his *Mémoires* (vol. 3, p. 61) that from the very outset he had had 'no illusions' about the success of this strategy. This is a contradiction of the key role of the counter-proposal in the contemporary debate, for which Caillaux shared responsibility. In any case Caillaux's opponents in 1913 did not regard this attack as 'illusory'.

76. According to Article 32 of the 1905 conscription law, each conscript served two years in the regular army, eleven years in the *réserve de l'armée active* and six years in the *réserve territoriale* (see Doumer, *La Loi militaire*, p. 176).

77. Messimy, *Souvenirs*, p. 117. See also Messimy, 'Le Problème militaire' (Paris, 1913), a collection of his essays published in pamphlet form in *Le Rappel* (7–17 May 1913). In his *Mémoires*, p. 99, Joffre examines this concept, which he considers unrealistic. However, he confuses the Paul-Boncour/Messimy counter-

proposal with that of General Pédoya. An account of the Paul-Boncour/Messimy counter-proposal is also given in Michon, *La Préparation à la guerre*, p. 164, and Ralston, *The Army of the Republic*, pp. 363–6. On the parliamentary debate, see p. 109, below.

78. Letter, 16 May, in BN, n.a.f. 16010, fos 341–2. De Mun emphasises, ibid., that he had agreed on this letter with Reinach and Montebello.
79. BN, n.a.f. 16014, fos 283–7.
80. See p. 50, above.
81. Poincaré, NJ (29 May). This was Poincaré's first personal reaction to the implementation of the *Trois Ans* since the formation of the Barthou government.
82. On Pau's statement to Parliament and the resulting problems for the government, see p. 103, below.
83. BN, n.a.f. 16014, fo. 287.
84. This is how Robert de Jouvenel, in his famous book of the same name (Paris, 1934), describes the syndrome of a parliament, without structured parties, split into groups gathered around prominent personalities.
85. Paléologue, *Au Quai d'Orsay*, p. 139 (= diary, 24 May). Strangely enough, there is no reference to the matter in either Poincaré's memoirs or his diary. On the enmity between Poincaré and Clemenceau, see p. 41, above. Following Poincaré's election to the presidency, Clemenceau had formally broken off all links with Poincaré; see Clemenceau's letter to Poincaré on 17 January 1913, quoted by Payen, *Raymond Poincaré*, p. 396 note.
86. *Gil Blas* (24 May).
87. See references in chap. 2, note 2.
88. *L'Humanité*'s interpretation (26 May) of the report in *Gil Blas*.
89. Detailed report in *Le Temps* (20–25 May).
90. For example, *Le Siècle* (22 May), which however blamed Barthou for the 'mutinies' in the same edition.
91. AN, F 7/13340, doss. Meurthe-et-Moselle, police reports (21 May).
92. *Le Matin* (23 and 24 May). The successive memoranda of the political police on the *Sou du Soldat* can be found in: AN, F 7/12911 (3 Jan. 1912); F 7/13333, doss. 1 (1 Dec. 1912); and F 7/13334 (July 1914).
93. RddM (1 July 1913). Evidence of the use of police reports in the detailed criticism of *La Vie Ouvrière* (20 July); see also BS (1 July).
94. *Le Matin* gave this statement a two-column report on its front page on 22 May.
95. Étienne's statement from *Le Temps* (24 May); see also DDF III/6 no. 609, Pichon to Delcassé, 25 May. According to Pichon, the 'mutinies' had not really been an expression of discontent in the barracks but a result of a secret campaign of revolutionary groups which would not spread, since the government had decided to pursue the 'ringleaders' and carry out searches the next day. Delcassé should inform the Russian government of these facts to set their minds at ease.
96. AN, F 7/13336, doss. 1 and 5: telegrams of 21 and 22 May.
97. AN, F 7/13343, doss. Saône-et-Loire, file 'Incidents' (22 May); F 7/13338, doss. Aveyron, file 'Incidents', nos 466, 469, 456; F 7/13340, doss. Meuse, file 'Incidents', reports of 21, 22 and 28 May, 16 June. See also AN, BB 18/2509, doss. 128 A 13, carton 76: report from the Montpellier prosecutor-general to the Minister of Justice, 26 May, stating that legal proceedings could not be opened, since there was no evidence whatsoever that the *Sou du Soldat* had been behind the Rodez unrest.
98. Precise details in AN, BB 18/2510, doss. 128 A 13, carton 165b.
99. In AN, F 7/13338–44, the results of the searches are listed in the annexes to the dossiers on the individual departments. My conclusions are based on this information and further material compiled by the Ministry of Justice in AN, BB 18/2509. Of the 136 dossiers in which charges were pressed by the various public prosecutors, only very few were followed up in the courts. Legal proceedings were turned down in nearly all cases, since the 'incriminating evidence' produced did not

permit the application of either the 1894 or the 1881 law on anti-militarist printed materials, because there was not sufficient evidence of direct instigation to disobedience. To quote an anecdote, lacking direct evidence for the 'anti-patriotism of the CGT', the Rouen state prosecutor put forward the fact that various contraceptives had been found in the labour exchange. Other public prosecutors were more frank in admitting that nothing of significance had been found (cf. AN, BB 18/2508, doss. 128 A 13, carton 51b).

100. Barthou's statement and the Senate discussion published in *Le Temps* (31 May).
101. BS (27 May).
102. Ibid. (20, 21 and 27 May).
103. *La Voix du Peuple* (1 and 7 June).
104. See p. 68, above.
105. BS (21 May). See also the statement in the anarchistic *Temps Nouveaux* (24 May) welcoming the fact that the government was about to put an end to the 'lethargy' in the revolutionary movement of recent years.
106. AN, F 7/13345, 'Agitation dans l'Armée', doss. 3, includes the essay mentioned by Yvetot. The sentence quoted was underlined by the authorities.
107. Ibid., F 7/13337, doss. 'Agitation contre la Loi de Trois Ans', reports from 21 May, and F 7/13570, doss. 9, contain a number of statements of this kind. On these plans, see also chap. 7, pp. 126–31.
108. Political police reports and memoranda in AN, F 7/13345, doss. 1 (5 and 26 June); F 7/13570, fos 132–5 (16 June); F 7/13571, doss. 2 (13 June). In the memorandum of 26 June it is maintained that there were plans to stir up a revolutionary strike in September 1913. For this reason it was appropriate to 'get hold' of the leaders as soon as possible. On the political and parliamentary consequences of these arrests, see p. 111, below.
109. BS (24 May); *L'Humanité* (25 May).
110. *L'Humanité* (26 May) and *Le Radical* (26 May) referred to the demonstrations as a *manifestation du peuple de Paris* which had included many patriotic Republicans. See also the bitter criticism in the anarchistic *Temps Nouveaux* (7 June): 'We had not been used to the CGT militants being so concerned about governmental stability. . . .'
111. Manifesto of protest of the CAP and SFIO parliamentary group in *L'Humanité* (1 June); but cf. AN, F 7/13337, doss. 'Agitation contre la Loi de Trois Ans', Prefect of Police report of 10 June, and F 7/13571, doss. 2, report M 75U (31 May).
112. *La Guerre Sociale* (9 July), quoted here from *L'Humanité* (10 July).
113. *Le Radical* (19 May).
114. See especially *Le Siècle* (25 May), refuting any links with the SFIO which had stirred up the 'children.'
115. See p. 83, and note 36 above.
116. Actually reported by *L'Humanité* (22 May).
117. See JOC, pp. 1531–4, 1543.
118. *Le Temps* (27 May): 'Retour au Bercail'.
119. In particular, the problem of how the measures planned by the government under Article 33/1905 were to be financed. The executive's prerogative to apply the emergency paragraph did not restrict Parliament's budgetary authority. The plans emerging at this time for a large loan to Russia faced the government with a further constraint: the full drawing of a loan at national level to cover armament expenditure was seen as a prerequisite for the loan to Russia (further details in chap. 6).
120. See p. 47, above.
121. *Le Temps* (24 May); in detail *Le Siècle* (25 May); *L'Information* (23 May); Poincaré, NJ (24 May), on a secret cabinet meeting that day which decided to increase excise tax: unfortunately the only sources available on the financing of rearmament and related issues submitted to the budgetary committee in May/June 1913 are the newspaper reports. The minutes of the budgetary committee meetings

during this period are listed in the AN inventory, but have disappeared from C 7426.

122. CE resolution in *Le Radical* (18 May).

123. JOC, pp. 1524–5 (22 May), presentation of the Bénazet report.

124. The following rates of progression were stipulated: up to 50,000 francs, 1 per cent; 50,000–100,000 francs, 2 per cent; and above 100,000 francs; 3 per cent. This new tax would therefore be applicable to around 250,000 taxpayers; see JOC, pp. 1565–6 (27 May). *Le Temps* (29 May) published the entire proposal. On the Dumont project, see also J.C. Allain, *Joseph Caillaux*, 1, *Le défi victorieux* (Paris, 1978), pp. 258–60.

125. Cf. *Le Radical* (29 May); *L'Humanité* (28 May); *Le Temps* (28 May); *La Petite République* (28 May); *La Liberté* (30 May); and *Le Figaro* (28 May).

126. *Journal des Économistes*, vol. 39 (July 1913), p. 184.

127. *Le Temps* (29 May) and *Le Gaulois* (29 May). In a similar vein, *La Liberté* (30 May).

128. Open letter from the *Union Générale*, published in *Le Reveil Économique* (18 June).

129. See p. 57, above.

130. The League's statement, sent to all the deputies, published in *La Liberté* (23 June). It is almost identical with the statement of the *groupe progressiste* in the Chamber (*La Patrie*, 16 June) and the UIE, *Le Reveil Économique* (11 June). See also *Journal des Économistes*, vol. 38, pp. 511ff.; ibid., vol. 39, p. 185; *Le Figaro* (28 May); and *La Patrie* (29 May). *La Liberté* (30 June) advised against the levying of a war tax on the German model; this, it stated would mean that the 'bourgeois' would not have enough to spend on luxuries, which in turn would impair industry and bring down wage levels.

131. *La Petite République* (30 May).

132. Caillaux, *Mémoires*, vol. 3, p. 61.

133. JOC, pp. 1596–1610, 1615–6 (29 May).

134. These deputies also stressed the need for an *impôt extraordinaire* in accordance with A. de Mun's doctrine (see p. 57, above.)

135. The finance committee's debate and resolution in AN, C 7470, doss. 1849, file 12/II.

CHAPTER 5. The Parliamentary Debate

1. Cf. the joint CAP and SFIO parliamentary group statement in *L'Humanité* (1 June), and Jaurès's statements, ibid. (2 and 3 June). The SFIO urged all left-wing Republicans to prevent the return to Mélinism, which was the government's objective.

2. JOC, pp. 1935–44 (16 June).

3. Ibid., p. 1337.

4. JOC, pp. 1652, 1664 (2 June).

5. Ibid., p. 1666.

6. This term generally refers to the antagonism between traditional and republican ideology which came to a head in the Dreyfus affair.

7. Several days later General Pau was replaced by Joffre without any comment. The government seems to have been so concerned about further velleities of the 1870 war hero and the embitterment of republican deputies that it dispensed with its initial aim of using Pau's authority to exert influence on Parliament (see p. 92, above, letters to Poincaré from de Mun and Reinach).

8. JOC, pp. 1693–4 (3 June), e.g. a banner read: 'For Joan of Arc, betrayed by her King and burned by her Church'.

9. In 1912 Poincaré, as head of government, had proposed the introduction of a

national holiday in honour of Joan of Arc. Weber, *Nationalist Revival*, p. 103, sees this as proof of a gradual *rapprochement* between 'national republicanism' and the traditionalist Right.

10. JOC, pp. 1767–8 (6 June).
11. Ibid., p. 2456 (4 July).
12. Ibid., p. 2459 (4 July).
13. For the Claussat interpellation on police activitiy in the May 1913 searches, see *L'Humanité* (14 June).
14. *Le Radical* (19 June) official bulletin. The left-wing republican *Siècle* advanced a similar opinion following the 'mutinies': see *Le Siècle* (23 and 25 May): 'le vrai bloc'.
15. AN, F 7/13342, doss. Rhône, report of 2 June.
16. Ibid., reports of 11 and 13 June. The chairman of the radical federation, Herriot, was one of the most adamant opponents of the *Loi de Trois Ans* in the Senate; cf. his statement in JOS, pp. 1311–22 (5 Aug.).
17. This was the position of F. Chautemps (JOC, p. 1653) and Augagneur (ibid., p. 1797) in particular. See also Michon *La Préparation à la guerre*, pp. 157–8. This motive frequently came to light in the campaign of the nationalist Right in favour of the *Trois Ans* (see chap. 3, pp. 53–8, above).
18. JOC, p. 1830; different figures but the same argument in Chautemps, ibid., p. 1656, and Thalamas, ibid., p. 1745; and even Joseph Reinach spoke out against the misuse of recruits (ibid., p. 1681). In the debate the soldiers serving in the colonies were often regarded as shirkers, since they were not available for the defence of *la patrie*; see *inter alia* JOC, p. 1661 (Chautemps and Vaillant); ibid., p. 1746 (Thalamas); and ibid., pp. 1814–15 (Augagneur).
19. See especially JOC, p. 1744 (Thalamas); and similar arguments in a statement of the Radical Party CE, in *Le Radical* (1 May).
20. In this context 'militaristic' refers to the syndrome of a military society established against civil society; the barracks are regarded as a stronghold of traditionalist values and a counterweight to republican and egalitarian tendencies. The essay by E. Lamy, 'L'Armée et la démocratie', in RddM, 69 (1885), pp. 835–72, is indicative of this concept.
21. Chautemps (JOC, pp. 1651–4, 1662–3); Thalamas (ibid., pp. 1689–70); Tissier (ibid., pp. 1787–90); Pédoya (ibid., p. 1828); Augagneur (ibid., pp. 1798–1802). On the theory of the integration of the reserves into the regular army (*encadrement*), see pp. 107–8.
22. Monteilhet, *Les Institutions militaires*, p. 282; Ralston, *The Army of the Republic*, pp. 308–9; Challener, *The French Theory*, p. 47; J. Godard, 'Les Lois sur le recrutement de l'armée', in *Revue Administrative*, 1962, pp. 36–40; and Kovacs, *French Military Legislation*, p. 6. For a criticism of the republican army constitution, see D. Porch, *The March to the Marne*, pp. 73ff. Unfortunately, Porch's bitter and exaggerated criticism of Ralston's work leads to an uncritical acceptance of the *société militaire* thought patterns of the time.
23. See J. Jaurès, *L'Armée nouvelle* (Paris, 1915), p. 16. 'It [the 1905 law] is the final term in a series of ambiguities. It is the final possible combination of the professional and caste army and the nation in arms.' On the problems of the concept of the 'nation in arms' in the 1905 law, see especially Thile, *Pouvoir civil et pouvoir militaire*, p. 33; in a similar vein, P.M. de la Gorce, *La République et son armée* (Paris, 1963), p. 80; and the Radicals' military programmes in J. Kayser, *Les grandes batailles du radicalisme, 1820–1901* (Paris, 1962), pp. 324, 327.
24. See especially J.M. de Lanessan, *Nos forces militaires* (Paris, 1913)—designed as a plea on behalf of maintaining two-year service! A detailed analysis of these shortcomings can also be found in the statement by the left-wing republican deputy, General Pédoya, JOC, p. 1884.
25. *Le Gaulois* (11 June); *Le Temps* (11 June), with details on the debate in the

Chamber and governmental decrees since 1906. See also Reinach, JOC, p. 1687.
26. JOC, pp. 1746–54 (5 June).
27. *Le Temps* (7 June).
28. *L'Humanité* and *La Lanterne* (both 6 June).
29. This is the title of a book published by Reinach in April 1913 in which he expounded on the Reinach/Montebello counter-proposal.
30. JOC, p. 2517 (8 July).
31. For a criticism of the mechanistic theory of drilling, see Monteilhet, *Institutions militaires*, pp. 284, 299; Ralston, *The Army of the Republic*, p. 361, refers to the sharp contrast between this concept and the original—'archetypal'—theory of the nation in arms. Challener, *The French Theory*, p. 82, sees the link between the offensive strategy and the drilling theory, but, like Ralston, wrongly assumes that this connection had been specified to Parliament and the public in the grounds for the three-year law.
32. See H. Paté, *Le Sacrifice, c'est le devoir, c'est le salut* (Paris, 1913), pp. 11, 20, 86–7, 97–8. This book is an authorised publication of the final report of the Chamber Army Committee. The author, Henry Paté, was the spokesman of this committee.
33. *Le Matin* (25 May); and in a similar vein, Paté's statement to Parliament, JOC, pp. 1812, 1891 (10/12 June).
34. See *inter alia*: Veillat (JOC, p. 1795); le Hérissé (ibid, p. 1649); Paté, *Le Sacrifice*, p. 55.
35. See *inter alia*: Girardet, *La Société militaire*, pp. 163–4; Challener, *The French Theory*, pp. 77–8; A. Mitchell, 'Thiers, MacMahon and the Conseil Supérieur de la Guerre', in *French Historical Studies*, 6 (1969), pp. 232–52, here: pp. 238–41; H. Guillemin, 'Jaurès dans l'action', in *Les Temps Modernes*, 21 (1965), pp. 776–815, here: pp. 793–796; and Kovacs, *French Military Legislation*, pp. 1–12.
36. This is in contrast to Chapman, 'Decision for War', pp. 83–7, and Sumler, 'Domestic Influences', op cit. (chap. 1 note 62 above), pp. 535–6. Both authors—pupils of A.J. Mayer—regard the parliamentary debate as an example of the political and social polarisation, which Mayer maintains was a general phenomenon of the time (see pp. 7–8, above). Compare this with the appropriate analysis by Monteilheit, *Institutions militaires*, p. 296: despite criticism of the objective 'bending of republican thinking' by militaristic influences, Monteilhet maintains that the left-wing Republicans agreed to the conscription law only because they regarded the *attaque brusquée* as a real danger.
37. See p. 91, above.
38. See p. 111, below.
39. JOC, p. 2347.
40. Ibid., p. 2350.
41. Ibid., p. 1804.
42. Ibid., pp. 2349–51.
43. Joffre, *Mémoires*, p. 99.
44. Both *Troisannistes* and *Antitroisannistes* criticised the counter-proposal's electoral interest. See *Le Temps* (3 July) and *L'Humanité* (10 June).
45. This refers to the parliamentary sitting in which Paul-Boncour expounded on the reasons for the counter-project.
46. Joffre, *Mémoires*, p. 99. Cf. La Gorce, *La République et son armée*, p. 118; Michon, *La Préparation à la guerre*, p. 164; and H. Contamine, *La Revanche*, p. 149. On events between Paul-Boncour's speech and the division on the counter-proposal, see, pp. 110–11.
47. See especially *Le Matin* (2 July), listing all the 'evidence' and the laws applied in this case. Yvetot was one of those arrested.
48. Statements of the CAP and the SFIO parliamentary group in *L'Humanité* (2 July).
49. BS (2 July),
50. See chap. 4, note 108.

51. Cf. the circulars of the heads of the political police dated 23 July, 3 September and 23 October (AN, F 7/13346, doss. 1–3). A further indication of the government's concern was the amendment of the governmental bill with the aim of dismissing the class of 1911.

52. See p. 110, above. *Le Temps* (3 July) warned all Republicans against voting for the Paul-Boncour/Messimy counter-proposal along with the Socialists, who, as 'accomplices of the CGT', wanted to open up the French frontier.

53. Votes against the counter-proposal were as follows: 71 *socialistes unifiés*, 114 *radicaux-socialistes*, 40 *radicaux*, 10 *gauches démocratiques*, 26 *républicain-socialistes*, 1 *groupe progressiste*, 1 ALP, 3 *non inscrits* (from *Le Temps*, (5 July).

54. It is interesting to note that on the day before the division on the Paul-Boncour/Messimy counter-proposal the SFIO presented Parliament with 730,000 signatures (see *L'Humanité* 3 July). In view of recent developments, this was given little attention by Parliament and the press.

55. JOC, pp. 2459–61 (4 July).

56. *Affichage* is Parliament's prerogative—in fact seldom used—to post speeches, etc., outside every town hall in France, making them semi-official.

57. Only 26 *républicain-socialistes*, and 44 *radicaux–socialistes* voted along with the Socialists against *affichage*.

58. *Le Temps* (6 July). Cf. *La Liberté* (6 July); *La Lanterne* (5 July); ARD, (6 July); *La France* (10 July); and *La Petite République* (6 July). At this time an extremely chauvinistic press campaign was launched against the SFIO and Jaurès in particular. Although the consequences of this daily smear campaign against Jaurès can hardly be overestimated, compared with the effect it was intended to have on Parliament, they remained episodic. Documentation on this agitation in: *Le Procès de l'assassin de Jaurès*, pp. 257–336 (= Paul Boncour's plea before the court of assizes). See also the forceful accounts by Guillemin, 'Péguy et Jaurès', op. cit. (Introduction note 34 above), and Rabaut, *Jaurès et son assassin*.

59. *L'Information* (4 June); ibid., the position of the 'Société nationale de la protection de la main d'oeuvre agricole'; the debate on all these issues in Parliament: JOC, pp. 2669–79 (16 July).

60. *L'Information* (10 June).

61. Poincaré, *Au Service*, vol. 3, p. 213.

62. Poincaré, NJ (2 July). The classes of 1910 and 1913 are the classes of recruits called up in the autumn of 1911 and 1914; see also ibid., 7 August.

63. JOC, pp. 2449–59 (4 July).

64. Ibid, p. 2475 (7 July). In press commentaries the Vincent amendment was generally regarded as a 'bomb' against the government bill: cf. *L'Information* (3/4 Aug.); RddM (15 July, 1 Aug.); *Le Gaulois* (12 Aug.); *La France* (9 July); *La France Militaire* (8 July); *L'Humanité* (8 July); and *Le Temps* (9 and 11 July).

65. No reference to the Vincent amendment to Article 18 in Sumler, 'Domestic Influences', pp. 535–6, although he regards the division on Article 18 as the main evidence for the polarisation theory (see note 36 above). The military historian Contamine criticises the 'egalitarian demagogy' of this amendment (*La Revanche*, pp. 150–1).

66. Jaurès feared that the 'incredible incoherence' of the government's action was bound to lead to a fresh outbreak of soldiers' unrest in the autumn (*L'Humanité*, 10 July).

67. *Le Temps* (18 July).

68. A group of *radicaux-Socialistes* deputies even voted in favour of the Escudier amendment, because this addendum finally highlighted the absurdity of the whole bill (see Augagneur, JOC, p. 2678); the result of the division in JOC, pp. 2685–6.

69. See *inter alia L'Humanité* (16 and 20 July).

70. See p. 108, above.

71. Result of the division: 244 votes to 36 (JOS, p. 1384).

72. Doumer was one of the most famous French colonial politicians; in 1931 he was elected President of the Republic.
73. P. Doumer, *La Loi militaire du 7 août 1913* (Paris, 1913), p. 23. This book is an authorised publication of the final report of the Senate Army Committee. The entire text of the law appears in its appendix. See also Doumer's statement to the Senate: JOS, p. 1300 (1 Aug.).
74. Clemenceau's statements: JOS, p. 1277 (31 July) and ibid., pp. 1332, 1340–2 (6 Aug.).
75. Ibid., p. 1298 (1 Aug.).
76. *Le Temps* 19 July (d.n.).
77. JOC, p. 2810.
78. Ibid., p. 2813.
79. Caillaux's group was comprised as follows: 96 *radicaux-socialistes*, 15 *radicaux*, 22 *républicain-socialistes*, 4 *gauche démocratique*, 3 *non inscrits*. Thirteen of the total of 140 deputies who had signed Caillaux's declaration did not vote with Caillaux in the final division (JOC, p. 2811); this should, however, be compared with the breakdown in *Le Temps* (21 July). Caillaux maintains that this statement was drafted along with Paul-Boncour (Caillaux, *Mémoires*, vol. 3, p. 69).
80. JOC, p. 2815 (19 July).
81. Precise details on the numerical strength of all the parliamentary groups in Bonnefous, *Histoire Pólitique*, vol. 1, p. 96.
82. *L'Humanité* (21 July); similarly, ibid. (3 and 20 July).

CHAPTER 6. The Completion of Plan XVII and the Question of the Russian Railway Loan, 1913

1. See p. 82, above.
2. On the 'short war' theory and its consequences on the military constitution see especially Challener, *The French Theory*, pp. 102–7, 134–5; in general Wallach, *Das Dogma der Vernichtungsschlacht*; T. Ropp, *War in the Modern World* (Durham, N.C., 1959), pp. 178–210; and L.L. Farrar, *The Short-War Illusion* (Oxford, 1973).
3. On the background to these decrees and their function, see Joffre, *Mémoires*, pp. 39, 142–3; and E. Carrias, *La Pensée militaire française* (Paris, 1960), pp. 296–7.
4. See chap. 2, note 8, above.
5. See Williamson, *Grand Strategy*, p. 224, and the sources mentioned.
6. Ibid., p. 221.
7. Joffre, *Mémoires*, p. 40.
8. For a summary of the *Bases du Plan XVII*, see *Les Armées françaises*, I, 1, pp. 18–29.
9. See p. 130, above.
10. See DDF III/6, no. 59, conversation with the Tsar, 24 March; ibid., no. 72, conversation with the Russian War Minister.
11. Williamson, *Grand Strategy*, p. 223, states that the implementation of the 'high-level and formal' agreements between the general staffs was a constant source of difficulty. Particular evidence of this can be found for 1913. However, Williamson's theory that these problems were a result of the latent mistrust between the military authorities is hardly appropriate.
12. See DDF III/7, no. 216, report from Laguiche, military attaché in St Petersburg, 26 June; Stieve, *Iswolski*, vol. 3, no. 936, Kokovcov to Sazonov, 14/27 June. See also ibid., no. 938, Sazonov to Izvolsky, 17/30 June. This interest and the interest of French financial circles in the prospect of Russia's economic take-off is clearly reflected in de Verneuil's final report on his visit to Russia: see DDF III/7, no. 309, de Verneuil to Pichon, 7 July. On de Verneuil's mission and the further negotiations, see R. Girault, *Emprunts russes et investissements français dans Russie*,

1887–1914 (Paris, 1973).
13. The exact amount of the planned loan is unknown.
14. See DDF III/7, no. 134, de Verneuil's report of 16 June, and Foreign Minister Pichon's note in the margin.
15. DDF III/7, no. 437 (21 July); ibid., no. 464, Pichon to Dumont, 24 July; Dumont's reply, ibid., no. 523 (2nd Aug.). On 8 August the French cabinet gave the go-ahead to de Verneuil's agreements (note on no. 523).
16. Ibid., and ibid., no. 521 (2 Aug.); DDF III/8, no. 62 (21 Aug.).
17. The minutes of this conference can be found in DDF III/8, no. 79. See also D. Geyer, *Der russische Imperialismus* (Göttingen, 1977) (*Kritische Studien zur Geschichtswissenschaft*, vol. 27), pp. 219–20.
18. See DDF III/8, no. 79, article 3; and ibid., no. 698, (Delcassé's report of 31 Dec. 1913). The 1912 agreements can be found in DDF III/3, no. 200 article 4. Girault, *Emprunts russes*, p. 68, gives an instructive outline of the 1913 agreements in map form.
19. DDF III/8, no. 104 (30 Aug.). The statement by the French chargé d'affaires that this reluctance did not reflect a real change in the position of the Russian government as a result of the recent general staff's agreements is disproved by ibid., no. 204, Doulcet to Pichon, 27 Setpember. On Kokovcov's attitude, see Geyer, *Der russische Imperialismus*, pp. 196–9.
20. See DDF III/8, no. 204 (27 Sept.), and no. 306, appendix I (10 Oct.). See also Joffre, *Mémoires*, p. 134.
21. 21 DDF III/8, no. 307 (11 Oct.).
22. Ibid., nos 392, 396 (28/29 Oct.). The fact that de Verneuil's proposal was rejected demonstrates that the French government was concerned primarily about strategics and that this concern was not merely a pretext for financial manoeuvring. De Verneuil proposed that his government should not only grant Russia an unconditional annual loan of 500 million francs but provide the Russian government with the outstanding amount required to construct the strategic railway lines. This solution, he argued, would satisfy both parties, especially since the loan would be an extremely profitable transaction in view of Russia's exceptional economic growth (see ibid., no. 469, 10 Nov.). In his report to the Tsar, Kokovcov surmised that the French government and the 'activity of individual credit institutes' had been behind de Verneuil's visit (see Stieve, *Iswolski*, vol. 3, no. 1169, here: p. 407). Taylor, *Struggle*, p. 501 note 32, also refers to such a link but without providing further explanation or evidence. A different account can be found in Geyer, *Der russische Imperialismus*, p. 198.
23. Cf. Kokovcov's report to the Tsar in Stieve, *Iswolski*, vol. 3, no. 1169, here: p. 402.
24. Pichon's report on his discussion with Kokovcov in DDF III/8, no. 485 (16 Nov.).
25. Ibid., appendix. The draft agreement (in German translation) is printed in Stieve, op. cit., vol. 3, no. 1177.
26. Stieve, op. cit., vol. 3, no. 1169, here: pp. 411–12.
27. See chap. 7.3 above.
28. Cf. the new, equally vague, formula proposed by Kokovcov on 13 December, in DDF III/8, no. 698, appendix I. This is also mentioned by Stieve, op. cit., vol. 3, no. 1177, Sazonov to Izvolsky, 3/16 December. On Izvolsky's approaches to the French government, cf. ibid., nos 1170–1.
29. DDF III/8, note on no. 622 (13 Dec.) and Stieve, op. cit., vol. 3, no. 1174, Izvolsky's report of 15 December.
30. Stieve, op. cit., vol. 3, no. 1177, Sazonov to Izvolsky, 3/16 December. The agreement became effective on 31 December (DDF III/8, appendices 2 and 3 to no. 698).
31. pp. 167–9, below; in general: Fischer, *Krieg der Illusionen*, pp. 481–515; I.V. Bestuzhev, 'Russian Foreign Policy, February-June 1914', pp. 106–7; Mommsen, *Die latente Krise*, pp. 87–90.

32. This is the theory of both Bestuzhev and Mommsen (see note 31 above). Fischer, op. cit., however, mainly attributes the deterioration of Russo-German relations to the German 'press war' against Russia in April 1914.
33. See Stieve, op. cit., vol. 3, no. 1169, here: pp. 415 ff., Kokovcov's report to the Tsar on his talks with Bethmann Hollweg and the Kaiser following his visit to Paris. Fischer, op. cit., p. 491, mentions identical instructions given by Neratov to the Russian ambassador in Berlin on 7 November.
34. The agreement was signed on 28 November 1913. Geyer's theory that Kokovcov had withdrawn his opposition, 'fearing further delays in the financial transaction' following the change of ministry in France (see Geyer, *Der russische Imperialismus*, p. 199), overlooks the core of the problem.
35. The Tsar to Delcassé, DDF III/9, no. 189 (29 Jan. 1914).

CHAPTER 7. Changes on the Domestic Front after the Adoption of the Three-Year Law

1. See chaps 4.4 and 5.2 above.
2. AN, F 7/13345, doss. 1, PP report, 1. bureau, cabinet du Préfet, 4 July.
3. Ibid., F 7/13570, fo. 161, PP report, 4 July.
4. See p. 35, above.
5. AN, F 7/13570, fo. 161.
6. Ibid., fo. 159, report 'M/8040', 3 July. See also the discouraged statement of the CGT secretary, Dumoulin (*La Voix du Peuple*, 13–20 July): 'It is all the worse for us if there are still so many workers who are so selfish and ignorant about matters of concern to their class that they believed the CGT could and should win without them'.
7. See pp. 62–8, above.
8. See *inter alia* BS (17 June) (Jouhaux), (18 June) (Hamp), (22 June) (Jouhaux), (24 June) (Picard). See also the commentary in *La Voix du Peuple* (13–20 July)— slightly chauvinistic, in the tradition of economic nationalism—which criticised the 'anti-patriotism' of French capitalists who, it maintained, preferred to oppose syndicalism rather than the Germanisation of France by German industrial goods. *L'Humanité* turned its attention to this problem early in 1914 and stressed in particular the fact that more and more foreign workers were being employed in French industry. However, the examples quoted by the newspaper—the smuggling in of Berber, Italian and German foreign workers—are not very convincing (see *L'Humanité*, 29 Dec. 1913, 1 and 14 Jan. 1914). Research into this question in the archives of the Ministry of Economic Affairs found no relevant material. Even the large estate of Albert-Thomas (who frequently raised this problem in Parliament and in the columns of *L'Humanité*) shed no further light on the matter (see AN., 94AP, Fonds Albert-Thomas, cartons 337–41).
9. '*Conférence ordinaire des Fédérations nationales et des Bourses du Travail ou Unions de Syndicats*', the official title of the interim congress held in the alternate years between the official CGT congresses.
10. See *Conférence ordinaire des Fédérations nationales et des Bourses du Travail ou Unions de Syndicats* (Paris, 1914), pp. 53–4. The minutes of the congress have evidently been altered on essential points, since they differ substantially from the minutes published in BS (16 July 1913). The latter version gives a closer reflection of actual events and corresponds with the detailed report of the *Sûreté Générale* observer (see AN, F 7/13583, doss. 4, report M 8087, 16 July).
11. Report 'M 8087'; also implied in *Conférence des Fédérations*, p. 57. Although the BS does not expressly examine this point, it confirms that a dispute between Constant and Jouhaux did take place.
12. Péricat was a determined advocate of the old *Hervéisme*. On 31 July 1914 he was

the only member of the CGT CC to call for mass strike action in protest against war; see Dubief (ed.), *Le Syndicalisme révolutionnaire*, p. 303. Péricat had already advocated political mass strike action in the event of war at the congress of Marseilles (1908). He was one of the forty-one Syndicalists classified as revolutionary who were arrested when war broke out. Péricat remained in detention for two years, the only one to suffer this fate; see Dolléans, *Mouvement Óuvrier*, vol. 2, p. 194, p. 216 note 6.

13. *Conférence des Fédérations* , p. 54; BS (16 July); report 'M 8087'.
14. *Le Temps* (16 and 17 July); *La Petite République* (16 July).
15. *L'Humanité* (29 July).
16. BS (17 July) (Jouhaux), (30 July) (Merrheim), (3 Sept.) (Merrheim); *La Vie Ouvrière* (20 July) (Monatte). On Merrheim's stand see also Dolléans, *Mouvement ouvrier*, pp. 167–76, 189–205. In a series of essays Jaurès tried to establish a theoretical basis for revolutionary practice (*L'Humanité*, 4–14 Sept.).
17. BS (2 Oct.). Opposition to the revolutionary trend is evident, e.g. in the resolution of the congress of the leather industry union (*Cuirs et Peaux*), emphasising the advantages of sabotage as a means of action (see *Le Temps*, 20 Sept.).
18. *La Vie Ouvrière* (5 Aug.).
19. For example, the resolution of the congress of the metal-workers' union, 9–12 September 1913; see BS (11 Sept.); *Le Temps* (12 Sept.).
20. BS (27 Aug.), 'Déclaration à propos de l'action confédérale'. See also Jouhaux's statement at the construction workers' congress (15 Apr. 1914). The CGT, he said, was still as revolutionary as it had been in 1895, but it had freed itself from blind activism and now aimed at fighting for social objectives at plant level; *action directe* and the use of violence were only secondary; the principal aim must be to bind the masses to the organisation, orienting the day-to-day struggle of the Syndicalists to the 'education and organisation of the working class' (BS, 16 Apr.; *Le Temps*, 17 Apr.). On the differentiation between reformists, revisionists and activists in the CGT, see also Westergard-Thorpe, *Towards a Syndicalist International*, pp. 40–1.
21. See *La Vie Ouvrière*, (5/20 Apr. 1914): 'Briand, Barthou, Clemenceau, Caillaux—let's paint them all with the same brush!'
22. See ibid., and AN, F 7/13271 doss. *Préparation du 1er mai, Paris et banlieue*, reports dated 28 March ꞏ ꞏd 8 April 1914. See also the manifesto of the *Comité Confédéral*, 7 April 1914, in Becker, *Le Carnet B*, p. 185: 'Assez de Boue! Place au Peuple!'
23. See especially *Le Radical* (8 and 10 June) on the wishes of a number of regional party congresses. See also *La France* (9 Aug.), manifesto from the chairman of the Seine party federation. *Le Temps* (27 June) reported on the formation of a committee of party deputies with the aim of drafting statutes of unity. See also Nordmann, *Histoire des Radicaux*, p. 184.
24. *Le Radical* (6 Oct.) (official bulletin).
25. On the composition of the Radical Party congresses, see D. Bardonnet, *Evolution de la structure du parti radical* (Paris, 1960), pp. 74–7.
26. *Le Temps* (8 Oct.); *Le Petite République* (15 Oct.); ARD (12 Oct.); *La France* (2, 5, and 17 Oct.). The opinion that the congress would fail to produce a new orientation for the party was very seldom voiced (see *La Liberté, 3 Oct.*).
27. *Le Radical* (3 Oct.), interview with Combes.
28. Combes's comment was an allusion to the defeat of the Boulangist movement after 1887 by the electoral reform pushed through with the aid of the radical majority in the Senate.
29. Caillaux to the Chamber, 29 May (JOC, p. 1607). In 1914 Caillaux actually carried this plan through (see p. 161, below).
30. Interview with the *Dépêche de Toulouse*, published in *Le Temps* (13 Oct.).
31. Caillaux later expressly qualified this programme as an attempt to merge 'moderate' and 'progressive' groups in a 'union of the Left', to quote contemporary language

(*Mémoires*, vol. 3, p. 61). J.-C. Allain, *Caillaux*, p. 406, refers to a letter from Combes to Caillaux, dated 19 September 1913, in which Combes refers to the reactionary and nationalistic 'goings on', spurred on by the Barthou government. This letter also contains a hint to Caillaux that he should stand for the chairmanship of the party. The contents of this letter do not accord with Combes's public statements; perhaps he felt that, despite the actual divergencies of the time, only Caillaux was in a position to lead the Left to victory against the forces of reaction.

32. *L'Humanité* (4 Oct.).
33. Ibid. (10 Oct.).
34. Ibid. (15 Oct.).
35. This opinion was shared by *L'Humanité* (17 Oct.) and *Le Temps* (18 Oct.). The following comments on the debate and resolutions passed at the congress are based on the daily reports in *Le Radical* and the official minutes of the congress, *Parti républicain, radical et radical-socialiste: Le Congrès de Pau* (Paris, 1914).
36. Camille Pelletan (1848–1914) was one of the most famous radical politicians. Formerly editor-in-chief of the anti-Boulangist *Justice*, he was a deputy from 1891 to 1912, Navy Minister in the Combes government and elected to the Senate in 1912. Pelletan was regarded as one of the most determined opponents of *Poincarisme*; see Berstein, *Histoire du Parti Radical*, pp. 76–7.
37. In his *Mémoires*, vol. 3, pp. 71–2, Caillaux maintained that he had stood for the party chairmanship to create an effective counter-weight to Poincaré's intention of curtailing the powers of Parliament with the help of the nationalist movement so that he could pursue his 'belligerent' foreign policy undeterred. However, this is not substantiated by Caillaux's action at the Pau congress. See also Wright, *Poincaré*, p. 86. Berstein, *Histoire du Parti Radical*, p. 73, overlooks the fact that the Buyssou motion which the Congress originally passed against Poincaré was later dropped following the energetic intervention of Caillaux himself!
38. *Le Temps* (21 Oct., 7 Nov.); *La Petite République* (22 and 24 Oct.); ARD (16 Nov.); *Le Figaro* (13 Nov.); RddM (1 Nov.); *L'Humanité* (28 Oct.); *La France* (29 Oct.); and *Le Républicain-Socialiste* (19 Nov.).
39. See p. 110, above, for the campaign against Dumont's national tax. See also *inter alia: Le Temps* (24 July); *Le Figaro* (22 July); and *Le Gaulois* (19 Aug.). Cf. JOC, pp. 2839, 2865 (21/22 July). Further examples in Chapman, *Decision for War*, pp. 112–13.
40. AN, F 7/13337, doss. 3, fo. 10 (26 July).
41. See p. 110, above.
42. JOC, p. 2260 (27 June).
43. Budgetary debate in AN, C 7426, vol. 5, fos 1–6.
44. This supplement to the taxes on the various income brackets contained the principle of the compulsory declaration of total income by every taxpayer. Statement of the budgetary committee in AN, C 7426, vol. 5, fos 1–6; also published in *Le Temps* (6 July), but with no reference to the disagreement of the government.
45. AN, C 7426, vol. 5, fos 23–4; *Le Temps* (17 July).
46. See *Information* (16 July) and Dumont's statement to the budgetary committee, AN, C 7426, vol. 5, fo. 25.
47. Ibid.
48. Noulens's proposal is published in *Le Temps* (18 July).
49. *Information* (24 July); AN, C 7470, doss. 1849, file 12/II, meeting on 22 July; at the meeting on 21 July (ibid.), the finance committee had voted against the budgetary committee and turned down the loan to cover the extraordinary costs accruing from rearmament, demanding a *contribution unique* instead. The fact that the finance committee abandoned its radical stance the very next day is presumably to be seen as a concession to the government.
50. *La France* (17 and 23 July).
51. *L'Humanité* (24 July).

52. See *Information* (23 and 25 July).
53. *Le Temps* (26 July).
54. From ibid. (15 Nov.) (d.n.); ibid., the official text of the draft budget.
55. Draft loan published in *Le Temps* (15 Nov.) (d.n.).
56. See *Le Temps* (16 May). *Le Matin* (16 May) published a statement to this effect by Dumont on page 1.
57. *Le Temps* (17 Nov.) (the financial week).
58. Ibid. (15 Nov.); *La Liberté* (16 Nov.).
59. Jaurès in *L'Humanité* (15 Nov.).
60. *Le Radical* (27 Nov.) published the ALP resolution. On 21 November the budgetary committee reduced the loan to 900 million francs (see JOC, p. 3654, spokesman Noulens's justification). See also *Le Temps* (23 Nov.; *Le Radical* 22 Nov.); and *Information* (26 Nov.).
61. On the resolution of Théodore Reinach's group, see *Information* (26 Nov.); *La France* (26 Nov.); RddM (1 Dec.); and *La Patrie* (3 Dec.). On the *Entente démocratique*'s resolution, see *Le Radical* (26 Nov.).
62. See *inter alia* Michon, *La Préparation à la guerre*, pp. 87–9, and P. Miguel, *Poincaré* (Paris, 1961), pp. 228–42. Chapman, 'Decision for War', p. 47, puts most of the blame for the obstruction of Caillaux's tax reform on Poincaré, who chaired the Senate finance committee for a number of years.
63. Poincaré, *Au Service*, vol. 3, p. 313; similarly, ibid., pp. 237–8. Poincaré's memoirs reflect the notes in his diary on this point (cf. Poincaré, NJ, 30 Oct., 16 and 29 Nov.).
64. This is implied in Poincaré, *Au Service*, vol. 3, p. 313; and expressly stated in Poincaré, NJ (30 Oct). Briand was of a similar opinion (see Caillaux, *Mémoires*, vol. 3, p.74). See also G. Suarez, *Briand*, vol. 2 (Paris, 1938), p. 464, according to which Briand criticised Barthou's 'enormous mistake' as a result of the pressure from financial circles.
65. See chaps 7, pp. 149–56, and 8, above.
66. Published in: *Le Temps* (17 Nov.), *Le Radical* (16 Nov.) and *La Petite République* (16 Nov.).
67. *La Petite République*, (16 Nov.).
68. Published ibid. (28 Nov.).
69. See especially ibid. (3, 4, 6 and 21 Nov.): criticism of the government's draft loan on the grounds that it was limited to covering the economically 'unproductive' military costs. Instead a loan of about 2 billion francs was demanded. Similarly, the moderately radical *France*, which turned away from Caillaux at this point (*La France*, 30 Oct., 10, 17 and 22 Nov. 1913, 19 Jan. 1914). *Le Temps* published a financial programme on 22 October which is typical of these opinions.
70. *La Liberté* (20 Nov.). Cf. ibid. (16 Nov.); similarly *Le Gaulois* (8 Dec.); *Le Figaro* (23 and 27 Nov., 2 Dec.); RddM (15 Dec.); *Le Temps* (16 Nov.); and CCEDF statement in *Le Temps* (2 Nov.).
71. JOC, pp. 3729–32 (2 Dec.).
72. See T. Reinach's statement to Parliament, JOC, p. 3707.
73. Ibid., p. 3663.
74. See chaps 1, pp. 44–52, and 4, above.
75. Poincaré, *Au Service*, vol. 3, p. 339.
76. Ibid., p. 341.
77. On 30 November—two days before the fall of Barthou—Caillaux had once again expounded on his views on defence policy at a Radical Party banquet: the demand for an improvement of the reserves' training, the modernisation of fortifications and a higher level of heavy artillery included the 'reintroduction, at least step by step' (*sic*) of the 1905 law, since no one could envisage straining the country excessively with rearmament in the longer term (see *Le Radical*, 1 Dec.).
78. Poincaré, NJ (4 Dec.); similarly Poincaré, *Au Service*, vol. 3, p. 341, and Caillaux,

Mémoires, vol. 3, pp. 81–2.
79. *Le Figaro* (8 Dec.; RddM (15 Dec.); *Le Gaulois* (3 Dec.); *La Patrie* (4 Dec.) and *La Liberté* (4 Dec.).
80. Poincaré, *Au Service*, vol. 3, p. 340.
81. Ibid., p. 342.
82. See p. 142, above.
83. Poincaré, *Au Service*, vol. 3, p. 343; Caillaux, *Mémoires*, vol. 3, p. 83.
84. See Bonnefous, *Histoire politique*, vol. 1, pp. 413–4, and the classification in *La Petite République* (9 Dec.).
85. As is clear in Poincaré's memoirs; cf. Poincaré, *Au Service*, vol. 3, pp. 345–6.
86. *Le Radical* and *L'Humanité* (both 7 Dec.).
87. *Le Gaulois* (3 Dec.); similarly ibid. (8 Dec.). See also *L'Oeuvre* (11 Dec.).
88. Poincaré, NJ (17 Jan. 1914).
89. Ibid. (18 Feb. 1914).
90. Ibid. (15 Feb. 1914).
91. In his memoirs Poincaré tries to cover up the hostility between himself and Caillaux. However, his diary, at times totally contradicting his memoirs, provides clear-cut evidence of this hostility, which intensified in the coming months as a result of the Doumergue cabinet's policies. Details of this will follow. Poincaré's diary is the best confirmation of Caillaux's description of his relationship with the President in his memoirs; see especially Caillaux, *Mémoires*, vol. 3, p. 84, on the first official visit of the new government to the President of the Republic and Poincaré, NJ (9 Dec.).
92. Of the 594 deputies in the Chamber, some 160 belonged to the Radical Party *groupe unifié* (see *Le Temps*, 11 Nov. 1913, and *Le Radical*, 23 Jan. 1914). Nordmann, *Histoire des radicaux*, p. 186, is of the opinion that the formation of the *groupe unifié* pushed the old *gauche radicale* towards the Right. However, the actual line of the *gauche radicale* in the subsequent period shows that this rather sweeping judgement is unsubstantiated.
93. Poincaré, NJ (6 Dec.).
94. Ibid.
95. Cf. his statement at a Radical Party banquet in May 1913 (*Le Radical*, 19 May).
96. *L'Humanité* (7 and 10 Dec.).
97. Caillaux, *Mémoires*, vol. 3, p. 80.
98. JOC, pp. 3745ff.
99. See pp. 36–8, above.
100. JOC, pp. 3746–51.
101. Ibid., pp. 3753–4.
102. Ibid., pp. 3745–6.
103. Ibid., p. 3759.
104. Ibid., pp. 3749–51.
105. *Le Temps* (23 Dec.; *La Petite République* (22 Dec.). The founding members included Briand, Barthou, Pichon, Millerand, Étienne, Klotz, Dumont, Morel, Chéron. Almost all these politicians had been members of the Barthou cabinet (see Suarez, *Briand*, vol. 2, pp. 457–8).
106. Quoted from ibid., p. 458.
107. *La Petite République*. (26 Dec.).
108. Briand's St Étienne speech. The following analysis and quotations are based on the version published in *La Petite République* (22 Dec.); the text of the speech given in Suarez, *Briand*, vol. 2, pp. 448–56, is of little use, since a series of highly important passages are omitted.
109. See in general R. von Albertini, 'Regierung und Parlament in der Dritten Republik', in *Historische Zeitschrift* 188 (1959), pp. 17–48, especially pp. 26–8; J.-C. Vénézia, 'Les Fondements juridiques de l'instabilité ministérielle sous la IIIᵉ et sous la IVᵉ République', in *Revue du Droit Public et de la Science Politique en France et*

à l'Etranger, 75 (1959), pp. 718–55; M. Dogan, 'La Stabilité du personnel parlementaire sous la IIIe République', in *Revue Française de Science Politique*, 3
(1953), pp. 319–48.

110. See Sembat, *L'Humanité* (24 Jan. 1914); similarly, *Le Radical* (8 Jan.).
Clemenceau's criticism of the FDG was almost identical; cf. Michon, *La
Préparation à la guerre*, p.187, and G. Wormser, *La République de Clemenceau*
(Paris, 1961), p. 282.
111. *Le Temps* (30 Dec.).
112. Cf. the resolution passed at the FDG inaugural meeting in which this organisational aim was brought to the fore. As regards the political programme of the new
movement, only the principles of anti-clericalism and moderate tax reforms were
mentioned; there was no reference whatsoever to the *Trois Ans!*
113. *Le Temps* (30 Dec.); *La Petite République* (13 Jan. 1914); and RddM (1 Jan. 1914).
114. *Le Matin* (30 Nov., 13 Dec.). P. Buneau-Varilla, editor of *Le Matin*, emerged
several months later as one of Caillaux's most bitter enemies (see p. 177, below).
115. Poincaré, NJ (9 Jan. 1914).
116. Ibid.
117. See p. 155, below.
118. *Le Temps* (27 Dec.). On the regional organisation of the trade associations prior to
1914 and the difficulties in setting up a national umbrella organisation, see G.
Lefranc, *Les Organisations patronales en France* (Paris, 1976), especially pp. 38–9,
45–6.
119. ARD (28 Dec.). See also ibid. (11 Jan. 1914), which refers to an FDG 'apostolate' to
which the other moderate republican groups had to subordinate themselves 'in
patriotic renunciation'.
120. On the composition of the CCEDF, see p. 58, above.
121. A detailed summary of the conference in *Le Reveil Economique* (17 Dec.); also
mentioned in Chapman, 'Decision for War', pp. 124–5, but with no reference to the
intention of intervening in political agitation.
122. Published in *Le Temps* (26 Dec.); see Chapman, 'Decision for War', p. 125.
123. The *Programme Économique* was first published in *Le Reveil Economique* (14 Jan.
1914). On the links between these groups and the *Comité des Forges* in the
background, cf. J. Boudet, *Le Monde des affairs en France* (Paris, 1936), pp. 106–7;
Bourgin, Carrère and Guérin, *Manuel des partis politiques*, pp. 237–42. The staff of
the UIE had close links with the ARD; cf. ARD (9 Feb. 1913).
124. *Le Reveil Économique* (25 March 1914).
125. Ibid.
126. Le Temps (14 Dec.).
127. *La Petite République* (14 Jan. 1914).
128. *mesures vexatoires*, as the conservatives generally referred to compulsory declaration of income and the inspection of tax returns by the authorities.
129. At the SFIO congress in Amiens in January 1914 Jaurès's tactics won the day,
despite the bitter opposition of the *Guesdistes* and the scepticism of many departmental federations. SFIO policy was now to be totally geared towards the fight
against the *Loi de Trois Ans* and *Briandisme*. Although the congress resolution also
deplored the 'faltering radicalism' of Caillaux, the party nevertheless declared its
readiness to fight along with all willing Radicals against the FDG, the 'father of the
three-year law', the 'parody of political organisation, the cartel of all veiled
reactionaries conspiring against democracy and the proletariat' (see *L'Humanité*,
29 Jan. 1914). On the problem of this bloc of the Left in the 1914 elections, see
chap. 9, especially pp. 201–10, below; see, in general, G. Krumeich, 'Zwischen
republikanischen und sozialistischen "Block": Die französischen Sozialisten vor
dem 1. Weltkrieg', in *Francia*, VII (1979), pp. 309–37.

CHAPTER 8. The Policy of the Doumergue/Caillaux
Government and the Fall of Caillaux

1. See p. 148, above.
2. Noulens had been the spokesman of the Chamber budgetary committee in 1913.
3. It is not possible to quote the exact figure, since the Barthou government had not differentiated between the extraordinary costs accruing from the *Loi de Trois Ans* itself and the armament costs in its draft loan, but had made an overall estimate of 900 million francs (see p. 140, above). According to Joffre, *Mémoires*, p. 57, this total was the sum of the armament programme submitted on 27 February 1913— 420 million francs—and the extraordinary costs of the *Trois Ans*. This means that Barthou had earmarked a maximum of 480 million francs for extraordinary expenditure as a result of the three-year law.
4. See Caillaux's statement to the Chamber of 15 January, in *Le Temps* (16 Jan.) (d.n.).
5. Jaurès's criticism (*L'Humanité*, 16 Jan.) that Caillaux's militarism was absorbing funds which could be better used for productive purposes was published the next day in the form of an SFIO parliamentary group resolution (ibid., 17 Jan.). Caillaux's action was ignored by the press of the non-radical Centre and by the Conservatives.
6. See p. 147, above. Caillaux's opponents observed this tactic with concern; see RddM (1 Jan. 1914 and 1 Feb. 1914). See also Poincaré, NJ (20 Jan. 1914): conversation with Ribot (President of the Senate), informing Poincaré of a conversation he had had with Caillaux. The latter had informed him that he did not intend to implement any further measures before the elections, but instead to gain time.
7. See Caillaux's letter to the chairman of the Chamber budgetary committee, read by Caillaux to the Chamber on 15 January, published in *Le Temps* (16 Jan.) (d.n.). Caillaux's measures were: cuts in the administration; transfer of the Moroccan expenditure from the regular budget; low additional taxes on a number of luxury goods; and re-estimation of expected state returns on the basis of the surplus from financial year 1913 and not, as was usual practice, from the last year but one.
8. Analysed in *Le Temps* (14 Jan.). (d.n.); published in complete form in ibid. (24 Jan.) (d.n.).
9. *Le Temps* (14 Jan.) (d.n.) and *Gil Blas* (14 Jan.), on Caillaux's statement to cabinet on 13 January. *Gil Blas*, close to Caillaux, was particularly well informed on governmental affairs in this period.
10. The Aimond proposal was first published in *Le Temps* (23 Dec. 1913).
11. *Les quatre vieilles*: taxes on personal estate, doors and windows, land tax, property tax. The new *cédules* system was generally known as 'general income tax'; see especially R. von Albertini, 'Die Diskussion um die franz. Steuerreform, 1907–1909', in *Schweizer Beiträge zur allgemeinen Geschichte*, 13 (1955), pp. 183–201, here: pp. 188–90; Allain, *Caillaux*, vol. 1, pp. 227–54.
12. See especially Touron's speech in the Senate on 14 February (*Le Temps*, 16 Feb.); and see in detail in Chapman, 'Decision for War', pp. 129–33. *Le Temps* (8 Feb.) accused Aimond of serving the Socialists' ends, just like Caillaux; so, similarly, did *La Liberté* (13 Feb.).
13. See Chapman, 'Decision for War', p. 129.
14. Speech on 19 February, published in *Le Temps* (21 Feb.), *Le Radical* and *Gil Blas* (20 Feb.).
15. Early in November 1913 a *Parti Républicain Socialiste* congress had resolved that, despite all scepticism regarding the SFIO's demand for an immediate reintroduction of the 1905 law, close cooperation with both the Radicals and the Socialists was desirable, especially in the field of tax policy. See the congress debate and resolution in *Le Républicain Socialiste*, (9 Nov.); see also Chapman, 'Decision for War', p. 117, who, however, wrongly regards this as a consensus on the *Trois Ans* issue.

16. Perchot was a member of the Radical Party executive committee and a friend of Caillaux.
17. *Le Temps* (27 Feb.); similarly *Le Figaro, Gil Blas* and *Le Radical* (all 26 Feb.); *L'Humanité* (2 and 3 March) was more sceptical; Allain, *Caillaux*, vol. 1, pp. 262–3, regards the Senate vote as a serious defeat for Caillaux.
18. The Dubois interpellation and the following debate from *Le Temps* (29 Feb.), also *Gil Blas, Le Radical* and *L'Humanité* (all 28 Feb.).
19. See p. 142, above.
20. Briand's accusation in his St Étienne speech (see p. 153, above) that Caillaux was a 'demagogic plutocrat' was in a similar vein. *La Petite République* (25 Feb.): 'Le Démagogue'. Caillaux was accused of being the head of an 'electoral enterprise', devoid of a statesmanly sense of responsbility, a 'bad shepherd' of whom the country must soon rid itself. The campaign against Caillaux (see chap. 8.3 above) also culminated in this accusation.
21. Jaurès in *L'Humanité* (28 Feb.).
22. Namely, the *ordre du jour Durand*, for the priority of which the government asked for a vote of confidence.
23. Much attention was given to Clemenceau's significant statement. He continued to advocate the *Trois Ans*, but added: 'I wish . . . it [the consription law] to be mitigated, since it only meets the most urgent requirements of our military defence by pressing heavily on our productivity and we must ask ourselves would it not be appropriate to look for more effective means' ('Homme libre', 17 Feb., quoted from *L'Humanité*, 18 Feb.).
24. As *Le Radical* (16 Feb.) correctly stated.
25. The *discours du Havre* was published in all the major newspapers and later distributed in the election campaign as a pamphlet. *Le Temps* (18 Feb.), 'France is with you', welcomed the FDG as a 'party of national security'. *Le Gaulois* (monarchist) described Briand and Barthou's speeches as the *magnificat* of the army and offered the participation of the monarchists in a Briand ministry!
26. Published in *La Petite République* (25 Feb.); further details in chap. 9.1 above.
27. The Doizy interpellation, discussed in the Chamber on 20 and 23 February. The whole of *L'Humanité*'s campaign against the three-year law from January to March 1914 was entitled 'The barracks of death': see details and documents in Krieger and Becker, *1914*, pp. 33–6.
28. The War Minister, Noulens', and Under Secretary Maginot's statements to Parliament on 20 and 23 February approved in detail in *L'Humanité* (21 and 24 Feb.).
29. *L'Humanité* (25 Feb.); a similar commentary by Jaurès in ibid. (24 Feb.). See also the commentary, ibid. (16 Feb.), in which Jaurès bemoaned the 'treason' of the government, but conceded that the 'reactionaries' great hatred of the government' compelled the SFIO to adopt a position of moderation. Its task until the elections would therefore be to break the wave of Briandisme.
30. See p. 197, below.
31. On the cadre law, see pp. 171–2, below.
32. See *L'Humanité* (17 Feb.).
33. Doumergue's governmental declaration; see also DDF III/9, no. 322 (17 Feb.).
34. P. Cambon, *Correspondance*, vol. 3, p. 56 (letter dated 9 Dec. 1913).
35. Izvolsky to Sazonov, 5/18 December 1913 (Stieve, *Iswolski*, vol. 3, nos 1179, 1181), and 19 December/1 January 1914 (ibid., vol. 4, no. 1198).
36. Conversation between Poincaré and Geoffray: Poincaré, NJ (11 Jan. 1914).
37. Poincaré, NJ (27 Jan. 1914); see also ibid. (23 Jan.).
38. Ibid. (1 Jan. 1914); according to Roman tradition, criminals were hurled into the depths from the Tarpeian Rock. In his memoirs Poincaré constantly endeavours to cover up his critical and at times hateful feelings towards the Doumergue/Caillaux government. Although he gives vent to some criticism of Caillaux's alleged endeavours to take over the reins of government (*Au Service*, vol. 4, p. 27), and also

expresses some regret at the fact that his own personal influence over governmental affairs was curtailed (ibid, pp. 12, 27), he nevertheless emphasises his full agreement with Doumergue's foreign policy (ibid., pp. 3, 9, 20, 27, 54, etc.; see also chap. 7, note 91 above).

39. On the attempts to partition the Portuguese colonies, see R. Langhorne, 'Anglo-German Negotiations Concerning the Future of the Portuguese Colonies, 1911–1914', in *Historical Journal*, 16 (1973), pp. 361–87; and J.D. Vincent-Smith, 'The Anglo-German Negotiations over the Portuguese Colonies in Africa, 1911–1914', in *Historical Journal*, 17 (1974), pp. 620–9.

40. Cf. Fischer, *Krieg der Illusionen*, pp. 443–6.

41. DDF III/9, no. 3, J. Cambon to Doumergue, 2 January 1914, and ibid., no. 171, P. Cambon to Doumergue, 27 January.

42. Ibid.

43. See DDF III/8, no. 607, and DDF III/9, no. 171, P. Cambon's reports of 10 December 1913 and 27 January 1914.

44. DDF III/8, no. 404, Paléologue's memorandum for the Colonial Minister, 30 October 1913; ibid., no. 640, Doumergue to P. Cambon, 17 December; ibid., no. 663, Lebrun to Doumergue, 23 December; DDF III/9, no. 116, circular from Doumergue, 20 January 1914.

45. This was the second part of the 1911 Morocco agreement.

46. Lebrun had already been Colonial Minister in Poincaré's 1912 cabinet and was a friend of the President (see Poincaré, *Au Service*, vol. 4, p. 28).

47. DDF III/8, no. 404, memorandum from Paléologue, 30 October 1913; ibid., no. 607, P. Cambon to Doumergue, 10 December; ibid., no. 663, Lebrun to Doumergue, 23 December; DDF III/9, no. 35, P. Cambon to Doumergue, 8 January 1914. In February 1914 Poincaré himself intervened in favour of this diplomatic solution (*Au Service*, vol. 4, p. 58).

48. DDF III/9, no. 116 (20 Jan. 1914).

49. Cambon assumed that the British government would refuse to conclude secret agreements which would prevent the implementation of the Anglo-German agreement.

50. DDF III/9, no. 171, P. Cambon to Doumergue, 27 January.

51. Poincaré, NJ (10 and 12 Feb. 1914); in contrast, Poincaré's memoirs, supposedly a true reflection of the notes in his diary: here (*Au Service*, vol. 4, p. 63) Poincaré, stresses Lebrun's and Doumergue's concern about the fate of the Portuguese colonies. Vincent-Smith, 'Anglo-German Negotiations' op. cit., otherwise most informative, fails to observe this dissent within the French government.

52. Poincaré, NJ (10 Feb. 1914).

53. Quoted from Poincaré, *Au Service*, vol. 4, p. 58. His conversation with Bertie strenghtened Poincaré's suspicions that Doumergue had not given the British ambassador sufficient information on the consequences the renunciation of Cabinda would imply for French interests (see Poincaré, NJ, 10 Feb.—this is not · mentioned in Poincaré's memoirs).

54. Poincaré, *Au Service*, vol. 4, p. 58.

55. DDF III/9, nos. 256 (10 Feb.) and 326 (18 Feb.).

56. Ibid., no. 326, Doumergue to P. Cambon, 18 February; ibid., no. 392, Doumergue's instructions to the attaché in Lisbon.

57. Ibid., nos. 326, 401, 408 and the note on no. 401.

58. Fischer, *Krieg der Illusionen*, p. 455.

59. Ibid., pp. 449–51; note the analogies with the difficulties of the French government mentioned here.

60. Poincaré, *Au Service*, vol. 4, p. 65, refers to this statement as a 'good move' on the part of Jagow. However, in his diary Poincaré expressed his concern that Germany was not really prepared to respect French rights under Article 16 of the 1911 treaty (see Poincaré, NJ, 13 Dec.).

61. Poincaré, *Au Service*, vol. 4, p. 69; and see note 49 above.
62. Poincaré later maintained that he had agreed with Doumergue to 'wait and see' (*Au Service*, vol. 4, p. 70). There is no reference to this in Poincaré, NJ (23 Feb.), but, on the contrary, the plan to prevail upon the British king 'before anything has been definitely accomplished'.
63. Fischer, *Krieg der Illusionen*, p. 456.
64. Mommsen, *Die latente Krise*, p. 88.
65. See pp. 123–4, above.
66. Cf. Stieve, *Iswolski*, vol. 3, no. 1186, Sazonov to Izvolsky, 14/27 December 1913; ibid., vol. 4, no. 1222, Sazonov to Izvolsky, 27 December 1913/9 January 1914.
67. Further details in Fischer, *Krieg der Illusionen*, pp. 494–7.
68. See DDF III/8, no. 689 (30 Dec.); and Stieve, op. cit., vol. 3, no. 1192, Izvolsky to Sazonov, 17/30 December 1913.
69. Albertini, *The Origins*, vol. 1, p. 545; cf. Taylor, *The Struggle for Mastery in Europe*, p. 501.
70. Poincaré, NJ (5 Jan. 1914). Poincaré expressly mentioned a conversation between Jagow and P. Cambon to Izvolsky (cf. DDF III/9, no. 3, 2 Jan. 1914), in which Jagow asked Cambon not to make the affair into a 'question of prestige', since this would make it impossible for the German government to yield, in view of the precarious situation at home.
71. Stieve, op. cit., vol. 4, no. 1199, Sazonov to Izvolsky, 20 December 1913/2 January 1914.
72. Poincaré, NJ (5 Jan. 1914). Izvolsky's report on this conversation does not mention this refusal, only the French doubts about the joint action of the *Entente* powers (cf. Stieve, op. cit., vol. 4, no. 1212).
73. Poincaré, NJ (13 Jan. 1914). The Franco-German negotiations were concluded on 15 February 1914 by a treaty which stipulated the financing of a stretch of the Baghdad railway line, but which in fact amounted to 'an agreement on the delimitation of mutual spheres of interest in the Ottoman Empire' (Mommsen,*Die latente Krise*, p. 76). Poincaré's allusion to a new 'Baghdad affair' refers to the imperialistic rivalries between the *Entente* powers which came to the fore in the first round of negotiations on the Baghdad railway project in 1911/12 (further details, ibid., p. 75).
74. DDF III/9, no. 138 (23 Jan.).
75. Poincaré, NJ (26 Jan. 1914): further criticism of Delcassé, ibid. (29 Jan.): 'Delcassé is once again most eager to adopt the Russian point of view'. The ill-feeling between France and Russia has also been described by J.F. Keiger, *France and the Origins of the First World War*, pp. 132–3. Keiger's view that Poincaré put pressure on Doumergue is unfounded; moreover the idea of Poincaré 'opposing Russia in order not to upset Germany' (ibid.) is hardly tenable.
76. Poincaré, NJ (26 Jan. 1914).
77. DDF III/9, no. 175, Boppe to Doumergue, 28 January.
78. Poincaré, NJ (29 Jan. 1914).
79. Ibid., with an express reference to the fact that Doumergue did not follow the advice to pass the instructions on to the ambassador.
80. Cf. DDF III/8, no. 619, 621, 627 (12–15 Dec. 1913); DDF III/9, no. 84 (14 Jan. 1914), no. 253 (7 Feb.) and no. 237 (8 Feb.); the text of Cambon's telegram of 26 January 1914 in Poincaré, NJ (27 Jan.), but not in DDF.
81. DDF III/9, no. 84 (14 Jan.).
82. Ibid., no. 119, Caillaux's memorandum on a conversation with Djavid Bey, 21 January; ibid., no. 128, almost identical instructions from Doumergue to Boppe, 22 January; see also ibid., no. 145, Doumergue to Delcassé, 24 January: Turkey's maintenance of the peace was the 'dominant question'.
83. DDF III/9, nos 159, 187, 197, 204, 207 (26 Jan.–3 Feb. 1914).
84. Poincaré, *Au Service*, vol. 4, p. 47: 'Therefore in Constantinople, as everywhere, it

is peace which defends France', with a direct reference to Doumergue's policy. In his memoirs Poincaré agrees with Doumergue that the preservation of peace in the Near East was the 'dominant question' (ibid., pp. 44, 54); this is in contrast with his constant fear of Doumergue's initiatives, evident in his diary, e.g. he believed that Doumergue had let himself be outwitted by the Italian government on the question of the joint intervention of the Great Powers. The only interest of the Triple Alliance powers was to project France as hostile to Turkey (NJ, 8 Feb. 1914). He further complained that this policy served only the 'egoism' of both Britain and Russia; the joint approach would mean 'the end of French interests in Turkey' (NJ, 8 and 14 Feb.). See also G. Hanotaux, 'Les Carnets de Gabriel Hanotaux', ed. Michel de Fonscolombe, in *Revue d'Histoire Diplomatique*, 91 (1977), pp. 5–142, 280–345, here: p. 127 note 404. Hanotaux, a close friend of Poincaré's and his adviser on foreign affairs, expressed the hope at the end of January 1914 that France would obtain 'legitimate advantages' from her support of Turkey.

85. See p. 123, above.
86. For example, the Tsar remarked to Delcassé that the endeavours of Germany to 'spread herself out' in Turkey—which had become apparent in the Liman affair—would lead to a 'collision, perhaps inevitable, in the near future, between German ambitions and Russian interests' (DDF III/9, no. 189, 29 Jan.).
87. The minutes of these conferences are published in Stieve, *Iswolski und der Weltkrieg*, pp. 234–66; cf. Bestushev, *Russian Foreign Policy*, pp. 106–8; Fischer, *Krieg der Illusionen*, pp. 504–11; Albertini, *The Origins*, vol. 1, pp. 547–50; Schmitt, *The Coming of the War 1914*, vol. 1, pp. 96–8.
88. See DDF III/9, no. 322, Paléologue's report, 17 February, of a conversation with the Tsar.
89. See the correspondence between Sazonov and Izvolsky, in Stieve, *Iswolski*, vol. 3, no. 1181, and ibid., vol. 4, nos 1198, 1217, 1218, 1223, 1224. At the end of 1914 Poincaré was still not convinced that the Russian government was prepared to respect the strategic agreements (Poincaré, NJ, 30 Jan.).
90. The Tsar to Delcassé, DDF III/9, no. 189 (29 Jan.).
91. See especially *L'Humanité* (17 Feb.).
92. Poincaré, *Au Service*, vol. 4, pp. 75–80. In personal talks with Doumergue, Poincaré persuaded his Premier to present the bill to Parliament as swiftly as possible, although some of Poincaré's political friends had urged him to use the cadre laws as a means of provoking an out-and-out confrontation between himself and the government. Poincaré noted the following on a conversation with Millerand (War Minister until January 1913): 'Millerand came to see me. He considers it necessary that I use my constitutional rights and send a message to the Chamber asking it to pass the bill on the constitution of the military units prior to the elections. The present cabinet has deprived me of much of my popularity; I was elected to act. I cannot be a president like Fallières and Loubet. . . .' (NJ, 4 March; similarly a warning from Reinach, ibid., 2 March). Immediately after the bill had been adopted by the Chamber on 12 March, Poincaré expressed his relief that he had paid no attention to Millerand's pessimism (NJ, 12 March).
93. See Joffre, *Mémoires*, pp. 39, 189: (a) 'Règlement sur la conduite des grandes unités', (b) Règlement sur le 'service des armées en campagne', (c) Règlement de manoeuvre de l'infanterie', and (d) 'Instructions sur la concentration'; ibid., a precise account of the significance of all these regulations for the offensive strategy.
94. Poincaré, NJ (2 Feb.).
95. See Poincaré, *Au Service*, vol. 4, p. 49, where this conversation with Joffre is related. However, the final sentence is omitted. Furthermore, Poincaré stresses .Joffre's alleged concern that the defensive(!) installations be completed in time in the case of German aggression.
96. See p. 160, above.
97. *Le Temps* (1 March).

98. Letter from the CCEDF, published in *Le Temps* (25 Jan.).
99. Resolution, published in *Le Temps* (28 Jan.); also mentioned in Chapman, 'Decision for War', p. 131.
100. See *Le Temps* (10 and 13 Feb.) and *La France* (12 Feb.). Further protests from various regional and national associations in: *Le Temps* (15 and 16 Feb., 10 March); ARD (1 Feb.); and *Le Reveil Économique* (14 Jan.).
101. See *Le Temps* (13 Feb.), *La Liberté* (13 Feb.) and *Gil Blas* (17 Feb.). *Le Radical* (13 Feb.) tried to portray this resolution as an unauthorised statement of 'some elements' of the Mascuraud committee. However, Mascuraud confirmed this resolution in *La Liberté* (18 Feb.).
102. P. Cambon alluded to this disparity in a letter to his brother Jules on 29 March in which he wrote that Carmichael, chairman of the CCEDF and Cambon's brother-in-law, was 'the only man in the whole of France' who had been able to organise resistance to Caillaux's proposals (P. Cambon, *Correspondance*, vol. 3, p. 64).
103. *Le Gaulois* (22 Jan.); cf. ibid. (8 Dec. 1913): 'Guerre à la Bourgeoisie' (= 'Guerre à la Nation').
104. See p. 152–3, above.
105. *La Petite République* (25 Feb.): 'Le Démagogue'.
106. *L'Humanité* (15 and 16 Jan. 1914, 14 and 15 March, and *Le Radical* (19 Dec. 1913, 3, 26 and 31 Jan., 14 March).
107. Cf. Bellanger, *Histoire Générale*, vol. 3, p. 350.
108. *Le Figaro* (19 Jan., 10, 12 and 13 March). Allain, *Caillaux*, vol. 1, pp. 236–7, 410–36, has a detailed account of *Le Figaro*'s campaign. Allain's account corresponds essentially to mine; the two are complementary on a number of details.
109. This also applies to the anti-Caillaux press: *La Petite République*, *Le Temps* and *La Liberté* generally went no further than publication of Calmette's accusations, whereby Caillaux's successive denials were also published. See also Poincaré, NJ (8 Jan.): 'Since Calmette could not produce any evidence, he should rather have kept his silence'; similarly, Poincaré, *Au Service*, vol. 4, pp. 30–1.
110. The text of the Fabre document was published in Bonnefous, *Histoire politique*, vol. 1, pp. 392–3.
111. Cf. p. 178, below: Poincaré's conversation with Barthou on 17 March.
112. Poincaré was concerned that the whole matter could give rise to a new Dreyfus affair which, in his opinion, could serve only Caillaux's interests, given the present scenario in domestic politics (NJ, 14 Jan.).
113. Poincaré's talks with Barthou, Caillaux and Briand are related here from Poincaré, *Au Service*, vol. 4, pp. 79–84. The accounts in Poincaré's memoirs have been partly supplemented, partly corrected, on the basis of the entries in Poincaré's diary (NJ, 14 and 16 March). Caillaux does not mention in his memoirs his talks with Poincaré on 14 and 16 March—presumably because they would have provided too obvious a contradiction of Caillaux's claim that Poincaré, filled with hate for Caillaux, had supported Barthou's intrigues (Caillaux, *Mémoires*, vol. 3, pp. 133–7).
114. See also *L'Humanité* (14 March): a statement by Jaurès demanding the publication of the Fabre document in order to find out the 'whole truth' and to punish 'all those responsible'.
115. Poincaré, NJ (14 March). Buneau-Varilla's plan to mobilise all the 'traders and grocers' is a further indication of the political ineffectiveness of the campaign of the business associations at this point; see chap. 7, note 118.
116. Caillaux, *Mémoires*, vol. 3, p. 117.
117. The text of the famous *Ton Jo* letter can be found in Bonnefous, *Histoire politique*, vol. 1, p. 389.
118. See *inter alia L'Humanité* (14 March).
119. Caillaux, *Mémoires*, vol. 3, p. 118; see also Poincaré, NJ (16 March). Several hours after the assassination of Calmette, Poincaré was informed by his confidant Pichon

that like Briand he had also been offered Caillaux's letters years previously. Pichon and Briand had, however, refused to use the letters in the political struggle against Caillaux.

120. See Poincaré, *Au Service*, vol. 4, p. 83, conversation with Caillaux.
121. RddM (1st April); *Le Temps* (18 March), and *La Petite République* (19 March).
122. Caillaux, *Mémoires*, vol. 3, pp. 133–7.
123. Poincaré, NJ (17 March). In Poincaré, *Au Service*, vol. 4, p. 90, the conversation with Barthou is mentioned but no details are given.
124. Following this conversation, Poincaré recorded in his diary his surprise that Barthou was on the one hand intent on being honest 'to the point of self-destruction', but on the other hand gave no justification for the fact that he had committed a 'vile deed by giving a journalist a document which he did not have the courage to use himself in the courts'.
125. Details of this *séance dramatique* in Bonnefous, *Histoire politique*, vol. 1, pp. 391–3.
126. Poincaré, *Au Service*, vol. 4, p. 90.
127. Ibid.
128. This meant interrogation of the witnesses under oath and a trial before a criminal court if false statements were made.
129. The conclusions of the committee of inquiry were published *inter alia* in *Le Temps* (3 Apr.). Bonnefous, *Histoire politique*, vol. 1, pp. 394–8, gives a detailed report but does not even mention the charges against Briand and Barthou! This is particularly strange, since Bonnefous himself was a member of the committee and protested against the accusations against Briand and Barthou (cf. *Le Temps*, 3 March).
130. See *Le Temps* (22 March) and ibid. (5 March) for the text of the Renoult proposal.
131. Quoted from *Le Temps* (1 Apr.); the Senate adopted the supplementary tax on 15 July (see p. 213, below). The introduction of an additional capital tax in accordance with the draft presented by Caillaux on 15 January was also 'ripe for a decision' by the end of the parliamentary session. On 29 March the Chamber finance committee adopted the essential points of this draft (see *Le Temps*, 31 March). On the new campaign of a number of trade associations, see ibid. (28 and 30 March).

CHAPTER 9. The 1914 Elections and their Political Consequences

1. See chap. 8, pp. 157–61, above.
2. See especially Goguel, *La Politique des partis*, p. 145: 'In the May 1914 general elections the two blocs of the established Order and the Movement confronted each other much more clearly than had been the case four years previously. The former demanded the maintenance of three-year service and rejected income tax; the latter the reintroduction of two-year service and tax reform.' In a similar vein Bourgin, Carrère and Guérin, *Manuel des partis politiques*, p. 12; Bonnefous, *Histoire politique*, vol. 1, p. 404; Michon, *La Préparation à la guerre*, pp. 193–4; Weber, *Nationalist Revival*, p. 137; and H. Goldberg, *The Life of Jean Jaurès* (Madison, Wis., 1962), p. 447. Chapman's view implies a certain contradiction. On the one hand, he correctly underlines the difficulties involved in the establishment of a 'bloc of the Left' in view of the disagreement among the Radicals on the defence question; on the other hand, he refers to a 'formidable progressive Bloc' (*Decision for War*, pp. 139, 146). Following the completion of the manuscript of the present volume, Becker's study, *1914: Comment les Français sont entrés dans la guerre*, was published. This includes an extremely precise and detailed analysis of the 1914 elections. Becker also adopts the polarisation theory in concluding that France had been divided into two camps by the three-year law and the issue of tax reform (pp. 63, 74). Becker backs up this theory by an exact calculation of the

number of candidates who had come out for or against the three-year law (pp. 69, 74). The present writer has deliberately not included this type of calculation, also carried out—with a lesser degree of precision—by *Le Temps* directly after the 1914 elections. On the basis of the above it is obvious that, regardless of whether a candidate was for or against the *Trois Ans*, he could still represent a welter of different political options.

3. *La Liberté* (16 May 1914).
4. See above, chap. 3, pp. 70–4.
5. Cf. L. Dubreuilh, *Le Socialisme, c'est la paix: Contre les Trois Ans* (Paris, 1914); and Dunois, *L'Action socialiste au Parlement*, pp. 6, 13–24. However, in a pamphlet published immediately after the war, the only justification the party gave for its line in the 'three years' ' dispute was the argument that the Socialists had rightly regarded the law as reactionary and superfluous, since, with respect to the 'salvation of the country', it had been less effective than the realisation of the concept of the nation in arms: *Le Parti Socialiste, la Loi de Trois Ans et la Guerre* (Limoges, 1919).
6. According to *L'Humanité* (10 Apr.), over 4 million of these pamphlets had already been circulated at this point.
7. *L'Humanité* (26 Apr.).
8. See p. 36, above.
9. CE manifesto in *Le Radical* (12 Apr.).
10. All these statements of policy were published in *Le Temps* (18 Apr.).
11. Doumergue's Souillac speech, published *inter alia* in *Le Temps* (20 Apr.).
12. *Le Radical* (26 Jan.).
13. Ibid. (26 Apr.); see also ibid. (15 Apr.). The electorate was urged to vote against any candidate who had concluded a 'pact with the Right' by supporting the three-year law. A candidate sponsored by the party who endorsed the *Trois Ans* was to be supported only if there were no radical *Antitroisanniste* running in that constituency.
14. *Le Temps* (14, 16 and 20 Apr.).
15. According to Cachin, *L'Humanité* (21 Apr.).
16. Ibid. (22 Apr.).
17. Published in *La Petite République* (25 Feb.).
18. See p. 149, above.
19. See p. 160, above.
20. See p. 155, above.
21. See *Le Reveil Économique* (29 Apr.–6 May); ibid. (13 May): 'There are only two parties: on the one hand, those who want to establish socialism, or at least pave its way, and, on the other, those who advocate economic liberty—which is the only means of assuring the *grandeur* and prosperity of France.'
22. Resolution of the *Assemblée des Présidents des Chambres de Commerce de France*, 28 March, in *Le Temps* (9 Apr.).
23. Published *inter alia* in *Le Temps* (12 Apr.) (d.n.).
24. This refers to the *Parti Républicain*, reviving a catchword from the Republic's years of struggle when all Republicans had for a time formed a front against the Monarchists.
25. See p. 149, above.
26. *L'Humanité* (16 March).
27. Barthou's statement of policy in *Le Temps* (18 Apr.).
28. See Briand's speech at the Élysée-Montmartre banquet, 1 April. Nearly all the leading newspapers published this speech in full; it was also circulated as an election pamphlet.
29. *La France* (12 Apr.); *La Petite République* (19 March).
30. See p. 141, above.
31. ARD (1 Feb.).

32. Ibid. (22 Feb.).
33. Ibid. (8 Feb.).
34. Ibid.
35. Published in ibid. (12 Apr.) and in *Le Temps* (10 Apr.) (d.n.).
36. See chap. 5.3
37. Report on the FR congress in *Le Temps* (5 Feb.) and *La Liberté* (3 Feb.).
38. Published in *L'Écho* (8 Apr.).
39. Published in *Le Temps* (12 Apr.) (d.n.) and *L'Écho* (13 Apr.).
40. See *Le Temps* (2 and 3 Feb.).
41. See APP B/a 1463, doss. 45,000–23, reports of 19 and 24 April; see also AN, F 7/12822, doss. 5, no. 1, report of 24 April on a pastoral letter from the Archbishop of Paris (and see *L'Écho*, 18 Apr.), and other examples of the active support given by the Catholic Right to die-hard *Troisannistes*.
42. See APP B/a 1463, doss. 45,000, reports of 30 May and 28 June 1913; now see also Sternhell, *La Droite révolutionnaire*, p. 144. Sternhell shows that the nationalist *Ligue des Patriotes* had been absorbed by the *droite classique* in the immediate pre-war years and developed into a kind of Praetorian guard of the ALP.
43. A compilation of incidents, and all the parties' posters and pamphlets from many departments, in AN, F 7/12822.
44. *Règlement de l'affichage électoral*, law of 20 March 1914. Cf. the criticism in *L'Humanité* (9 Apr.) and *L'Écho* (21 Apr.) on the impairment of the electoral campaign of the parties which had no adequate counterweight (e.g. local and regional newspapers).
45. See AN, F 7/12822, doss. 6, no. 15, and APP B/a 1463, doss. *Divers*: instructions from the Prefect of the Police (10 Apr.) following an order from the Ministry of the Interior.
46. On the reasons for the Syndicalists' reluctancy, see chap. 8, pp. 126–31, above. It is difficult to pinpoint the reasons for the reticence of the *Action Française*. It is possible that the disappointment that domestic *Poincarisme* had lost momentum following the fall of Barthou led them to withdraw, resigned, from day-to-day politics. The AF circulated only three posters in Paris manifesting its 'general doctrine' without any real intention of entering the election campaign (see APP B/a 1463, doss. 45,000, report dated 25 Apr.). The same presumably applies to the *Ligue des Patriotes*, which was faced with an additional problem: its political leader, Paul Déroulède, had died in February 1914.
47. *Le Temps* (27 Apr.). Candidates whose platform covered only specific local demands were regarded as 'unserious'.
48. *Le Radical* (25 Apr.).
49. According to *inter alia Le Temps* (25 Apr., 1 May); *La Petite République* (28 Apr.), *La France* (28 and 29 Apr.), *Le Gaulois* (28 Apr.), *L'Écho* (28 Apr.) and *La Liberté* (29 Apr.): 'The policy of *entente* with the parties of revolution and degradation leading the enemies of *la patrie* represents profound immorality... this is killing... the Radical Party.'
50. The basis for these and subsequent calculations is provided by the valuable statistics in *Le Temps* (28 Apr. fos 1–7), showing for each constituency both the size of the electorate and the number of votes polled by each candidate. As far as possible, the parties to which candidates belonged, or by which they were sponsored, are also specified; precise election figures, giving the numbers polled by the Radical Party, can be found in Berstein, *Histoire du Parti Radical*, pp. 78–80.
51. Published *inter alia* in *Le Temps* (28 Apr.) (d.n.).
52. Ibid. (29 May).
53. Ibid. (28 Apr.) (d.n.); *La Petite République* (28 Apr.). *Le Radical* (28 Apr.) referred to these statistics as an admission of the defeat of the FDG, since they qualified all the dissident left-wing groups as a bloc. The Radical Party itself was satisfied with the publication of the statistics of the Ministry of the Interior, which did not give a

separate classification of the seats won by the *radicaux unifiés*.
54. *L'Humanité* (28 Apr.).
55. Cf. *Le Radical* (28 Apr.); *L'Humanité* (29 Apr.); *La Petite République* (28 Apr.), *Le Temps* (28 Apr., 1 May); *Le Gaulois* (28 Apr.); *La France* (28 Apr.); *L'Écho* (28 Apr.); and *La Liberté* (28 and 29 Apr.).
56. *Le Radical* (28 Apr.); and in a similar vein, *L'Humanité* (29 Apr.).
57. *La France* (28 Apr.); and similarly, *La Petite République* (29 Apr.).
58. Published in *Le Radical* (6 May).
59. *L'Humanité* (29 Apr.).
60. Ibid. (30 Apr.).
61. See chap. 7, note 129.
62. CAP manifesto published in *L'Humanité* (1 May).
63. These figures are based on the statistics published in *Le Temps* (12 May), and the daily reports in *Le Temps*, *Le Radical* and *L'Humanité* (30 Apr.–10 May) on electoral agreements in all the constituencies.
64. According to *Le Temps* (10 May).
65. FR manifesto published in *Le Temps* (6 May).
66. *L'Écho* (5 May); cf. *Le Radical* (6 May).
67. ARD manifesto published in *Le Temps* (5 May).
68. Statement by the FDG steering committee in *Le Temps* (30 Apr.); cf. *La Petite République* (2 May).
69. FDG manifesto published in *La Petite République* (7 May); cf. *Le Temps* (7 May).
70. *Le Temps* (12 May). Bonnefous, *Histoire politique*, vol. 1, p. 405, quoted these figures as 'official'; however, no official statistics on the affiliation of the elected deputies were published—this would in any case have been in contradiction of the principle of uninominal voting.
71. *Le Radical* (12 May).
72. See Bonnefous, *Histoire politique*, vol. 1, pp. 19, 185.
73. This table of the SFIO's gains and losses is based on statistics in *Le Temps* (12 May 1914). Department by department, *Le Temps* shows which of the deputies elected in 1910 were re-elected/not elected in 1914, and which candidates were elected in the first ballot. The SFIO's share of the poll, expressed in percentage brackets, is taken from Rémond, *Atlas historique*, p. 119. The percentage brackets ×–7 represent the following: × = 0 per cent; 1 = 0–5 per cent; 2 = 5–10 per cent; 3 = 10–15 per cent; 4 = 15–20 per cent; 5 = 20–25 per cent; 6 = 25–30 per cent; 7 = 30 per cent +.
74. This is also the opinion of Becker, *1914: Comment les Français sont entrés dans la guerre*, pp. 78–80.
75. *L'Humanité* (11 May).
76. Ibid. (16 May); in a similar vein, ibid. (12 May) (Cachin).
77. Resolution published in *L'Humanité* and *Le Temps* (2 June) (d.n.).
78. Ibid.
79. Shortly after the elections, 182 deputies had already registered as *radicaux unifiés*; See *Le Radical* (10 June).
80. See *Le Radical* (2 June) and *Le Temps* (4 June) (d.n.).
81. *ordre du jour du bureau du Comité Exécutif* in *Le Radical* (30 May), adopted by the CE plenary on 3 June; cf. *Le Temps* (3 June).
82. Doumergue's statement published in *Le Temps* (3 June).
83. See *L'Humanité* (2 June) and *Le Radical* (2 June).
84. *Le Temps* (30 May) (d.n.).
85. Poincaré, NJ (24 May).
86. DDF III/10, no. 194, Cambon to Doumergue, 3 May.
87. *discours de Lyon* published in Poincaré, *Au Service*, vol. 4, pp. 130–1.
88. *L'Humanité* (26 May).
89. See especially the 'open letter to M. Poincaré' from the editor of the monarchist

Gaulois, A. Meyer, in *Le Gaulois* (15 May); also *L'Écho* (20 June); *La Liberté* (7 June); further demands of this kind in Poincaré, NJ (15–26 May).

90. According to Poincaré, NJ (5 June).
91. *discours de Rennes*, published *inter alia* in *Le Temps* (2 June) (d.n.).
92. *L'Humanité* (2 June).
93. Cf. Poincaré, NJ (5 June), where, in his conjectures on the likely composition of the governmental majority, he stresses that the SFIO will undoubtedly agree with the Radicals on every issue—except the *Trois Ans!*
94. See Poincaré, NJ (2 June).
95. Viviani's statement of policy published in *Le Temps* (5 June).
96. First published in *Le Temps* (7 June).
97. See *Le Radical* (7 June) and *Le Temps* (7 June) (d.n.); also Poincaré, *Au Service*, vol. 4, p. 130, which corresponds with Poincaré, NJ (6 and 7 June).
98. An impressive account of these negotiations is given in Poincaré, *Au Service*, vol. 4, pp. 152–5, an almost word-for-word reproduction of the entries in his diary.
99. The Ribot ministry, regarded as strictly conservative, was unanimously welcomed by the conservative press: cf. *Le Gaulois* (11 June); *Le Temps* (9 June); *L'Écho* (12 June); and *La Liberté* (11 June), see also Poincaré, *Au Service*, vol. 4, pp. 155–60. Here, however, M.E. Schmidt, *Alexandre Ribot: Odyssey of a Liberal in the Third Republic* (The Hague, 1974) is of interest. Schmidt observes that Ribot was originally extremely sceptical about the three-year law and quotes from Ribot's diary to the effect that he now only supported the upholding of the conscription bill to avoid creating the impression of a 'sort of [French] abdication abroad'.
100. See Poincaré, NJ (9 June), on a conversation with Noulens, War Minister in Doumergue's cabinet, who refused to accept a portfolio in a non-radical ministry: 'I [Poincaré] remarked to him that he would be assuming a grave responsibility by refusing to support a cabinet formed to defend the military law'.
101. Published in *Le Temps* (13 June) (d.n.).
102. See p. 180, above.
103. *Le Temps* (12 June); ibid., an almost identical resolution of the Radical Party Seine federation; ibid. (10 June), resolution of the Radical Party group; ibid., resolution of the *républicain-socialistes*.
104. From *Le Temps* (14 June).
105. *ordre du jour Combrouze/Berger* from *Le Temps* (13 June).
106. 102 *socialistes-unifiés*; 25 *républicain-socialistes*; 165 *radicaux unifiés;* 14 others (see Bonnefous, *Histoire politique*, vol. 2, pp. 8–10).
107. Cf. *L'Humanité* (13 June); *Le Radical* (13 June); *Le Gaulois* (16 June); and *L'Écho* (14 June).
108. According to Goguel, *Géographie des Elections*, pp. 44–5.
109. *L'Humanité* (13 June); cf. *L'Écho* (20 June) and Poincaré, *Au Service*, vol. 4, p. 161.
110. *L'Humanité* (8, 9 and 10 June).
111. Ibid., (13 June).
112. See Poincaré, NJ (13 June); similarly, Poincaré, *Au Service*, vol. 4, p. 162.
113. Ibid., p. 164.
114. According to Poincaré, NJ (13 June).
115. From *Le Temps* (18 June).
116. Analysis of the division in *Le Temps* (18 June).
117. *L'Écho* (17 June); see also *La Liberté* (18 June): 'Echec au bloc'; *L'Oeuvre* (18 June); and *Le Temps* (18 June). Only *Le Gaulois* (16 June) was of the opinion that Viviani was independent of Jaurès and Caillaux and would therefore 'sacrifice' both public finances and national defence.
118. *L'Humanité* (17 June).
119. This is also the opinion of Becker, *1914: Comment les Français sont entrés dans la guerre*, p. 82.

120. CE statement in *Le Radical* (18 June).
121. *L'Humanité* (17 June). This was also the hope of *Le Radical* (17 June).
122. See p. 148, above.
123. *Le Temps* (21 June) continued to bemoan the determined 'demolition' of French credit by all sorts of *unifiés*. However, in the rest of the conservative press there is virtually no criticism to be found of this measure, once so controversial. The trade associations also remained silent on this issue.
124. See p. 180, above.
125. *Le Temps* (23 June) (d.n.); ibid. (24 June), publication of the proposal.
126. On 13 July the St Petersburg stock exchange newspaper published an article, 'inspired' by the War Minister Suchomlinov, headed 'Russia is ready, France must be ready also'; see Michon, *La Préparation à la guerre*, p. 197, and Weber, *The Nationalist Revival in France*, p. 195 note 66.
127. From *Le Temps* (3 June). No denial followed.
128. Paléologue, *Au Quai d'Orsay*, pp. 293–4.
129. See especially *L'Humanité* (13 June). Michon, whose account of the *Trois Ans* debate generally follows the contemporary line of argument of the Socialists, expressly refers to an 'intimidation campaign' (*La Préparation à la guerre*, p. 197).
130. Poincaré, NJ (16 June).
131. Ibid. (4 July). On 4 and 6 July *L'Éclair* and Clemenceau's *Homme Libre* published reports on Messimy's intention (cf. Weber, *Nationalist Revival*, p. 142).
132. Cf. Poincaré, NJ (8 July): Viviani had simply replied 'we shall see. . . .' (i.e. when Parliament reconvenes in the autumn of 1914). Messimy stressed in his memoirs that the Premier, Viviani, had given him express instructions to draft amendments to the three-year law (Messimy, *Souvenirs*, pp. 124–5). However, Poincaré's diary suggests that the initiative came from Messimy himself (NJ, 16 June, 4 and 8 July).
133. Poincaré, NJ (4 July).
134. Messimy, *Souvenirs*, p. 125.
135. Ibid., with obvious criticism of Poincaré's silence on the matter.
136. See p. 46, above; a detailed account of Humbert's speech is in Bonnefous, *Histoire politique*, vol. 2, pp. 17–18.
137. Humbert's speech was published as a pamphlet: Charles Humbert, *L'Armée: sommes-nous défendus?* (Paris, 1914).
138. This speech, entitled 'Ni défendus ni gouvernés', is published in G. Clemenceau, *Discours de guerre* (Paris, 1968), pp. 19–37.
139. See Weber, *Nationalist Revival*, pp. 142–3; now also presumably the definitive study by Becker, *1914: Comment les Français sont entrés dans la guerre*, pp. 125–36.
140. *L'Humanité* (14 July).
141. Poincaré, NJ (26 June); ibid. (3 July), a similar conversation with Tardieu, editor-in-chief of *Le Temps*.
142. Ibid. (20 June).
143. Albertini, *The Origins*, vol. 2, pp. 295, 536–9, 584.
144. Ibid., pp. 588, 593.
145. J. Isaac, *Un Débat historique: 1914, le problème des origines de la guerre* (Paris, 1933). On Isaac's work see also J. Droz, *Les Causes de la Première Guerre Mondiale* (Paris, 1973)), pp. 35–42.
146. Isaac, *Un Débat historique*, p. 196.
147. Ibid., p. 217 (italics in the original). In contrast, P.M. Kennedy, in agreement with L.C.F. Turner, has observed recently that Russian mobilization had no influence on the mechanics of German mobilization; see P.M. Kennedy (ed.), *The War Plans of the Great Powers* (1978), Introduction.
148. Isaac, *Débat historique*, p. 196.
149. Ibid., p. 216.
150. On J. Keiger's new assessment of Poincaré's diaries, see above, p. 245 (note 35). In

my opinion, there is no adequate source to substantiate Keiger's view that 'during the July crisis Poincaré was the principal decision maker in foreign policy with Viviani acting as a mere puppet' (ibid., p. 164).

151. See chap. 1, pp. 28–30, and chaps 2, 6 and 8, pp. 161–72. above.
152. This refers to the plans of the War Minister, Messimy, to present an amendment to the three-year law in the autumn of 1914 (see p. 214 above).
153. Poincaré, NJ (16 July); ibid. (18 July), another discussion with Viviani. Poincaré was at first shocked at Viviani's ignorance of matters of foreign policy and tried to 'put him in the picture'. Poincaré's diary (B.N., n.a.f. 16027, fos 133–5) contains a copy of an extract from Paléologue's diary (i.e. that of the ambassador in St Petersburg) which differs substantially from the later published version (M. Paléologue, *La Russie des Tsars pendant la Grande Guerre*, Paris, 1921). This document, which evidently contains previously unpublished passages from the original diary, gives impressions on Viviani's visit to St Petersburg not included in the published version. The following is an extract from the entry dated 20 July 1914: 'However, I [Paléologue] talked to Viviani, Sazonov and Izvolsky. Alas, Viviani, awkward and sullen, found nothing to say. One felt his mind was elsewhere. After a few minutes of awkward and laboured conversation, he took me aside and asked abruptly, "What news from Paris? Have you any telegrams for me? . . . To think that the Caillaux trial [the trial of Madame Caillaux for the assassination of Calmette] is opening at this very moment! . . . What are we bloody well doing here anyway?" (*sic*) . . . Viviani is neither acquainted with the ways of the world, nor has he firmness of character . . . he is violent, timid and vulgar, enveloped in a gloomy silence.'
154. See Poincaré, *Au Service*, vol. 4, pp. 236–7, 246–8.
155. Albertini, *The Origins*, vol. 2, p. 188.
156. According to Poincaré, NJ (20 July); cf. Poincaré, *Au Service*, vol. 4, p. 237, which states that the Tsar had simply raised the problem briefly and 'discreetly'.
157. From Poincaré, NJ (21 July); in a similar vein, Poincaré, *Au Service*, vol. 4, pp. 246–8.
158. This tends to be Albertini's interpretation: see Albertini, op. cit., vol. 2, pp. 194–7.
159. Quoted from Poincaré, NJ (21 July); similarly Poincaré, *Au Service*, vol. 4, p. 254.
160. See Poincaré, NJ (21 July); this is not mentioned in Poincaré's memoirs.
161. See ibid. (22 July).
162. See Albertini, op. cit., vol. 2, p. 210.
163. See chap. 8, pp 161–72, above.
164. This is in contrast to Albertini and Fay who regard Poincaré's 'stubbornness' towards the British proposal as a 'capital charge' against him (see Albertini, op. cit., vol. 2, p. 210, and the reference to Fay's comment).
165. Poincaré, *Au Service*, vol. 4, p. 276.
166. Ibid., p. 288.
167. Albertini, op. cit., vol. 2, p. 590.
168. See ibid., the conclusions on the basis of Viviani's despatches to Paris. On the problem of Russo-Serbian relations, see in particular J. Stengers, 'July 1914: Some Reflections' in *Annuaire de l'Institut de Philologie et d'Histoire Orientales et Slaves*, vol. 17 (1963–5), pp. 105–48. Stengers clearly shows that Poincaré's views were shared by the leading statesmen in Berlin and Vienna and also illustrates how the pressure of public opinion forced the Russian government into supporting Serbia after the Austria-Hungarian ultimatum to the latter.
169. Poincaré, NJ (25 July). D. Lieven, in *Russia and the Origins of the First World War* (London, 1984), p. 141, quotes a highly interesting report on a meeting of the Russian cabinet on 24 July 1914, drafted by the Finance Minister, Peter Bark, who was present. The report, now in the Bakhanetec archives at Columbia University, shows that the Austrian ultimatum to Serbia and the stirring of Russian public opinion urged the Russian leaders, initially in fact reluctant, to change course and

offer unconditional support to Serbia.
170. See the detailed and presumably definitive account by Albertini, op. cit., vol. 2, pp. 295, 303.
171. Quoted from DDF III/11, no. 138.
172. Albertini, op. cit., vol. 2, pp 583, 591–3.
173. Poincaré, NJ (27 July).
174. See Albertini, op. cit., vol. 2, pp. 591–3; DDF III/11, no. 50 (25 July).
175. See Albertini, op. cit., vol. 2, pp. 304–8.
176. As a note in the margin, Poincaré, NJ: '27 July evening'.
177. Poincaré, *Au Service*, vol. 4, p. 337.
178. Poincaré, NJ (27 July; entry dated '27 July evening').
179. Albertini, op. cit., vol. 2, p. 345.
180. See note 178 above.
181. Ibid.; it should be added that the storm abated somewhat when more precise news arrived from London and Paris. On 28 July Viviani actually sent a telegram to London in which, with Poincaré's approval, he agreed to Britain's proposal to include Belgrade in the planned talks between Vienna and St Petersburg and to call on Austria not to take any steps against Serbia in the meantime (Poincaré, NJ, 28 July; the same version in Poincaré, *Au Service*, vol. 4, p. 329).
182. See p. 27, above.
183. Cf. Joffre, *Mémoires*, pp. 117–18, and Albertini, *The Origins*, vol. 2, p. 598.
184. Cf. Messimy's conversation with the Russian military attaché in Paris, Ignatiev, 29/30 July 1914 (Messimy, *Souvenirs*, pp. 181–2).
185. This tends to be Albertini's assessment (i.e. op. cit.), although he considered that the basic responsibility lay with Germany.
186. When Izvolsky brought the news of Russia's mobilisation against Austria-Hungary on 29 July, no such warning was given. However, this was probably due to the fact that on 27 July the German government had let it be understood that Germany would mobilise only if Russia mobilised against her or attacked Austria-Hungary (see Schmitt, *The Coming of the War*, p. 94). Poincaré maintains in his memoirs that the Russian mobilisation against Austria-Hungary had been a new source of concern to him (Poincaré, *Au Service*, vol. 4, p. 374). Given his earlier concern that Russia was being too passive, this seems barely credible. Unfortunately a number of pages are missing from Poincaré's diary from 29 July, so that we have no authentic source on the cabinet meeting that day or on the reaction to Izvolsky's news.
187. DDF III/11, no. 305 (30 July).
188. Ibid., no. 301.
189. Poincaré, *Au Service*, vol. 4, p. 385.
190. Albertini, op. cit., vol. 2, pp. 608, 618–9.
191. Poincaré, NJ, 30 July (the present writer's italics).
192. See Albertini, op. cit., vol. 2, p. 536.
193. See Poincaré, *Au Service*, vol. 4, p. 449.
194. Poincaré, NJ (3 July). In his *Mémoires* (vol. 4, p. 449), Poincaré stated that Viviani's reply to von Schoen had been given with his approval and that this reply was further evidence that France had tried to preserve peace to the very end.
195. Poincaré, NJ (31 July); and in contrast see Poincaré, *Au Service*, vol. 4, p. 458.
196. Poincaré, NJ (1 Aug.): Poincaré's notes on the course of the cabinet meeting on the afternoon of 1 August are confirmed, almost word for word, by the records of the Under Secretary of State, Abel Ferry. See Abel Ferry, *Les Carnets Secrets* (Paris, 1957), p. 27.
197. See P. Renouvin, *Les Origines immédiates de la guerre* (Paris, 1927), 2nd ed., p. 217.
198. Poincaré, NJ (30 July); cf. Poincaré, *Au Service*, vol. 4, p. 415.
199. Ibid., p. 404.
200. Poincaré, NJ (1 Aug).

201. Ibid. The conversation with Izvolsky—but with no reference to this problem—is also mentioned in Poincaré, *Au Service*, vol. 4, p. 495.
202. Quoted from Poincaré, NJ (3 Aug.); Poincaré maintains that the feeling of relief was the general mood in the cabinet. This can scarcely have been the case. The other members of the cabinet were undoubtedly relieved, not because of precise calculations, but because of the wish to bring things finally to an end. On this mood in August 1914, after weeks of highly tense diplomatic activity, see especially Isaac, *Un Débat historique*, pp. 104–5.
203. SFIO manifesto, 28 August 1914, quoted from Kriegel and Becker, *1914*, p. 232.

Bibliography

I. Unpublished Sources

A. *Archives Nationales (Paris)*

1. Série C:
Assemblée Nationale: Elections; Synthèses; Sessions; Projets de Loi; Procès-Verbaux des séances des commissions; Pétitions; Lois et Résolutions

7419: Armée; durée de service; cadres; organisation
7420: Armée coloniale; objets divers
7421: Commission de l'Armée: procès-verbaux des séances
7426: Commission du Budget, 1913
7439: Défense nationale: compte spécial
7470: Commission de législation fiscale: procès-verbaux
7471: Impôts sur le revenu, sur le capital

2. Série F:
Versements des Ministères:

a) F 1a 3518–3519: Circulaires émanées du Ministère de l'Intérieur: originaux (1912–1915)
b) F 7: Police Générale:
12722: Mélanges (1902–1916)
12773: Grèves: instructions ministérielles, plans de protection, emploi des troupes et usage des armes, dessous politiques, chronologie des grèves (1849–1914)
12811: Sociétés de préparation militaire (1909–1913)
12821: Election de Poincaré, 1913
12822: Elections législatives, 1914
12863: Action Française 1912–1915
12864: Camelots du Roi 1909–1913
12873: Ligue des Patriotes 1907–1925
12911: Antimilitaristes 1912–1917
12932: Incidents de Nancy, 1913
13030: Contre la Loi Millerand (25.3.1912); Modifications des articles 4/5 de la loi de 1905
13065: Sabotage 1907–1927
13072: Congrès SFIO (1905–1920)
13073: Le Parti Socialiste et les Ministères (1910–1914)
13074: Notes politiques sur le parti socialiste
13075: Notes et presse concernant Jean Jaurès
13270: Le premier mai 1913

13271: Le premier mai 1914
13327: Les socialistes contre la Guerre
13332: Antimilitarisme et sabotage, 1910–1913
13333: Le Sou du Soldat 1912–1914
13334: Le Sou du Soldat
13335: Agitation contre la Loi de Trois Ans. Départements D – H
13336: Lutte contre l'agitation contre la loi de trois ans 1913–1914
13337: La Loi de Trois Ans:
    Doss. 1–3: Interpellation de M. Claussat
    Dossier: Agitation contre la loi de trois ans (Dép. Seine)
13338–13344: Agitation contre la loi de trois ans. Rapports et notes par Départements,
    1913–1914
13345: a) La Loi de Trois Ans
    b) Agitation dans l'Armée
13346–13347: Agitation dans l'Armée (suite)
13570: La CGT (1911–1914)
13571: La CGT et les partis politiques (1906–1916)
13583: (CGT). Conférences des Fédérations et des Bourses
13963: Réponses des préfets aux circulaires du Ministère de l'Intérieur (1913–1914)

c) F 9: Affaires Militaires:
1433: Préparation militaire obligatoire, 1913–1917

d) F 12: Commerce et Industrie:
8193: Voeux émis par des groupements professionnels, 1907–1912

e) F 30: Finances:
228: Projet d'émissions de rentes 3 % perpétuelles, en vue de subvenir aux dépenses
    militaires extraordinaires de la défense nationale et de l'expédition du Maroc

3. Serie BB 18: Ministère de la Justice. Division criminelle
2508 Doss. 128 A 13, 1–51: Rapports des procureurs généraux sur les faits d'antimili-
    tarisme survenus dans leurs ressorts
2509 Doss. 128 A 13, 52–136: idem
2510 Doss. 128 A 13, 137–165: idem

4. 94 AP: Fonds Albert Thomas:
Cart. 338–343: Affaires militaires, question coloniale, relations économiques interna-
    tionales, 1908–1913

B. *Archives du Ministère de la Guerre (Paris-Vincennes)*

Etat-Major de l'Armée; Conseil Supérieur de la Guerre, 1 N 11, Doss. CXLII – CXLIV

No. 837: Exposé de Motifs [Loi de Trois Ans], Exemplaire officiel
    839: Modifications au régime de recrutement: Note de Présentation au Conseil
        Supérieur de la Guerre, 3. 3. 1913 (secret)
    840: Conseil Supérieur de la Guerre: Procès-verbal de la séance du 4 mars 1913
        (secret)
    845: Plan XVII, Note de Présentation (18. 4. 1913)—Bases du Plan
    846: Conseil Supérieur de la Guerre, procès-verbal de la séance du 18 avril 1913
    848–852: Conseil Supérieur de la Guerre, Séance du 24 avril 1913
        ('note de présentation', 'rapports', i.a.)
    853: Conseil Supérieur de la Guerre: Procès-verbal de la séance du 24 avril 1913

C. *Archives de la Préfecture de Police (Paris)*

B/a 748: réunions publiques (1914)

752: Rapports mensuels du Préfet au Gouvernement (1910/1913)
769: Rapport quotidien, janv.-avr. 1913
1463–4: Élections législatives de 1914
1499: Anarchistes. Menées, Propagande (1907–1914)

D. *Bibliothèque Nationale (Paris), Département des Manuscrits, Nouvelles Acquisitions Françaises (n.a.f.)*

1. Archives Poincaré:
n.a.f. 15992–16018: Lettres reçues
n.a.f. 16024–16027: Notes Journalières (NJ), 26.12.1912–August 1914

2. Fonds Eugène Etienne: n.a.f. 24327

3. Fonds Joseph Reinach: n.a.f. 24882–24884

E. *Internationaal Instituut voor Sociale Geschiedenis (Amsterdam)*
Guesde-Archief
439/1–453/3: Papers of Jules Guesde, 1913–1914
649/1–649/4: Election material, 1914

F. *Archives Départementales*

1. A.D. Aveyron (Rodez):
 5 M 22–25: Elections législatives (1906–1914)
11 M 7   : Maintien de l'Ordre; Police Générale
23 M 5   : Manifestations politiques (1869–1935)

2. A.D. Côte d'Or (Dijon):
20 M 550: Manifestation contre la guerre organisées par la CGT
20 M 551: Projet de loi relatif au service militaire de trois ans. Consultation
          ministérielle; rapports de Police; manifestations pour ou contre
Supplément 2593/4: Elections législatives (1913–1914)

3. A.D. Loire (St. Etienne):
 3 M 55–56 : Elections législatives 1914: instructions, correspondance, rapports, ren-
             seignements, professions de foi, affiches
10 M 158   : Police Générale: la campagne contre la loi de trois ans, 1913
19 M 32–37 : Anarchistes (1912–1914)
93 M 5   : Syndicats et Coopératives: propagande antimilitariste; tendances à
             l'extrême gauche; influences socialistes; manées anarchistes

4. A.D. Haute-Loire (le Puy):
3 M 3   : Elections législatives 1910 et 1914 (affiches, rapport)
6 M 133–141: Politique générale; délits politiques; écrits et cris séditieux; manifestations
             politiques diverses
7 M 67–68 : Sûreté générale: Circulaires, correspondance, réunions publiques

5. A.D. Meuse (Bar-le-Duc):
3 M 36   : Elections législatives 1914

6. A.D. Tarn (Albi):
II. M/3 93–97: Elections aux Chambres législatives 1914
IV. M/2 98   : Police Générale: Grèves diverses; rapports sur la politique; manifesta-
               tions du 1er mai (1910–1913)

II. Published Sources

A. *Diplomatic Correspondence*

Ministère des Affaires Etrangères. Documents Diplomatiques Français (1871–1914), III. Série (1911–1914), vols. 3–11, Paris, 1931–36

Stieve, Friedrich (ed.): Der diplomatische Schriftwechsel Iswolskis, 1911–1914, 4 vols., Berlin, 1924

'. . .L'abominable vénalité de la presse . . ., d' après les documents des archives russes', Paris, 1931

B. *Parliamentary Minutes*

Journal Officiel de la République Française, Chambre des Députés
Serie I: Débats parlementaires (1913–1914)
Serie II: Documents parlementaires (1913–1914)

Journal Officiel de la République Française, Sénat
Serie I: Débats parlementaires (1913)

Individual publications

Paté, Henry: Le Sacrifice, c'est le devoir, c'est le salut. La loi de recrutement de 1913, Paris, 1913 (authorised publication of the Minutes of the Army Commission of the Chamber).

Doumer, Paul: La loi militaire du 7 août 1913, Paris, 1913 (authorised publication of the Minutes of the Army Commission of the Senate).

C. *Congress Reports*

Confédération Générale du Travail. Le Congrès du Havre (16–23 septembre 1912), Le Havre (1912)

Conférence ordinaire des Fédérations nationales et des Bourses du Travail ou Unions de Syndicats, tenue les 13, 14 et 15 juillet 1913, Paris, 1914

Parti Socialiste (SFIO): 10ᵉ Congrès national tenu à Brest, 23–25 mars 1913, compte-rendu sténographique, Paris (1913)

Parti Républicain radical et radical socialiste: Le Congrès de Pau, Paris, 1914

Le Prolétariat contre la guerre et les trois ans, Paris (1913) (contains i.a.: compte rendu du Congrès Extraordinaire de la CGT, tenu à Paris les 24 et 25 novembre 1912)

D. *Newspapers and Periodicals 1913–1914*

L'Action Française
L'Alliance Républicaine Démocratique
L'Aurore
La Bataille Syndicaliste
L'Echo de Paris
Le Figaro
La France
La France Militaire
Le Gaulois
Gil Blas
L'Humanité
L'Information économique et financière
Journal des Economistes

La Lanterne
La Liberté
Le Matin
L'Oeuvre
La Patrie
Le Petit Parisien
La Petite République
Le Radical
Le Reveil Economique
Le Républicain Socialiste
La Revue des deux Mondes
Le Siècle
Socialisme et lutte de classe
Le Temps
Les Temps Nouveaux
La Vie ouvrière
La Voix du Peuple

III. Monographs

Actes du Colloque 'Jaurès et la Nation', Toulouse, 1965

Agulhon, Maurice and Nouschi, André, *La France de 1914 à 1940*, Paris, 1971

Albertini, Luigi, *The Origins of the War of 1914*, vols. 1, 2, Oxford, 1952 (reprint 1967)

Albertini, Rudolf von 'Die Diskussion um die französische Steuerreform, 1907–1909', in *Schweizer Beiträge zur allgemeinen Geschichte*, 13 (1955), pp. 183–201

―――, 'Regierung und Parlament in der Dritten Republik', in *Historische Zeitschrift*, 188 (1959), pp. 17–48

Allain, Jean-Claude, *Agadir 1911*, Paris, 1975

―――, *Joseph Caillaux*. Vol. 1, *Le défi victorieux*, Paris, 1979

Allix, Edgar and Lecerclé, Marcel, *L'Impôt sur le revenu*, Paris, 1926

Ambrosi, Christian and Ambrosi, Arlette, *La France 1870–1975*, Paris/New York, 1976

Anderson, Robert D., *France 1870–1913. Politics and Society*, London, 1977

Andréani, Roland, 'L'Antimilitarisme en Languedoc Méditerranéen avant la Première Guerre Mondiale', in *Revue d'Histoire Moderne et Contemporaine*, 20 (1973), pp. 104–23

―――, 'Le Languedoc méditerranéen et le retour au service de trois ans (1913–1914)', in *Recrutement, Mentalités, Sociétés: Colloque international d'histoire militaire*, Montpellier, 1974, 1975, pp. 317–24

Andrew, Christopher M., *France Overseas: the Great War and the Climax of French Imperialism*, London, 1981

―――, 'Déchiffrement et diplomatie: le cabinet noir du Quai d'Orsay sous la IIIe République', in *Relations Internationales*, 3 (1976)

Les Armées Françaises dans la Grande Guerre, ed. Ministère de la Guerre, Etat-Major de l'Armée, Service Historique, pt. I, vol. 1, Paris, 1923

Arnold, Joseph C., 'French Tactical Doctrine, 1870–1914', in *Military Affairs*, 42 (1978), pp. 61–7

Arum, Peter M., 'Du syndicalisme révolutionnaire au réformisme: Georges Dumoulin (1903–1923)', in *Le Mouvement Social*, 87 (1974), pp. 35–62

Auffray, Bernard, *Pierre de Margerie (1861–1962) et la vie diplomatique de son temps*, Paris, 1976

Baker, Robert P., 'Socialism in the Nord, 1880–1919', in *International Review of Social History*, 12 (1967), pp. 357–89

Bardonnet, Daniel, *Evolution de la structure du Parti Radical*, Paris, 1960

Barraclough, Geoffrey, *From Agadir to Armageddon*, London, 1982

Barral, Pierre, *Le Département de l'Isère sous la IIIe République*, Paris, 1962
———, 'Géographie de l'opinion sous la IIIe République', in *Information historique*, 25 (1962), pp. 149–54
Barrès, Maurice, *Mes Cahiers*, vol. 10, *1913–1914*, Paris, 1936
Baumont, Maurice, *La Troisième République*, Lausanne, 1968
Becker, Jean-Jacques, *1914: Comment les Français sont entrés dans la Guerre*, Paris, 1977
———, *Le Carnet B. L'antimilitarisme vu par les pouvoirs publics*, Paris, 1973
Bellanger, Claude, *Histoire Générale de la Presse Française*, vol. 3, Paris, 1972
Berstein, Serge, *Histoire du Parti Radical*. Vol. 1, *La Recherche de l'Age d'Or, 1919–1926*, Paris, 1980
Bestuzhev, I.V., 'Russian Foreign Policy February–June 1914', in *Journal of Contemporary History*, 1 (1966), pp. 93–112
Bloch, Roger, *Histoire du Parti Radical*, Paris, 1968
Bomier-Landowski, Alain, 'Les groupes parlementaires de l'Assemblée Nationale et de la Chambre des Députés de 1871 à 1940', in François Goguel and Georges Dupeux (eds.), *Sociologie électorale*, Paris, 1951, pp. 75–89
Bonnefous, Georges, *Histoire Politique de la IIIe République*, vols. 1, 2, Paris, 1965, 1967
Boudet, Jean, *Le Monde des Affaires en France*, Paris, 1936
Bouju, Paul M. and Dubois, Henri, *La Troisième République*, Paris, 1967
Bourgin, Georges/Carrère, Jean/Guérin, André, *Manuel des partis politiques en France*, Paris, 1928 (2nd ed.)
Bron, Jean, *Histoire du mouvement ouvrier français*, vol. 2, Paris, 1970
Bruhat, Jean and Piolot, Marc, *Esquisse d'une histoire de la C.G.T. (1895–1965)*, Paris, 1966
Bury, J.P.T., *France, 1814–1940*, London, 1969
Caillaux, Joseph, *Mes Mémoires*, vols. 1–3, Paris, 1942–7
Cairns, John, 'International Politics and the Military Mind: the Case of the French Republic, 1911–1914', in *Journal of Modern History*, 25 (1953), pp. 273–85
Cambon, Paul, *Correspondance 1870–1924*. Vol. 3, *1912–1924*, Paris, 1946
Campbell, Peter, *French Electoral Systems and Elections since 1789*, (2nd ed.) London, 1969
Carrias, Eugène, *La pensée militaire française*, Paris, 1960
Carroll, Eber M., *French Public Opinion and Foreign Affairs 1870–1914*, New York, 1931 (repr. London, 1965)
Cazalis, Emile, *Syndicalisme ouvrier et évolution sociale*, Paris, 1923
Centenaire de la Troisième République. Actes du Colloque de Rennes, 1975, Paris, 1975
Challener, Richard D., *The French Theory of the Nation in Arms*, New York, 1955
Chapman, Geoffrey W., 'Decision for War. The Domestic Political Context of French Diplomacy, 1911–1914', diss. Princeton, 1971 (ms.)
Chastenet, Jacques, *Histoire de la Troisième République*. Vol. 4, *Jours inquiets et jours sanglants, 1906–1918*, Paris, 1955
Chevallier, Jean-Jacques, *Histoire des institutions politiques de la France moderne*, Paris, 1958
Clemenceau, Georges, *Discours de Guerre*, Paris, 1968
Collins, D.N., 'The Franco-Russian Alliance and Russian Railways, 1891–1914', in *The Historical Journal*, 16 (1973), pp. 777–88
Compère-Morel, Adédodat, 'Die Präsidentenwahl in Frankreich', in *Die Neue Zeit*, 31 (1913), pp. 617–21
Contamine, Henri, *La Revanche*, Paris, 1957
———, *La victoire de la Marne*, Paris, 1970
Debierre, Charles, *La Démocratie sociale*, Paris, 1910
Derfler, Leslie, *President and Parliament. A short history of the French Presidency*, Boca Raton, 1983
Desveaux, Emile, *Le Parti Radical et la question sociale*, Paris, 1910
Dogan, Mattei, 'La stabilité du personnel parlementaire sous la IIIe République', in *Revue Française de Science Politique*, 3 (1953), pp. 319–48

Dolléans, Edouard, *Histoire du Mouvement Ouvrier*. Vol. 2, *1871–1920*, Paris, 1957

Dommanget, Maurice, *Edouard Vaillant*, Paris, 1956

Drachkovitch, Milorad M., *Les Socialismes Français et Allemand et le Problème de la Guerre*, Geneva, 1953

Droz, Jacques, *Les causes de la Première Guerre Mondiale*, Paris, 1973

Dubief, Henri (ed.), *Le Syndicalisme Révolutionnaire*, Paris, 1969

Dubreuilh, Louis, *Le Socialisme, c'est la Paix. Contre les Trois Ans*, Paris, 1914

Dunois, Amédée, *L'Action socialiste au Parlement, 1910–1914*, Paris, 1914

Dupeux, Georges, 'La Troisième République, 1871–1914', in Georges Duby (ed.), *Histoire de France*. Vol. 3, Paris, 1972, pp. 119–48

Duroselle, Jean-Baptiste, *La France et le Français, 1900–1914*, Paris, 1972

Duverger, Maurice, 'L'Eternel Marais. Essai sur le centrisme français', in *Revue Française de Science Politique*, 14 (1964), pp. 33–51

——, *Les Partis Politiques*, Paris, 1951

Ehrmann, Henry W., *Politics in France*, Boston, 1968

Engerand, Fernand, *Le Secret de la Frontière*, Paris, 1918

Escaich, René, 'L'influence des présidents de la République', in *Ecrits de Paris*, 237 (1965), pp. 64–76

Farrar, Marjorie M., 'Politics versus Patriotism: Alexandre Millerand as French Minister of War', in *French Historical Studies*, 11 (1980), pp. 577–609

Ferry, Abel, *Les Carnets secrets (1914–1918)*, Paris, 1957

Fiechter, Jean-Jacques, *Le socialisme français: de l'affaire Dreyfus à la Grande Guerre*, Geneva, 1965

Fischer, Fritz, *War of Illusions*, London, 1975

Gascouin, Général F., *Le Triomphe de l'Idée*, Paris, 1931

de Gaulle, Charles, *La France et son Armée*, Paris, 1945

Georges, Bernard and Tintant, Denise, *Léon Jouhaux. Cinquante ans de syndicalisme*, Paris, 1962

Geyer, Dietrich, *Der russische Imperialismus*, Göttingen, 1977

Girardet, Raoul, *La société militaire dans la France contemporaine*, Paris, 1953

Godard, Jean, 'Les lois sur le recrutement de l'Armée', in *Revue administrative* (1962), pp. 36–40

Goguel, François, *Géographie des élections françaises sous la Troisième et la Quatrième République*, Paris, 1970 (2nd ed.)

——, 'L'influence des systèmes électoraux sur la vie politique d'après l'expérience française', in idem (ed.), *Nouvelles études de sociologie électorale*, Paris, 1954, pp. 74–81

——, *La Politique des Partis sous la IIIᵉ République*, Paris, 1973 (4th ed.)

—— and Grosser, Alfred, *La Politique en France*, Paris, 1975 (5th ed.)

Goldberg, Harvey, *The Life of Jean Jaurès*, Madison, 1962

Gorce, Paul-Marie De La, *La République et son armée*, Paris, 1963

Grossheim, Heinrich, *Sozialisten in der Verantwortung. Die französischen Sozialisten und Gewerkschafter im ersten Weltkrieg 1914–17*, Bonn, 1978

Guillemin, Henri, 'Jaurès dans l'action', in *Les Temps Modernes*, 21 (1965), pp. 776–815

——, *Nationalistes et nationaux (1870–1940)*, Paris, 1974

——, 'Péguy et Jaurès', in *Les Temps Modernes*, 18 (1962), pp. 72–108

Girault, René, *Emprunts russes et investissements français en Russie, 1887–1914*, Paris, 1973

Hanotaux, Gabriel, 'Les carnets de Gabriel Hanotaux, edited by Michel de Fonsco-lombe', in *Revue d'histoire diplomatique*. 91 (1977), pp. 5–142, 280–345

Haupt, Georges, *Der Kongreß fand nicht statt. Die sozialistische Internationale 1914*, Vienna, 1967

——, and Howorth, Jolyon, 'Edouard Vaillant, délégué au Bureau Socialiste interna-tional: correspondance avec le secrétariat international (1900–1915)', in *Annali della Fondazione G. Feltrinelli*, 17 (1976), pp. 209–305

Herzfeld, Hans, *Die deutsche Rüstungspolitik vor dem Weltkrieg*, Bonn/Leipzig, 1923

Hoffmann, Stanley, *Sur la France*, Paris, 1976

Isaac, Jules, *Un débat historique: 1914, le Problème des Origines de la Guerre*, Paris, 1933

Jauffret, Jean-Charles, 'Armée et pouvoir politique', in *Revue Historique*, 270/1 (1983), p. 97–144

——, 'L'image de l'armée britannique devant le Parlement français et le Conseil Supérieur de la Guerre de 1871 à 1900', in *Forces armées et systèmes d'alliance. Colloque international d'histoire militaire (1981)*, Montpellier, 1983

Jaurès, Jean, *L'Armée Nouvelle*, Paris, 1915

Joffre, Joseph, *Mémoires du Maréchal Joffre*, vol. 1, Paris, 1932

Joll, James, *1914. The Unspoken Assumptions*, London, 1968

——, 'War Guilt 1914: A Continuing Controversy', in Paul Kluke and Peter Alter (eds.), *Aspects of Anglo-German relations through the centuries*, Stuttgart, 1978, pp. 60–80

——, *The Origins of the First World War*, London, 1984

Jouvenel, Robert de, *La République des camarades*, Paris, 1914

Julliard, Jacques, 'La CGT devant la guerre', in *Le Mouvement Social*, 49 (1964), pp. 47–62

Kayser, Jacques, *Les grandes batailles du radicalisme, 1820–1901*, Paris, 1962

——, 'The Radical Socialist Party as a Party of Government in the Third French Republic', in *Parliamentary Affairs*, 13 (1960), pp. 318–28

Keiger, John F., *France and the Origins of the First World War*, London, 1983

Kennedy, Paul M (ed.), *The War Plans of the Great Powers, 1880–1914*, London, 1979

Kovacs, Arpad F., 'French Military Legislation in the Third Republic', in *Military Affairs*, 13 (1949), pp. 1–12

Kriegel, Annie, 'Patrie ou Révolution: Le mouvement ouvrier français devant la guerre (juillet—août 1914)', in *Revue d'histoire économique et sociale*, 43 (1965), pp. 363–85

——, and Becker, Jean-Jacques, *1914. La Guerre et le mouvement ouvrier français*, Paris, 1964

Krumeich, Gerd, 'L'offensive "à outrance" et la crainte de "L'attaque brusquée": Problèmes politiques et militaires de la Loi de Trois Ans de 1913', in *Forces armées et systèmes d'alliance. Colloque international d'histoire militaire et d'ètudes de défense nationale (1981)*, Montpellier, 1984, pp. 474–81

——, 'Zwischen republikanischem und proletarischen "Block": Die französischen Sozialisten vor dem 1. Weltkrieg', in *Francia*, 7 (1979), pp. 309–37

——, 'Poincaré und der "Poincarismus" ', in *Francia*, 8 (1980), pp. 429–53

——, 'Raymond Poincaré et l'affaire du "Figaro" ', in *Revue Historique*, 264/2 (1980), pp. 365–73

Lachance, Paul F., 'French Youth and the Debate over the Three-Year Law', in *Proceedings of the Sixth Meeting of the Western Society for French History*, San Diego, 1978, pp. 353–60

Lamy, Etienne, 'L'Armée et la démocratie', in *Revue des Deux Mondes*, 69 (1885), pp. 835–72

De Lanessan, Jean-Marie, *Nos forces militaires*, Paris, 1913

Langhorne, Richard, 'Anglo-German Negotiations Concerning the Future of the Portuguese Colonies, 1911–1914', in *Historical Journal*, 16 (1973), pp. 361–87

Lavau, Jean, *Partis politiques et réalités sociales*, Paris, 1953

Lefranc, Georges, *Le Mouvement Syndical sous la Troisième République*, Paris, 1967

——, *Le Mouvement Socialiste sous la Troisième République*, Paris, 1975 (2nd ed.)

——, *Les organisations patronales en France*, Paris, 1976

Legrand-Girarde, *Un quart de siècle au service de la France*, Paris, 1954

Leroy, Maxime, *La coutume ouvrière. Syndicats, bourses du travail, fédérations professionelles, coopératives. Doctrines et institutions*, 2 vols., Paris, 1913

Liddell Hart, Sir Basil H., 'French Military Ideas before the First World War', in Martin

Gilbert (ed.), *A Century of Conflict, 1850–1950, Essays for A.J.P. Taylor*, London, 1966, pp. 136–44

Lieven, David, *Russia and the Origins of the First World War*, London, 1984

Ligou, Daniel, *Histoire du Socialisme en France, 1871–1961*, Paris, 1962

Martin, Benjamin F., *Count Albert de Mun. Paladin of the Third Republic*, Chapel Hill, 1978

Massé, Jean, 'Aperçus sur l'antimilitarisme ouvrier dans le département du Var avant 1914', in *Cahiers d'histoire*, XIII (1968), pp. 193–208

Maurin, J.R., *Armée, Guerre, Société. Soldats languedociens, 1889–1919*, Paris, 1982

Maurras, Charles, *La Contre-Révolution spontanée*, Lyons, 1943

Mayer, Arno J., 'Causes and Purposes of War in Europe, 1870–1956: A Research Assignment', in *Journal of Modern History*, 41 (1969), pp. 291–303

——, 'Domestic Causes of the First World War', in Leonard Krieger and Fritz Stern (eds.), *The Responsibility of Power*, New York, 1967, pp. 286–300

——, *The Persistence of the Old Regime. Europe to the Great War*, New York, 1981

Mayeur, Jean-Marie, and Rebérioux, Madeleine, *The Third Republic from its origins to the Great War, 1871–1914*, Cambridge, 1984

Mazgaj, Paul, *The Action Française and Revolutionary Syndicalism*, Chapel Hill, 1978

Merlier, M.G., 'De Grandmaison, Penseur et Ecrivain militaire', in *Actes du 87e Congrès National des Sociétés Savantes (1962)*, Paris, 1963, pp. 529–41

Messimy, Adolphe, *Mes Souvenirs*, Paris, 1937

——, *Le problème militaire*, Paris, 1913

Michon, Georges, *La Préparation à la Guerre: La Loi de Trois Ans (1911–1914)*, Paris, 1935

Miquel, Pierre, *Poincaré*, Paris, 1961

Mitchell, Alan, 'Thiers, MacMahon and the Conseil Supérieur de la Guerre', in *French Historical Studies*, 6 (1969), pp. 232–52

Mommsen, Wolfgang J., *Die latente Krise des Deutschen Reiches, 1909–1914*, in Just, Leo (ed.) *Handbuch der Deutschen Geschichte*, IV, 1, Frankfurt, 1972

——, 'Domestic Factors in German Foreign Policy before 1914', in *Central European History*, 6 (1973), pp. 3–43

Monteilhet, Joseph, *Les institutions militaires de la France, 1814–1924*, Paris, 1926

Nicolet, Claude, *Le Radicalisme*, Paris, 1967

Nordmann, Jean-Thomas, *Histoire des Radicaux 1820–1973*, Paris, 1974

Oncken, Emily, *'Panthersprung' nach Agadir. Die deutsche Politik während der zweiten Marokko-Krise 1911*, Düsseldorf, 1981

Ornano, Roland de, *Gouvernement et Haut-Commandement en régime parlementaire français*, Aix-en-Provence, 1958

Paléologue, Maurice, *Au Quai d'Orsay. A la veille de la tourmente. Journal 1913–1914*, Paris, 1947

——, *La Russie des Tsars pendant la Grande Guerre*, vol. 1, Paris, 1921

Paix-Séailles, Charles, *Jaurès et Caillaux*, Paris, 1920

Le Parti Socialiste, *La Loi de Trois Ans et la Guerre*, Limoges, 1919

Payen, Fernand, *Raymond Poincaré*, Paris, 1936

Pedroncini, Guy, 'Stratégie et Relations Internationales: La Séance du 9 Janvier 1912 du Conseil Supérieur de la Défense Nationale', in *Revue d'histoire diplomatique*, 91 (1977), pp. 145–58

Persil, Raoul, *Alexandre Millerand*, Paris, 1949

Poidevin, Raymond, *Les relations économiques et financières entre la France et l'Allemagne de 1898 à 1914*, Paris, 1969

——, and Bariéty, Jacques, *Les relations franco-allemandes, 1815–1975*, Paris, 1977, vols. 1–4

Poincaré, Raymond, *Au Service de la France*, vols. 1–4, Paris, 1926–1927

Porch, Douglas, 'L'armée française et l'esprit d'offensive, 1900–1914', in *Annales de l'Université des Sciences Sociales de Toulouse*, 25 (1977), pp. 155–87

——, *The March to the Marne. The French Army, 1871–1914*, Cambridge, 1981

Possony, Stefan T. and Mantoux, Etienne. 'Du Picq and Foch. The French School', in E.M. Earle (ed.), *Makers of Modern Strategy. Military Thought from Machiavelli to Hitler*, Princeton, 1943, pp. 206–33

Prélot, Marcel, *L'Evolution politique du socialisme français*, Paris, 1939

Le Procès de l'assassin de Jaurès, Paris, 1919

Rabaut, Jean, *Jaurès et son assassin*, Paris, 1967

——, *Jaurès*, Paris, 1971

Ralston, David B., *The Army of the Republic*, Cambridge (Mass.), 1967

Rappoport, Charles, 'Der Gewerkschaftskongreß von Havre', in *Die Neue Zeit*, 31 (1913), vol. 2, pp. 47–52

Rebérioux, Madeleine, 'Jaurès et l'unité ouvrière', in *Pensée*, 120, ns, (1965), pp. 57–76

——, *La République Radicale? 1898–1914*. Vol. 11 of *Histoire Nouvelle de la France Contemporaine*, Paris, 1975

Reinach, Joseph, *L'armée toujours prête*, Paris, 1913

Rémond, René (ed.), *Atlas historique de la France contemporaine*, Paris, 1966

——, *La Droite en France*, Paris, 1968 (3rd ed.)

Renouvin, Pierre, *La crise européenne et la première guerre mondiale*, vol. 19 of *Peuples et Civilisations*, Paris, 1969

——, *Les origines immédiates de la Guerre*, Paris, 1927 (2nd ed.)

Ridley, F.F., *Revolutionary Syndicalism in France. The Direct Action of its Time*, Cambridge, 1970

Rinaudo, Yves, 'L'opposition à la loi de trois ans dans le Var', in *Provence Historique*, 20 (1970), pp. 162–83

Ropp, Theodore, *War in the Modern World*, Durham (N.C.), 1959

Saatmann, Inge, *Parlament, Rüstung und Armee in Frankreich 1914/18*, Düsseldorf, 1978

Schmidt, Martin E., *Alexandre Ribot: Odyssey of a liberal in the Third Republic*, La Haye, 1974

Schmitt, Bernadotte E., *The Coming of the War, 1914*, vol. 1, New York, 1930 (reprint 1966)

Seager, Frederic, 'Joseph Caillaux as Premier, 1911–1912. The Dilemma of a Liberal Reformer', in *French Historical Studies*, 11 (1979), pp. 239–57

Seignobos, Charles, *L'Evolution de la IIIᵉ République (1875–1914)*. vol. 8, *Histoire de la France contemporaine*, Paris, 1921

Serman, William, *Les officiers français dans la nation 1848–1914*, Paris, 1982

Setzen, Joel A., 'Background to the French Failures of August 14. Civilian and Military Dimensions', in *Military Affairs*, 42 (1978), pp. 87–90

Steiner, Zara, S., *Britain and the Origins of the First World War*, London, 1977

Stengers, Jean, 'July 1914: some reflections', in *Annuaire de l'Institut de Philologie et d'Histoire Orientales et Slaves*, 17 (1963–5) pp. 105–48

Sternhell, Zeev, *Maurice Barrès et le nationalisme français*, Paris, 1972

——, *La Droite Révolutionnaire. Les Origines Françaises du Fascisme*, Paris, 1978

Stieve, Friedrich, *Iswolski und der Weltkrieg*, Berlin, 1924

Stone, Norman, *The Eastern front 1914–1917*, London, 1975

Suarez, Georges, *Briand*, vol. 2, *1904–1914*, Paris, 1938

Sumler, David E., 'Domestic Influences on the Nationalist Revival in France, 1909–1914', in *French Historical Studies*, 6 (1970), pp. 517–37

——, 'Opponents of war preparedness in France, 1913–1914', in S. Wank (ed.), *Doves and Diplomats: Foreign Offices and Peace Movements in Europe and America in the Twentieth Century*, Westport (Conn.), 1978

Taylor, A. J. P., *The Struggle for Mastery in Europe*, London, 1954 (reprint 1967)

Thaden, Edward D., *Russia and the Balkan Alliance of 1912*, University Park (Penns.), 1965

Thile, Lucien, *Pouvoir civil et pouvoir militaire*, Paris, 1914

Thomson, David, *Democracy in France since 1870*, Oxford, 1969 (5th ed.)

Tixier, Gilbert, 'Poincaré et le redressement français', in *Revue politique et parlementaire*, 57 (1955), pp. 185–91

Touchard, Jean, *La gauche en France depuis 1900*, Paris, 1977

Trachtenberg, Marc, 'The Social Interpretation of Foreign Policy', in *Review of Politics*, 40 (1978), pp. 328–50

Travers, T.H.E., 'The Offensive and the Problem of Innovation in British Military Thought, 1870–1915', in *Journal of Contemporary History*, 13 (1978), pp. 531–53

Trotabas, Louis, *Les finances publiques et les impôts en France*, Paris, 1937

Turner, L.C.F., 'The role of the General Staffs in July 1914', in *Austrian Journal of Politics and History*, 11 (1965), pp. 305–3

———, 'The Russian Mobilization in 1914', in *Journal of Contemporary History*, 3 (1968), pp. 65–89

Vénézia, Jean-Claude, 'Les fondements juridiques de l'instabilité ministérielle sous la IIIᵉ et sous la IVᵉ République', in *Revue du droit publique et de la science politique en France et à l'Etranger*, 75 (1959), pp. 718–55

Vincent-Smith, James D., 'The Anglo-German Negotiations over the Portuguese Colonies in Africa, 1911–1914', in *Historical Journal*, 17 (1974), pp. 620–9

Wallach, Jehuda D., *Das Dogma der Vernichtungsschlacht*, Munich, 1970

Watson, David R., *Georges Clemenceau. A Political Biography*, London/New York, 1974/1976

Weber, Eugen, *The Nationalist Revival in France, 1905–1914*, Berkeley, 1959 (reprint 1968).

———, 'Un demi-siècle de glissement à droite', in *International Review of Social History*, 5 (1960), pp. 165–201

———, *Action Française. Royalism and Reaction in 20th Century France*, Stanford, 1962

Weigold, Marily E. 'National Security versus Collective Security: The Role of the Couverture in Shaping French Military and Foreign Policy (1905–1934)', PhD, St John's Univ., NY, 1970 (ms.)

Reichsarchiv (ed.), *Der Weltkrieg 1914 bis 1918*. Vol. 1, *Kriegsrüstung und Kriegswirtschaft*, Berlin, 1930

Wesseling, Hendrik L., *Soldaat en Krijger: Franse opvattingen over leger en oorlog, 1905–1914*, Assen, 1969

Westergard-Thorpe, Wayne, 'Towards a Syndicalist International: The 1913 London Congress', in *International Review of Social History*, 23 (1978), pp. 33–78

Williamson, Samuel R., *The Politics of Grand Strategy. Britain and France Prepare for War, 1904–1914*, Cambridge (Mass.), 1969

Wilhelm, Julius, 'Das Problem der "Deux France" ', in idem, *Beiträge zur romanischen Literaturwissenschaft*, Tübingen 1956, pp. 15–35

Winnacker, Richard A., 'The Délégation des Gauches, in *Journal of Modern History*, 9 (1937), pp. 449–70

Wormser, Georges, *La République de Clemenceau*, Paris, 1961

Wright, Gordon, *Raymond Poincaré and the French Presidency*, Stanford, 1942 (reprint, New York, 1967)

Zeldin, Theodore, *France 1848–1945*, vols. 1–2, Oxford, 1973, 1977

Ziebura, Gilbert, *Die deutsche Frage in der öffentlichen Meinung Frankreichs von 1911–1914*, Berlin, 1955

———, Die Dreyfus-Affäre und das Regierungssystem der Dritten Republik, in *Historische Zeitschrift*, 191 (1969), pp. 548–61

Index